HORMONES *of* LIFE

HORMONES *of* LIFE

Endocrinology, the Pharmaceutical Industry, and the Dream of a Remedy for Sterility, 1930–1970

Christer Nordlund

Science History Publications/USA
a division of
Watson Publishing International LLC
Sagamore Beach
20011

First published in the United States of America
by Science History Publications/USA
a division of
Watson Publishing International LLC
Post Office Box 1240,
Sagamore Beach, MA 02562-1240, USA
www.shpusa.com

Library of Congress Cataloging-in-Publication Data
Nordlund, Christer, 1970–
[Hormoner för livet. English]
Hormones of life : endocrinology, the pharmaceutical industry, and the dream of a remedy for sterility, 1930–1970 / Christer Nordlund.
p. ; cm.
Includes bibliographical references and index.
ISBN 978-0-88135-475-1 (pbk.)
1. Chorionic gonadotropins. 2. Aktiebolaget Leo. 3. Pharmaceutical industry—Sweden—History—20th century. 4. Infertility, Female—Hormone therapy. I. Title.
[DNLM: 1. Aktiebolaget Leo. 2. Chorionic Gonadotropin—history—Sweden. 3. Advertising as Topic—history—Sweden. 4. Drug Industry—history—Sweden. 5. History, 20th Century—Sweden. 6. Infertility, Female—drug therapy—Sweden. WK 920]
QP572.C53N6713 2011
618.1'7806—dc22

2011009110

(ISBN 978-0-88135-475-1)

Designed and typeset by Publishers' Design and Production Services, Inc.

Manufactured in the USA.

CONTENTS

FOREWORD

THIS BOOK IS ABOUT HORMONES, or more precisely, about hormone drugs developed and used to treat sterility. As such, it is also about the idea that involuntary childlessness is a problem that can be solved with biomedical means. At its center stands Gonadex, a drug that upon its launch in Sweden in 1948 sounded awfully promising, but which never really achieved the success expected. My intent is to show how this long-forgotten drug came into being and was marketed, but also what happened afterward. One of the primary aims of the present volume is to demonstrate how complicated the pharmaceutical innovation process can be, and in that way make an empirically based contribution to the current debate on innovation theory. This is not a history of hormones in general but rather a biography of Gonadex.

The book does however have a broader, historical perspective, using Gonadex as a prism to illuminate the development of reproductive endocrinology, its early involvement in the population question and the introduction and establishment of hormone drugs in gynecological practice during the period 1930–1970. I chose to delve into this subject partly due to my interest in the grand scientific, medical, financial and political visions invested in the early hormone preparations. It was only after the project was well underway that I realized that I too was part of that history, which of course did nothing to lessen my resolve. I see the book primarily as a contribution to the history of biomedicine and endocrinology, a field of research hitherto dominated by contributions from the UK and the USA, but my goal has also been to provoke thought and reflection on the scientific, financial and mass medial dimensions of modern health care in general.

Hormones of Life was first published in Swedish in 2008. It was partly based on some of my earlier publications, notably "Hormones for Life? Behind the Rise and Fall of a Hormone Remedy (Gonadex) against Sterility in the Swedish Welfare State," *Studies in History and Philosophy of Biological and Biomedical Sciences* 38 (2007). Its publication in a slightly revised English edition is the result of having been fortunate enough to receive a Young Researcher Award by Umeå University in 2009, which financed the translation and defrayed some of the production costs. Thanks to Boel Berner and

Arkiv Publishers for providing consent and to Neale Watson for adding it to his Science History Publications/USA imprint. SHP has long supported the historical study of science and technology in Sweden and becoming part of this tradition is an honor indeed.

Most of the work on this book was conducted at the Department of Historical, Philosophical and Religious Studies at Umeå University, the Swedish Collegium for Advanced Study in Uppsala and the Max Planck Institute for the History of Science in Berlin. Each of these academic environments has enriched my studies and I wish to take the opportunity to thank both my geographically far-flung colleagues and those who made these visits possible: the Max Planck Society, Riksbankens Jubileumsfond, the Swedish Collegium for Advanced Study, the Swedish Foundation for International Cooperation in Research and Higher Education, and Umeå University.

Without access to adequate source material, this book could never have been written. First and foremost, I would like to thank Pfizer for permission to enter and comb the archives of Aktiebolaget Leo (Helsingborg), and former Leo employees (now pharmaceutical historians) Jerker Ahlin, Rolf Lundgren and Erik Helmer, who expertly guided me through the voluminous collections. Thanks also to the staff of the Regional State Archives of Uppsala, the Stockholm County Council Archives, the National Archives in Stockholm, the Foundation for Economic History Research in Banking and Enterprise in Stockholm (for access to the Knut and Allice Wallenberg Foundation's Archives), Carolina Rediviva, Umeå University Library, the Swedish Academy of Pharmaceutical Sciences, Christina Lärkner, Ann-Margret Sundius, and my informants and interlocutors Egon Diczfalusy and the late Rolf Luft.

Along with Tore Frängsmyr and Soraya de Chadarevian, who long ago helped me draft the broad outlines of this book, I would also like to thank those who have been kind enough to read, comment and discuss all or part of the manuscript with a keen, critical gaze: Jerker Ahlin, Boel Berner, Egon Diczfalusy, Jenny Eklöf, Leif H. Eklund, Karin Frisendahl, Kerstin Hagenfeldt, Kjell Jonsson, Anders Lundgren, Rolf Lundgren, Lennart Nordenfelt and Inge-Bert Täljedal. Special thanks to my friend and colleague Stephen Fruitman, who carried out its translation with care and finesse.

Finally, my warmest thanks to Clara. The Swedish version of this book was dedicated to our son Leonard. So it's only right that the English one be dedicated to his little sister. Happy birthday, Maj!

Berlin, 23 January 2011
Christer Nordlund

HORMONES *of* LIFE

INTRODUCTION

> We are always told who originated a discovery or technique, we are rarely told how it fared thereafter.[1]
>
> *John V. Pickstone*

On the evening of 10 June 1948, a sensational press conference was held in Stockholm. Arranged by pharmaceutical company Aktiebolaget Leo (Helsingborg), its main attraction was a lecture featuring one of Sweden's most esteemed physicians, Professor Axel Westman. The purpose of the event was to announce that Leo, in close collaboration with Westman and his colleagues at the Women's Clinic of the Royal Caroline Hospital,* had succeeded in developing a new, highly advanced hormonal preparation. With reference to the scientific term for the type of hormone used—gonadotropin—the new drug was dubbed *Gonadex*.

This drug, it was stated, possessed the unprecedented ability to help sterile women become pregnant; it could literally create life. It could also be used to treat a number of other diagnoses, including menstrual problems and menopausal discomfort. Furthermore, thanks to its unique clinical purity, Gonadex was completely free of side effects, in contrast to earlier hormone replacement drugs. All this made Gonadex a drug the likes of which had never before been seen, which, as the press reported the next day, amounted to nothing less than a "Swedish triumph."[2]

Radio and newspapers explained that Gonadex—this "amazing medical discovery"—was an innovation of nearly inestimable value whose significance related to several different levels. Gonadex was a victory for science, a breakthrough for modern, research-based medicine and, just as important, on its way to becoming a commodity with a worldwide market for the expanding, internationally-oriented Swedish pharmaceutical industry.[3]

---

*Today, the English translation of "Karolinska Sjukhuset" and "Karolinska Institutet" is "the Karolinska Hospital" and "the Karolinska Institute." In the past, however, they were translated as "the Royal Caroline Hospital" and "the Royal Caroline Institute." In this book, these original translations are used.

Since Gonadex could contribute to increasing the population, it was also reckoned as having political and economic connotations, at the same time as it was expected to have an existential influence on the many living in involuntarily childless marriages and thereby missing out on having "real families." The government could look forward to a sought-after increase in the population. And for those women and men who had waited in vain for the joy a baby provided, a new era of hope had begun.

Gonadex was without doubt a most remarkable product for its day. Together with Pharmacia's blood substitute Macrodex and Astra's local anesthetic Xylocain, it belonged to the first, exclusive host of so-called "original preparations" introduced in Sweden during the 1940s.[4] Moreover, Gonadex was one of the very first Swedish preparations to emerge from the exciting field of hormone research. The positive coverage it received in the Swedish press, on the other hand, was far from unique. Rather, it was typical of how journalists in the period following the Second World War breathlessly reported on domestic scientific and medical discoveries with terms like "progress," "breakthrough," and "groundbreaking."[5] Similarly typical is the fact that the media seem to have nothing more to say about Gonadex after 1948, by which time the drug was no longer seen as newsworthy. Thus it was probably difficult for the public at large to gage the extent to which the enormous expectations roused by Gonadex had been justified.

Interestingly, an analogue to this mass medial focus can be found in the historiography of science and medicine. As historian of science John V. Pickstone has indicated, it is actually uncommon for historians to follow up on new discoveries and technologies; as a rule, focus lies on investigating how the discovery or technology was created, not on what happened next. So proved to be the case with Gonadex. In Lennart Norgren's study in economic history, *Kunskapsöverföring från universitet till företag: En studie av universitetsforskningens betydelse för de svenska läkemedelsföretagens produktlanseringar 1945–1984* [The transfer of knowledge from university to company: A study of the importance of university research for the introduction of new products in the Swedish pharmaceutical industry, 1945–1985], the only scholarly study the present author has been able to locate that actually mentions Gonadex, the origins of the preparation are described in a few paltry sentences as the result of a collaboration between Leo and the Royal Caroline Hospital, distinguished by its high level of purity, just like the media reported. According to Norgren, Gonadex became a "base product" which helped kick off research and development in a new field—endocrinology—at Leo, whence other products were generated in a distinct chain of events. One of these spin-offs was Homogonal, another gonadotropin preparation intended for the treatment of sterility, which Leo began marketing in 1967. However, the reader learns nothing about the fate of Gonadex after its launch, other than that in time, it came to be prescribed in combination with Homogonal.[6]

Perhaps Gonadex can be seen as a medical breakthrough and a catalyst for Leo's innovation system. It all depends on the perspective. However, behind such sterilized and contextless images, a much more complicated and exciting story lays waiting to be told. This is the story of *Hormones of Life*.

PREMISES AND QUESTIONS

Once considered a medical miracle, now as good as forgotten, the hormone replacement drug Gonadex is the subject of the present book. I chose Gonadex as an object of study because its story connects with so many historically important issues concerning the interaction between science, industry, medicine and the mass media. For the purposes of this study, the many questions have been boiled down to the following fundamental few: Why did a highly-respected scientist like Axel Westman choose to collaborate with private enterprise, and on closer inspection, what were the consequences of this collaboration? Why did Leo, best known in Scandinavian homes for its headache tablet Albyl, devote its resources to developing advanced hormone preparations of this specific type? What evidence exists to prove that Gonadex really worked at the time of its public launch? Why was Gonadex described the way it was in the daily press?

My interest in Gonadex was first piqued by the fact that it roused such high expectations in an era characterized by powerful faith in social engineering and the possibilities of medical science to improve society. As indicated, there was a general perception that Gonadex would help involuntarily childless couples to finally become parents, to the benefit of both themselves and society at large. This perception impelled me to investigate how social and existential expectations of biomedical research come into being, but also find out what happened if said expectations were not met. I have simply been curious to know what happened after the launch of the drug that summer evening in 1948. How did doctors, researchers, and the childless react to the news? Did they even react at all?

Considering that it is impossible to successfully treat all involuntarily childless couples even today, one wonders whether Gonadex really was the medical triumph and profit-generating "worldwide commodity" it was hailed as being? If not, how did the pharmaceutical industry and researchers involved react, and what was the eventual fate of Gonadex? And what was the actual relationship between Gonadex and its successor, Homogonal? These follow-up questions are a concerted effort at taking Pickstone's criticism seriously, as is the conviction that the significance of an innovation and its possible success can only be assessed after it has left the laboratory and the factory and its real life-cycle begins.[7]

Another reason for delving into this subject is that it can help deepen our understanding of the therapeutic culture characterizing the burgeoning Swedish welfare state, especially insofar as the population question was concerned. In previous historical research, the reform policies of the Social Democratic Party, including its notorious sterilization programs, have been characterized as highly distinctive. Eugenics, racial biology and theories of heredity are usually invoked as the scientific foundation upon which the sterilization program was based.[8] However, ought not endocrinology and research on hormonal preparations intended to cure sterility also be considered in that political context? Can sterilization implemented in order to reduce the number of "undesirable" elements in the Swedish welfare state and the treatment of sterility for the purpose of increasing the number of "desirable" ones be seen as two sides of the same coin? That would entail a whole new interpretation of the ideological motives informing the development of sterility treatment. In *Guldägget: Föräldraskap i biomedicinens tid* [The golden egg: Parenthood in the age of biomedicine], ethnologist Susanne Lundin emphasizes the significance of the democratic assumption that having children not only constitutes a basic, biological need but also a *right* that ought to be met.[9] But beyond this individualistic assumption there may also be a more collectivist ideal, wherein the development of sterility treatment is instead motivated by its conceivable significance to society at large.

By analyzing the expectations and biomedical and industrial efforts behind the creation of Gonadex, deconstructing the mass media's image of the drug, and following up what happened after its launch, I intend to show how the origin and development—including the marketing—of Gonadex played out. One of the aims of the present book is to demonstrate how complicated such an innovation process can be, and in that way attempt to make an empirically sound contribution to the current debate about innovation theory.[10] However, the book also has a broader historical aim, which is to observe, through the prism of Gonadex, the development of reproductive endocrinology and its early connection with the population question and the introduction and establishment of hormone replacement drugs in gynecological practice in Sweden during the period stretching from 1930 to 1970. In other words, I assume the task of studying other hormone preparations as well, both those preceding Gonadex and those following in its wake, Homogonal in particular. I have also attempted to chart the more general debate about the pros and cons of hormone replacement therapy as a medical technique.

The present volume is primarily a contribution to the history of endocrinology and biomedicine but also wishes to give rise to thought and reflection on the scientific, financial and mass medial dimensions of modern health care. In order to clarify the latter aim, I shall begin by locating the subject of this book in its greater historical context.

THE NEW PHYSIOLOGY BEFORE THE ARRIVAL OF THE NEW BIOLOGY

Gonadex is associated with a branch of the life sciences dealing with hormones and hormone treatment, which since the beginning of the twentieth century has gone under the name of "endocrinology." From initially being regarded with skepticism by professional physicians and researchers, endocrinology fairly blossomed in the interwar era. In an era that lionized anything "modern," endocrinology roused enormous expectations, both scientific and therapeutic. To distinguish it from classic, nineteenth-century physiology, British physiologist Edward Schäfer (1850–1935; after 1918 Sir Edward Sharpey-Schafer) referred to it as "the new physiology."[11]

One set of opinions announced that the "endocrinologists" who dedicated themselves to this field had in a very short space of time achieved revolutionary physiological and chemical insight into how the human body worked, and envisioned them helping to explain, treat and cure all manner of disease, eventually controlling the very "life processes" themselves. As the title of a book published in 1935 proclaimed, the endocrinal organs were "The Glands of Life."[12] Solving the mystery of sterility was an attractive challenge, though only one of many.[13] There were also researchers who wished to influence and expand mental capacity and eventually profoundly transform society.[14] As I have mentioned elsewhere, some endocrinologists even dreamed of improving the entire human race with the help of hormonal eugenic therapy, which they saw as much more effective than the clumsy techniques thus far offered by the burgeoning discipline of genetics.[15] Without diminishing the exertions of the early geneticists, one can agree with the assertion of historian of biology Nicolas Rasmussen that "in the first half of the twentieth century, hormones took pride of place as life's master molecules, and the endocrinologist took precedence over the geneticist as the scientist offering the means to control life."[16] In such circumstances, the fact that leading research sponsors like the Rockefeller Foundation in the United

States, the Wellcome Trust in England and the Wallenberg Foundation in Sweden awarded healthy endowments to hormone research in the middle of the last century is easy to understand.

Expectations of the dividends endocrinology would pay were also very much financial. Seeing hormones as the next big thing, the fast-growing pharmaceutical industry actively supported and conducted research and development in the field. In fact, collaboration between business and academia had already been established at the turn of the century. Thus the pharmaceutical industry was an important factor in the creation of hormonal preparations—and in their popularity. Numerous hormone medicaments were launched in the 1930s and 1940s almost as miracle cures, pitched with advertising promising the safe, effective and affordable treatment of an abundance of diagnoses. "Miracle drug" and "wonder drug" were superlatives used to describe, for example, the adrenal cortex hormone cortisone, which after the Second World War began being manufactured for therapeutic use. In 1949, before any clinical tests had been run and side effects documented, newspapers around the world claimed that cortisone, together with the equally new pituitary hormone ACTH (adrenocorticotropic hormone), could be used to successfully treat Addison's Disease, rheumatic fever, gout, inflammation of the eyes, arthritis, psoriasis, sundry skin and blood diseases, sclerosis, osteoarthritis, anemia, and high blood pressure. Thus the fuss made over Gonadex can be described as typical of the period.[17]

In the past few decades, the relationship between hormones and genes has evolved in a manner quite the opposite of what Rasmussen described. From a comprehensive historical perspective, the "hormone model" has been replaced by the "DNA model." Hormonal drugs are still widely prescribed throughout the world, and research into many and varied hormones is ongoing and intensive. But as historians of medicine Sheila M. Rothman and David J. Rothman state in *The Pursuit of Perfection* (2003), the greatest therapeutic and financial hope has now been placed on "gene therapy" rather than "hormone therapy."[18] And insofar as creating life in the future is concerned, it is not a needle filled with hormones being dreamt of, but rather new biotechnologies: cloning, new variations of in vitro fertilization (including pre-implantation genetic diagnostics in order to create "genetically-designed" offspring), even ectogenesis, where the entire pregnancy occurs outside the body.[19] At the same time, the bio-scientific view of mankind as a biological entity has changed; the older idea, that mankind is driven by its hormones, has been complemented with the notion that it is ultimately driven by its genes. For the last couple of decades, this branch of research, influenced by molecular biology and molecular genetics and closely affiliated with business and government, has been referred to as "the new biology."[20]

Against a backdrop in which biological and medical thought, as well as therapeutic practice and the industrial system are all considered to be undergoing a radical restructuring, interest in the modern history of biomedicine has dramatically increased. Since the grand promises and great expectations which we today use to characterize genes are undeniably reminiscent of the ones used little over a half-century ago to describe hormones, it has been indicated that there is much to learn from the fate of endocrinology.[21] History of course does not repeat itself, and comparisons made over such long stretches of time ought to be conducted with caution. Still I am convinced that historical studies of the "new physiology" and its connections with the pharmaceutical industry provide perspectives and provoke speculation of import to today's discussion of the "new biology" and its connection with the gene technology industry. At the very least, such study serves to remind us that the "biotechnological century" did not begin in the 1980s, but rather the 1880s.[22]

A CONTROVERSIAL ISSUE

Research interest within the cultural sciences has heretofore focused mainly on verbal and visual representations of the human body, its functions and component parts, and on biomedical diagnoses and treatments implemented at clinics and hospitals which implied that an increasing number of private, social and political problems had been incorporated into the biomedical frame of reference—the "biomedicalization" of medical services and health care. This transformation of individual human bodies into collective, medical objects, faceless "cases," has become a central theme of critical study.[23] However, even modern, scientifically tested drugs, including hormonal preparations, that were developed, mass-produced and prescribed within the so-called "therapeutic revolution," have come under increasing scrutiny.

Of course, traditional pharmaceutical history has long recorded the development of various drugs and drug research, but almost exclusively those that proved in hindsight to be the most successful. This bias has since been rectified. Studies of medicines are conducted in many different disciplines and from widely varied perspectives, which has resulted in a more nuanced historiography. By not taking the drugs and their therapeutic capabilities for granted and approaching them as a "critical stranger" instead, attempting to open, analyze and contextualize the "black boxes" they tend to turn into after having become established and expounded upon in the medical and pharmaceutical literature, has become the prime strategy of many researchers.[24]

At the same time, studies of drugs undertaken by the cultural sciences have stirred up some controversy. This is partly due to the fact that the object of study often belongs to contemporary history, sometimes still being used regularly in medical practice, which may mean that powerful private, professional and financial interests are in play, but also because drugs are exceptional artifacts whose consequences have been (and are) far from unambiguous. The development of new, effective, mass-produced drugs is undeniably a central element in the foremost success stories of science and industry. Think of the millions of lives prolonged by vaccines, penicillin and insulin alone. Together with other modern medical techniques, drugs comprise without a doubt research's "greatest benefit to mankind," in the words of historian of medicine Roy Porter.[25] However, ever since the tragic consequences of the sedative thalidomide, once considered completely harmless but which proved to have catastrophic side effects by the 1960s, modern drugs have become a social issue of an entirely different dignity.

Other issues include not only the difficulties in predicting short- and long-term negative side effects but also unambiguously determining their positive effects.[26] In turn, these problems are part of an even larger complex of issues dealing with the relationships between the pharmaceutical industry, the life sciences and medical practice and issues of transparency.[27] In the anthology *Contested Ground* (1996), sociologist Peter Davis concretizes this fraught situation aptly when he writes, "Tensions are inevitable because of the complicated moral and symbolic character of pharmaceuticals. Medicines are profitable commodities that are potentially toxic, but that also have the power to heal. In this respect they possess a distinctly postmodern aspect with moral and symbolic ambiguity."[28]

The problematic with the type of pharmaceuticals dealt with in this book is reinforced by the fact that broadly speaking, they belong to reproductive technology, which has always been the subject of much debate in ethical and religious quarters. Practitioners have been accused of jeopardizing the stability of the traditional family and the stability of society as a whole and alternatively preparing the way for the technocratic "brave new world" Aldous Huxley once warned against.[29]

The field has furthermore attracted the interest of numerous gender theoreticians, who have contributed to problematizing technology from various power and gender perspectives. One recurring standpoint is that the development of reproductive technology has taken place in cultures dominated by men, and that this has influenced its design and use in a gender stereotypical, unequal manner. Due to a culturally construed power structure stemming from perceptions of "male" and "female," men have dominated (and profited from) the construction of these techniques, while women, who have been the prime consumers, have been forced to live with the risks and side effects. One of the most vocal critics, Gena Corea, has gone so far as to claim that reproduction technology is by extension an expression of the compulsion of men to exercise power and control, and that its existence is the result of a scientific race for glory and prestige, rather than a genuine desire to help those in need.[30] However, gender research criticism has not primarily concerned itself with whether or not trying to assist couples incapable of having children via the biomedical route is wrong. Rather, it emphasizes the fact that similar technologies could have been developed in other, more equable, less costly ways, had only the biomedical and therapeutic culture been different.[31]

The history and social consequences of modern pharmacy can of course be painted in black and white, but my approach as an historian of science and ideas makes it incumbent upon me to illuminate and investigate both problems and conflicts, merits and mutually-agreed upon solutions—not to praise or condemn, but to facilitate a more profound understanding of the recent past and thus the times in which we live.[32] Further historiographic perspectives informing this volume will be discussed in the section immediately below. Readers uninterested in theoretical and methodological discussions can skip straight to the next chapter without fear of losing the narrative thread.

ARTIFACT BIOGRAPHY AND NETWORK ANALYSIS

Historical studies of modern pharmaceuticals make different historiographic demands on research than traditional historical studies of medical treatments do. In their thought-provoking introduction to the anthology *Biographies of Remedies* (2002), historians Godelieve van Heteren, Marijke Gijswijt-Hofstra and Tilli Tansey write:

> Whilst the historiography of therapies has gained enormously in breadth and sophistication, the call for a history of "remedies" signals yet another important shift: "remedies" evokes other semantic registers than those produced by "therapies." The term "remedies" focuses interest on concrete objects of healing. It evokes notions of production. It

> directs attention to the buzz of productivity and commerce linked to the worlds of healing.[33]

The authors stress that historical research on pharmaceuticals ought to reckon in many factors beyond basic laboratory work and clinical practice, including the means of production and processes of commodification. It is however also important to show how these factors cleave to one another. There are a variety of models from which to choose. Researchers who are themselves engaged in the life sciences sometimes prioritize a linear, almost evolutionary model to describe the birth of a drug: from basic research to clinical testing to medical application.[34] A similarly linear model is also suggested in Norgren's above-mentioned study, which deals with how ideas, solutions and research competence is "transferred" from university to industry. That such transmission occurs is undeniable but it needs to be emphasized that ideas, solutions and research competence is transferred in the opposite direction as well, from industry to academia. Pharmaceutical research is not just about innovation and theoretical knowledge but also material culture. Academic pharmaceutical research exploits a wide variety of resources, from simple standardized substances to the advanced machinery industry has at its disposal. In turn, both academic and industrial research laboratories are dependent on experimental and clinical environments where substances are tested, prescribed and evaluated. Ideas for new drugs can also spring from these environments.

The development of a drug does not necessarily end the moment it goes on the market. In fact, its life cycle has just begun. When it is actually put into use, new and previously unexpected effects can reveal themselves, which can lead to the modification of the preparation or the genesis of new ones. New diagnoses may also manifest themselves. Philosopher Rein Vos likens drugs and disease to dance partners: when one takes a step, the other follows as closely as possible. Vos' point is that it is impossible to accurately predict who will lead and who will follow. "Presumably diseases are just as frequently important in the innovation of therapies, just as drugs can be invented which reveal new aspects of a disease."[35] Since medicine goes through development and fine-tuning in association with testing and treatment, clinical practice is also a significant element in the history of the drug. The distinction between historical studies of the preparation on the one hand and treatment on the other should thus not be exaggerated.[36]

The guiding theoretical principle of the present study is that drugs are techno-scientific artifacts which come into being and are used and developed within the framework of a "medico-academic-industrial complex," where the boundaries between science, technology and medicine are blurred and where academic knowledge development, industrial product development, and clinical practice are apprehended as mutually-influential rather than separate processes.[37] According to this perspective, what eventually gets to be a commercial drug cannot be taken for granted; drugs are not necessarily the result of a given, intra-academic knowledge accretion converted into industrial product development and ending up on the pharmacy shelf. Nor is it given that the drug's significance for the patient or society will be exactly as planned; no drug has only one, single effect and the diagnoses for which the drug is prescribed are not always those for which it was developed. Further complicating the situation is the fact that the drug can both affect the body of the user and influence her attitude toward its significance and consequences. Which can in turn influence the opinion of others. As far as hormonal preparations are concerned, this complicated relationship between "biology" and "society" can be characterized in a variety of ways. One intriguing proposal is, as sociologist Celia Roberts does, to call hormonal drugs "biosocial actors."[38]

Thus a drug can have different meanings over time. It can undergo "identity shifts," even have "multiple personalities," depending on where and how it is used by different social groups. It can at one and the same time be the object of research in a laboratory, a medical tool in the clinic, a product on the market, and a biomedical symbol in popular culture.[39] One way of capturing such a protean identity is to study the preparation biographically. Since the term "biography" refers to a written account of the life of a human being, this suggestion may seem odd at first glance.[40] But the term should be understood metaphorically rather than taken literally. It implies approaching the object of study through its *life cycle* rather than the history of a particular discipline, a particular business, a particular individual, illness, patient group or discovery. Much as the biography of an individual, *artifact biography* can use its study object as a prism through which to view larger social phenomena and events, in the present instance the development of reproduction endocrinology, the population question and the introduction and establishment of hormonal drugs in gynecological practice.[41] Though the current number of drug biographies is modest, especially considering how many influential drugs have come (and gone) during the last fifty years alone, several outstanding examples can be found.[42]

Inspired by sociologist of science Bruno Latour, historians of medicine Vivien Walsh and Jordan Goodman have recommended that the biographical approach be complemented with an actor-network analysis, "which offers the research and narrative strategy of following the object wherever it leads, thus allowing a relationally-based biography to be constructed."[43] Such an analysis localizes the varying actors and things which over the course of time are "enrolled" in the medico-academic-industrial complex and lays bare common interests and channels of communication. It also shows that as a new drug is born and "stabilized" as a reliable medical instrument, new social categories tend to be created and "stabilized," too. I have to some extent been influenced by this perspective, especially insofar as concerns the benefits of the network metaphor for describing the relationships between the socially heterogeneous actors who created (and re-created) Gonadex and elucidating the interplay between academic knowledge development, industrial product development, and clinical practice. This also explains that we are dealing not only with formal, organizational collaborations (what nowadays are usually referred to as "clusters") but also informal and unofficial connections. However, I make no claim to follow the methodological and conceptual program outlined by Latour and his colleagues.

In summation it can be said that I study the development of Gonadex over time by simultaneously studying the networks which contributed to said development. However, network analysis needs a starting point from which to proceed, and I have chosen Aktiebolaget Leo (Helsingborg). I deviate from the main current of business economics network research insofar as I do not see Leo merely as a collective actor, but rather as a coalition of diverse individuals each with his own interests and resources.[44] Moreover, I regard Leo's network both as a "production network" and a "distribution network."[45] These networks should not be construed as detached or successive, but rather overlapping and concurrent. Nor should they be perceived as closed and immutable. As I see it, networks always exist in larger intellectual, political and socio-economic contexts, and though they may be relatively stable, they are subject to change over time.

With reference to previous research into the development of biological drugs in the Western world during the period under investigation, I shall introduce four key practices, central to the work of the pharmaceutical companies, to which production and distribution networks contributed. I call them "consultation," "procuration," "standardization" and "mediation."

CONSULTATION, PROCURATION, STANDARDIZATION AND MEDIATION

As with other techno-scientific artifacts, biomedical products are based on a combination of scientific, technical and industrial knowledge. In *Ways of*

Knowing (2000), John V. Pickstone writes that by this is meant both ways of *knowing*—systematics, analysis, experiment, synthesis—and ways of *doing*—craftsmanship, techniques of rational production, systematic innovation.[46] Historian of science Anders Lundgren has uttered similar thoughts about the chemical industry. Like Pickstone, Lundgren calls attention to the fact that it is based on various types of knowledge, which he categorizes as "analytical knowledge," "synthetic knowledge" and "scale-up knowledge," respectively. "Scale-up knowledge" refers to the ability to transform small-scale laboratory experiments into large-scale production, an ability essential to the pharmaceutical industry. In turn, these different types of knowledge can be linked to the needs of industry. Lundgren first and foremost highlights the obvious financial needs of industry, which demand new knowledge in order to generate new, profitable products. However, he also focuses on the ideological need of industry for scientifically founded arguments to support the marketing of these products.[47]

In the interwar period, well-established companies like Leo naturally had their own resources in the form of capital, technical infrastructure and permanent staff. However, this was not always enough to create, design and sell new techno-scientific artifacts. In order to procure the necessary raw materials as well as manufacture and control the quality of the drug, companies were compelled to enroll external competence. Visible association with recognized expert researchers was also decisive for ideological reasons, in order for the company to be deemed reputable and ethical.[48] Thus pharmaceutical companies were forced to devise production networks in which university researchers and hospital physicians served as essential nodes.

The fact that academics and physicians collaborated with private enterprise was not unproblematic at the beginning of the twentieth century; on the contrary, academia viewed such collaboration with some skepticism. Many, though not all, cherished the ideal that science should remain free to pursue the truth, independent of worldly interests. At the same time, this was an age in which the pharmaceutical industry was riddled with quacks and snake-oil salesmen.[49] In the United States, pharmacists working in the industry were actually refused membership in the American Society for Pharmacology and Experimental Therapeutics. The society wished to avoid, as it stated, "every external influence which would be inimical to the scientific interests of pharmacology."[50] However, during the 1930s and 1940s this distrust began to erode, partly due to the fact that scientists realized that their own research could benefit from the financial and material resources the industry availed them.[51] As Nicolas Rasmussen put it, a change in the "moral economy" of the drug company-medical scientist collaboration took place.[52] These associated researchers contributed to raising the prestige of the pharmaceutical industry, which in turn attracted young academics looking for work and new careers beyond the hallowed halls.[53] Some companies, like Organon in The Netherlands (est. 1923), were in fact created at the initiative of academic scientists.[54]

Experts who could conduct technical, laboratory and clinical research were hired as consultants, either "general" or "specialist" according to the typology of historian of medicine John P. Swann. The former arrangement meant that university scientists with high academic status, broad competence and a comprehensive network of contacts were contracted as scientific advisors. They worked closely with management and were charged with supervising strategic choices of new research projects and products in one or several fields of medicine. Thus their influence on the company was sizable. They also had the task of contributing to the reputation of the company and its products by dint of their personal reputations, and facilitate the future recruitment of staff and its contact with political and other outside interests.[55]

"Specialist" consultants were researchers hired on an ad-hoc basis as experts in their particular field, be it chemistry, microbiology or pharmacology. These individuals were particularly valuable for companies having trouble attracting enough sufficiently competent staff. But specialist consultants were also hired by companies with no such recruitment problems in order to quickly impart the latest news from the "research front" to their staff. In contrast to general consultants, who were usually faithful to one, single company, specialist consultants typically offered their services to several different firms, sometimes all at once.[56]

The production network of the pharmaceutical industry has a further significant material aspect, which ultimately concerned access to natural resources. Producing drugs was not merely a matter of maintaining a well-stocked cabinet of chemical substances. Large-scale production of many types of hormones (so-called "biologicals") also required subcontractors who could be counted on to deliver raw materials with prompt regularity. For these hormones were made from fresh, organic material. It was therefore imperative that the companies establish steady, reliable contacts with the places from whence this raw material came, which included slaughterhouses, farms, hospitals and nursing homes.[57] Scientists in the midst of conducting hormone research also required access to an uninterrupted flow of raw material, which, as sociologist of science Nelly Oudshoorn has shown, intensified the necessity for more or less formal collaboration—infrastructural arrangements—between academy, industry and wholesale suppliers.[58]

Purifying a hormone in the laboratory for industrial production is one thing. Having the resulting drug approved as medicine, convincing physicians to prefer and prescribe it, and moreover, convincing patients to take it, is another. To achieve this a distribution network insuring that the drug be accepted, publicized, sold and used was essential. Such a network included clinics and laboratories with doctors and researchers who prescribe, test and evaluate the preparation *after* it leaves the factory. The network might also incorporate other pharmaceutical companies functioning as distributors to foreign markets. Furthermore, studies of new drugs were usually conducted by special quality-control authorities. The main controlling body in Sweden at the time of the emergence of Gonadex was the National Pharmaceutical Laboratory (NPL) under the auspices of the Royal Board of Medicine. This institute inspected and assessed the properties and possible side effects of the drugs but also determined the extent to which they were "standardized" in conjunction with international guidelines.

In the present context, standardization refers to heeding the formal compliance to use particular instruments and methods in order to facilitate testable and reproducible measurements in different laboratories. This in turn leads to the manufacture of authorized examples considered "standards," which serve as reference objects or units.[59] In order to effect harmonization throughout the pharmaceutical world, scientists have collaborated since the 1920s in stipulating international standards for biological pharmaceutical substances. Initially, this effort was coordinated by the State Serum Institute in Copenhagen and the National Institute for Medical Research in London under the auspices of the Health Section of the League of Nations. After the Second World War, responsibility passed into the hands of the World Health Organization (WHO) and its Expert Committee for Biological Standardization (ECBS).[60]

The goal has been to achieve consensus on how biological substances are defined, how their potency should be determined, and which units were to be used in order to arrive at rational, universal solutions. In practice, however, these solutions have, for better or worse, often proven temporary, pragmatic and dynamic.[61] For standardization also concerns standardized values about what was considered reliable and what skills were considered adequate for the job at the time. In *The Invisible Industrialist* (1998), historians of science Jean-Paul Gaudillière and Ilana Löwy characterize the situation in the following manner: "It is about standardized items being similarly produced, as well as judging these items to be reliable means of operation and evaluation. It also refers to judging individuals to be reliable when using these adequate means."[62] A pharmaceutical company intent on marketing a new drug was required to defer to these complicated conditions, but so was the body inspecting the finished product. Maintaining a good mutual relationship was in everybody's best interests.

Marketing departments and public relations firms also comprised an essential node in the distribution network. The bigger pharmaceutical companies had their own, in-house "information departments" which made sure that the country's physicians were regularly called on and convinced of the excellence of their wares. And in turn, salesmen, or "pharmaceutical consultants," gathered opinions and information from their clients for the company; communication was a two-way street. By distributing ads directly to physicians, pharmacists and scholarly periodicals, they were considered ethically acceptable, as opposed to advertisements in the daily papers. In addition, the mass media were approached indirectly, for example by inviting journalists to tour the company's facilities or issuing press releases later quoted in the news.

Scientific consultants played a role in marketing and public relations, too. Physicians and medical researchers have in fact been deeply involved in introducing new drugs, not only through consultant work and clinical trials but also by actively collaborating with industry in identifying and creating new markets. From ethnographic studies of the practices of developing and introducing drugs to treat so-called "female sexual dysfunction," sociologist Jennifer R. Fishman declares that public medical experts act as "mediators."

> Clinical trial researchers play integral and often purposeful roles in bringing new sexual dysfunction drugs to market, by making them publicly acceptable and by legitimating their clinical uses. In this capacity, researchers often position themselves as mediators between pharmaceutical companies and regulatory agencies, the professional medical community, and potential consumers of new drugs.[63]

As an example, Fishman states that today, medical researchers relay information about clinical trials at a variety of medical gatherings, like continuation courses, and by increasing public awareness about new diagnoses and treatments via Internet websites. At the same time, medical researchers pass information and knowledge from clinics to companies; and this channel of communication is also multi-directional. Medical researchers acting as mediators between pharmaceutical companies and consumers (doctors and patients) when, and even before, new drugs are introduced is however nothing new, even if the precise form of mediation has changed over time.[64] In this study, the contributions of Axel Westman will be closely scrutinized.

SOURCES AND SCOPE

One of the circumstances explaining the lack of historical studies of modern pharmaceuticals is the difficulty in gaining access to adequate source material. This difficulty does not lie in the fact that private pharmaceutical companies have been less diligent in archiving their documents than their public counterparts, but rather that these archives are often only open to company employees. To gain access as an external researcher requires special consent, and to be granted consent requires negotiation. Whether these negotiations will lead to consent is impossible to predict, as it depends on company policy and how it is interpreted. This at least has been my experience.

After lengthy negotiations, I had the pleasure of finally being permitted to visit and use parts of the archives of Aktiebolaget Leo (Helsingborg). These studies, undertaken in the autumn of 2003 and spring of 2005, were conducted with the permission of Pfizer, who then owned the archives.[65] The empirical foundation upon which the present volume rests consists mainly of material from Leo. I have had the opportunity of studying documents on Gonadex, Homogonal and other sex hormone drugs developed and sold by Leo, mostly in the form of incoming and outgoing correspondence pertaining to development and marketing. However, I have not been able to systematically partake of documents concerning the actual running of the company, which has considerably limited my efforts to follow the company's decision-making process. This obstacle has been partly overcome thanks to the company chronicle *Från Leopiller till nicorette* [From Leo pills to nicorette] (2002), which is based on source material from the same archives.[66] Other information, including the registration and control of Leo's pharmaceutical products, has been gleaned from the papers of National Pharmaceutical Laboratory (NPL), housed in the National Archives in Arninge (NAA), Stockholm.

Leo's papers were archived by then-owner Pharmacia in the mid-1990s in cooperation with the non-profit Scanian Industrial Archives. These in-house archives, which came to be known as the "Leo Historical Archives" (LHA) were located in the company's former plant in Helsingborg. Despite some thinning out while being catalogued, it turned out to be a rich collection featuring some 7,000 volumes of registered, somewhat haphazardly sorted documents covering the years 1920 to 1986. Today, the Leo Historical Archives are no longer housed in the plant, having been moved to the Scanian Industrial Archives' premises (also placed in Helsingborg) in 2005, where its contents will eventually be made available to researchers. In the present bibliography, references to the volumes of documents from the Leo

Historical Archives follow the system used in the original archive. Whether or not the same system will be employed in the Scanian Industrial Archives has yet to be determined.

Another source of invaluable material to the composition of this book is the Archives of the Women's Clinic of the Royal Caroline Hospital (WCA), housed in the Stockholm County Council Archives (SCCA). I have gone through twenty-four document volumes containing incoming and outgoing letters from the period 1920–60. This archival material includes correspondence between Leo and Axel Westman and other scholars and physicians. I have used these letters as sources to study relationships and communication between the various actors. On the other hand, I have not come across any minutes or other archival material from the hormone laboratory of the clinic offering details of laboratory research on either Gonadex or any other preparation. Nor have I been able to find archives dedicated solely to Axel Westman, either at the university or any of Sweden's other public archives. Along with those already mentioned, I have gleaned facts about Westman and his activities from the Regional State Archive of Uppsala, the archives of the Knut and Alice Wallenberg Foundation (KAWF) in Stockholm and through interviews with two of his colleagues, Egon Diczfalusy and Rolf Luft, and his daughter, Ann-Margret Sundius.

From the archives of the Women's Clinic of the Caroline Hospital I have also perused letters to and from private individuals, especially in order to study user attitudes toward Gonadex and other hormone drugs. In accordance with Swedish law, these letters are classified, which means that details that may in any way breech "the privacy of the individual" may not be published. For this reason, private correspondents will not be referred to by name, nor will their income bracket or profession be made evident. Letters will instead be referred to by date and whether the writer was male or female, as "name withheld (F)" and "name withheld (M)" respectively. However, since hormonal sterility treatment was an expensive undertaking, we may presume that as a rule, the writers belonged to the upper social classes, though of course every rule has its exception. It would also have been interesting to study the medical effects of Gonadex and Homogonal directly from patient files, but this has proven impossible to arrange. A general image of the outcome of treatments has however been possible to compile thanks to the internal reports with which Westman and other scientists provided Leo.

I wish to advise the reader that several of the documents I have used are not originals but rather photocopies, transcriptions or drafts. This is the case with all the letters from the Women's Clinic sent to private households and some to other recipients. In instances where I have not had access to original letters, I have also made do with transcriptions of outgoing mail from Leo, the Knut and Alice Wallenberg Foundation and the NPL. Documents from Leo have in many cases been duplicated and circulated within the company. One and the same document, letters included, can therefore have been sent to a number of individuals simultaneously. Furthermore, sometimes specifications as to who has written the letter are missing. When the name is unclear, I have consistently listed "LHA" as remitter. In order not to overtax the footnotes, I have omitted such detailed source information. The source of each is however always made clear.

This book is also based on a large amount of published material, particularly books, scholarly articles and op-ed commentary in domestic and international periodicals of medicine, endocrinology and pharmacology from the beginning of the century to the 1970s. I have systematically gone through the Swedish journals in these fields—*Farmaceutisk Revy* [Swedish pharmaceutical review], *Svensk Farmaceutisk Tidskrift* [Swedish pharmaceutical journal] and *Svenska Läkartidningen* [Swedish medical journal]. Otherwise the selection has been made with the help of summaries and bibliographies. I have also made use of press material, primarily in order to follow the launches of Gonadex in 1948 and Homogonal in 1967, respectively, but also in order to provide insight into the public debate on endocrinology. To this end, the collections of press clippings stored in the Leo Historical Archives and the Knut and Alice Wallenberg Foundation Archives along with those (for the years 1939–55) of the administrative and personnel departments of the Royal Caroline Hospital in the Stockholm County Council Archives have proven invaluable.

OUTLINE

The basic narrative strategy chosen for this book maintains a biographical approach, which means that the history of Gonadex is presented chronologically: from cradle to grave, as it were. This account is complemented throughout with an analysis of the production and distribution networks within which Gonadex was developed and marketed, dealing partly with the main practices of the network—consultation, procuration, standardization, mediation—and partly with the broader political, socio-economic and mass medial context of which the network itself was a part.

Hormones of Life is divided into three sections, each containing three chapters. The first section, "Tradition," is intended to provide background and context from three different, if overlapping, perspectives. Chapter One describes the early development of endocrinology from the perspective of the history of ideas, with particular focus on so-called "sexual endocrinology." Much of the medical terminology necessary to the lay reader's understanding of the story is introduced here. The second chapter introduces Axel Westman and his notions on the significance of endocrinology for gynecology in general and the scourge of sterility specifically. It also investigates the role of sterility and sterility research in relation to the federal government's population policy. In Chapter Three, I present Leo, its gradual orientation toward endocrinology, and the establishment of Sweden's first hormone laboratory. Together these chapters cover the period from the turn of the century to the early 1940s.

The second section, "Innovation," takes place during a few years at the end of the 1940s and deals with the origins, marketing and reception of Gonadex. Thus the story becomes more concentrated. In Chapter Four, I show how the substance which would become Gonadex was developed, tested and registered as an original preparation. Chapter Five relates the grandiose launch of the product and the image of the drug as construed by the mass media. Chapter Six describes how it was received by physicians, scientists, experts and invested members of the public. Together these chapters facilitate a comparison between the official image of Gonadex and the one Leo wished to portray. In turn, these images are problematized by contrasting them with how Gonadex functioned in practice.

The third and final section, "Development," shows how work on perfecting the drug continued after its launch and how its identity went through several changes between 1949 and 1986, when Gonadex was finally deregistered as a drug. In Chapter Seven I analyze Leo's strategies for altering Gonadex and having it accepted as a drug, during the course of which we witness how both Leo's gonadotropin research network and public debate about hormone preparations were transformed in the years immediately following its launch. In Chapters Eight and Nine I demonstrate how pituitary glands from both calves and human beings were introduced to reproductive endocrinological research and therapy, and the effect this had on Leo's continued efforts in the field of sterility, at which point its gonadotropin drug Homogonal, from 1967, enters the spotlight.

Finally, the present volume rounds off with a concluding analysis summarizing first the collaboration between Leo and Axel Westman and then Gonadex and its protean identity. Through discussion of the continuous development of reproductive technology during the 1970s and 1980s, I come full circle and revisit the relationship between the new physiology and the new biology.

PART I

TRADITION

CHAPTER ONE

Hormones and Hormone Therapy: Historical Background

As a rule, a biography begins with a background sketch establishing the links between the main actors and their historical context. A drug also has a background, belongs to a tradition, which requires extrapolation in order for its origin and character to be intelligible. Thus this chapter opens with an overview of the foundation of endocrinology as a field of research and therapeutic practice. Thereafter it proceeds to delineate how first sex hormones and later gonadotropins became the focus of interwar endocrinology. The chapter makes no claim to originality but is rather an introduction to the world of hormones, largely based on previous historical research. Other, more political and material aspects of Gonadex' historical background will be investigated in the two following chapters.

INTERNAL SECRETION AND ORGANOTHERAPY

It has been said that drugs containing hormones are among the most widely distributed and prescribed in the history of medicine. And indeed, today it is almost impossible to imagine a world without them.[1] Still, the history of hormone preparations is not long. At the turn of the last century, hormones were still an unknown quantity to the great majority, physicians included. On the other hand, at least some doctors were familiar with something known as "internal secretion." The term, generally attributed to French physiologist Claude Bernard (1813–1878), refers to the fact that certain organs produce chemical substances, which flow straight into the bloodstream and have a direct effect on the body.[2] This knowledge led to a partially new view of mankind's health and physiology.

In the first half of the nineteenth century, physiological understanding of the body and the central functions of life were greatly a matter of the relationship between the brain, the nervous system and the cells. Glands too, the subject of exhaustive medical study ever since the seventeenth century, were considered regulated by the electrical currents of the nerves. In 1812, zoologist George Cuvier claimed that the nervous system *was* the entire organism and that all other systems were subordinate to it.[3] During the second half of the nineteenth century, this tendency began to be broadened by researchers throughout Europe, who meant that certain types of disease, like life itself, could not be explained without considering the effect of internal secretion on the organism and its biological evolution.[4] How the reciprocal relationship between the "electrical nervous system" and the "chemical internal secretion system" was to be interpreted aroused heated debate, but it was initially assumed that both functioned in entirely different ways and completely independent of one another. A simile later made popular was that the nervous system was like a telephone switchboard with its network of cables and wires, while internal secretion resembled radio waves, transmitted by a wireless station and only caught by receivers tuned in to the broadcaster's wavelength.[5]

Along with bacteriology, research on internal secretion established an explicit collaboration with practical medicine early, a process historians have called medicine's "laboratory revolution."[6] From the outset, research on internal secretion was conducted at both medical clinics and academic laboratories, which implied that in practice, it was as much applied medicine as basic physiology.[7] One common starting point was the fact that the chemical composition of internal secretions was necessary to the physiological processes of the body, but that in too small or too large amounts it could also cause disease. In a manner almost reminiscent of the humoral pathology of the ancient Greeks—according to which disease occurs due to an "imbalance" between bodily fluids—questions of how the quantity of these substances could be adjusted and "balanced" were posed. What could be removed, what could be added, and how could the effect of such treatment be gauged and controlled?

Internal secretional illnesses were initially treated surgically, by removing or replacing sections of the glands. Beginning in the 1870s, it was not uncommon for gynecologists in the United States and in some European countries to remove ovaries (one or both) not only in order to treat infection and tumors but also mental and nervous complaints, often referred to as "hysteria." Thus many women were deprived of what we today would consider normally functioning ovaries.[8] Also well known are the "revitalization methods" developed by Viennese physiologist Eugen Steinach (1861–1944) and Parisian surgeon Serge (Samuel) Voronoff (1866–1951) at the beginning of the century, which entailed the rejuvenating of older men in particular. Their method consisted of operating on the tissue of the testicles and vas deferens but also included transplantation of testicular tissue harvested from deceased young men or monkeys. For a time, this treatment was quite routine, especially in the United States, even if it was the subject of much debate.[9] Functioning sex glands were literally regarded as fountains of youth.[10] As a doctor quoted in the *New York Times* said in 1921, "With a perfectly balanced endocrine system one would live forever. In fact, your fountain of youth lies within yourself."[11] Less well known is the fact that gynecologists in an analogous manner performed ovarian transplants in an attempt to treat women suffering from sterility and early-onset menopause, among other things. The American surgeon Robert Tuttle Morris (1857–1945), for example, implanted pieces of ovaries (about the size of a pea) donated from fertile women into numerous women who had been subject to ovariotomy.[12]

Parallel to the surgical alternative, physicians and researchers tried to create drugs out of extracts from organs considered to produce internal secretion. At University College in London, injections of extracts from animal pancreas and thyroid glands were tested in the 1890s in an attempt to treat diabetes and myxoedema (the edema and dry skin seen in primary hypothyroidism). These tests were deemed successful and encouraged further research.[13] The most famous of these early attempts to manipulate internal secretion remains however those which entailed testicular extracts from puppies and hamsters performed in the late 1880s by French physiologist and neurologist Charles-Édouard Brown-Séquard (1817–1894), first on laboratory animals and then on himself. Brown-Séquard, who succeeded Claude Bernard as the chair of medicine at the Collège de France, maintained that geriatric debility was the result of decreased production of internal secretions and that injections of these extracts could have a bracing, vitalizing effect. Similar experiments were also being conducted on women in Paris, but in this case the injections contained ovarian extracts taken from guinea pigs. These methods created quite a sensation and sex gland extracts, sometimes called "Brown-Séquard fluids," were soon being prescribed to individuals with a variety of diagnoses, from hysteria to tuberculosis and cholera.[14]

Organ drugs were embraced by the burgeoning pharmaceutical industry and spread quickly across Europe and across the ocean to the USA, where the press and advertising proclaimed that the elixir of life—the much sought after *elixir vitae* of the alchemists—had finally been discovered.[15] The use of similar preparations, sold in pill, powder or liquid form and based on one or more glands from different animals, was referred to as "organotherapy."[16] The term recurred in the titles of books and periodicals and even the names of a few businesses, including the British Organotherapy Company, Ltd. Like other "patent medicines," however, organotherapy was beset by suspicion. Physicians, researchers and esteemed medical journals were all skeptical about rejuvenation remedies à la Brown-Séquard, protesting that organotherapy was at best ineffective and at worst potentially harmful to the patient. As an editorial in the *British Medical Journal* explained in 1893:

> Manufacturing chemists are making extracts not only of thyroid, but of nearly every organ in the body, even including the pituitary body, this last for the cure of acromegaly. We find medical men writing of these ideas and of the cures achieved in the most sanguine strain, and often upon no better evidence than quacks produce for their "cures."[17]

As late as the first decades of the twentieth century, top-selling organ preparations were being dismissed as sheer quackery. Gynecologists in particular complained that mass-produced sex gland drugs rarely performed satisfactorily, at least no better than their own, "homemade" extracts. In turn, the gynecologists were criticized by physiologists for using preparations whose effects had yet to be confirmed experimentally.[18] For pharmaceutical companies wishing to maintain a serious reputation, dabbling in this field was risky business.

FROM ORGANOTHERAPY TO ENDOCRINOLOGY

Systematic animal testing proved that certain organ preparations did in fact have palpable physiological effect. Together with theoretical and experimental advances in biochemical research on internal secretion, this contributed to maintaining medical interest. When relatively pure chemical substances began to be produced from gland extracts, great expectations were raised about their use in concentrated form as potent, "scientific" drugs.

The first substance purified from the internal secretion of an endocrine gland was christened "epinephrine." The substance was isolated from secretions of the adrenal medulla in 1901 and launched the same year by the American firm Parke, Davis and Company under the name "Adrenalin" (without the "e"). Adrenaline immediately entered into regular medical use where it served as an anesthetic and in the treatment of hypotension, cardiac arrest and respiratory distress brought on by asthma attacks and allergic reactions.[19] A chemically synthesized adrenal preparation followed some six years later when Meister, Lucius and Brüning of Germany introduced Suprarenin.[20] Another internal secretional substance adopted early on by medicine and quickly commercialized was thyroid gland extract. Thyroxin was isolated during the First World War and marketed by the American firm Squibb. It took ten more years before synthetic thyroxin was also made available.[21]

At the beginning of the twentieth century, the term "hormone" was introduced to signify the biologically active substance in internal secretions. The word originates in the Greek verb *hormao*, which means "set in motion," "urge," "stimulate."[22] Its coining is usually attributed to English physiologist Ernest Starling (1866–1927) of University College in London. In 1905 he defined a "hormone" as a chemical substance produced in one of the organs and transported via the bloodstream to other locations in the body in order to exercise an influence and regulate or coordinate the evolution of the organism.[23] A metaphor made popular by Starling referred to hormones as the "chemical messengers" of the body. After Starling, other definitions were proposed. That it long proved difficult to reach a consensus in this matter is suggested by Swedish scientist Axel Westman in his book *Hormoner* [Hormones] (1940).

> It might seem that [defining hormones] is unnecessary, given how often internal secretion, hormone research and organotherapy are spoken and written about nowadays. In actual fact, however, it is no easy task to stipulate what best be included in the term "hormone."[24]

As seen, the terms "internal secretion" and "organotherapy" recurred well into the 1900s, though their use fell off successively with the establishment of the more academic sounding "endocrine" and "endocrinology." The word "endocrine" also has Greek roots in *endon*, which means "inside," and *krino*, which means "separate" or "differentiate." It began to be used to designate glands that produced internal secretions, as in the expression "endocrine glands" and "endocrine organs."[25] In 1906 it was suggested that endocrinology be used to denote the theory of endocrine glands, their secretion in the form of hormones and their diseases.[26] Practitioners in the field would thus henceforth be known as "endocrinologists."

Endocrinology became the umbrella term for a variety of expertise and practice, but a new academic discipline or medical specialty in the conventional sense had yet to emerge.[27] Worth noting, however, is the fact that a multidisciplinary society dedicated to the subject was created in 1917, the Association for the Study of the Internal Secretions (ASIS), renamed The Endocrine Society in 1952. The association consisted of physicians, researchers and pharmaceutical manufacturers in the United States, though it long served as an international society.[28] One of the original founders of ASIS was the famous (and in some medical circles infamous) Henry R. Harrower (1883–1934), a physician and manufacturer of organ preparations who tirelessly propounded the benefits of hormone therapy and published the handbook *Practical Hormone Therapy: A Manual of Organotherapy for General Practitioners* (1914). His advice to the eager physicians was simply to use the trial-and-error method: if one preparation did not work as expected one could always try another one.[29] Harrower was also the first editor of ASIS's pioneering journal, *Endocrinology*.[30] Optimism within the ranks of the new society was rife, as evident by the introduction to the first issue.

> There has been, during the recent period, in no department of medicine more activity manifested than that which has characterized the study of the glands of internal secretion. — Indeed, the interest in endocrinology has been widespread not only among alert internists and surgeons, but also among experimental pathologists and physiologists, pathological anatomists and histologists, comparative anatomists and embryologists, pharmacologists, and biological chemists. The nature of the ductless glands, previously obscure, has been recognized; and the new principle of a regulation and correlation of the functions of the different bodily organs by "chemical messengers," or "hormones" (in addition to the earlier recognized principle of nervous regulation), has been generally accepted.[31]

It should be recalled, however, that endocrinology still remained controversial at the time of the foundation of ASIS. A struggle over epistemological privilege ensued between various scientific and medical professions and debate on dubious vitalization cures raged regularly.[32] When the dust finally settled, only a few organ and hormone drugs with proven effect were marketed before 1917.[33] As numerous scholars have indicated, the reputation of the field was even shakier outside the United States. Though it had its partisans, endocrinology as both concept and practice long remained a bone of contention.[34] As far as the present author can tell, no organizational impulses in the form of societies for the advancement of endocrinological research in Europe can be detected until after the Second World War. But once it did take hold, the professionalization process progressed that much faster.[35]

The definitive medical and commercial breakthrough came with the introduction of insulin, extracted from the pancreas and launched in the early 1920s, first and foremost as a weapon in the fight against diabetes.[36]

While the results of treatment with the new drug were not unequivocally positive, they were a significant improvement on what had been achieved in previous years. "If endocrinology had no other triumph to its credit than the discovery of insulin, that alone would be a sufficient reward for all the labors that have brought science to its present state," observed a report published in 1936.[37] This breakthrough was achieved through intimate collaboration between Eli Lilly and Company in the United States, scientists at the University of Toronto in Canada and a string of medical clinics.[38] Insulin not only brought fortune to sufferers of diabetes but also to Eli Lilly, the scientists and their university. In 1923, two of the many individuals involved, physician Frederick Banting (1891–1941) and physiologist John Macleud (1876–1935) were awarded the Nobel Prize in Physiology or Medicine. Insulin went on sale in Sweden a year later, a topic to which I shall return in Chapter Three, as it has significance for the understanding of Leo's status in the field of hormones.

The unprecedented success of insulin contributed to raising expectations on the clinical side of endocrinology and drawing attention to the value of close collaboration between industry and the academy. There was no longer any doubt that the functions of the human body could, at least provisionally, be manipulated with the help of hormones. The hope was to be able to treat and cure medical problems—hormonal imbalances—but also improve, "refine," things about the human body that contemporary society accepted as perfectly normal. According to historians of medicine Sheila M. Rothman and David J. Rothman, "The initial discoveries held out the promise that endocrinology would empower medicine both to correct gross abnormalities, whether they were physical, mental, or behavioral, and then also to improve normal functioning. Hormones might be able to refashion the self."[39] Against this backdrop of optimism not only regular research financiers but also a number of pharmaceutical companies began to invest heavily in endocrinology.

SEX HORMONES IN FOCUS

During the interwar period, the endocrinological debate and research in the Western world focused in no small degree on sex glands and sex hormones. In the United States (as well as Europe), this was at least partly due to the interest the Rockefeller Foundation expressed in financing research, which served to scientize politically sensitive issues of reproduction, birth control, sexuality, prostitution, gender roles and eugenics. For decades the Foundation channeled funds to researchers through the Committee for Research in

Problems of Sex (CRPS), established by the National Research Council in 1921. The CRPS was a direct descendant of the Rockefeller-funded Bureau of Social Hygiene, founded in 1913. Of all available entry points into the broad complex of the "problems of sex," the CRPS chose to prioritize hormone research, which it felt could provide a solid scientific basis upon which other fields could build.[40]

The lion's share of the CRPS's socially motivated subsidies to sex hormone research was allocated to research groups at the University of Chicago, Berkeley and Cornell, and to specialist research centers at Yale, Columbia and the University of Wisconsin. The Rockefeller Foundation also sponsored hormone research abroad, including that of Axel Westman and his team at Lund University.[41] In 1937, the Foundation also organized a Committee on Endocrinology, further strengthening the hand of hormone research. This multidisciplinary investment proved highly successful over time, and contributed to the extraction of internal secretions from sex glands and discovery of the presence of several sex hormones. Estrogen, first known as "the ovarian hormone," was produced in 1923 and isolated in pure form six years later. The first major compilation of results was produced when a member of the CRPS staff, Edgar Allen, a zoologist and professor of anatomy at Yale, published the now-classic *Sex and Internal Secretions: A Survey of Recent Research* in 1932. When the second, revised edition was published seven years later, the volume had swollen to more than 1,300 pages.[42] But the Americans were of course not alone. Significant contributions to the field were made in Europe over the same stretch of time. Two networks have been cited as particularly influential, one in Holland headed up by pharmacologist Ernst Laqueur (1880–1947) and his research team at the firm Organon and the Pharmacotherapeutic Laboratory in Amsterdam, and the other in Germany, where Adolf Butenandt (1903–1995) and his team were working for Schering AG and the Kaiser Wilhelm Institute for Biochemical Research in Berlin.[43]

Endocrinological research on sex glands and sex hormones had an enormous effect on the view of mankind. As historian Julia Rechter has demonstrated in her dissertation "'The Glands of Destiny'" (1997), a theoretical model was formulated in which both the biology and culture of mankind were related to the influence of sex hormones. "Hormones, in the 1920s," writes Rechter, "were everywhere and could do anything."[44] However, the greatest amount of interest on behalf of both the research community and the pharmaceutical industry was focused on what was considered the "female" sex hormone. One significant reason was the accepted medical notion that sexual biology played an immensely larger role in the lives of women than it did for men. Sex hormones became central to the understanding of the biological evolution and constitution of women in terms of menstrual cycle, fertility, pregnancy and menopause.[45] They were also considered as having a decisive effect on what was seen as the typically female physique as well as female behavior on the whole. The Swedish journal of medicine *Svenska Läkartidningen* bluntly stated that sex hormones were the "actual content" of women's lives.[46] Late eighteenth-century biological notions of the "specifically feminine" as emanating from the ovaries had now boiled down to an idea of the essence of femininity being chemical, comprised of sex hormones.[47]

The reorientation of sexual endocrinology in the direction of the female body was strengthened in its resolve by the fact that while the medical landscape was dotted with women's clinics, corresponding clinics for the male sex were non-existent. With sex hormones gynecologists had found a new scientific language and new theoretical and practical tools. A series of so-called "female illnesses," both somatic and psychological, were immediately related directly to hormones. One classic diagnosis of the utmost significance to what follows below was "menstrual imbalance" or in medical terminology, "amenorrhea." This Greek-derived, Latin neologism, meaning roughly "non-monthly flow," referred to the non-occurrence of menses in women of a fertile age (who were neither pregnant nor nursing). The diagnosis was subdivided into primary amenorrhea, which means that menstruation has never occurred, and secondary amenorrhea, where menstruation ceases for an extended period. Many arguments in favor of treating the disorder with hormones were broached. As historian of ideas Karin Johannisson points out, menstruation was understood almost as a barometer of women's health.[48] The endocrinological conclusion that menstruation and ovulation were interrelated raised suspicions that amenorrhea could be a symptom or even the cause of infertility. Another reason was based in psychology and concerned the fact that since menstruation was so strongly associated with female existence, when it stopped the afflicted individual risked suffering an identity crisis.[49]

Even conditions previously perceived as completely normal were now conceptualized and diagnosed as hormone imbalances. The phenomenon of "premenstrual stress" (PMS) was established as late as 1931. In this manner, the number of female diagnoses considered to require treatment with sex hormones increased rapidly and became during the course of the 1930s ten times as big as the corresponding diagnoses for men. Via this biomedicalization process the breadth of usage, along with the market for drugs based on sex hormones appeared nearly infinite; every woman was a potential client, and for years to come, to boot.[50] And the market grew even larger when gynecologists began advocating hormones in an attempt to forestall possible hormonal imbalances in order to prevent, for example, miscarriage. The fact that numerous companies in both Europe and the United States began manufacturing sex hormones was a result of this view of women but also the realization that they could be produced in a relatively cheap and effective manner.

NEW METHODS OF PRODUCTION AND QUALITY CONTROL

Since the end of the nineteenth century, organ preparations had mainly been produced out of endocrine gland extracts. For a long time even the first sex hormone drugs were drawn from the same source, which greatly increased the demand for human and animal (especially swine and cattle) ovaries and testicles. Companies needed colossal quantities of biological material in order to manufacture their drugs, but so did endocrinal researchers in order to conduct experimental studies, develop methods for extracting and synthesizing hormones, test their physiological effect and analyze their chemical structure. Under such circumstances, where raw material and research material were practically the same thing, competition for resources was fierce. In order to meet this demand, new networks and infrastructural arrangements consisting not only of pharmaceutical companies and universities but also suppliers like hospitals, gynecological clinics, slaughterhouses and farms emerged. Some universities and firms even started their own farms, raising livestock as well as laboratory animals.[51]

Sex glands actually contain miniscule amounts of sex hormones; for every gram of concentrated hormone extract literally tons of biological material was required. Thus the harvesting of this raw material was understandably complicated and costly. More effective methods were called for and several different ones were tried. Researchers in England even attempted to make do with ovaries from blue whales, a method which, partly due to preservation difficulties, was not particularly successful.[52] Toward the end of the 1920s however, a new, more attractive source emerged. Two research gynecologists at the Charité Hospital's Women's Clinic in Berlin, Selmar Aschheim (1878–1965) and Bernhard Zondek (1891–1966), published a series of reports claiming that relatively large amounts of sex hormones were excreted into the blood and urine of expectant women and pregnant mares.[53] Zondek also chanced across female sex hormones in the urine of stallions (and in even greater concentration in their testicles), discoveries which proved that the sex hormone was not as gender specific as had previously been assumed.[54]

On the contrary, during the course of the 1930s a consensus was reached that both types of hormones could be found in both men and women. "Male" and "female" sex hormones, or estrogen and androgen, would henceforth be defined according to their chemical structure rather than gender. This did not however prevent the two types of hormones from continuing to be associated with their respective sexual attributes.[55]

The detection of sex hormones in urine had huge value to both research and industry. Here was a "residual product" that could be recycled. Urine had previously proven important in the industrial production of salpeter, ammonia and manure.[56] During the 1930s it became the prime ingredient in the manufacture of sex hormones. Expectant women and pregnant horses suddenly became key resources and the collection of urine for the purpose of producing hormones developed into a minor industry of its own.[57] The fact that many expensive hormone drugs were derived from lowly urine was likely unknown to many of those who took them, though the fact was occasionally mentioned in advertising. The name of one of the most widely prescribed estrogen drugs in history, Premarin (Ayerst Laboratories from 1942) is in fact an acronym for "*pre*gnant *mar*e's ur*ine*."[58]

The discovery of this stable, inexpensive and readily accessible natural resource further contributed to coaxing researchers and pharmaceutical companies to concentrate their hormone studies on sex hormones, especially "female" ones. Scientists had certainly learned that "male" sex hormones could also be produced from urine and testicle extract, and sex hormone therapies for men were being developed to treat enlarged prostates, male menopause (defined as a marked reduction in sexual potency, libido, mental capacity and vitality), erectile dysfunction and even homosexuality.[59] But expectations were low and the medical use of such drugs comparatively modest, due to the fact that male sex hormones were expensive to produce and medical interest in male reproduction was slight. As mentioned above, there was no male counterpart to gynecological practice and thus no obvious context in which comprehensive clinical studies of men with "hormone imbalances" could be conducted. The profession probably also wanted to avoid the risk of being accused of prescribing unreliable revitalization cures in the wake of Brown-Séquard. However, research into and use of male sex hormones slowly gained momentum after 1935, when they began to be manufactured synthetically, generally for the treatment of cancer.[60] As long as testosterone (including anabolic steroids) has been available, it has also attracted the unwelcome attention of athletes, body-builders and others who wished to increase their physical capacity artificially, as is well documented.[61]

FIGURE 1 Notions of "feminine" and "masculine" are reproduced in endocrine theory as well as in the marketing of sex hormone drugs. Organon–Pharmacia's Menformon, which contained female sex hormone, was marketed with a female gender symbol and a (headless) woman's body. *Hormoner* 6 (1942).

The turn toward "female" sex hormones in hormone research and the pharmaceutical industry thus had cognitive, institutional and material aspects. However, the history of experimental biology is evidence that it has not been unusual for research to be restricted and dictated by the availability of raw material. Summarizing her survey of the evolution of reproduction physiology in the United States during the first half of the twentieth century, sociologist of science Adele E. Clarke states that "[t]he availability of and familiarity with particular biological materials surely did much to shape the pace, direction, and even the content of research in reproductive physiology and no doubt in other fields as well."[62] The circumstances are familiar today, for example when genetic research is stimulated by the type of biological material which happens to be locally available through biobanks.[63]

Another issue raised during the infancy of sexual endocrinology was that several different methods could be used to determine and describe the potency and effect of hormone drugs. Wild variation abounded in both scientific reports and the brochures issued by pharmaceutical companies. Furthermore, hormones were known by different names in different

FIGURE 2 Organon–Pharmacia's Neo-Hombreol, which contained male sex hormones, was marketed with a male gender symbol and a reproduction of two men battling over a woman in J. P. Molin's bronze statue *Bältesspännare*. *Hormoner* 6 (1942).

countries. This discrepancy made it exceedingly difficult to scientifically compare hormone preparations. It also complicated decisions about dosage and treatment for health care professionals. With this in mind, the Health Section of the League of Nations began arranging international conferences on pharmacological endocrinology in order to achieve consensus on guidelines. The goal was international standardization.

The two first conferences were held in 1932 and 1935 at the National Institute for Medical Research in London and hosted by its director, Sir Henry Dale, the foremost authority on the standardization of biological substances.[64] At the first "International Conference on Standardization of Sex Hormones," female sex hormones unsurprisingly topped the agenda. A biological test created by Edgar Allen and fellow American Edward Doisy in 1923 was chosen to determine the potency of estrogen. Doisy was a biochemist who was both a member of the CRPS and on the payroll of the American pharmaceutical giant Parke-Davis. In conducting these tests, the ovaries of female mice or rats were removed. The animals were then treated with hormones, whereupon cell change in the vagina was monitored. If the changes showed that the animal had gone into heat, then the hormone had had the desired effect.[65] The need for standardizing male sex hormones, the corpus luteum ("yellow body") hormone and the pituitary hormone was also discussed, but all agreed that the time was not yet ripe for deciding their fates.

The next conference, aptly advertised as the "Second Conference on the Standardization of Sex Hormones," also spent a great deal of time discussing estrogen. Since discovering that there was not just *one estrogen* but rather a *variety of estrogens* (estrone, estriol and estradiol), previous directives were in need of recalibration. Decisions were also made concerning the standardization of the corpus luteum hormone and the male sex hormone, or androsterone. In determining the latter, the so-called "cockscomb test" was chosen, which consisted of comparing the difference in a castrated rooster's comb before and after hormone treatment.[66] During both conferences it was also agreed that for each and every type of hormone, a standard preparation would be chosen as the international benchmark against which other drugs could be calibrated. Dosages would then be determined in international units of measurement, initially referred to as "mouse units," "rat units" and "cockscomb units."

It was in the best interests of reputable pharmaceutical companies to follow the guidelines sanctioned by the League of Nations as closely as possible. Information assuring that the drug was standardized according to international guidelines was also widely used in advertising since it testified to the quality control of the product. At the same time, standardization was both time-consuming and costly. The work needed to be performed in a laboratory environment by skilled personnel and with the help of a large number of animals suitable to the task. However, even when companies hired external experts and strove to meet standardization demands, problems emerged. Exact measurements were complicated simply because no two laboratory animals were the same. Moreover, the introduction of new measuring techniques was accompanied by a new view of the standard preparations, whose potency had been determined using obsolete technology. This issue will be illustrated further at the conclusion of Chapter Six.

GONADOTROPIN OR GONADOTROPINS?

In early sexual endocrinology, sex glands were often ascribed the status of the body's most valuable endocrine glands, a status they seem to have retained to this very day in the popular imagination. The historiography of endocrinology is also to a large extent shaped by the history of sex glands, classical sex hormones and ideas about their significance regarding sex and gender identity.[67] In the field of endocrinology itself, however, this status was partly challenged by a tiny, pea-shaped gland located beneath the brain known as the hypophysis or pituitary gland. Based on clinical observation recorded since the turn of the century by Harvey Cushing (1869–1939) and other physicians, and backed up with solid experimental support in the 1920s, the notion that there existed an intimate connection between this gland and the sex glands took hold. Injections of pituitary extract and transplants proved to have a palpable effect on the sex glands and their hormone production: immature laboratory animals rapidly entered puberty. A similar effect, though in the opposite direction, occurred when an animal's pituitary glands were carefully removed. Adult animals lost their sex drive and ability to procreate, while in younger animals, sexual maturity abated.[68]

The conclusion reached was that the hormone production of the sex glands was ultimately governed or regulated by the hormone production of the hypophysis (the frontal lobe of the pituitary gland, to be precise). This hormone should thus be regarded as a dominant sexual hormone, the very driving force behind the sexual functions of the organism. Or as Axel Westman put it concisely in 1931, "the hypophysis hormone is primary, while the ovarian hormone is secondary."[69] Since it seemed to act in the same manner in both males and females, it was also classified as a "universal" sexual hormone. In naming the sex gland-stimulating hypophysis hormone, English-speakers chose "gonadotropin" (from the Greek *tropos*, "turn" or "direction"), while in German it was originally dubbed "prolan" (probably from Latin's *proles*, "progeny").[70]

As was the case with sex hormones, research on gonadotropin was developed in close collaboration between the academy, health care and the pharmaceutical industry. Germany initially took the lead under the direction of Zondek and Aschheim who, with the assistance of chemical and pharmaceutical conglomerate I. G. Farben, began harvesting *Hypophysenvorderlappenhormon*, or prolan, for laboratory studies and therapeutic use. Since large quantities of pituitary glands were even more difficult to acquire than sex glands, the need for an alternative source was acute.[71] The problem seemed to have been radically resolved when urine from pregnant women proved to contain not only sex hormones but also gonadotropin-like substances in rich quantities. The amount that could be procured from one liter of urine was equal to what could be extracted from thirty average human pituitary glands.[72] The substance was tested on mice and rats and when the anticipated effect manifested itself, the assumption was made that urinary gonadotropin was identical with the hormones of the hypophysis.[73] And so gonadotropin too began to be manufactured on a large scale and used in gynecological practice, mainly for diagnoses associated with the function of the pituitary gland.

The discovery of an abundant supply of gonadotropin in the urine of pregnant women also had diagnostic significance, becoming the starting point for the first endocrine-based pregnancy test, the "Aschheim-Zondek pregnancy reaction." Women in the early stage of their pregnancy deposited a urine sample at their local clinic. The urine was injected directly into female baby mice, who were put down after several days and examined. If the gonadotropin level was high, it would manifest itself in a characteristic transformation of the undeveloped genitalia of the mouse. If the mouse became sexually mature, then pregnancy was indirectly established. For their pregnancy reaction test as well as their research into the function of gonadotropin from the pituitary gland, Aschheim and Zondek were repeatedly nominated for the Nobel Prize in Physiology or Medicine. Although deemed "praiseworthy," they were never deemed prize-worthy.[74]

Soon, however, research on gonadotropin became complicated and controversial as Zondek and Aschheim proposed that the gonadotropin hormone actually consisted of *two different hormones* that affected the gonads in different ways. One reason for this conclusion was the observation that prolan seemed to be able to both stimulate and impede the production of sex hormones and thus ovarian maturation and ovulation, depending on how long treatment lasted. The difference was indicated by the terms "prolan A" and "prolan B." The former was described as a "follicle-stimulating hormone," which regulated the development of the gestational sac, and the latter as a "luteinizing hormone," which stimulated the egg to loosen and the gestational sac to become a yellow body.[75]

This division was met with approval from scientists who claimed they could confirm the existence of the dual postulate.[76] Others retorted that the actual number of pituitary gonadotropins was *three*, while still more dismissed the division altogether, partly due to the fact that these hormones appeared extraordinarily difficult to extract in a pure form.[77] In Sweden, Axel Westman considered the existence of two separate gonadotropins, A and B, but he maintained that there might in fact only be a single hormone, whose effect varied according to quantity. It might be, he reasoned, that follicle maturity was stimulated by a small dose of hormones, while the subsequent luteinization process required a heavier one. "Do Prolan A and B really exist?" was a question also posed by chemist Erik Jorpes, who in *Svenska Läkartidningen* in 1934 indicated that the experimental proof of the two factors was not terribly convincing.[78]

The situation was further complicated when gonadotropin was also discovered in the tissue of pregnant women (primarily in the placenta) and their fetuses. The question then arose as to whether urinary gonadotropin really should be considered a genuine hypophysis hormone or if instead it was a "placental gonadotropin." Or to put it another way: did the placenta function as an independent endocrine gland or was it merely a "storage space" for the pituitary hormone? In order to clarify that gonadotropin could both originate in the hypophysis and occur in the placenta, the term "human chorionic gonadotropin" (hCG) began to be used to denote the latter ("chorion" being the term for the outermost fetal membrane). One of the first hCG preparations, Organon's Pregnyl (originally called "Pregnon") of 1931, initially contained hormones extracted directly from the placenta. This raw material was however soon replaced with urine from pregnant women, which afterward became the common platform material in the production of human chorionic gonadotropin.

Another gonadotropin-like substance was discovered in the blood serum of pregnant horses, which later variant was appropriately dubbed "pregnant mare serum gonadotropin" or PMSG.[79] Since horses were a resource in relatively large supply at the time, the technique of extracting gonadotropin from horse blood was quickly adopted by the pharmaceutical industry. Examples of commercial hormone drugs available from dispensaries include Boots Pure Drug Company's Antostab, Roussel Laboratorie's Gonadyl and the British Drug House's Serogan.

Were pituitary gonadotropin, human chorionic gonadotropin and mare serum gonadotropin in fact identical and non-species specific (even if produced by different organs)? Were they three different, species-specific substances, one of which occurred in two different variants? Or were these variants two separate substances (prolan A and prolan B)? These issues comprised the theoretical core of the gonadotropin debate which would persist for decades, and which we shall encounter again and again in the course of this narrative. An attempt at reaching consensus was made in 1938 when the Health Section of the League of Nations launched an international project to standardize gonadotropins. At the "Third Conference on the Standardization of Sex Hormones" held at the Palais des Nations in Geneva, international standards for hCG and PMSG were ratified (along with the pituitary hormone prolactin), but not for the pituitary gonadotropin. On the other hand, the nomenclature was standardized, so that prolan A became "follicle-stimulating hormone" (FSH) while prolan B became the "luteinizing hormone" (LH).[80] That there was in fact some kind of difference between the various gonadotropins was clear, but not what that difference precisely meant and whether they actually were two different hormones.[81] Much more effort would be required before consensus could be reached.

The latter part of the period described in the present chapter, the years 1925 to 1940, has with good reason been called the "endocrinological gold rush." It has also been dubbed "the heroic age of reproductive endocrinology."[82] Several different types of sexual hormones—estrogens, androgens and gonadotropins—were identified and marketed in drug form. Among the tone-setting companies contributing to this development were, alongside Eli Lilly and Parke-Davis, Organon, Schering and the Swiss firm Ciba.[83] Leading Scandinavian hormone drug manufacturers included Løvens kemiske Fabrik in Denmark and Leo in Sweden. The medical side dealt with hormonal imbalances of various kinds, and whether or not they could be tackled with hormone preparations. One idea proposed a close connection between abnormalities in the pituitary gland, menstrual problems and sterility, and suggested that gonadotropins would be effective in treating involuntary childlessness.[84]

But even if gonadotropins could theoretically fulfill an important function in gynecological practice, it was far from certain that it would happen.[85]A key issue remained the quality and standardization of the drug. As the chemist Erik Jorpes stated, "From both strictly physiological and practically therapeutic perspectives, there is still a good deal left to be clarified. In any case, there is reason not to be hasty in judgment of this new hormone therapy, until one is convinced that the preparation has been applied with satisfactory results."[86] The hope was that gonadotropins, like sex hormones, could be manufactured chemically. But since gonadotropins are proteins, not steroids, with a particularly complex structure, they posed challenges to both chemical description and synthetization. This is one significant part of the scientifically complicated background against which Leo designed and launched Gonadex.

CHAPTER TWO

Axel Westman, Endocrinology, and the Population Question

THIS CHAPTER INTRODUCES the man hailed as the "inventor" of Gonadex by the daily press, gynecologist and endocrinologist Axel Westman (1894–1960). It focuses on Westman's career and research profile, but also discusses his contributions to popular science and the ongoing political conversation. Special emphasis is placed on his dream of treating sterility with hormone therapy, proposing that this vision should be seen in the context of the contemporary discourse on population issues. As shall become apparent in this and the following chapter, Westman belonged to an elite of research entrepreneurs who enjoyed high academic status, were both actively engaged in formulating research policy and popularizing its results, and who at the same time worked hand-in-hand with the pharmaceutical industry.[1] In order to understand Gonadex and the attention it attracted, it is necessary to be aware of the elevated academic and public status Westman commanded.

ENDOCRINOLOGY AND "MODERN" GYNECOLOGY

When Axel Westman entered the debate on the nature and significance of sexual hormones in earnest at the beginning of the 1930s, he had just been named Professor of Gynecology and Obstetrics at Uppsala University and Chief of Medicine at its hospital's Women's Clinic.[2] He had arrived after studying general medicine and surgery at the Caroline Institute in Stockholm, teaching at the National Childbirth Institute, also in Stockholm, and holding posts including temporary chief medical officer at Sabbatsberg

FIGURE 3 Portrait of Axel Westman, oil on canvas by Bo Beskow 1944, which hangs in the Rydbergska rummet at the Royal Caroline Hospital, Stockholm. *Courtesy the Karolinska Institutet.*

Hospital's provisional obstetrics section and assistant lecturer in obstetrics and gynecology at the Caroline. So Westman was a physician specializing in gynecology and obstetrics, historically a surgical specialty in Sweden since the 1860s.[3] However, he was also a scientist, driven by immense ambition.

Despite such impressive merits, Westman was unschooled in the endocrinological tradition. His initial forays into scientific study were oriented toward morphology, histology and radiation therapy. His first publication was an article on the cell structure of the mucous membrane of the fallopian tubes in 1916, while two subsequent publications accounted for the results of his study of X-ray and radium radiation in the treatment of genital disease.[4] Nor can his doctoral dissertation, *A Contribution to the Question of the Transit of the Ovum from Ovary to the Uterus in Rabbits* (1926), upon completion of which he became an associate professor (*Docent*) of obstetrics and gynecology, be categorized as a study in endocrinology.[5] Detailing how the egg is transported from the ovary via the fallopian tubes to the uterus, it was conducted with the help of cannula, "windows" cut into the stomachs of laboratory rabbits through which the movement of the ovaries and fallopian tubes could be monitored and even filmed. The dissertation is primarily a study of muscle movement, but it also relates the mechanisms of the reproductive organs to endocrinological suppositions, which suggests that Westman had begun to be influenced by the new theories of internal secretion.[6]

After defending his thesis, however, most of Westman's clinical and experimental research dealt with hormones and their effect on the structure and function of the female genital organs, and the relationship between the sex glands and the hormone production of the cerebrum, by which Westman can be said to have introduced an endocrinological perspective to Swedish gynecology. Central to this commitment was his conviction that traditional gynecology, based primarily on mechanical techniques and surgical intervention, would benefit from the new, biochemical lab research endocrinology represented. In this way, gynecology, generally designated low status among the medical sciences, could become "modern." Westman also argued that a new, endocrinological gynecology would have a major effect on treatment and care and by extension society at large.

Westman presented these social and medical possibilities in a series of articles written in the 1930s. His most resolute "manifesto" on the relevance of endocrinology was delivered in the form of the inauguration lecture "Den moderna hormonforskningens betydelse för gynekologien" [The significance of modern hormone research to gynecology], that he gave upon assuming his professorship in Uppsala in 1932.[7] Westman staked out the path history was taking by stating that gynecology, after first having been characterized by surgical intervention and then X-ray and radium therapy, was now entering a revolutionary new epoch—the "hormonal" era. This new epoch, which he himself represented, was exemplified by the fact that physicians' view of genital disease had now become "determined by the recently acquired insight that the functions of the genital organs were largely regulated by so-called hormones or the products of internal secretion, and that the deepest cause of numerous illnesses could be found in disturbances of the endocrinal organs."[8] Close collaboration between clinic and laboratory was therefore a necessity. It was time for the diagnostic and surgical gynecologist to also become a laboratory scientist.

From a medical standpoint, Westman explained, the theory of internal secretion had relevancy for all members of society. And yet his lecture—like all his early articles on hormones—dealt exclusively with the discovery of the "female" sex hormones (referred to as "estrogen" and "progestin"), their centrality to female biological development, the function of female sexual organs and specific diseases associated with said organs.[9] At the same time, Westman emphasized that the hormone production of the ovaries was not isolated but rather influenced by hormones from the frontal lobe of the pituitary gland. As mentioned above, the sex glands were described as the "master glands" of the human body in previous decades. But in the 1930s their status was on the verge of changing. The pituitary gland, maintained Westman, had now "advanced up the ranks of organs of internal secretion which we know have a crucial effect on the development and existence of the individual."[10] However, the internal secretion of the pituitary gland was in turn influenced by the sex gland hormones, so these different glands interacted. Even if the hypophysis was the superior organ, it was hardly an absolute dictator. As another endocrinologist later put it, the endocrine system was instead more of a democracy, where even subordinate organs could exercise influence on the body's politics.[11]

The fact that pure hormones were being produced and made available in drug form was another subject Westman touched on in his lecture, at the same time presenting the scanty amount of hormone therapy currently available to gynecological practitioners. "Thus we now have at our disposal a highly effective oestirin drug manufactured from ovarian follicles, a provisionally none too dependable corpus luteum extract containing progestin, and finally a highly-effective pituitary hormone preparation . . . not produced by the hypophysis but rather the placenta or urine of child-bearing women."[12] According to Westman, injection of such preparations would make it possible for specialists to provide rational treatment of what he called "functional" genital disorders, among which he included developmental abnormalities in puberty and menstrual and menopausal imbalances. The specific hormone drug and dosage would be determined from case to case based on analyses of hormone counts in the blood and urine of the patient. More exact Westman could not be at that time.

The enthusiastic arguments in favor of hormones and the need to integrate the insights of endocrinology with medical practice recur in the lecture "Könsutvecklingen och den inre sekretionen" [Sexual development and internal secretions], which Westman held at a meeting of the Swedish Federation of Nurses and which was subsequently published in the first issue of their house organ in 1934.[13] The lecture is reminiscent of his speech in Uppsala, though this time Westman also mentions "psycho-endocrinology," an aspect of hormone study broached by American endocrinologist Louis

Berman in 1928 as a theory of the significance of hormones for personality, character and mental health.[14] As his prime example Westman offers Johann Wolfgang von Goethe, whose periods of intense productivity were said to have coincided with bouts of erotic fervor.

> According to our way of seeing, the strange connection between periods of renewed creativity and redoubled ardor must be the result of periods of increased production in the internal secretional glands, which charge the emotions with the excitement necessary for them to blossom while at the same time instilling the instincts with an intensity usually only found in the first flush of youth.[15]

Westman thereby posited the possibility of explaining human behavior endocrinologically, including the differences between masculinity and femininity.[16]

Psycho-endocrinology never became one of Westman's major professional interests. In the end, his fundamental attitude seems to have been that the healthy human being, as opposed to other "hormonally-fated" mammals, was as a rule master of his endocrine organs; hormonal impulses were sensibilized but not regulatory.[17] On the other hand, Westman was careful to point out that the endocrine system in fact acted in concert with the nervous system, which could cause endocrinal illnesses to crop up as a result of psychological issues and vice-versa. Westman thus adopted a holistic view usually identified with American physiologist Walter B. Cannon (1871–1945) and his famed book *The Wisdom of the Body* (1932), which contends that hormones, nerves and psychological experiences are bound up and interact with one another in an intricate system.[18]

Axel Westman published another text on the value and future significance of hormone research typical of this period in *Olösta gåtor och aktuella problem* [Unsolved mysteries and contemporary problems] (1937), a collection of essays intended for popular consumption.[19] His text is interesting since it stands as an early example of how adept Westman was at conveying his ideas beyond medical circles. The volume anthologizes the opinions of internationally renowned researchers who replied to a questionnaire on the most pressing issues and goals of natural science issued by the national daily *Svenska Dagbladet*.[20] Lisa Meitner and Max Born, for example, discuss the structure of atomic nuclei, while Thomas Hunt Morgan explicated the latest discoveries on the structure of chromosomes. Among this illustrious company Westman took the opportunity to speak of the blessings to come from endocrinology in treating diverse women's diseases.

> Many problems still await their solution, but considering the intense efforts currently being exerted in endocrinology, we have every reason to believe that our options will soon rapidly increase in a successful struggle against different sexual abnormalities and a variety of genital diseases, the most profound reason to search for disruption in the normal function of the endocrine organs.[21]

The basic premise Westman presents here and in the other articles is that gynecology as science and medical practice would benefit considerably from the new, chemically based endocrinology. As we shall see below, he was passionate about one particular therapeutic mystery: sterility.

INFERTILITY AS ENDOCRINOLOGICAL PROBLEM

Infertility and sterility has been described in written culture for at least two thousand years. The inability of certain women to procreate is a theme which turns up both in Genesis, where fecundity is depicted as a gift God can choose to give or to take away, and in the *Corpus Hippocraticum*, the Hippocratic Canon of ancient Greece which compiles a wide variety of medical issues.[22] Similarly ancient is the perception that infertility is highly undesirable. In other words, people tend to want to reproduce. Modern medical literature on childlessness proceeds from the same perception, though the reasons vary. In a Swedish inquiry, *Utredning och behandling av ofrivillig barnlöshet* [Study and treatment of involuntary childlessness] (1993), gynecologist Ann Lalos maintains that "[t]he urge to reproduce is apparently fundamentally human. In religious, cultural and social norms, the childless marriage has through time been regarded as a great misfortune."[23] These norms have of course not stopped some individuals and couples from creating families through other bonds than strictly biological ones or freely choosing to be childless.

It has also been common to see infertility as part of the "nature of things" or Divine Providence, i.e. that it is not everyone's lot in life to have children and there was nothing to be done about it.[24] At least in theory, because at the same time, sundry "fertility rituals" have existed for a very long time in very many cultures. Ethnologists have shown that in Swedish peasant society, the oral tradition contains detailed instructions for curing infertility. Outdoor, springtime intercourse was apparently one stimulus, while a little animal blood smeared on the lips of a pregnant woman would prevent damage to the fetus. Clerical blessings were also considered beneficial.[25] However, new ideas and new hope began to emerge in the eighteenth and nineteenth centuries when childlessness began to be defined within a modern, medico-scientific frame of reference. The inability to procreate thus became converted, from a social state into a medical condition. Furthermore, as Margaret Marsh and Wanda Ronner clearly explain in *The Emty Cradle* (1996), this process of medicalization brought about a certain cultural transformation: "from an emphasis on coping with childlessness through social means, such as participating in the rearing of others' children, to dependence on medical intervention."[26]

Medical science wanted to prove that the natural order of things was in fact an "unnatural order," a whim of capricious nature that could be righted, if not right now then eventually. But while childlessness began to be interpreted as a treatable medical condition, a new perception of the nature of things was established, according to which the female reproductive system had a given purpose, and that purpose was procreation. If a woman could not be fertilized then something was "wrong," and like other "wrongs" this needed to be analyzed and corrected, regardless of whether the woman was otherwise perfectly healthy. Physicians and researchers were certainly not unaware of the fact that infertility could depend on the male party as much as the female (and that certain venereal diseases often caused the problem). And yet in both theory and practice, medicine primarily fixed its gaze on the female body—on "sterile woman" rather than "infertile couples." Owing to that, as gender researchers have remarked, chronic childlessness came to be perceived primarily as a "woman's problem," which in turn engendered new issues, ideological as well as medical.[27]

Since the end of the nineteenth century, a variety of medical methods for treating involuntary childlessness have been tried and abandoned. Different methods have dominated different periods and cultures, partly due to changes in the parameters of diagnosis and interpretation but also social, political and economic realities, which historian of medicine Naomi Pfeffer has shown in her important account of the history of infertility treatment, *The Stork and the Syringe* (1993). The treatment focused upon in the present volume concerns attempts to influence, or stimulate, the ovaries of barren women, in order to rectify the failure to ovulate and create the requisite conditions for conception. The methods have varied also within this framework. Some physicians have considered X-ray analysis and radium radiation of both the ovaries and the brain the most accessible route to ovulation. For decades, the often serious side effects this could cause proved no obstacle.[28] Parallel to "physical" radiation therapy, gynecologists began treating infertile women (and men too to a certain degree) with "chemical" hormone therapy.

Sporting pharmaceutical-sounding names like Fertilinets, Pregnantol, Juvigold, and Bioglan, a considerable number of organ preparations containing extracts from one or several endocrine hormones were marketed as medicine for the treatment of sterility. These would later be driven from the market by more exclusive and much more expensive hormone drugs. In seeking to remedy non-ovulation the female sex hormones estrogen and progesterone were mainly used. For a while, thyroxin was also prescribed liberally, since it was the one hormone considered capable of influencing the entire endocrine system, reproductive apparatus included. Gonadotropins of different shapes and degrees of purity were also tested. "Pluriglandular" treatments, in which more than one type of hormone was used either simultaneously or in a specific consequential order, were also common and would remain so. No imaginable combination seems to have been left untried.[29]

In Scandinavia, Axel Westman was one of the most powerful advocates of hormone therapy as a solution to the sterility problem. His take on the issue is made plain in his second inaugural lecture, entitled "Sterilitet och sterilitetsbehandling" [Sterility and its treatment].[30] It was held on 4 May 1935 in Lund, to which Westman was summoned to succeed the legendary Elis Essen-Möller (1870–1956) as professor and chief medical officer of obstetrics and gynecology at the university's clinical institute, located at the county hospital.[31] In it, Westman described sterility and its various treatments from a number of different angles, continuing to focus exclusively on female genitalia.[32] Sterility was characterized as a disease that like all other diseases should be diagnosed and treated *medically*. He makes no distinction between women who are involuntarily childless, those who cannot conceive but do not consider it a problem, and those who have chosen to remain childless.[33] Westman discussed both anatomical and physiological matters and the conventional techniques available for localizing and treating them rationally, radiation therapy included. The connection between infertility and psychology was also mentioned.[34] But another theme to which Westman attached great significance was "the recent discoveries made by hormone research, particularly insofar as the ovarian hormones' effect on the uterus and its mucous membrane are concerned."[35] These hormones, referred to as "estrin" and "progestin" in 1932, are now called "folliculinum" (or "follicle-stimulating hormone") and "yellow body hormone" (or "corpus luteum hormone").

According to Westman these two hormones, produced in exactly the right amount—neither too much nor too little—were absolutely essential to the normal fertilization and development of the egg. Moreover, they cause secretion in the mucous membrane of the vagina, without which spermatozoa cannot survive, leaving the egg unfertilized. If "normal" production of these hormones is disrupted, the inevitable result is sterility. With support in these findings, Westman argued that it was also necessary to conduct sex hormone analyses during gynecological examinations of sterile women. He further explained that hormone imbalances in the ovaries may occur for several different reasons, and even be related to imbalances in other, internal secretional glands in the body. Once again, he returned to the role of the magic pituitary gland.

> Recent research suggests that the function of the ovaries is highly dependent on the activities of the hypophysis. It is under the influence of the hormones of the hypophysis that initial pubertal ovarian maturity occurs, and the presence of an adequate amount of pituitary hormones is an absolute must for the continued functioning of the ovaries.[36]

In other words, if the internal secretion of the pituitary gland were disturbed, it would affect the hormone production of the ovaries as well. This was the reason why in examining a purportedly sterile patient, the function of her hypophysis should also be checked, by analyzing blood or urine. If analysis proved that the patient suffered from some form of hormone imbalance, there was treatment at hand in the form of hormone therapy. In such cases (and provided the patient did not suffer from any other serious anatomical, physiological or psychological problems), sterility could be overcome with aggressive treatment. "Facts from the literature show that modern hormone therapy is highly valuable, and my own experience has taught me that a relatively large number of cases of sterility are caused by imbalances of the sort in question, and are therefore receptive to hormonal therapy."[37] In conclusion, Westman stated that progress in the field of endocrinology had contributed to a transformed, more positive attitude toward sterility. The solution is within reach, as long as we allow budding research to blossom.

> While surgical therapy has most likely come as far as it can, forms of hormonal treatment are still under development. Comprehensive experimental and clinical research is required before definitive guiding principles for the treatment of sterility can be drawn up. At that point our odds of helping the numerous women visiting their doctor due to sterility will be greatly enhanced.[38]

Westman dreamed of a therapeutic hormonal remedy for sterility, a dream he came to share with others in time, including family practitioners and their involuntarily childless patients.

POPULATION POLICY AND STERILITY

Considering his research profile and the fact that he was a gynecologist, it comes as no surprise that Axel Westman became involved with the issue of sterility; how appropriate that he chose a stork as the symbol gracing his personal bookplate.[39] Nor was he the only gynecologist who lectured and conducted research on the endocrinal basis of sterility or cherished hopes of one day being able to successfully treat barren women with hormone therapy. In the significant book *Human Sterility*, published in 1934, Samuel Meaker of the medical school at Boston University had indeed promoted the field when he suggested that endocrinological disturbances occurred in more than fifty percent of all infertile couples.[40] But at that point in time, the problem of hormonally based sterility had yet to attract much attention on the international research front.

For a long time in America, according to the testimony of endocrinologist George Corner, it proved hard to get practicing gynecologists interested in endocrinology and laboratory scientists interested in concrete clinical problems like sterility. It did not begin climbing up the list of priorities until after the Second World War and even then, it did so as but one component in a broader research field including reproduction, fertility and techniques for planned parenthood.[41] Another indication that the subject was generally a postwar phenomenon is the number of societies for the study of reproduction founded with the cessation of hostilities. After the American Society for the Study of Fertility, established at the end of the war as a medical science complement to the Endocrine Society, the British Society for the Study of Fertility was founded in 1949, the French Société Nationale pour l'Étude de la Stérilité et de la Fécondité in 1955, and the American Society for the Study of Reproduction in 1967. The International Fertility Society was established in 1953 and it was not until 1969 that the national federations were gathered under the umbrella of the Federation of Fertility Societies.[42]

Axel Westman's focus on sterility as early as the 1930s can be related to the political and socioeconomic context in which he acted—the burgeoning Swedish Welfare State and its visionary social program, which began taking shape as soon as Prime Minister Per Albin Hansson formed the country's first Social Democratic government in 1932. This program addressed the need for increased democracy, education, public health and social and economic justice. The so-called "population question" was also included on the agenda, spurring discussion about the "quality" of the populace and how the "folk material" could be prevented from degenerating and in fact be improved.[43] This theme connects with the ideas of Social Darwinism and racial hygiene that became institutionalized in Sweden as early as 1921 with the establishment of the National Institute of Racial Biology in Uppsala.[44] But first and foremost, the population question was based on the fact that nativity rates in Sweden, as in numerous other European countries, had dropped steadily since the end of the nineteenth century. Contemporaneous with what historical demography now calls the "fertility transition," some fifty million Europeans had emigrated to America and other destinations abroad.

Dwindling nativity in Europe caused alarm for one particular political reason, summarized by historian Maria Sophia Quine: "For political leaders as much as for distinguished intellectuals, the drop in the birthrate threatened to endanger the nation's prospects for continued prosperity and progress."[45] The idea that there was a direct connection between population growth and national prosperity and between low nativity and national anxiety was vehemently expressed by Italian demographer Corrado Gini (1884–1965), who in the late 1920s formulated an organic theory of civilization. Every civilization passes through a predetermined number of stages of development, from birth and growth to maturity and dotage. According to Gini, these stages corresponded with the nation's degree of "fertility." A nation whose birth rate was decreasing was ageing and on its way to becoming completely sterile. For old nations like France, Great Britain and Sweden, this theory did not bode well. On the other hand, the future looked bright for a young, "virile" nation like Italy. In this way, the imperial ambitions of Mussolini received scientific backing; Gini was presented with a medal by *Il Duce* himself.[46]

In Sweden the debate was momentously influenced by a controversial book written by the social democrats and scholars Alva and Gunnar Myrdal in 1934, *Kris i befolkningsfrågan*—Crisis in the Population Question.[47] From the presumption of a *de facto* decrease in population, the Myrdals warned not only of the risk for reduced national productivity but the eventual disappearance of the Swedish race altogether. They also emphasized the importance of maintaining the high standard of Swedish "folk material"; in an oft-cited phrase they referred to the "radical sifting-out of extremely undesirable individuals" now made possible with the passage of new sterility legislation in 1934. According to this law, sterilization could be performed either on race hygienic grounds, due to "illness and physical defect," or social grounds, including the inability to provide adequately for one's own children.[48]

However, the authors invest greater hope in the government's ability to stimulate childbirth by enlarging the social safety net. They recommended a more civic-minded and economically egalitarian family policy, including housing allowances, free pediatric care, free daycare and free schooling.

Crisis in the Population Question was a radical book that essentially deals with the need to create a new kind of society better suited to an era in which the agrarian economy was giving way to an urban, industrialized society. The population question was to be solved through scientifically based political reform; the Myrdals actually made no direct demands on the life of the lone individual. But accompanying this plea for social justice was the expectation, an almost tacit demand, that healthy, young people promptly marry and raise a family. The goal was three children per family, the average rate in agrarian society before the nativity rate began its nosedive in the 1880s, in order, as sociologist Eva Palmblad put it, to encourage healthy reproduction "in the service of the nation."[49] The conviction that the production of new citizens was a way to take responsibility and contribute to social development was expressed in a variety of ways, though probably never as explicitly as in the informational literature aimed at the country's potential parents. This kind of rhetoric about the duty of bearing children recurs long after the 1930s.[50]

Like many others, Axel Westman was affected by the population debate, but he also participated personally. In common with the Myrdals, he insisted that the population question was mainly social or socio-medical in character. As the leading expert on obstetrics and gynecology in Sweden, he stressed the unique role expanded maternity and pediatric care would have. But he also declared that the question was complex in nature and deserved to be examined from every possible angle. In his inaugural address in Lund, Westman thus maintained that "the lively discussion currently being conducted in nearly all quarters on the question of our nation's population has actualized all the issues which in one way or another are tangential to the measures to be taken in order to increase the size of the population."[51] At least one of these questions was of a strictly medical nature, i.e. the fact that many Swedish couples were *involuntarily* childless. According to a poll conducted by statistician Sven Wicksell in 1932, the number might be fifteen percent or more.[52]

In other words, there were many married couples that wanted to have children but were simply biologically incapable of doing so. Which is why research on sterility and infertility aimed at discovering adequate treatment was important, not just for the individuals involved, said Westman, but also for society and the nation itself. "It must be in the greatest interest of society that women who wish to have children, but who are sterile for one reason or

FIGURE 4 The booklet *A och O för blivande mödrar* [*The ABCs of motherhood*] (1943) advised Sweden's mothers-to-be that, "Every woman deserves to experience happiness and prepare to perform a duty. Happiness is the child, for whom any healthy woman, even unconsciously, longs. Duty is the entreaty of life that the race endure."

another, receive all the help medicine can provide."[53] From this perspective, facilitating pregnancy was as urgent as preventing unwanted ones through sterilization, contraception and in exceptional cases, abortion.[54] Linking sterility to the population question was met with the approval of numerous physicians and Westman's notions on how best to tackle sterility were also considered politically relevant.[55] Ideas like his were, however, not unique to Swedish therapeutic culture in the 1930s and 1940s but were also current abroad, for example in Italy, Germany and Israel.[56]

Though the population question was treated with the utmost seriousness by both the right and the left in Swedish politics, opinion was divided on the comprehensive reform proposal tabled by Gunnar and Alva Myrdal. To study the issue a government population commission was appointed which from 1935 to 1938 submitted a total of eighteen action plans in line with the policies of the welfare state. Along with the members appointed to the commission, the Department of Health and Social Affairs called in a number of external experts. Not surprisingly, Axel Westman was one of them. Westman's contribution consisted mainly of two texts written for the *Betänkande i sexualfrågan* [Report on sexuality] (1936), the fruit of an inquiry led by Gunnar Myrdal—one on involuntary sterility and one on hygienic and medical indications for preventive birth control. Here he reiterated that the sterility question was intimately related with the population question.

> When seeking clarity as to the factors that influence our population either positively or negatively and the measures taken to halt declining nativity, the matter of involuntary sterility, its cause and its treatment must be paid considerable attention.[57]

Likewise he pointed out the many causes of sterility and emphasized once again that hormone research and hormone therapy lay in the nation's best interests. Interestingly, this time he recommended "intensive" hormone therapy not only for sterile women but for sterile men as well.

By the time the Population Commission was debriefed in 1939, the financial market had become precarious and the political situation further complicated by the outbreak of the Second World War. Sweden now had a coalition government, which prioritized national military preparedness and food supplies. Preserving peace and the nation's liberty went before everything else. Child allowances and maternity aid were allocated and a decision on preventive health care taken, but other measures intended to stimulate child birth rates were temporarily relegated to the sidelines. While nativity did increase somewhat, the debate surfaced with renewed energy at the beginning of the 1940s. Sweden, it was said, not only needed an external defense strategy but an internal one as well. Demands for following up and supervising of the work of the Population Commission were raised from various quarters and in 1941 a Population Committee was set up by the government which, chaired by State Secretary Tage Erlander, continued its work until 1946. This time both Westman and his colleague gynecologist Sune Genell submitted reports, both of which emphasized the political value inherent in the research and treatment of sterility.

In a controversial book entitled *Vårt folk och vår framtid* [Our people and our future] (1940), conservative physician Gunnar Biörck emphatically reiterated the notion of the incontestable role played by women in their role as child-bearers, "for to bear children is an absolutely necessary civic duty." Equating women's duty to procreate with men's duty to perform military service was attacked by Social Democrats Inga Thorsson and Birgitta von Hofsten, who not only protested that Biörck reduced women to one-dimensional sexual beings but also reminded him that not all women were capable of getting pregnant.[58] The latter thread was also taken up by Genell, who remarked in the Swedish journal of medicine that increased nativity was not only a matter of social welfare and goodwill. "The prospect of enticing people through public or privately sponsored propaganda to have more children is limited at best. Increasing the chances for those *who want to but cannot have children* is surely a more rewarding task."[59] Thus one proposal Genell made to the Population Committee was that state-of-the-art hormone labs ought to be opened in clinics throughout the country so that as many as possible could benefit from the emerging endocrinological expertise.

Axel Westman offered his own data and petitioned the committee to subsidize scientific research on sterility. He believed however in contrast with Genell that if the government could indeed dispense funds to build laboratories, they should all be concentrated on the premises of the newly-completed Caroline Hospital, so that sterility research at its women's clinic could be expanded.[60] That Westman chose that particular environment was hardly surprising given that he had left Lund in 1943 for a professorship at the Caroline Institute and position of chief of the hospital's brand-new women's clinic. In the course of the discussions of the Population Committee, the question of whether involuntarily childless couples could obtain government subsidy for medical treatment arose. A bill proposing grant reform was presented to the upper house of parliament in 1945.[61] Though it referred directly to an article on sterility and its treatment written by Westman for the ambitious reference work *Sexuallivet i modern belysning* [Contemporary sexuality] (1944), he himself appears not to have commented on the motion.[62]

Finally, it should be noted that interestingly enough, the connection between the population question, sterility and endocrinology was also articulated in the contemporaneous policy inquiry on "the promotion of medical research." In this inquiry, conducted at the behest of the Ministry of Ecclesiastic Affairs and eventually laying the foundations for the creation of the National Medical Research Council in 1945, Westman once again acted as a consultant.[63] According to reports, the new research council would prioritize two comprehensive categories of research: social and military medicine. Beyond that other specialized priorities were indicated; in one of its appendices marital sterility is declared a fundamental aspect of the population question.[64] Thus once again Westman appeals for greater resources to be made available.

> With our increased understanding of the physiology of the sexual sphere, it has become possible to counteract sterility in both women and men through surgery and specific treatment . . . . Owing to this and the public discussion of the population question, the interest of the general populace has also increased markedly. It is apparent that these matters call for continued scientific research.[65]

Sterility and its treatment was not the central question addressed by the government inquiries discussed above, but was relegated to the periphery. Scrutinizing the reforms actually carried out as a result of the Population Committee, the establishment of a national child allowance in 1947 was most likely the most important. Though it should be noted that sterility research was not left empty-handed, which says something about just how complicated the history of science can be.

To summarize then, the political debate on falling nativity rates influenced Axel Westman when formulating his research program on sterility and its treatment. In turn, he was invited to give expert testimony before government inquiries, where he called for the state to earmark new funds for research. As shall be discussed in more detail below, his wish was granted when the Swedish government helped subsidize the expansion of the women's clinic at the Caroline Hospital. This proves that science and politics do not necessarily comprise two solitary spheres of activity. It also proves that it is impossible to determine whether politics shapes science or vice-versa; rather, it seems that science and politics develop together, not side-by-side but hand-in-hand, in a mutually beneficial relationship.[66]

Historians rarely discuss reproductive research and therapy as aspects of the emerging welfare society or the population question.[67] When intense debate broke out in the 1990s on the Swedish welfare state's social and medical engineering, it was mainly the negative side of reproductive control that was aired, especially the forced sterilization of physical and mental "deviants" relegated to the periphery of society. The scientific discipline featured most prominently in the latter-day debate was the genetics that laid the ground for race biology, which in turn served as a source of inspiration for the sterility campaign.[68] Considering that some sixty thousand individuals, the majority women, were sterilized between 1935 and 1975 (when the law was repealed), telling its history is a matter of significant public interest. However, the efforts of Westman and his colleagues to *cure* sterility ought also to be told. The positive and negative practices to control and aid reproduction engendered by the population question should be seen as two sides of the same coin.[69] Bearing in mind both aspects illuminates the fact that the medical interventions developed against the backdrop of and together with the population question and the normative ideals of welfare society touched even the most well-situated members of society, for involuntary childlessness paid class divisions no heed. Of course, the chances of the wealthier members of society being examined and treated by a specialist were much better.

It is difficult to state with any certainty the exact number of people who actually received hormone treatment for pregnancy during this era, though it is probably considerably lower than the number sterilized. Though society expected its women to become mothers, there was no authorized treatment of the barren comparable to the so-called "compulsory sterilization" campaign.[70] The differences between the two however pose no obstacle to our understanding of endocrinological assisted reproduction as an aspect of the history of the Swedish population question.

ENDOCRINOLOGY AS PUBLIC SCIENCE

The well-versed reader of modern Swedish literature is aware that the new ideas about hormones were part and parcel of the burgeoning welfare state. Gunnar Ekelöf put the phenomenon to its most concise use in his poem "Till de folkhemske," collected in *Non Serviam* in 1945. The poem, which can be read as a collectivist dystopia aimed at the over rationalized, detailed social project which the Myrdals represented, tells of pristine, hygienic children untouched by human hands and clouds made square for reasons of aesthetic conformity. He also offers this image of the modern home as a routinized beehive.

> Each day turns to night and sexless vitamin drones swarm home in order of seniority, Svea, Queen of the Hormones, jealously guarded by imposing sentries.[71]

Hormones also play a role in Eyvind Johnson's novel *Grupp Krilon* (1941), the first volume in a trilogy taking the moral temperature of Sweden during the Second World War. It features a passage in which dancer Ann Band Farlane asks her doctor to tell her everything he knows about those peculiar endocrine glands. "That stuff about hormones is so interesting, she said wearily. We have glands and all kinds of things which do work for us and guide us and scratch our backs and make us feel lazy or lively."[72] Did not she herself remind him of a hormone, she wonders. The doctor obliges by expounding on the fundamentals of endocrinology to the best of his ability, but reminds her that he is no expert in the field and that "she could look up all the information he can give her about hormones in any reference book or popular science article."[73] The latter suggestion is hardly pulled out of thin air, since so many popular publications were readily available, many of them written by Axel Westman.

Westman actively promoted the professionalization of endocrinology in Sweden in a way reminiscent of his contemporary, Gunnar Dahlberg, who energetically struggled to establish the discipline of human genetics. Another trait he shared with Dahlberg was his extensive publicistic efforts.[74] Alongside brief articles and interviews in daily newspapers, weekly magazines and on radio, he discussed the new discoveries in a series of popular guides and textbooks.[75] A number of these books were reprinted several times and some were translated into other Scandinavian languages, suggesting a relatively wide audience. Two books published in 1940 while he was in Lund deserve special attention. The first is simply entitled *Hormoner*—Hormones—and

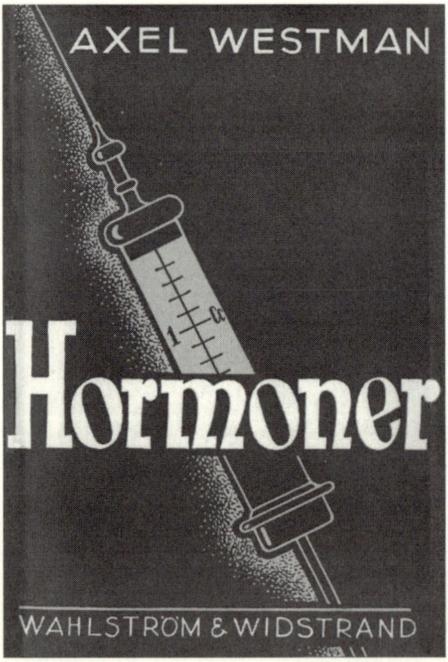

FIGURE 5 Axel Westman was a prolific author of general interest books on endocrinology and gynecology. One of these is *Hormoner* (1940), which, in the words of critic Pehr Henrik Törngren, was "factually impeccable and confidently written."

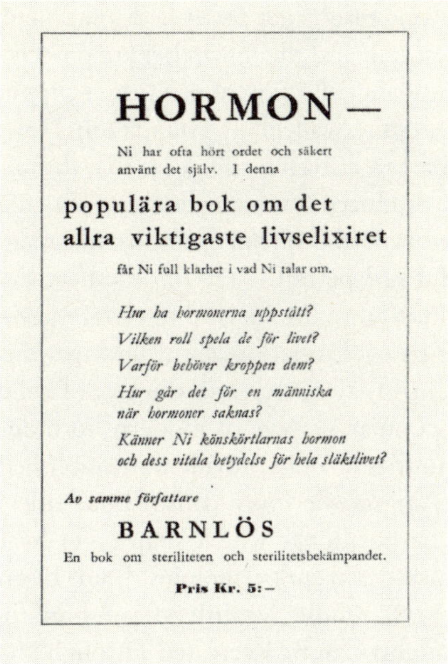

FIGURE 6 At the outset of the twentieth century, it was common to associate hormones with the sought-after *elixir vitae* of the ancient alchemists. The blurb on the back cover of Westman's *Hormoner* (1940) proclaims that this is a book about "the greatest elixir of life of them all" and "its vital significance to the entire race."

was the broadest introduction to the theory of endocrinology to date: the physiology of the dominant endocrine glands, their hormone production and the way these hormones influenced evolution, health and reproduction. The second, *Barnlös: En bok om barnlösheten och sterilitetsbekämpandet* [Childless: A book on sterility and its prevention], is more medically-oriented and can be described as an expanded edition of previously discussed essays on the reproductive organs, procreation, internal secretion and sterility. It too proceeds from the population question, but is not aimed merely at an audience of professional physicians, nurses and politicians, but directly at men and women suffering or at risk of suffering from sterility.

The critical sociologist of science might interpret these books, like the articles from the 1930s, as the means by which Westman "sold" endocrinology in the research policy market in order to gain acceptance and funding for his own scientific interests.[76] The same could be said about Westman's frequent appearances in the media spotlight. The fact is that financiers not only care that scientific results get published in academic forums but also monitor how the research and the researcher are portrayed in public; this is indicated by the abundant collection of newspaper clippings about Westman found in the archives of the Wallenberg Foundation. However, an empathetic reading is as plausible as a critical reading, i.e. that through the popular educational material he produced, so characteristic of the era, Westman honestly wished to inform, educate and spread optimism in a manner which rigorous scholarly articles did not permit.[77] He hoped therewith that insight into the importance of lifestyle to the survival of certain, central "hygienic laws" would increase and that information about new treatment methods would contribute to minimizing resignation in the face of childlessness.[78]

A number of popular surveys of modern hormone research and the therapeutic opportunities it could provide were published in other countries at the same time. Among the more conspicuous titles were *Hormonerna som forma livet* [The hormones which shape life] by Eugen Steinach in Vienna and New York-based endocrinologist Louis Berman's *New Creations in Human Beings* (1938), whose Swedish edition bore the slightly ominous subtitle, "How Mankind Can Be Recreated Through Hormone Therapy."[79] As endocrinologists, Steinach and particularly Berman were visionaries, if not utopians. Both advocated hormone therapy as a miracle cure promoting physical and mental vitality, thereby improving and prolonging life. Berman went so far as to claim that hormone therapy was a way to hasten biological evolution and create "ideal men." When mankind had finally reached its apotheosis, when the physiological and biochemical foundation had been laid, he could then create the perfect society. In *New Creations in Human Beings* he boasted immodestly:

> The endocrine glands constitute in their integrated totality a governing directorate of the personality. Because they are his governors, Man must learn to govern them before he can learn to govern himself. The finest chemical machine in the universe, himself, thereby becomes a malleable instrument in his own hands. He can turn out, through its manipulations, newer and better models of himself, or remodel himself nearer to his heart's desire.[80]

Such refinement would not be the purview of a tiny elite, according to Berman. Like so many other scientists in the US, he was strongly influenced by the social and political questions of the interwar period, and advocated global hormone-based eugenics for the betterment of all mankind.[81]

Compared with the books of Steinach and Berman, which were received with skepticism and likened to overheated science fiction in Sweden,

Westman's more modest prose met with high praise. In a review published in the daily *Dagens Nyheter*, psychiatrist and psychoanalyst Pehr Henrik Törngren wrote that *Hormoner* was "clear and concise in form, lucidly formulated, and factually beyond all knowledgeable, trustworthy criticism." *Barnlös* was met in similarly glowing terms.[82] Alluding to authors like Steinach and Berman, *Stockholms-Tidningen* mentioned that much had been written and fantasized about concerning the ability of science to help create "the super-homo of tomorrow" with the aid of hormones, but that the dream of an elixir of life would surely never be fulfilled. This however did not hinder the paper from praising the school of endocrinological research Westman represented. "For once dreamers and utopians find themselves on solid ground, for hormone research offers sensational results and discoveries which indicate revolutionary developments on an almost daily basis."[83]

By this time Westman had accrued tremendous scientific credibility and with time was offered many prestigious academic appointments. In the terminology of sociologist Pierre Bourdieu one can say without exaggeration that Westman possessed a great deal of cultural and symbolic capital within the field of medical science.[84] That however does not necessarily mean that everyone shared his perception of the significance of hormone research to medicine and gynecology. International controversy had raged throughout the 1920s and by the 1940s, endocrinology was still considered controversial in some medical circles. Even physicians who were sympathetic to endocrinological research could say that the "record speed" to which the diagnosis "endocrinal imbalance" was resorted was worrisome, that hormone therapy had become more based on "fashion" than sense.[85] In a survey in the *Journal of the American Medical Association* (1940), physician Robert Tilden Frank concluded that faith in the gospel of endocrinology had become so fervent that there was a risk other diagnoses would be overlooked.[86]

In Denmark a "hormone dispute" had even broken out, which ended in court. The dispute began when a professor of internal medicine, Cai Holten, publically stated that the vaunted sexual hormone drugs had actually proven something of a disappointment. Holton's skepticism was refuted by physician Johanne Christiansen who threw all her support behind hormone therapy and worried that such criticism could frighten away patients in need of treatment. She in turn was met by the opposition of another professor of internal medicine, Erik Warburg, who warned that the "hormone clan" presented inconclusive research data as if it were established scientific fact. Things got so out of hand that Christiansen eventually sued Warburg for defamation of character.[87]

Skepticism toward the practical value of hormone research can be illustrated in a most concrete manner by a letter sent by physician Gideon Vilhelm Törnqvist to Axel Westman's predecessor in Lund, Elis Essen-Möller.[88] Törnqvist speaks of a well-attended meeting of the Physician's Society in Uppsala on 4 May 1942, where "Hormone Vestman" appeared as the featured lecturer. His speech, entitled "Hormonal Treatment Methods in Gynecology," was said to have been about rabbit does, ovarian hormones, the pituitary gland and the neural pathways running from the brain to "the pituitary gland lately of such note."[89] He writes that he has no doubt that Westman's research will one day have practical use, but is still upset that this new science has been given so much attention at the cost of practical doctoring. His own experience treating genital problems proved that many women could become well "without injections" through "exercise and physical exertion in the fresh air." Westman paid no regard to the significance of environment and lifestyle, according to Törnqvist, who observed acidly, "This scientific idol worship at the expense of good, critical, practical work does not bode well for the future of medicine. Render unto Caesar that which is his. Too much about hormones and their adorers."

Törnqvist's objections can be read as a reaction to how the complex function of the female body had begun to be reduced to molecules in a lab. But his criticism can also be interpreted as a contribution to "boundary-work" in the sense sociologist of science Thomas Gieryn used it, in this case as an attempt to protect the status and craft of the practitioner from the rapidly multiplying number of laboratory researchers crowding into medicine and garnering so much attention from the mass media.[90] To the question of the relationship between endocrinology and gynecology we shall return. But first, let us get to know the company that launched Gonadex on the world, Aktiebolaget Leo (Helsingborg), and discover what happened when it crossed paths with Axel Westman.

CHAPTER THREE

Lion of the North: Leo and the First Hormone Drugs

Gonadex was part of an international tradition of endocrinological research and treatment, and came into being against the backdrop of a political debate on the need to find a cure for sterility. But like all other modern drugs, Gonadex was also firmly rooted in industry. An essential component in the history of Gonadex is the company which launched it, Aktiebolaget Leo (Helsingborg) and its wide network of contacts. This chapter presents Leo, its early interest in developing hormone drugs and its first urine-collection campaign, conducted to acquire the raw material necessary to manufacturing the drugs. It also includes a discussion of the government regulations the pharmaceutical industry was compelled to follow in the first half of the twentieth century. In conclusion, I investigate how Axel Westman was recruited by Leo and how their collaboration was institutionalized in the form of Sweden's first hormone laboratory. This lab was of great significance since it functioned as a platform for endocrinological research while simultaneously contributing to the institutionalization of endocrinology in gynecological practice.

THE BIRTH OF A BUSINESS

In Europe, mass-produced medicine has a history that stretches back to the Industrial Revolution in the first half of the nineteenth century. Before that, the manufacture of drugs was a cottage industry maintained by monks, chemists, pharmacists, physicians and other medical experts. These pre-industrial preparations, known as *materia medica*, were mainly extracted from the vegetable kingdom, though animal and mineral components were also used. Their concoctions were available through all kinds of vendors, though for centuries the main formal source was the local apothecary (from *apotheke*, Greek for "storehouse").

In the historical literature, the subsequent transition from handicraft to industry is usually described as an evolution proceeding along two parallel lines. One proceeds from big apothecaries where, with the help of mechanized pill-making machines, a surplus of certain medicaments began to be produced for sale to other retailers. The other line embarks from the chemical industry, particularly the German dye industry, which had begun using industrial methods to effectivize production of pharmaceutical substances and also found a market for its waste products.[1] These factory-made drugs prepared according to recipe were called "patent medicines," a term adopted in the 1880s which had negative connotations for many apothecaries. This skepticism was partly based on the perception that products manufactured on a large scale could never be as precise as those blended by hand, but also in fear for the future of their profession.[2]

Toward the end of the nineteenth century, these two traditions were fused and institutionalized as more or less self-contained businesses specializing in medical preparations. Germany led this development with Great Britain, France, Switzerland and the United States close behind. Aside from mass-producing and selling approved drugs, some of these companies saw it their task to attempt to develop new and better drugs, among whom we find Wellcome in England and H. K. Mulford Company and Park, Davies and Company in the US.[3] In Sweden, pharmaceutical production was first industrialized in the form of a small-scale chemical and instrument manufacturing industry materializing around the turn of the century, at the same time as the industrialization process writ large had its breakthrough in the country. Faith in the financial opportunities offered by industry and technology was strong, and new businesses were encouraged and subsidized by both the government and by young, exuberant investment capitalists.[4] However, the prohibition on anyone other than licensed apothecaries from manufacturing medicine was not repealed until 1913 with the passing of the Apothecary Products Bill, which went into effect 1 July the following year. Before that, and stretching back to the 1680s when the profession was regulated through royal decree and an official pharmacopoeia, apothecaries maintained exclusive rights to drug production. And according to the new law, industrially produced pharmaceuticals could still only be sold by apothecaries.[5]

Aktiebolaget Leo (Helsingborg) belonged to the first generation of drug companies founded in Sweden against the background of the expansion of industry and drafting of new legislation to regulate it.[6] The firm's statutory meeting was held on 23 July 1914—just before the outbreak of the Great War—and one year later, on 17 July 1915, it was officially registered with the Royal Patent Office. The business set up shop in the port of Helsingborg which, with its 30,000 residents, was the country's fifth-largest city. The firm of AB Ferrosan was established there at the same time, serving as something like a development company for Leo.[7] Aside from the nearby cities of Stockholm and Södertälje, where Energon (renamed Pharmacia shortly thereafter) and Astra were founded in 1911 and 1913, respectively, Western Scania became something of a stronghold for the burgeoning pharmaceutical industry in Sweden.

Aside from such strictly pharmaceutical companies working in conjunction with pharmacies were a number of other factories and post-order firms manufacturing strength-enhancing preparations and nutritional supplements of varying quality sold via advertisements in the daily and weekly press. The extent to which these medicaments were to be classified as drugs, foodstuff or generic "chemical-technical articles" and whether they should be sold by pharmacies or not was a hot topic in the ongoing "quackery debate."[8] The question of quackery was however complex and concerned much more than which drugs the Swedish Academy of Pharmaceutical Sciences and other professional authorities could give their seal of approval. Treatments as many and varied as homeopathy, chiropractics, naprapathy, massage, spa cures and vegetarianism were assiduously debated. According to sociologist Eva Palmblad, the question came down to "the opinion of the medical profession as to who has the right to treat, which is the right method—and who is the right patient."[9] Being accepted by the pharmaceutical and medical profession was one of the greatest challenges faced by the early drug industry.

In its first years, Leo had no intention of developing its own drugs. In common with so many contemporary pharmaceutical companies, it restricted its activities, as is recorded in its first articles of association, to "the manufacture and sales of pharmo-chemical and nutritional preparations."[10] As a matter of fact, Leo was not even an independent company but rather the subsidiary of a Danish concern founded in 1908, when Løveapoteket, a Copenhagen pharmacy, began manufacturing its own medicine. The company first called itself "Københavns Løveapoteks kemiske Fabrik" but subsequently shortened its name to "Løvens kemiske Fabrik" and was generally referred to simply as "Løvens." Its trademark was "Leo."[11] The intention was that Leo in Helsingborg would serve as a "bridge" between Løvens and the Swedish market, which had opened up with the above-mentioned new legislation. Though Leo was routinely referred to as a "Swedish" company manufacturing "Swedish quality drugs," it would remain in Danish hands until the 1980s. Although direct control of Leo by Løvens kemiske Fabrik would only last until 1946, when the latter was bought by Danish pharmaceutical firm H. Lundbeck and Co.[12]

After a few slow years during the war, when access to raw materials was limited and tools nearly laid down, the business took off in the latter half of the 1920s. Proper factory facilities had been found in the industrial neighborhood of Stattena in Helsingborg, a small workforce hired, a catalogue prepared (the first, published in 1921, featuring a mere ten items), marketing systematized and financial reward reaped. Some of the first products offered for sale were Leotol cough drops, a fish oil called Grasinol and the laxative Leopiller. But real financial return came in the form of the analgesic Albyl, created at Løvens kemiske Fabrik which, after its launch in Sweden in 1924 became synonymous with "aspirin." The pill, which contained salicylic acid and magnesium oxide, was gentle on the stomach, convenient, inexpensive and most of all, effective.[13] But also important to Leo's success was being granted permission to introduce the North American hormone drug insulin to Sweden.[14] Leo's insulin was extracted from the pancreatic glands of swine at the Nordic Insulin Laboratory in Copenhagen, which had secured the rights to manufacture insulin in Scandinavia through the connections of Nobel Prize laureate August Krogh. Leo secured the Swedish distribution rights to insulin, calling it "Insulin Leo," due to the fact that the main financier and chairman of the board of the Nordisk Insulinlaboratorium was Danish pharmacist and industrialist August Kongsted (1870–1939), who also helped found Løvens kemiske Fabrik and Leo.[15]

Insulin Leo quickly became a popular tool in the fight against diabetes, one of the scourges of the burgeoning welfare state.[16] Its effect was instantaneous, almost miraculous. "The *effect of insulin* is made known as all symptoms disappear," Leo wrote in its second catalogue, issued in 1924.[17] As usual when an effective drug is introduced, insulin was tested to see if it could treat other afflictions, including schizophrenia, psychosis and anorexia.[18] Altogether this led to an enormous market demand for insulin and in order to meet it, the company expanded on both sides of the Straits of Öresund.[19] At first, insulin was sold in pill form, to be dissolved in water before being injected into the patient. This was followed by ampoules containing insulin in liquid form.[20] Insulin Leo was followed by a series of other insulin drugs, all manufactured by the Nordisk Insulinlaboratorium.[21] It was contractually obliged that all insulin drugs coming from the Nordisk Insulinlaboratorium contain the word "Leo" in their name, a practice which continued until the 1980s.

The introduction of insulin earned Leo the reputation of being a modern, science-based pharmaceutical company—a "hormone business." It also led to Løvens and therefore also Leo being in direct contact with the very latest in hormone research and therapy. Presumably they listened closely to this *frontier talk*—testimony as to how far the front lines of research had been pushed at any given moment and pledges of the knowledge and opportunities to come as that boundary is passed—which spread throughout endocrinological and pharmaceutical circles on both sides of the Atlantic. Pushing the boundaries of science, however, came at a cost, primarily financial but also social and ethical, and this cost threw up new boundaries as to how far researchers, institutions and science-based businesses could afford to go. Outlay needed to be motivated, which was done in the form of visionary expectations about the significance of this new knowledge for individuals and society as a whole.[22]

As previously mentioned, hopes were high during the interwar years about the scientific, medical and financial opportunities endocrinology might offer. It was squarely in the forefront of biomedicine, comparable with today's molecular biology and genetics, which motivated continued investment. Research and development went hand in hand. The enormous success insulin brought to Eli Lilly led numerous companies to seek connections with leading researchers in order to try and replicate its success by launching hormones extracted from other endocrine glands.[23] So too Løvens and Leo. Half of the seventeen original preparations Leo developed and launched between 1948 and 1972 were hormone-based.[24] The biological and medial motives behind this investment is made clear in an ad campaign draft from the 1940s, where Leo made the following assertions about the might of the hormone.

> In recent years, hormone treatment has become a factor to reckon with in the therapeutic arsenal. In minimal quantities, these substances intervene in the complicated processes of the organism. For it is hormones which determine whether a person will grow tall or short, fat or thin, it is hormones that decree constitution and even personality. Hormones have a decisive significance in the area of sexuality. Developmental abnormalities, disruptions in the normal menstruation cycle, all can be traced to the influence of hormones.[25]

LEO'S FIRST URINE COLLECTION CAMPAIGN

When Gonadex was put on the market in 1948, it was Leo's first own hormone drug and probably one of the very first developed in Sweden at all.

But it was hardly the first sex hormone drug Leo manufactured and distributed. However, Leo's involvement in the hormone industry was inextricably interwoven with the research and development being conducted at Løvens kemiske Fabrik in Denmark. Like many others who went into the hormone business, insulin led to sexual hormones. At the end of the 1920s, the company began collaborating with physicians at the University of Copenhagen, including pathologist Oluf Thomsen and gynecologist Christian Hamburger, and within a few years was marketing both female sex hormones and gonadotropins.[26] These early preparations proved to have enormous significance for the direction Leo's subsequent interest in endocrinology took. As we shall see, Gonadex was the result not only of an international drug tradition, but a local one as well.

The mainstays of the roster of sexual hormones available from Løvens and therefore also Leo were a series of drugs named Physex, Ovex, Lutex and Antex. The first was Physex Leo which entered its catalogue in 1931. Its name would have you assume that Physex had something to do with the hypophysis and so it was. At least according to the catalogue copy, which states that the drug contains hormones from the frontal lobe of the pituitary gland. Furthermore, it is intended to be used by members of both sexes to treat a number of different diagnoses: "Impotence in younger men without organic cause, certain forms of amenorrhea and dysmenorrhea, dystrophia adiposogenitalis, pituitary developmental inhibition, neurasthenia, likewise effective as a stimulus to irregular milk secretion in nursing mothers."[27] A few years later however, the text has been altered to read that Physex is a gonadotropic hormone, which "is possibly entirely or partially created by placenta" and which is manufactured from the urine of pregnant women.[28] In other words, Physex did not contain hypophysis gonadotropin but rather human chorionic gonadotropin (hCG). This change is part and parcel with the difficulties mentioned in Chapter One in actually determining exactly where gonadotropins originate.

Its second sexual hormone drug, Ovex Leo, debuted in Leo's catalogue in 1932, described as containing the "cyclus hormone" of the ovary (also called "folliculinum" and later "estrone"), hence the choice of product name. Ovex contained female sex hormones and was intended exclusively for women, to treat a number of diagnoses including some it shared with Physex: "Primary and secondary amenorrhea, dysmenorrhea, climacterium praecox and ordinary menopausal complaints, symptoms of deficit after having undergone an ovariectomy, infantilism and hypoplasia of the female genital organs, and particularly sterility caused by the latter."[29] Two years later several more diagnoses were added, including certain skin diseases.[30] It is possible that sex hormones used in the production of Ovex were initially extracted from the ovaries, but the main ingredient, as shall be shown below, was urine from pregnant brood-mares.

Physex and Ovex were quickly followed by Lutex Leo and Antex Leo, appearing in the catalogues of 1934 and 1935, respectively. Lutex was described as a corpus luteum hormone (or "progestin") that could also be used to treat women with a number of varying diagnoses, including reduced production of the corpus luteum hormone ("forms of metropathia cystica haemorrhagica"), chronic miscarriage, the threat of miscarriage or premature delivery, and abbreviated menstrual intervals. Its contents were first manufactured from the extract of porcine ovaries. Like its predecessor Physex, Antex was presented as a gonadotropic hormone from the frontal lobe of the hypophysis—its name probably taken from the Latin *anterior*—but here, too, no mention is made of the fact that it is not produced directly from the pituitary gland but rather from the blood of pregnant mares. In other words, Antex contained brood-mare serum gonadotropin. The first time Antex appears in the catalogue it is recommended to be taken together with Ovex and only for the treatment of primary amenorrhea.[31] It is noteworthy that Physex, Ovex and Antex were also advertised as veterinary medicines for treating sterility and irregular heat cycles in horses.[32]

Aside from these four, classic Leo drugs, a number of combination drugs emerged in the 1930s, like Klimovex Leo, Ferrovex Leo, Neurovex Leo and Thyrovex Leo, all of which contained Ovex and some other component, and all of which proved short-lived. A testosterone drug named Virex Leo was introduced in 1935. It contained hormones extracted from animal testicles and was intended for men suffering from sexual afflictions caused by frayed nerves, fatigue or depression.[33] Another category of hormone drug introduced to the European market at the time contained extracts from animal pituitary glands, mainly from sheep and pigs. Leo appears never to have sold this kind of gonadotropin preparation, despite some initial interest.[34]

The sexual hormone drugs Leo sold during the 1930s were all essentially manufactured by Løvens kemiske Fabrik in Denmark. The one exception was Ovex, which Leo began manufacturing at the behest of Løvens. In order to do so, an adequate physical infrastructure was necessary, staffed with pharmaceutically and technically competent personnel. In the early 1930s a new building was raised in Helsingborg, containing offices, production lines and laboratories, while the old factory premises were turned into a synthesis laboratory in which old methods could be improved and new drugs manufactured. A small detached outbuilding was also constructed for ether extraction. An extraction apparatus was purchased from the German firm Friedrich Heckman and retrofitted to suit Leo's needs. In 1934, it was reported that outfitting the new "hormone factory" was now complete and manufacturing was in full swing.[35] The following year a total of seventy-nine employees were on the payroll.

In order to procure raw material, Leo took its cue from Aschheim and Zondek's discovery that female sex hormones could be extracted from the urine of pregnant mares. At the suggestion of Løvens, representatives of the firm approached farmers in the Scanian countryside and by 1933, had gained access to approximately one hundred horses scattered throughout the region.[36] Through this early production network what can be called Leo's first urine collecting campaign was started.[37] In brief, each farmer was paid to gather urine from all the pregnant brood-mares in his stables and saved it in a special well Leo installed on the premises.[38] The urine was then shipped to Leo's factory where it was transferred to barrels in a storage facility popularly known as the "Piss House" before extracting its precious hormonal contents. Plenty of correspondence between Leo and local farmers has been preserved and it turns out that urine collection could be a complicated procedure, as this 1939 letter to Anders Andersson of Allarp, Södervidinge, attests.

> Since we plan on using some urine during the period 1 October–1 March, allow us to hereby inquire if it would be advantageous to you to deliver urine according to the enclosed conditions [urine from pregnant mares for the production of drugs, payment of 12 öre per liter]. We request that you inform us of the number of mares from which you intend to deliver urine and send samples from same. We enclose a self-addressed, stamped envelope for your answer.[39]

Andersson had been retained by Leo before and that they would submit this new request indicates that he was considered a reliable supplier. Andersson replied that he was still willing to sell them horse urine, but that delivery posed certain practical problems.

> To answer your esteemed letter of the 24th of this month about the delivery of urine, I can inform you that this year I have 4 covered mares, one has been pronounced pregnant by the veterinarian, and from the remaining three I shall send urine samples for testing. However, as far as the price is concerned, 12 öre is now too little, since labor costs have risen so much that I can no longer employ any other workers than those who perform the most essential tasks. It takes quite a lot of time to keep the area behind the mares clean so that the urine can reach the drains, as well as straining and collecting and transporting to the station.[40]

Leo replied that as far as the price was concerned, an additional two öre per liter would be added, payable upon delivery.[41] The following day, Leo informed Andersson on its test outcome. "The analysis of the urine samples from your mares gave a positive result for Rut and Alva, from whom delivery may immediately begin, while the results were negative for Kinett, from whom we await new samples. Canisters, strainers and receptacles can be picked up at our facilities. N.B. We do not accept delivery on Saturday or the day before public holidays."[42] In an historical perspective, letters like these can seem trivial, but it was through such direct communication that important ground was prepared for what would become an advanced effort at drug manufacture.

In the 1940s, the rate was raised to twenty-two öre per liter, exceeding the amount farmers were getting for their milk.[43] That Leo paid so handsomely for horse urine surprised many but some still hesitated to participate since they were expected to collect it themselves, a prospect few found attractive. In time, Leo took over more of the transportation process, either in milk cans loaded onto a flatbed or in tanker trucks.[44] According to head of research Ove Fernö (1916–2007), Leo bought a total of 50,000 liters of horse urine annually, from which approximately a half a kilo of estrone was extracted, used mainly in the manufacture of Ovex.[45] Leo's collection of horse urine proceeded in this manner up until the 1950s, when it became easier and more cost-effective to manufacture estrone synthetically. The stench of the stable finally lifted from the factory grounds to the grateful relief of its urban surroundings. An article in the local news testifies to the fact that the odor emanating from Leo's facilities could be trying. "The whole area stinks. We need gas masks. We can't have the tiniest window open and still the smell of horses is everywhere."[46] But even if Leo stopped using *horse* urine, they did not stop using urine to produce its hormones. Urine collection on a large scale continued to be pursued by the company for decades to come, as we shall see below.

Aside from a physical infrastructure, technical personnel and access to raw materials, Leo required medical competence in order to develop, test and produce and, not the least, market hormonal drugs in a scientifically acceptable manner. By establishing contact with prominent medical researchers, Leo demonstrated that it was a serious and ethical company. Like other contemporary pharmaceutical companies, Leo strove to recruit academic researchers as external consultants. At first, these consultants were given very limited remits beyond lending the company scientific credibility via their titles.[47] However, circumstances changed once new marketing legislation was introduced in Sweden.

A state-run pharmaceutical lab with supervisory powers had existed in Sweden since 1915, when a special laboratory unit was set up at the Department of Forensic Chemistry at the Swedish Medical Institute. When the latter was dissolved in 1918, the lab was granted the status of independent authority and named the National Pharmaceutical Laboratory (NPL), working under the auspices of the Royal Swedish Board of Medicine. The initial task with which the NPL was charged was to inspect drugs in accordance with the prevailing pharmaceutical product regulations and determine whether or not they should be classified as licensed articles. It also conducted inspection tours of factories and wholesalers and performed pharmaceutical studies for the Board of Medicine.[48]

When a promulgation on trade with "pharmaceutical specialties" (a term which replaced the older "patent medicines") took effect, the duties of the NPL were multiplied significantly.[49] Before a new factory-produced medicine could be made freely available in pharmacies, it had to be registered. Applications required submitting facts including the name of the specialty, its characteristics or composition, how it was manufactured, the dimensions of its packaging and price. Advertising material intended for circulation need also be enclosed. Samples of the drug were to be submitted for testing, which would verify whether the facts were correct but also if the drug satisfied "appropriate pharmaceutical standards." The NPL conducted its inspection and the Board of Medicine decided if it qualified for registration, which was valid for five years, and thereafter it must be renewed.[50]

The new legislation made tougher demands on the industry. In order to guarantee that a new drug be approved, companies were compelled to make sure that they delivered what they promised. One way of fulfilling this requirement was to hire experts and resort to external competence, i.e. consultants, which is exactly what Leo did. Georg Kahlson (1901–1982) was recruited in 1936. A pharmacologist and physiologist with a degree from Lund University, Kahlson was put on retainer as general consultant supervising production and fact-checking informational material on each new drug Leo launched. Through Kahlson, contact was made with Hungarian-born chemist Adam Deutsch (1907–1976), who was hired in 1938 to manage the company's research laboratory and synthetization department. Other scientists enlisted around this time included physician Sven Ingvar (1889–1947) of the University Hospital in Lund and Ingeborg Leisering, who had previously served as Bernhard Zondek's research assistant in Berlin.[51] Its roster of external hormone expertise was thus eminently qualified. During the first years Leo sold sexual hormones, they were standardized and manufactured in Denmark under the supervision of Oluf Thomsen.[52] But when Leo began producing Ovex itself as the new Swedish pharmaceutical specialties legislation came into effect, it entered into a collaboration with the Women's Clinic in Uppsala with research gynecologists Axel Westman and Sune Genell.

LEO'S WANDERING HORMONE LAB

In his 1932 inaugural address in Uppsala, Professor Axel Westman maintained that modern gynecology demanded new skill sets. The gynecologist needed to become an endocrinologist and in doing so adopting experimental methods. Due to his scientific background, Westman emphasized the value of research, of producing new knowledge which by extension could lead to improved health care. But experiments and hormone analyses required specific material prerequisites. Physicians and researchers had to have modern, well-equipped laboratories at their disposal, something which at that point in time was only a "future goal."[53] This requirement, together with the need for animals on which to experiment, industrially-purified hormones and a variety of indispensable but expensive instruments, was probably the most important reason why Westman agreed to work with Leo. The company financed the construction and maintenance of a certain laboratory at the Women's Clinic in Uppsala, which has subsequently gone down in history as "Sweden's first hormone laboratory." Regardless of whether or not this was in fact true (what is meant by "laboratory" is a question of semantics), Leo was undeniably one of the first companies to finance and materialize laboratory study of hormones in an academic environment.[54] Thus Leo helped make the scientific riddles confronting Westman and his colleagues "doable."[55] Inversely, it can be claimed that government employee Westman and his consultant colleagues were among the first in the country to actively collaborate with the private pharmaceutical industry. Thus this case can be added to the many examples of a so-called "Mode 2" or "Triple Helix" relationship—where university researchers collaborate closely with both government and industry—which occurred long before the end of the twentieth century, when this terminology was introduced to designate the ostensibly new research climate.[56]

I have been unable to ascertain exactly how the laboratory came into being or how the collaboration between Leo and Westman was consolidated. A letter from Leo to Westman dated 6 November 1933 proclaims, "We welcome the Professor as supervisor of standardization for our hormone drugs."[57] Leo also informed Westman that he was free to order subscriptions to international periodicals and that the company would happily contribute funds to hire lab assistants. Another document simply states, "Professor Westman of Uppsala University [has] joined the staff of our hormone factory."[58] Looking back, Westman tells the following version of the story.

> Upon assuming the post as head of the obstetrics and gynecology clinic of the Academic Hospital in Uppsala in 1932, I came into increasingly closer contact with AB Leo in Helsingborg. It was at a point in time when hormone research in obstetrics and gynecology was becoming more topical. Biological pregnancy reactions were performed and therapeutic trials with hormone drugs for a variety of functional ovarian disorders had begun. Said pharmaceutical firm was highly interested in this new direction in research and considered it one of its duties to try and manufacture effective hormone preparations. Thus we agreed to collaborate and a very modest hormone laboratory was equipped with the support of AB Leo in an attic above the clinic.[59]

Properly outfitting this attic laboratory was not entirely dependent on the generosity of Leo. In a letter from Westman to the Directorate of Academic Hospital dated 20 October 1933, he mentions that hormone analyses were relegated to an old bathroom and the lab animals kept in cages in the basement.[60] Westman finds these conditions far from satisfactory and therefore asks the directorate for funds to build a hormone lab in the attic above the Women's Clinic. This would help fortify the efforts of scientific hormone research, efforts that Westman described as "wholly dedicated to practical goals and whose ongoing results will directly benefit health care."[61] The directorate granted him the asked-for sum, which suggests that the hormone lab was already under construction when Westman was hired, though it was Leo who paid for the equipment and operating expenses.[62]

In this, Leo followed in the footsteps of Organon and Schering in Holland and Germany, respectively, both of which had developed successful field collaborations with gynecologists and gynecological clinics. Through these relationships companies gained access to raw material in the form of glands removed from patients and the urine of pregnant women. The arrangement also meant the new hormone drugs could be tested in a clinical environment and ultimately increase sales.[63] Westman successively introduced new drugs into his clinical work and together with his many public appearances, essays and books contributed to whipping up interest in hormone therapy. Furthermore, his endocrinological expertise, unparalleled in Sweden, lent indirect luster to the same drugs he had a hand in producing.[64] Westman was not unaware of this, for as he later admitted in a letter, "It was in the financial interests of Leo to subsidize the laboratory since most of the hormone drugs were manufactured by the Leo factory in Helsingborg."[65]

Another good reason for Leo to choose to finance an external lab at this time was the new quality demands imposed on hormonal drugs at the beginning of the 1930s. A central component in these guidelines concerned the international standardization of the drugs, and an important task of the hormone lab in Uppsala was to perform such standardization tests. In practice, the tests were conducted not by Westman but rather his assistant, gynecologist Sune Genell (1897–1960), another qualified endocrinologist. Educated in Lund, Genell had shown an early interest in sexual endocrinology and, like Westman, contributed actively to introducing new findings to the Swedish medical corps.[66] After further studies in laboratory technology at the Women's Clinic at the municipal hospital of Berlin-Spandau, headed by Bernhard Zondek, he was on the staff of the Women's Clinic in Uppsala when Leo hired him as specialist consultant on 1 June 1933.[67]

Genell's first assignment consisted of standardizing Ovex, Lutex and Physex as they rolled off the conveyor belt, checking and confirming the strengths of the dosages in conformance with the international norms. He was also free to offer advice during the production process in the Helsingborg factory and assist in composing advertising copy. In return, Genell received an undisclosed annual sum but also unlimited free samples for the clinic, along with access to lab animals, chemicals and other laboratory utensils.[68] However, it was Axel Westman who ruled the roost and thus Genell's activities as well. The distribution of labor between the two is apparent in a catalogue Leo published in 1934. "Biologically standardized in accordance with the Allen-Doisy Test by Dr. Sune Genell under the supervision of Dr. Axel Westman, Professor of Obstetrics and Gynecology at Uppsala University."[69]

Westman and Genell spent a long time as Leo's leading consultants in the field of sexual hormones. Since Westman was both a practicing chief medical officer and veteran researcher with high academic status he was the ideal partner, providing medical competence to the development and supervision of Leo's products and contributing to its reputation as a science-based concern. A further bonus was the fact that Westman had so many contacts in the research field, to which Leo acquired indirect access by adding him to its network. From having been a specialist consultant Westman evolved into general consultant to the firm. The collaboration between Leo and the clinic in Uppsala did not last long, however. When Westman moved to Lund Hospital in 1935 to assume the reigns of its women's clinic, he brought the hormone lab with him. This indicates that Leo was more concerned with its relationship with Westman than the clinic in Uppsala that, all things considered, was rather weak from a scientific viewpoint.

Between its founding in 1894 and the doctoral thesis of Leif Wide in 1962 (on the chorionic gonadotropin, as fate would have it), the staff had only three Ph.Ds to its credit.[70]

At first, the conditions for conducting experimental hormone research were modest in Lund, too; the lab was located in a display room the clinic had at its disposal. However, material conditions improved after a few years when Leo's funding was complemented by generous grants from the Rockefeller Foundation. Four new rooms were allocated to the hormone lab in the clinic's basement and modern equipment was purchased, vastly intensifying the pace of research, which continued to mainly concentrate on the female sexual cycle and its "disruptions," the hormones of the ovaries, function of the fallopian tubes and movement of the egg in the uterus.[71] While this work was going on, Westman embarked on his internationally renowned experiments in neuro endocrinology, dealing with the relationship between the sex glands, the pituitary gland and the hypothalamus, in an effort to discover the significance of the latter for the gonadotropic functions of the hypophysis.[72] Also involved in this research was Dora Jacobsohn (1908–1983), a physician from Germany who had fled upon the Nazi seizure of power and was hired as Westman's assistant in Uppsala in 1934. After her time at the women's clinic in Lund, she moved over to the Department of Physiology, where she collaborated with another of Leo's famed consultants, Georg Kahlson.[73]

Sune Genell also made the move to Lund. He worked with Westman at the clinic in Lund for several years before choosing to strike out on his own at Malmö General Hospital, where he became chief of medicine after defending his thesis in 1938. Genell continued to make his services available to Leo. A pamphlet published by the company in 1940 makes it clear that the relationship between Westman and Genell remained unchanged. "Antex Leo, Lutex S Leo, Ovex Leo and Physex Leo were all standardized by *Dr. Sune Genell*, M.D., Associate Professor of Obstetrics and Gynecology at Lund University and Chief Medical Officer of the Women's Clinic of Malmö General Hospital, under the supervision of *Dr. Axel Westman*, M.D., Professor of Obstetrics and Gynecology at Lund University."[74] Genell continued to champion endocrinological practice, making it hardly surprising that it became a significant discipline at the new women's clinic in Malmö General Hospital, opened in 1944.[75]

Alongside his research and practice, Westman embarked on a swift and successful administrative career, being named director of Lund Hospital in 1940. His work in Lund came to an abrupt end in 1942, however, when he assumed the professorial chair at the new Women's Clinic of the Royal Caroline Hospital. On the move again, he took Leo's hormone lab with him. Leo continued to finance its day-to-day expenses for another full decade. The contract between Leo and the Caroline Hospital called for premises at the clinic to be let for a "hormone laboratory to be run by the company." Leo would provide the equipment, some of which was shipped from the clinic in Lund, while the hospital would pay for the utilities. As in Uppsala and Lund, the hormone lab would be used to check and develop Leo's products. But the clinic could also make use of the lab's resources for a fee.[76]

The relocation of the hormone laboratory to Stockholm was featured prominently in the local daily *Stockholms-Tidningen*, which reported that the Caroline Hospital could now boast of the foremost laboratory of its kind in Scandinavia, a place filled with wildly rotating centrifuges and retorts in which incomprehensible "chemical magic" took place. As the paper noted, the staff consisted not only of two male doctors, Harald Johansson[77] and Erik Nordlander, but also a number of "young ladies" in charge of the lab animals. "With practiced and gentle hands they treat the little creatures in a way no man can imitate."[78] A special unit for sperm analysis was also created, which in time grew into its own specialized laboratory.[79] This was an early but not unique attempt to broaden the scope of activity to include male patients. When additions were built onto the Malmö General Hospital women's clinic, Sune Genell was given his own hormone laboratory, where he too began conducting sperm diagnoses.[80]

The Women's Clinic at the Caroline Hospital was not suited to large-scale research and the lab premises made available soon proved far too cramped. The lab animals were apparently stored in a former lecture hall.[81] In order to have the premises enlarged to make room for a proper research section, Westman applied for a hefty grant from the Knut and Alice Wallenberg Foundation in 1945.[82] The application sought funding for both construction work and new equipment, but only the latter was granted, on the condition that the expansion of the clinic be contracted to another party.[83] Soon the government stepped in with financial support. After pressure from the Caroline Hospital, the Swedish Parliament allocated funds to the planned expansion in 1947—exactly what Westman had requested two years earlier in his submission to the Population Inquiry.[84] In addition, extra funding was allocated to laboratory diagnosis and treatment of sterility. Thus one step at a time, sexual endocrinological research in Sweden established itself in a medical environment through both private and state sponsorship. The dream of finding a cure for sterility now had a chance to come true.

PART II

INNOVATION

CHAPTER FOUR

Inventing Gonadex

IN THIS CHAPTER, I will survey the discussions and scientific and industrial efforts of Leo's production network preceding the launch of Gonadex at the press conference held in Stockholm in June of 1948. We have reached the point in this biography where it is time to treat the birth and early adolescence of its subject. We begin with a description of the turbulent political and economic climate in which Leo decided to invest by developing its own original preparations, though I show that Gonadex was actually not entirely a brand-new drug but rather an elaboration of an older drug, developed abroad. I continue by studying the process that led to the new artifact and the scientific evidence provided by the firm defining suitable areas of use when seeking to register the drug. Finally, I describe how Leo initiated a new campaign to accumulate the raw material necessary to its increased rate of hormone production.

THE SECOND WORLD WAR: A TURNING POINT FOR THE SWEDISH PHARMACEUTICAL INDUSTRY

When the industrial revolution reached Sweden in the 1890s, industry expanded slowly but surely through the interwar years and the Second World War. The transition from agrarian to industrial society can be said to have been complete by the early 1940s, when the percentage of industrial jobs exceeded farming's for the first time. This evolution continued with undiminished momentum in the decades immediately following the cessation of hostilities, an era of prosperity that has been called the "golden age of Swedish industry."[1]

The pharmaceutical industry followed this pattern. Its robust expansion can be illustrated by the fact that sales to retail pharmacies increased more than twelve-fold between 1924 and 1945. At the same time, the percentage of pharmacy-produced products declined significantly. Pharmaceutical specialties manufactured by Swedish companies eventually comprised a greater percentage of total retail sales than all the other items together (including in-house preparations, import products, homeopathic remedies and sundries like bandages, fruit salts, and toothpaste).[2] Domestic businesses had "conquered" the Swedish market and due to the Second World War, which entire sectors of the massive German pharmaceutical industry failed to survive, now had access to a large export market. Drugs were coveted barter in so-called "counter trade" and after the war, the opportunity to export to war-torn nations with limited access to pharmaceuticals presented itself. Circumstances had combined to make the mid-century Swedish pharmaceutical industry appear as a promising business with a glowing future. Perhaps even more foreign markets could be conquered?[3]

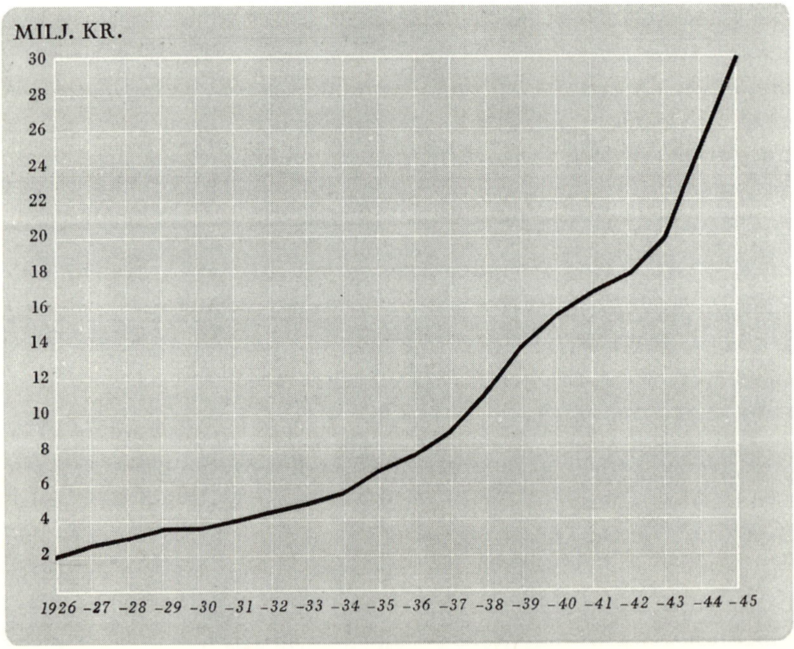

FIGURE 7 The Swedish pharmaceutical industry grew slowly but surely in the interwar period and expanded substantially during the Second World War. This diagram depicts the sales development of the seven largest Swedish companies (including AB Leo) on the Swedish market, 1926–45. *Svensk Läkemedelsindustri* (1946).

At the same time, the industry underwent an organizational transformation from small-scale production and manufacturing units to full-scale research, development and marketing entities. Models for this process were thick on the ground, especially in the United States, where successful industrial research labs like Merck Research Laboratory (and the Merck Institute for Therapeutic Research), Lilly Research Laboratories, the Squibb Institute for Medical Research and Abbott Research Laboratories had been set up during the interwar years.[4] Up until the 1930s, the dominant strategy in Sweden had been to exploit foreign innovation. Now the ambition was to begin developing preparations domestically. As factories were being built, state-of-the-art research labs were being outfitted to conduct analyses and create syntheses, which attracted an increasing number of highly qualified full or part-time staff—engineers, physicians, pharmacists and researchers.

These investments soon paid off, as several new drugs were introduced to the medical market. Vitrum's anticoagulant Heparin, launched in 1936, is usually referred to as the very first wholly Swedish original drug. During and after the war, it was followed by Ferrosan's own anticoagulant, Apekumarol, in 1942, Pharmacia's blood substitute Macrodex (Dextran) in 1947, Astra's local anesthetic Xylocain and Ferrosan's antituberculant PAS (1948), and Kabi's plasma Albumin (1949). The companies marketed a number of other products simultaneously, including diagnostic tests and medical equipment.[5]

The circumstances in which the Swedish pharmaceutical industry found itself in the mid-1940s are reflected in the personnel working for seven of the leading manufacturers. Together, Astra, Ferrosan, Hässle, Leo, Pharmacia, Tika and Vitrum employed a total of 1,382 individuals, of whom one hundred and sixty-six were degree-holding academics and engineers. On top of this, the companies hired some sixty researchers and medical professionals as scientific consultants.[6] In the USA, lasting bonds were forged between manufacturers and universities (not only in the pharmaceutical field but also chemistry and electrical technology), and most other Western nations, including Sweden, soon followed.[7] Alongside creating an expansive labor market for academics, the industry began awarding prizes and jobs to deserving individuals, as well as financing research at colleges, universities and larger hospitals through grants. Institutions that soon assumed a leading role in pharmaceuticals included the Royal Caroline Institute, the Royal Caroline Hospital, Stockholm University and the medical faculty of Uppsala University.[8] Both the actual and the psychological barriers between science and commerce certain doctors and research academics had hitherto attempted to maintain began eroding, only to collapse altogether in the

1950s. Biomedical research and development of pharmaceuticals became both *big science* and *big business*, and thus also *big politics*.

Another notable example of the integration of industry, academy and medicine is the Swedish Endocrine Society, established in 1945 as a counterpart to the American Association for the Study of the Internal Secretions (ASIS). According to the first paragraph of its charter, the society would serve as a federation of Swedish endocrinologists and "other individuals interested in endocrinology,"[9] referring of course to researchers active in the many different branches of endocrinology, but also to practicing physicians and, tellingly, even representatives of the pharmaceutical industry. One of the initiators of the association and its first secretary, too, was the head of the Swedish offices of Organon at Pharmacia, German pharmacologist Frederik Paulsen.[10] The same year the society was founded, it applied to be granted the status of a separate section of the Swedish Society of Medicine.[11] Since its membership did not consist strictly of medical professionals, the proposal had difficulty obtaining a hearing, but was eventually granted nonetheless. The fact that the name of its first chairman was Axel Westman likely facilitated the handling of the matter.[12]

Established Swedish firms competed for customers with domestic pharmacies but also with leading foreign enterprises. During and immediately after the war, major investments were made in the development of drugs and biomedical research, which contributed to flooding the market with new preparations, most of them bearing American labels.[13] Furthermore, companies were forced to deal with the many tiny firms that still distributed medically dubious patent medicines with no little success through newspaper and magazine advertisements. They were compelled to appear as the most reliable alternative, which meant that they had to convince the public that a modern, harmonious and fruitful marriage of science and industry had been entered into in Sweden, too. Pharmaceutical companies thus blithely described themselves as being part of a "science-based industry," though as historian of technology Wolfgang König put it, it could just as well be called "industry-based science."[14]

The brochure *Svensk läkemedelsindustri* [The Swedish pharmaceutical industry], compiled by the seven, above-mentioned firms in May 1946 under the editorial hand of Leo's managing director, Svante Wiström (1893–1965), reveals how these businesses thought. Its main purpose was to present a united front protesting against legislative and administrative policies deemed unfair to the domestic pharmaceutical industry from a commercial standpoint, preventing what the authors themselves considered the healthy, natural course of development. The main problem they intended to address was not the current supervisory legislation, but rather the fact that the table of medicinal rates, the *de facto* price list stipulated by the government, seemed to benefit retail pharmacies at their expense.[15] Against the background of a motion presented to the lower house of parliament in 1944, and in protest against increasing government influence over the private sector, the brochure can also be seen as a salvo from the opposition in the "command economy" debate.[16] The motion called for an inquiry into the nationalization of the entire pharmaceutical sector in order to achieve a more rational organization and eventually, cheaper prescription drugs. An inquiry was in fact convened in 1946, but a bill was never introduced.[17] But aside from taking up matters of a political nature, the companies also used the opportunity to provide insight into the industry and its efforts to develop and manufacture products with the help of science. This was of course also political posturing.

A number of the arguments broached in *Svensk läkemedelsindustri* are similar in tone to the sales strategies of the mid-twentieth century pharmaceutical industry. First and foremost the companies want to assure the public that they guarantee the precautions safeguarding Swedish drugs, precautions backed up by scientific method. "Meticulous control has always been a mainstay in the manufacture of Swedish drugs, which extends through all stages in the production of a first-class, reliable product, not just with respect to the chemistry, physics and bacteriology, but pharmacology, toxicology and clinical therapy as well."[18] This safety-mindedness contributed, secondly, to the high quality for which Swedish medicine was renowned. "What now characterizes Swedish specialties—the industrially-manufactured drugs of today—is their high quality and homogeneity, achieved through thoroughly tested methods of fabrication under the above-mentioned watchful eye, which is further assured by the inspectors of the National Pharmaceutical Laboratory."[19] Moreover, the consumer can be certain that their ads are always ethical and the price of Swedish-produced drugs reasonable. "The Swedish pharmaceutical industry has from its very beginnings stood for quality workmanship, trustworthiness in advertising and moderation in pricing."[20] For these reasons, Swedish drugs were said to have won the trust and support of the Swedish medical and pharmaceutical corps during the "difficult formative years." Further support is finally mustered from off-shore medical and pharmaceutical experts. What is not mentioned, however, is the *effect* of any of their drugs. In common with the advertising of so many other products of "Swedish quality" from this era, it is instead implied that anything produced by the Swedish pharmaceutical industry functioned outstandingly, if not better than their foreign counterparts. A similarly positive image of the expanding Swedish pharmaceutical industry is expressed a few years later in the popular science periodical *Teknik för alla* [Technology for all], where the modern pharmaceutical factory is presented as the embodiment of the advances of science and technology for the good of all. "Compared with other industries, like milling, mining and shipbuilding, it is still young. But it has already earned such esteem that it will undoubtedly also earn a place among those businesses in the world which strive not merely for the best of one nation, but of all mankind."[21]

Since Swedish companies competed with local retailers, foreign companies and "purveyors of patent medicine," it was important for them to present a united front, which is the impression given by *Svensk läkemedelsindustri.* In reality, of course, they competed with each other as well, and at the end of the day, the question that preoccupied the head offices of each was how to deal with domestic competitors. What strategy did Leo choose in the mid-1940s?

INVESTING IN A "LINE OF HORMONES"

By the middle of the 1940s, Leo had become a well established and, in Scandinavian terms, medium-sized business concern.[22] Between 1927 and 1935, staff size had tripled from twenty-five to seventy-nine. Ten years later, the total payroll was up to almost one hundred and seventy employees plus consultants—twelve researchers and physicians as full-time general consultants and seventeen researchers, physicians and veterinarians as part-time specialist consultants.[23] A new factory had been built and a new synthesis lab was up and running, and production and research had expanded and broadened successively.[24] The company had some five hundred drugs on the market distributed in roughly 1,500 different packages. Annual sales approached five million SEK. Aside from the off-site hormone laboratory, there was a research section with a staff of ten, a biology lab, a chemical lab, a physiological lab and a separate "pollen group" conducting allergy research.[25] At the center of this new research organization was the abovementioned Svante Wiström, a pharmacist who had first been recruited with the launch of insulin in 1923. Wiström had now earned the highest confidence of the company board, being named vice-president in 1945 and given a place on the directorate, where he was put in charge of research, development, sales and information, which in practice meant that he served as director of marketing. Civil engineer Ove Fernö, named head of research in 1946, and engineer Bertil Högberg (1918–1999), recruited the same year, played other key roles.

As is emphasized in the book *Från leopiller till nicorette*, Leo's new research arm cultivated its relationship with the external hormone lab (relocated to the Royal Caroline Hospital in Stockholm during the war) very carefully.[26] This was strategically sound, since Leo had attained prominence in the field of sexual hormones, at least insofar as hormone preparations was concerned, according to the pamphlet *Sexualhormonpreparat Leo*, six thousand copies of which were distributed to physicians, medical students and pharmacists. In the 1944 version, eight different types of hormones are listed as available in various quantities and packaging, all of which have been standardized and tested by Leo's scientific consultants. "Dosage instructions are largely based on empirical knowledge acquired at the Women's Clinic of the Caroline Hospital and the Women's Clinic in Lund under the direction of Professor Axel Westman, and the Women's Clinic in Malmö under the direction of Associate Professor Sune Genell."[27]

Aside from the old standard-bearer Ovex Leo, two other preparations containing varieties of estrone were available, Ovex B Leo and Glycovex Leo.[28] The primary source of estrone was still urine from pregnant brood mares. Synsteron Leo was also available, a drug made from synthetically manufactured estrogen. There was also Lutex S Leo, containing synthetically produced progesterone, and two familiar gonadotropin drugs: the chorionic gonadotropin Physex Leo and the pregnant mare serum gonadotropin Antex Leo. With the exception of Antex, which was also intended for men, all these drugs were intended to treat diverse disorders of the female sexual cycle. While the pamphlet mentions a special hormone preparation exclusively for men, Virex S Leo, which contained synthetic testosterone and was recommended for the treatment of "disorders of the hormonal function of the testicles," this drug was said not to be available when it went to press.[29]

In fact, Leo was not only having trouble providing customers Virex at that time. Most of the drugs listed in the 1944 edition of *Sexualhormonpreparat Leo* were still being made in Denmark by parent company Løvens kemiske Fabrik. Leo itself had yet to produce its own original hormone drug. This was not considered a problem during its build-up phase; exploiting innovations made elsewhere was a way for Leo, in common with other companies, to quickly establish a presence on the Swedish market.[30] However, during the Second World War, when Denmark was occupied by the Germans and trade with the West was frozen, import was rendered tricky and it is reasonable to assume that the number of Leo's hormone drugs were in short supply, at least for the time being. This circumstance in combination with increased domestic competition, was problematic, but also offered an organizational opportunity. To quote management researchers Marcie J. Tyre and Wanda J. Orlikowski, the situation contributed to opening a "window of opportunity."[31] Leo was confronted with the question of whether it should increase production of hormone preparations. In fact, maybe it was time for Leo to start *developing* its own drugs? The war brought problems and opportunities to Løvens kemiske Fabrik, too, during which it began the first Scandinavian production of penicillin and entered into the new, very promising field of antibiotics, which would eventually assume a dominant position in the research and development department of the company.[32]

Its stable of consultants loudly championed the notion that Leo should seize the opportunity to partly alter its routines. In the autumn of 1944, Leo's managing director Carl Holtman (1896–1986) wrote to Axel Westman informing him of the company's plans to invest in what he called a "line of hormones." Westman's delight at the news and his eagerness to be involved is obvious in his reply to Holtman. "As you understand, it greatly pleases me that the Company intends to increase production of hormone drugs and like you, I find it propitious that we continue to collaborate in the manner hitherto pursued."[33] On 11 November, a few days after this exchange, a meeting was arranged between Westman and Leo's representatives Adam Deutsch and Paul Kallós at the Caroline Hospital's women's clinic. Westman explained that the "incorporation of the domestic manufacture of hormone preparations, sexual hormones and others, [is] of the greatest significance."[34] According to Westman, Leo was the one company in Sweden suited to succeed in such an endeavor. He repeated that he was eager to participate in the work himself and recommended that collaboration between Leo and his women's clinic "not only proceed according to plan but deepen and expand."[35]

Furthermore, Westman recommended that Leo begin developing its own hormone drugs. His interest in the significance of the pituitary gland for the endocrine system continued unabated, and he suggested manufacturing freeze-dried hypophyses. The company did not care much for that idea, since organ implants had previously proven to have immunological issues. But that the company was otherwise prepared to undertake a major investment in hormone research is made plain by a memo dated 29 December 1944, which states that a variety of female sex hormones had already been manufactured and the possibility of producing several more was currently under consideration. It goes on to say that both Antex and Physex would shortly be going into biological testing and production. "Attempts at further purification of these preparations are underway."[36]

Sune Genell also applauded investing in sexual hormone drugs in a meeting with Deutsch and Kallós in Malmö on 4 April 1945. The purpose of the consultation was to hear Genell's opinions on Leo's current stock of hormone preparations. Did they work? Were the recommended doses adequate? How did Leo's drugs stack up in comparison with its main competitor Pharmacia (distributor of Organon's hormone drugs)? Deutsch and Kallós were also curious to hear what Genell thought about the need for other hormones. Genell, now chief of medicine at Malmö General Hospital, stated that it was of "great significance and import" that Leo begin manufacturing its own hormones, mentioning in particular the gonadotropins Antex and Physex. While the urine of pregnant women was necessary in order to produce Physex, Genell had a concrete suggestion as to how this raw material could be collected at the prenatal clinic in Malmö. In their report on the meeting, Deutsch and Kallós wrote that

> [Genell] believes that in the majority of cases, it would suffice that Leo provide bottles of chloroform and hire a shipping agent to take charge of the packing and transportation of the bottles when notified by the clinic. In a number of instances, a small payment for the urine would certainly assure the acquisition of larger amounts of material. Dr. Genell is willing to oversee the operation in Malmö together with us.[37]

Two days later, a meeting brought Westman, Deutsch, Kallós and Leo's managing director Carl Holtman together. Also in attendance was a German chemist named Thomas Rosenberg, who had entered the orbit of Leo and the Nordic Insulin Laboratory during the war. The theme of the meeting was Leo's planned investment in new hormone preparations and the discussion focused on one specific sort—pituitary gland hormones.[38] Westman urged research and development of hypophysis-based medicine like prolactin and growth hormones, but also reiterated his wish that Leo produce and test freeze-dried hypophyses. As far as gonadotropin hormones were concerned, it was pointed out that testing had shown that the biological effect could vary widely depending on whether they had been produced from the urine of pregnant women or the blood of pregnant horses, or if real pituitary glands were used as the starting material. This, replied Westman, was a matter deserving further investigation.

THE DREAM OF A PURE GONADOTROPIN

The meetings held between Leo and its consultants in the mid-1940s were in all probability crucial for the direction Leo took in the future. Just how crucial is hard to say, since the documentation to which I have had access does not contain any information about decisions made by the board in this matter. It should also be repeated that Leo had been bought by H. Lundbeck and Co in 1946, so its break with Løvens kemiske Fabrik can have played some role. In any event, Leo and Westman undertook a series of collaborative development projects dealing with the pituitary gland hormone prolactin and preparations intended for the treatment of sterility.[39] Such drugs had been on the market for several years now, but in his earlier mentioned book *Barnlös* (1940), Westman commented on them and their use in the following terms.

> Hormone treatment of sterility is comparatively new. Only in most recent years have scientists been able to produce preparations of sufficient strength. In such circumstances it is natural that our knowledge has not grown particularly large, and solid parameters for treatment have not been established. But development moves quickly forward and we have every reason to believe that in the future, hormone treatment of sterility will lead to better results than those hitherto achieved.[40]

Westman undeniably had good reason to expect that future hormone therapy would be better than what was available at the time of writing. A number of clinical tests with existing sex hormone drugs had indeed been conducted, and there were also several positive instances of treatment that had been both literally and figuratively fruitful. But on the whole, hormone therapy had had very little impact on the treatment of sterility.[41] According to some practitioners, it was a "thankless task," no more than firing a "shot in the dark."[42] On the other hand, medical treatment of involuntarily childless women had increased significantly in Sweden. Of all the patients admitted to the Women's Clinic in Lund between 1931 and 1941, the number undergoing treatment for sterility increased from 0.6% to 13%. In Stockholm the rate of increase was even more marked, from a mere one percent in 1933 (Sabbatsberg Hospital) to a whopping 35% in 1943 (Caroline Hospital). During 1943 alone, four hundred and sixty women underwent treatment at the latter clinic. Westman's personal conclusion was that sterility and its treatment had finally achieved prominence in the nativity debate. In turn this had engendered a transformation in the "psychological attitude" of the general public toward the population question.[43] This interpretation of the state of affairs was probably correct. As Marsh and Ronner have put it: "Changes in the culture, rather than scientific advances or greater technological expertise, have been and still are the forces most likely to bring a rush of infertile patients to clinicians' offices."[44]

Apparently the outcome of these visits and treatments proved often positive. According to published statistics, almost one-third of the patients eventually became pregnant and bore healthy children.[45] However, the question still remained as to the exact contribution made by the new hormone preparations. Westman's own studies from 1944 appear to show that surgery or other mechanical operations remained the preferred method. In 1944's *Sexualhormonpreparat Leo*, "sterility and frigidity" were still included among indications, and Westman recommended specific drugs from the Leo catalogue for treating these diagnoses. But promises as to the expected effect of the drugs were modest to say the least.[46] Another problem was that the drugs could cause a number of undesirable side effects. Only a few years hence, Westman would testify to the fact that "the drugs we have hitherto had at our disposal can cause considerable side effects. Fever, nausea, and other complications are not unusual in conjunction with treatment."[47]

Leo's gonadotropin drugs Physex and Antex were two of the problematic preparations to which Westman referred. They were intended (either separately or together) for women who suffered from a lack of hypophysis gonadotropin, resulting in low sex hormone production and a failure to ovulate. Sterility was one of several diagnoses for which they were prescribed.[48] Prescribing chorionic gonadotropin and pregnant mare serum gonadotropin had become common clinical practice for a strictly material reason; it was simply much cheaper and easier to manufacture hormones from urine and blood than from human pituitary glands.[49] It was however far from proven that chorionic gonadotropin and pregnant mare serum gonadotropin had the same clinical effect as "genuine" hypophysis gonadotropin. In biological experiments conducted on small animals like rats, mice, hamsters and rabbits, the substances all acted on the sexual glands in an expected and similar manner. But when experiments were conducted on lab animals whose pituitary glands had been removed, the results were far less encouraging. In contrast to hypophysis gonadotropin and pregnant mare serum gonadotropin, chorionic gonadotropin had sometimes no effect whatsoever.

Furthermore, during the 1940s it was reported that chorionic gonadotropin had no discernable effect on the sexual glands of primates, whose physiology is similar to man, either with or without the pituitary gland. Ovulation could be attained artificially at times, but only if the injection of chorionic gonadotropin was preceded by treatment with pregnant mare serum gonadotropin.[50] If these observations proved correct, then the various types of gonadotropin were in all likelihood not identical. It was therefore not surprising that their effect on hormonal disorders were but slight. Doubt about the medical value of chorionic gonadotropin began to spread. In the citation index *Hormoner*, pharmacologist and businessman Frederik Paulsen admitted in 1942 that "unfortunately one can say that the great expectations raised, especially in the field of gynecology, when Aschheim and Zondek in Germany and Smith and Engle in America discovered the effects this hormone [hCG] had on ovaries in animal experiments, have not been met."[51]

But there was a difference of opinion on the biological effects and clinical value of chorionic gonadotropin.[52] Axel Westman, who had been studying various types of gonadotropic hormones since the late 1930s maintained that the observed difference between rodents and primates was partially the result of the fact that the doses given the latter were far too weak.[53] This objection was not uncommon. Since the 1920s, the standard reply to the question as to why commercial sexual hormone drugs did not work was that they were simply too feeble.[54] The quandary was that when treatment was intensified, so were the undesirable side effects. Similar problems had however occurred in the use of other types of hormones, including insulin, and the standard solution to that problem had been to attempt to make the drug as chemically pure as possible. In other words, theoretical opinion still insisted that side effects were caused by "pollutants" in the drug, not the hormone itself.[55]

In light of this situation, and in combination with the conviction that the struggle against infertility was a significant aspect of the population question, not to mention the fact that Leo was braced to beef up its in-house arsenal of drugs, there were more than enough reasons to attempt to produce absolutely pure gonadotropins. Since they should ideally not cause any side effects whatsoever, these improved drugs could be injected in very strong doses and thus, predicted Westman, be more effective than their predecessors. Important to note is that Westman also argued that a pure chorionic gonadotropin would also be a valuable "scientific instrument" in endocrine research in and of itself. Through clinical treatment, new and significant knowledge about the effect of chorionic gonadotropin on the human body would accrue.[56]

Thus there were political, medical and scientific impulses for Leo to roll up its sleeves. There were also financial reasons. Not that a drug of this nature would generate enormous profits via retail sales, since the market was adjudged too small. However, it might open the door to the much more lucrative international market.

THE DEVELOPMENT OF "NEW PHYSEX"

Upon consultation with Axel Westman, Leo chose to create new hormone preparations by "updating" Physex and Antex. Like their older versions,

"New Physex" and "New Antex" would be comprised of gonadotropins extracted from the urine of pregnant women and the blood of brood mares, but in a much purer form. Work on the new Physex will be discussed below, for it was that work which eventually led to Gonadex. Leo's efforts to create an alternative to Antex, which indirectly resulted in Homogonal, will be dealt with in Chapters Eight and Nine.

I have been unable to study the course of chemical research on the new variant of Physex in detail, since I could not unearth any extant notes on everyday lab routines.[57] Nor has it been possible to say exactly how the clinical trials were conducted. The source I have been compelled to rely upon is an article published by Lennart Claesson, Bertil Högberg, Thomas Rosenberg and Axel Westman, "Crystalline Human Chorionic Gonadotrophin and Its Biological Action," submitted for publication on 13 February 1948 and appearing the same year as the first article in the first issue of the periodical *Acta Endocrinologica*, where Westman was editor-in-chief.[58] Resorting to a published paper to describe "science in action" is naturally problematic from a source critical perspective. However, the overriding purpose of the present discussion is to provide a narrative of the collaboration between Leo's research department and the Caroline Hospital's Women's Clinic and create a foundation for later discussion of the published results and the profile Gonadex would assume.

As mentioned above, attempts at "further purifying" drugs like Physex had begun as early as 1944, when Leo first decided to invest in a "line of hormones." But the project only really gained momentum two years later, when the break with Løvens kemiske Fabrik was a fact. First and foremost, the goal was to develop a technique of analysis that rendered the production of chemically pure chorionic gonadotropin from urine possible. Worth noting is that these purification efforts were not performed by Westman or any other external researcher, but by the staff at Leo's chemical lab in Helsingborg, under the aegis of engineer Bertil Högberg, who had joined the firm in 1946. Before this he had worked in Stockholm with the distinguished biochemist Hans von Euler and later, under Westman at the hormone lab of the Caroline Hospital.[59] Thus Högberg and Westman were already well acquainted and it is not unlikely that Westman had something to do with the former being recruited by Leo. Another participant was Thomas Rosenberg, an expert in protein chemistry, and he too had had previous contact with Westman.[60]

According to "Crystalline Human Chorionic Gonadotrophin and Its Biological Action," Leo's purification efforts were rewarded when, by modifying an older technique (whose first step consisted of absorbing the hormone with the aid of benzoic acid), a pure substance that crystallized in the shape of delicate, transparent needles was produced. This crystalline substance was tested with electrophoresis, a relatively new method for separating charged molecules from one another. Afterwards the research group concluded that the substance was completely pure and homogeneous. It was a good thing that Leo had access to an electrophoresis machine, and that Högberg was familiar with the technology. The group had achieved its first goal, one that no one had achieved before.[61]

While isolating the sought-after hormone, researchers tested the biological activity of the substance on baby female mice. The experiments, conducted at the hormone lab of the Women's Clinic by medical student Lennart Claesson, showed that the purified preparation caused the expected effect on the animals' sex glands and that its strength was proportionately potent. It was concluded that each milligram was equal to less than six to eight thousand international units (IU). However, the results of these biological trials were not entirely unequivocal—the sex glands of the animals were apparently not affected the same way each time. The research group interpreted this phenomenon by referring to the guiding principles of endocrinology, which stated that the chorionic gonadotropin introduced interacted with the more or less substantial amount of gonadotropins produced by the animals' own pituitary glands. This interpretation was reinforced when experiments with hypophysectomied rats produced consistently negative results; the added hormones had no native hormones with which to interact. In order to obtain further support, similar experiments were conducted on rabbits.[62]

The medical value of these purified preparations was still an open question, at least in practice. In order to determine this, Leo had to rely not only on Westman but also on his patients at the Women's Clinic. Westman selected approximately thirty women on whom to test the effect and possible toxicity of the drug. After having been injected with increasingly stronger doses over the course of a few days, both intramuscularly and intravenously, Westman declared that the new drug had no side effects whatsoever, exactly as he had hypothesized. Only one patient reacted negatively, and Westman's explanation was that it was probably an allergic reaction.[63] Two mitigating circumstances should be mentioned, though. First of all, Westman did not have a control group or conduct any other kind of blind test, which was not considered necessary in those days. Secondly, no long-term risk calculation was made. This is not surprising, either, because in the therapeutic culture of the 1940s, "risk" was still synonymous with injurious or toxic effect produced directly by treatment. If no such effect was immediately made manifest, the substance was considered safe for use, as long as administered by a qualified physician.[64] It is not known if the women knew they were part of a privately financed research project, nor whether they gave their informed consent.

Ten of them went on to act as study objects in order to more closely investigate the effect the new drug had on the ovaries. A week after they received a series of strong doses, abdominal incisions were made in order to inspect their ovaries. Westman found that the ovaries of most of the women showed signs of growth, while between two and seven developed ovarian follicles, which he interpreted as proof that the injections had had results. That these follicles could have developed before or without the aid of the injections seems not to have occurred to him. Westman also measured the estrogen content in the women's urine in order to discern the degree to which the injections had affected the hormone production of their ovaries. The study, which began three days before the injections were administered and ended two days after the last injection, indicated a certain temporary rise directly after the first injection. The results supported the idea that pure chorionic gonadotropin stimulated the ovaries to increase production of estrogen.

Some of Westman's patients had been diagnosed with amenorrhea, due to low levels of hypophysis gonadotropin, and these patients reacted well to treatment insofar as menses commenced.[65] All in all this proved, according to the authors of the article, that there was no longer any doubt that chorionic gonadotropin was in fact effective in the treatment of human beings. "The action of the injected chorionic gonadotrophin combined with that of the insufficiently functioning pituitary may give rise to a gonadotrophic effect of complete value."[66] The results were even more convincing if combined with small doses of the drug Antex, making the synergy effect all the more distinct. Even better results would probably be achieved once pregnant mare serum gonadotropin too was available in chemically pure form.

REGISTERING GONADEX

The results of the initial experiments with the new, crystalline chorionic gonadotropin were discussed at a meeting held on 17 January 1948. Though the experimental phase was not yet complete, it appeared clear that New Physex was superior to its predecessor, for no side effects manifested themselves, despite the fact that the preparation had been injected in "very large doses."[67] As far as the uses to which it could be put, it was suggested that New Physex could be used to treat the same indications as the old variant, and others as well: "The clinical tests currently being conducted at the Women's Clinic may furthermore eventually lead to the investigation of new indication fields for the preparation."[68] After the meeting, Leo entered into a period of intense activity culminating in the public launch of Gonadex five months hence. This activity consisted partly in rapidly organizing a campaign to collect urine from pregnant women in order to scale up production of chorionic gonadotropin, and partly in preparing a marketing strategy for the new product. However, before looking more closely at that, I will first compare the published results of the experiments with the description of Gonadex composed when the drug was registered as a new pharmaceutical product.

The article "Crystalline Human Chorionic Gonadotrophin and Its Biological Action" can be categorized as a strictly academic affair. Its main purpose is to describe the method used by Leo to chemically produce and purify chorionic gonadotropin from the urine of pregnant women and to argue that the product obtained was of pure, crystalline and electrophoretically homogeneous form. The latter conclusion was based primarily on chemical evidence, but visual representations in the form of photos taken through the microscope depicting needle-like structures in seventy and two hundred and fifty times magnification were also employed. These images were considered important proof of the purity of the substance and would later be frequently used in the marketing of Gonadex. The results of tests conducted to determine the biological and clinical effects of the new drug were also included. The summary message was that crystalline chorionic gonadotropin had a measureable effect on the gonads, and that it was neither toxic nor caused undesirable side effects. Photographs of ovaries that had undergone treatment and showed clearly developed follicles were displayed as visual evidence as well.

The medical effects were however presented as preliminary, and as far as the value of the drug was concerned, the tone, as is common in scientific articles, was cautious.[69] It is also stated that the drug ought to be combined with a pregnant mare serum gonadotropin (like Leo's Antex) in order to achieve maximal effect.

> If these preliminary results can be verified on a greater material, it would mean a new pathway to the effective treatment of amenorrhea related to pituitary hypofunction. Furthermore it seems to be obvious from the investigations described above that combined treatment with pregnant mare serum gonadotropin specially increases the chances of a successful therapy in amenorrhea.[70]

The authors maintain that menstruation can be affected but say nothing about the possibility of successfully treating sterility. Nor do they mention that the research was conducted in order to refine Leo's Physex or that the substance would be used in the new drug Gonadex. Instead, the smooth transition from "New Physex" to "Gonadex" first appeared in a Swedish-language article published by Axel Westman in *Svenska Läkartidningen* shortly after the Stockholm press conference. This article, which more or less recycles the content of the article in *Acta Endocrinologica*, was entitled "Klinisk prövning av choriongonadotropinet 'Gonadex Leo'" [Clinical Trial of the Chorionic Gonadotropin 'Gonadex Leo'].[71] No evidence is provided here either that Gonadex could have a positive effect on sterile women. It is however stated that tests are currently being conducted.

> The new drug is being subjected to continued clinical trials, primarily for the treatment of patients suffering from amenorrhea. In addition, cases of sterility caused by failure of the corpus luteum function and in instances of threatened or habitual miscarriage, which likewise can be attributed to faulty secretion of yellow body hormones.[72]

A further article on the same subject was published in 1948. In the Nordic medical journal *Nordisk medicin*, Westman's younger colleague Rolf Luft (1914–2007) predicted that major endocrinological problems would be solved now that chorionic gonadotropin was available in crystalline form. But he presented no other clinical evidence than that already accounted for by Westman et al.[73]

As made evident by these three articles, great things were expected of crystalline chorionic gonadotropin, even though development and testing was far from complete. It is likely that Leo felt that more time was needed before the drug would be "ready," while at the same time wishing to get it out on the market at soon as possible. On 16 February, a representative of Leo explained in a letter to Harald Johansson of the hormone lab that, "I don't think we can wait as long as the fall to launch the drug, since news about New Physex has been leaking out bit by bit and will cause the competition to redouble their own efforts."[74] And in fact Leo did not wait until autumn, but rather filed the first registration papers with the Royal Board of Medicine on 16 April 1948, applying to register Gonadex in three dosage strengths, 5,000 IU, 10,000 IU and 20,000 IU. A little over a week later, Leo requested to change the name of the old Physex to Gonadex.[75] Upon being granted permission, Leo also submitted a new application requesting that the new drug take over the old one's dosages of 300 IU, 600 IU and 1,500 IU (for both common Physex and the veterinary preparation of the same name). In accordance with the legislation of 1934, the application contained both a description of the proposed field of use of the drug and its name, packaging, price and advertising mock-ups.[76]

Leo sought to register Gonadex for the treatment of a remarkably long list of indications, made more remarkable by the fact that from the previously mentioned experimental and clinical trials, it was far from certain how the new drug was to be used. The "profile" Gonadex eventually received was the result of a series of assumptions based partly on information culled from the endocrinological literature and results achieved by other researchers with other types of chorionic gonadotropin preparations. The declaration refers to the following indications for women: metropathia haemorrhagica cystica, amenorrhea, infertility, habitual miscarriage and sterility due to reduced or failed function of the corpus luteum. Despite the fact that Gonadex, as far as I have been able to discern, had only been tested on women, several indications for men were also listed, including cryptorchidism, dystrofia adiposogenitalis and impotence.[77]

Given the paltry number of clinical studies conducted at the Caroline Hospital upon which it could base its application, one suspects that Leo inflated the indication field in order to stimulate use and market demand. But even if that were the case, professor Axel Westman had (one must assume) scrutinized and approved the application before it was submitted.[78] Despite the plethora of indication fields, the recommended dosage was imprecisely formulated, stating little more than that Gonadex could be "injected intravenously once or repeatedly, depending on the nature of the case and obtained effect."[79] No mention is made of the fact that Gonadex ought possibly be complemented with Antex or some other, similar drug. It should also be noted that Gonadex was priced relatively low. Converted to cost per international unit, it was cheaper than its namesake but also cheaper than the (non-crystalline) counterparts manufactured by the competition, like Organon-Pharmacia's Pregnyl, Bayer's Prolan, British Drug House's Gonan and Parke, Davies and Company's Antuitrin S. That Leo was aware that the low price would raise a few angry eyebrows is apparent in a marginal note that states, "We have to be prepared to face frenetic opposition from the competition, especially Pharmacia-Organon."[80]

It is commonly assumed that before a drug is put on the market, it has undergone rigorous testing by independent experts. Back in 1946, the pamphlet *Svensk läkemedelsindustri* assured that industrially manufactured drugs in Sweden were renowned for the scrupulous control to which they were subjected, which was further guaranteed by inspection conducted at the National Pharmaceutical Laboratory.[81] This has however not always been the case and it certainly was not with Gonadex.[82] According to the prevailing regulations for pharmaceutical specialties, it was possibly to receive a temporary permit to sell a new drug before the requisite external scrutiny had been completed. In the case of Gonadex, it took no more than a month after Leo submitted its application before the Board of Medicine declared that the drug "may be sold pending final approval of the application."[83] Thus until further notice, Gonadex had been approved for sale and placed on the so-called "free list," which meant that it could be tendered in retail pharmacies in Sweden.[84] Two weeks later, the drug was packed and ready for delivery.[85]

LEOS' SECOND URINE COLLECTION CAMPAIGN

In order to produce its own hormone drugs in Helsingborg, Leo needed to establish lasting relationships with diverse sources of raw material. As long as Leo only manufactured Ovex, it needed only to woo horse owners in the local countryside. But when it invested in its "line of hormones" during the war and expanded its repertoire, Leo needed a much larger number of suppliers in its production network. One new enlistee was the Scanian Abbatoir Cooperative, which had begun stockpiling slaughter residue like pituitary glands, brains, adrenal glands, thyroid glands, ovaries, testicles and gall for pharmaceutical companies.[86] Correspondence from 1942 between Leo and the Cooperative shows that Leo was interested in rather sizeable quantities. After a request from Leo, a slaughter house in Kävlinge replied that it was prepared to deliver up to twenty-five kilos of frozen bovine and porcine ovaries a week at a cost of five and a half crowns per kilo, while another in Åstorp could supply three hundred hog stomachs for forty-five öre a piece.[87] Later in 1948, Leo ordered a grand total of 1,000 kilos of frozen testicles. Together with equine urine, such raw material went into the manufacture of hormones.[88]

As the 1940s came to a close, Leo kicked off two additional campaigns to collect biological material. One involved the collection of blood from pregnant mares, for the manufacture of Antex. Leo began by collating a register of all the horse-breeders and veterinarians in the region. The latter were contacted first, a price was agreed upon, and Leo's agents began knocking on the doors of local farmhouses. Armed with a list of local vets, they could immediately suggest the name of a vet who could perform the bloodletting. The veterinarians, many of whom the farmers were already familiar with, functioned as a link between the company and the raw material it craved. A list headed "Contractors of Mare's Blood" contains the names of roughly thirty horse-breeders who owned more than a hundred horses. The number of vets under contract was twenty-six. The mares were bled of five or six liters at a time, after which the blood was shipped to Leo via parcel package in dedicated three-liter containers infused with anti-coagulants. Each liter of blood earned the owner four crowns, while the vets were paid twenty crowns per letting. This procedure was not entirely risk-free, and that is why the mares and their fetuses were insured at Leo's expense.[89]

The other campaign involved the collection of raw material with which to produce New Physex, i.e. Gonadex. In order to do so, Leo needed access to urine from pregnant women and Leo's network of consultant contacts proved its value once again. The first urine used in the development of New Physex had probably come from Sune Genell's clinic in Malmö, suggested by directives he issued in 1945. However, when production of Gonadex began in earnest, the campaign focused on Stockholm instead, mainly the clinic Westman oversaw. On 17 January 1946 it was estimated that the campaign would yield twenty-five to forty liters a day, enough to manufacture 1 to 1.5 million IU of chorionic gonadotropin.[90] However, this was not considered enough, and a second campaign was launched in Helsingborg. In April 1948 the company calculated that Helsingborg could easily provide twelve liters of urine per day, an amount that could surely be multiplied several times over if the company ran a "systematic advertising campaign."[91] After a few years, the catchment area was expanded to include prenatal clinics in the Gothenburg region, thus covering all of southwest Sweden.

Pregnant women visiting any one of the clinics belonging to Leo's network were asked to provide a urine sample in the service of the pharmaceutical industry. In order to increase compliancy, each received a fee commensurate with the amount of urine delivered. Some preserved receipts show a fee of one crown per liter, but the amount may have varied from clinic to clinic.[92] However, the success of the system was contingent on the willingness of nurses and midwives to oversee the procedure on top of their regular duties. When Leo realized their irreplaceable value, it introduced a commission for those willing to get their patients to sign up for the campaign: two crowns per name.[93] The urine was subsequently shipped to Leo's industrial park in Helsingborg. According to an account statement from 1950, Leo's raw material costs for Gonadex in Stockholm, Helsingborg and Gothenburg that fiscal year ran to just over SEK 25,000, including shipping.[94] While it was an expensive and complicated arrangement, it worked and insured a steady supply of raw material necessary for the large-scale production of Gonadex.

CHAPTER FIVE

Launching Gonadex

GONADEX WAS A MILESTONE for Leo and the Swedish pharmaceutical industry as a whole. After thirty-five years spent producing and distributing other companies' hormone preparations, Leo was set to sell a drug which it had created (almost) itself in concert with prominent researchers. That company pride swelled is not hard to imagine, nor is the fact that Leo wanted value for the resources it had invested in the off-site hormone lab, research and development, and readying its factory for large-scale production. Expectations ran high that Gonadex would prove profitable, on the national market initially but then also abroad. As the following chapter shows, the launch and marketing of Gonadex was characterized by this sense of confidence. From a media history standpoint, the present chapter analyzes the advertising and public relations strategies Leo employed and the role played by Axel Westman in creating public perception of Gonadex as a remarkable new treatment for sterility.

LEO'S ADVERTISING CAMPAIGN

If a pharmaceutical company intends to introduce a new drug to a highly competitive market, establishing solid networks of production and distribution are absolutely essential. Within the latter, the manufacturer offers the consumer information about the product and data about the needs and desires of the consumer are relayed back to the manufacturer. Physicians play a central role in distribution networks, since it is they who prescribe the drugs to their patients, thereby effectively functioning as "consumption directors."[1] In light of this structure, marketing efforts were primarily aimed at physicians. This meant that companies were loath to call their marketing "advertising," preferring instead "information campaigns," which signaled scientific objectivity.[2] It was also common for them to refer to their own practices as "ethical" while distancing themselves from ostentatious ads in the daily and weekly press thumping the drum for patent medicines. Behind closed doors, however, the pharmaceutical industry used the term "propaganda."

Over the course of the first half of the twentieth century, resources invested in marketing increased at the same pace as investment in research. By the mid-1940s, the seven leading pharmaceutical companies in Sweden were investing equal amounts in both.[3] Leo's campaigns were coordinated by a special "propaganda section." Part of its budget paid the salaries of so-called "propagandists," salesmen or pharmaceutical consultants, whose job was to travel up and down the country visiting doctors in their clinics. During these visits, the doctors were provided with information about the new drugs, while the propagandists availed themselves of the situation to collect data from the "field." The information they passed on might concern a particular physician's familiarity with Leo's products or his hopes that other necessary products were in the offing. Thus the relationship was one of give-and-take. In order to succeed at their task, it was important that the propagandists be well-acquainted with the pharmaceutical world, which is why most received some pharmaceutical training. They also attended special courses designed to familiarize them with the firm and its products and to learn the art of effective and trustworthy persuasion. An effective salesman was one who appeared to be an informant possessed of high ethical standards.[4]

Aside from face-to-face meetings, advertising space was bought in medical and pharmaceutical journals like *Svenska Läkartidningen* and *Svensk Farmaceutisk Tidskrift* and flyers, pamphlets and guides were printed and distributed to physicians and pharmacists. Leo was also a constant presence at meetings and conferences and arranged visits to its factory for journalists, organizations, academic societies, local politicians, physicians, pharmacists and students. Some of these tours were reported breathlessly in provincial papers. As long as the journalists covering the pharmaceutical beat lacked critical perspective, companies could exploit them as free advertising space.[5]

In order to fully appreciate the extent of Leo's propaganda campaign, consider that in 1941 the company's propagandists paid visits to roughly 1,350 physicians, all of whom were provided with free literature. Thirteen flyers and six press sheets loaded with testimonials were also mailed out. On top of this, a large number of price lists were compiled—rate sheets for pharmacists, physicians, veterinarians and a catalogue of dental products.[6]

Leo estimated it would soon visit twice as many physicians annually. Such aggressive marketing naturally took plenty of money and time but the people running Leo's information department reasoned, quite presciently, that "the future success of a pharmaceutical company depends on the way in which it disseminates information about its products."[7] Selling drugs, like any other product, was not simply a question of supply and demand; it behooved the industry to *create* a demand. This tactic was taken to surprising extremes, especially in the United States. By the end of the 1950s, several of the largest corporations testified before the Senate that marketing funds were quadruple the size of the money spent on research and development.[8]

SELLING GONADEX

There is a standard to which physicians are held dictating that they ought not participate in the marketing of pharmaceuticals, especially if they themselves have a financial interest in any of the products. The World Medical Association International Code of Medical Ethics of 1949 states specifically that doctors "shall not receive any financial benefits or other incentives solely for referring patients or prescribing specific products" and "should use due caution in divulging discoveries or new techniques or treatment through non-professional channels."[9] This standard has largely been upheld insofar as physicians seldom participate directly in marketing campaigns. However, that does not mean that they had not participated indirectly. The norm can be problematized if one analyzes doctors as mediators between business and the consumer. The matter addressed below is whether Axel Westman mediated information about Gonadex and if so, what impact did it have on sales?

To begin with, I would suggest that the above-mentioned articles in *Acta Endocrinologica* and *Svenska Läkartidningen* were in fact aspects of a conscious marketing strategy. The former was not only biased because Westman was editor of the journal in which it appeared, but also because Leo financed its publication. In September of 1947, Westman and Hjalmar Wijnbladh, chairman and standing secretary of the Swedish Endocrinology Association, respectively, wrote to Leo in order to inquire as to whether the company would be interested in contributing to the establishment of a Scandinavian periodical dedicated to endocrinology. In order to gain the industry's trust, the association made clear that a number of prominent researchers and physicians supported the project.[10] Westman and Wijnbladh promised that the journal would be widely distributed among general practitioners and that its ads would feature state-of-the-art design layout. "We dare hope for your support of the planned undertaking, insofar as it offers both increased opportunities for publishing endocrinological research and

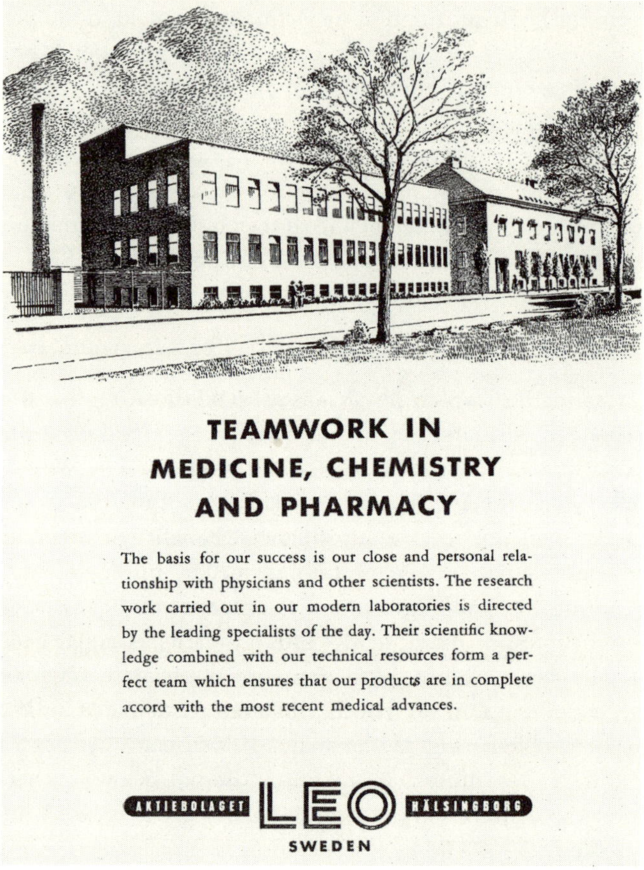

FIGURE 8 The maiden issue of *Acta Endocrinologica*, edited by Axel Westman, was published in August 1948. In it appeared the first article on crystalline chorionic gonadotropin, the ingredient in Gonadex, as well as a display ad on Leo's successful collaboration with physicians and other scientists.

the advantages of an advertising medium whose readership has a particular interest in hormone preparations and related medicines."[11]

Leo agreed to contribute funds and also used the first issue of *Acta Endocrinologica* in its campaign to launch Gonadex. This led not only to publication of the article co-written by Westman, Högberg and Rosenberg, his colleagues at Leo. In May of 1948, the company wrote Westman to propose the insertion of "prestige advertising space on page 3" of each issue.[12] The first issue contained numerous ads for diverse hormone drugs taken out by companies like Astra, Organon, Park, Davies and Company, Ciba and Løvens kemiske Fabrik. But the advertisement Leo took out and which recurred in several future issues, was not for a specific drug but for the company itself and its modern, science-based business plan.[13]

Leo's close involvement with the Swedish Endocrine Society continued apace as it helped finance a Scandinavian convention held in Stockholm in the fall of 1948, hosted by Westman, and featuring lectures on gonadotropins on its agenda.[14]

Svenska Läkartidningen also proved accommodating toward Westman. His article contained nothing new from a scientific perspective, simply recapitulating the contents of its English-language original. The difference was that the name "Gonadex Leo" appeared in its title and was reiterated by Westman in its conclusion. In essence, the article served as a sort of information text about the new drug. This time, Leo wished to synchronize the appearance of the first ad for Gonadex in *Svenska Läkartidningen* with the publication of Westman's article. As is stated in a letter to Westman: "We propose the insertion of an ad in Svenska Läkartidningen . . . in the same issue for which your article on Gonadex has been accepted."[15] This would assure the company twice the exposure and scientific weight in the most widely read Swedish medical journal of the day. A later missive from Leo to Westman dated 27 May 1948 summarizes the publicistic collaboration between the parties.

> Since pages 1–18 of number I of Acta Endocrinologica have been pressed and delivered to the publisher . . . our participation in this issue is complete. We have been in contact with Svenska Läkartidningen, which has promised to make room for your article on crystalline gonadotropin in no. 24 of the eleventh of June, on the condition that you deliver the manuscript this week. In accordance with the agreement, we will be taking out an ad for Gonadex, which is enclosed for your approval.[16]

The article "Klinisk prövning av choriongonadotropinet 'Gonadex Leo'" [Clinical testing of the chorionic gonadotropin 'Gonadex' Leo] was submitted to *Svenska Läkartidningen* at the end of May and published a few days after the Stockholm press conference at which Gonadex Leo was launched. *Acta Endocrinologica* took a little longer, not appearing in print until August.[17] It should be noted that this type of well-executed synchronization was not unique to Gonadex. When a drug called "AH 51" was just about ready for registration in October of 1951, the necessity that "publishing clinical results be coordinated with the launch of the preparation" was brought up at a meeting at Leo headquarters.[18]

The ads for Gonadex were studiously designed to mediate their message both linguistically and visually, by now standard industry procedure and a strategy that Leo, together with Axel Westman, had already applied to sell older preparations. In the spring of 1947, discussions concerned how advertising copy should be complemented with symbolic images. Among the suggestions were a picture of a mare with her newborn foal, or a mother and child.[19] These images were both relevant and traditional. In *Vitamania* (1996), her study of the culture history of vitamin supplements, medical historian Rima Apple points out that interwar American ads for health products typically did not focus on the product itself but rather its consequences—either how badly things could go if the product in question was not used, "the negative appeal," or how well things would turn out if it was, "the reason why." In either instance, the technique uses both emotional and intellectual arguments.[20] Mother and child (like mare and foal), alluding to the fact that sterility has been overcome or the risk of miscarriage avoided, are typical "reasons why." In advertisements for a variety of hormone drugs, this image recurs time and again, e.g. in both Schering's and Pharmacia's gonadotropin campaigns. A not-insignificant detail in this context is that "mother with baby" is one of the primary motifs of Christian iconography, symbolizing that Jesus, through divine intervention, was born of the Virgin Mary. A hitherto barren woman bringing forth new life was in its way also miraculous, though now it was not God, but endocrinology, or more specifically hormone drugs, taking the credit for the wonder.

Other ideas as to how to present Gonadex visually and textually were broached, but the picture Leo finally settled on featured no sentient beings. Instead, an illustration that accentuated the unique purity and scienticity of the preparation was chosen. As early as March 1948, it was suggested that the ads should show "a microphotograph of chorionic gonadotropin crystals on for example a bright blue field, against which the crystals would stand out in polarized light," i.e. the kind of photograph appearing in scientific articles about Gonadex. Furthermore it was recommended that boldface type be used for the section of copy explaining that Gonadex consisted of "crystallized" chorionic gonadotropins, as well as perhaps mentioning how effective it was in comparison with other, older drugs on the market.[21] The final results largely followed these recommendations, which is why the image appearing in the flyer for Gonadex is reminiscent of an abstract work of art.[22] In line with the results of the experimental and clinical studies, the reverse side explained that Gonadex "stimulates follicle growth and estrogen production," and that it was a beneficial "substitution therapy in cases of hypophysis insufficiency" without risk of side effects. Photographs of treated

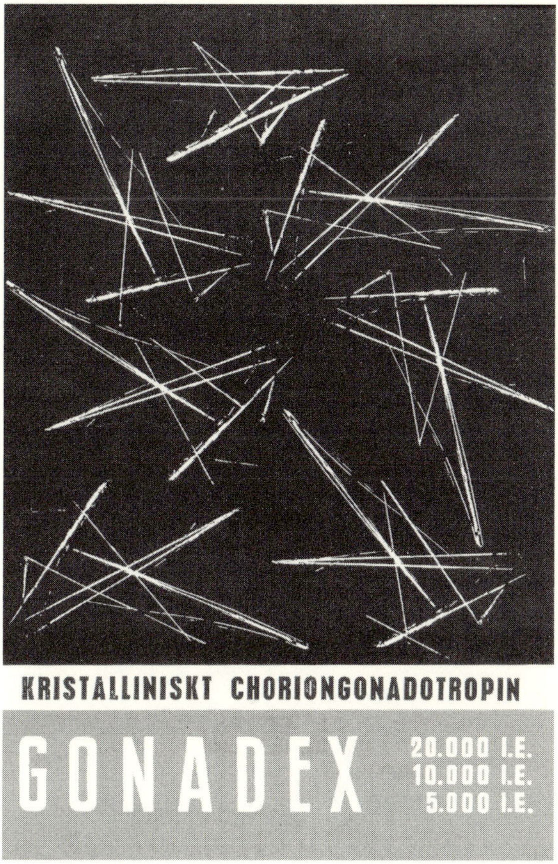

FIGURE 9 In the first Gonadex print ad, a microphotograph of chorionic gonadotropin crystals appears. The crystals symbolized the purity and therefore the reliability of the drug.

ovaries said to show the intensive follicle growth caused by Gonadex were also inserted.[23]

The photo of the crystals signaled that the drug was pure, high quality and therefore entirely safe. This aspect too was a common element in advertising pharmaceutical specialties, as with health products in general.[24] The goal was to gain a reputation for reliability among the medical corps. The unique purity of Gonadex was also emphasized in the rest of the marketing campaign, in pamphlets and similar texts published in 1948.[25] However, Leo not only stressed the drug's intimate relationship with modern research labs but also its close relationship with a healthy body. One the

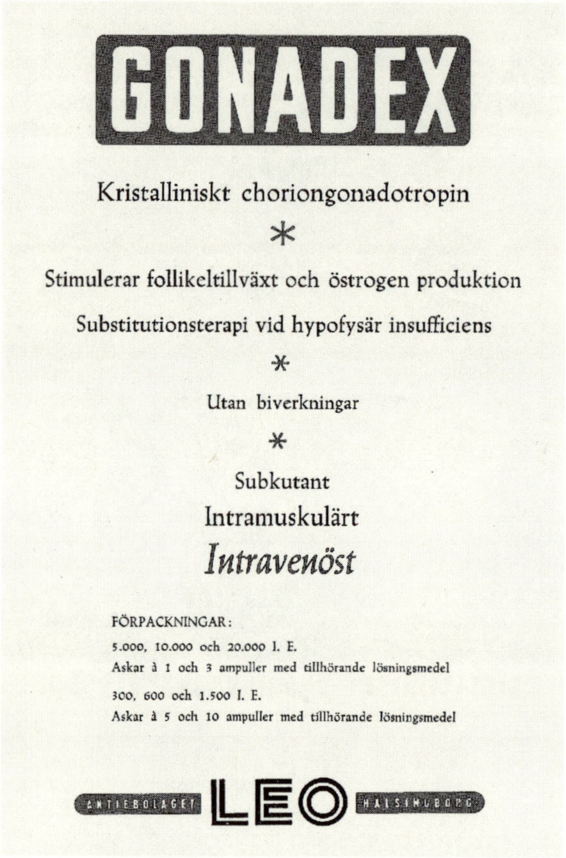

FIGURE 10 As the copy of this 1948 ad makes evident, Leo explicitly accentuated the fact that Gonadex contained "crystalline" chorionic gonadotropin. The drug was said to stimulate both follicle growth and estrogen production without causing any side-effects. Note that the potencies listed range all the way up to 20,000 IU.

one hand, Gonadex was the result of highly-advanced biomedical research, which produced a hormone that could be used in its absolutely purest form, one that was "electrophoretically homogeneous" and "crystalline." On the other, Gonadex was completely "natural," extracted from common urine and containing a substance produced by all healthy pregnant women. In addition, Leo availed itself of what historian of ideas Roger Qvarsell has called "authoritative reasoning," a form of rhetoric intended to convince the consumer that the drug did in fact deliver on its promises.[26]

Similarly, Leo targeted the medical corps, who were expected to recommend Gonadex to their patients. But academic articles and advertising flyers were only one part of the campaign Leo orchestrated, according to a strategic document entitled "P.M. angående publicity för Gonadex" [Memo re: Publicity for Gonadex] composed in mid-February 1948, three months before the Board of Medicine approved the new drug.[27] The document lists seven bullet points concerning a planned press conference.

1. An interview with Prof. Westman should be arranged as soon as possible. This interview should be conducted by an experienced journalist, either one of those suggested by the Swedish Telegram Bureau . . . or perhaps one Professor Westman has been in contact with previously, e.g. Sand of Stockholm-Tidningen. All facts and medical data ought to be mentioned in the article.
2. Simultaneously, we ought to compile full and varied photographic material. All pictures of Prof. Westman and the drugs ought to be taken immediately or as soon as possible.
3. Premises for the press conference should be reserved well in advance. We heartily recommend the Grand Hotel in Stockholm.
4. As soon as the necessary preparations are complete, a personalized letter should be delivered to the editors-in-chief of the Stockholm papers, which clearly states that it is a truly revolutionary preparation with the full weight of Professor Westman behind it.
5. At the press conference itself, members of the press should each be provided with a transcript of the above-mentioned interview and photographic material. Furthermore, Prof. Westman and representatives of AB Leo will answer questions. It would also be appropriate to invite noteworthy local physicians.
6. Along with members of the daily newspapers, we should invite representatives of Vecko-Journalen and other weekly or trade journals of interest for our public relations.
7. For PR purposes, the articles should be translated and distributed in England and the USA via our foreign ad agency contacts to suitable newspapers and magazines. A list should be compiled in advance.

The document concludes by urging one last time that this preliminary spadework be carried out as soon as possible. As we shall see below, the staff at Leo generally followed these instructions to the letter, culminating in the much-anticipated press conference. Leo made a conscious decision to spread information and propaganda with the aid of scientists via the various news media, which gave the channels to the general public wider range.[28] In this Leo was ahead of the curve, but it was not alone. Rather, it had been inspired by the latest public relations strategies from the States that gained a foothold on Swedish soil after the Second World War. The Swedish Association of Advertising Agencies had just arranged its first course in "Corporate Public Relations" and press departments were springing up in government agencies, private organizations, trade associations, and some of the heavy industries. As media and communications expert Larsåke Larsson points out, public relations had served different needs in different sectors, but as far as the private sector was concerned, this need usually involved the launch of single products.[29] In Leo's case, the goal was "publicity for Gonadex."

A CONFERENCE FOR THE PRESS

The press conference was intended for the eleventh of July, the same day Westman's article in *Svenska Läkartidningen* was set for publication. But when it turned out that another major public event was scheduled for the same day—a visit by the British Navy—Leo chose to move it to Thursday, the tenth of June. Two drafts of the invitation were produced in accordance with point number four, above. Both state that AB Leo had the pleasure of inviting the recipient to attend a lecture by Professor Axel Westman at the Grand Hotel in Stockholm at six PM. According to the first version (which Westman himself preferred), the lecture would simply describe the manufacture of crystalline chorionic gonadotropin. The other version claimed that Westman would account for the "sensational results" of his hormone research. Note that neither version mentioned that the actual reason for the event was to launch a new commercial product.[30]

Highlighting Westman's presence was a smart move. Today, respected medical professionals regularly attend and even call press conferences to report new research results. But in the 1940s it was a rare event in Sweden, partly because press conferences in general rarely dealt with medicine but mainly because the medical community was particular about maintaining its integrity and ethical stance. Members of the corps who publically collaborated with private interests risked being labeled irresponsible and in the worst case allying themselves with quacks. Thus it was to be expected that Leo's press meeting aroused plenty of interest and curiosity.

At the conference, Leo's sales reps handed out freshly printed flyers and pamphlets as attendees awaited the main event, Axel Westman's address. It proved to be a proper academic lecture on female genital illnesses and their treatment, and on the joint effect of sexual and hypophysis hormones on the ovaries.[31] Westman also spoke in general terms about how diverse hormone preparations for the treatment of genital illness were produced and the difficulties circumscribing such therapy. He explained that treatment had previously been unreliable and gone amiss since there were no hormonal preparations pure enough or strong enough. He only mentioned the ostensible topic of the evening, pure, crystalline Gonadex, as he was wrapping up, without mentioning his own contribution to the manufacturing process, giving the impression that he had been summoned from without to inspect Gonadex with his critical scientific eye in order to give it his seal of approval before the assembled press.

According to his lecture notes, Westman stated that

> Swedish pharmaceutical factory Leo has begun shipping a new hormone drug, called "Gonadex," which satisfies the highest demands. The drug, which is the result of years of effort by the factory's chemical research staff, is of such high-grade purity that it can be manufactured in crystalline form, something that has previously proven impossible. It can be injected directly into the bloodstream without fear of side effects, which makes a high and very precise dosage possible.[32]

As in his scholarly articles, Westman was restrained in his assurances of the therapeutic benefits of Gonadex. All he said was that results achieved with Gonadex had so far been "largely encouraging" and that there was therefore good reason to expect that "another step forward had been taken in the struggle against functional genital diseases, among which involuntary sterility and abnormal haemorrhaging in young women may gain the greatest benefits."[33] In other words, the ultimate goal was in sight but still somewhat out of reach.

It is reasonable to assume that Westman believed in Gonadex and that he was eager to see the drug implemented in gynecological practice as soon as possible. He was aware that evidence of the physiological effects of Gonadex was tentative, but he probably felt that the older preparations available were inferior. At the same time, Westman's participation in the press conference should be seen as a component in Leo's well-orchestrated marketing strategy—on the strength of his name alone, Westman attracted journalists and lent Leo's launch of a commercial product scientific legitimacy. Why else had Leo not asked one of its own chemists or engineers to hold the lecture? For it was they, and not Westman, who had succeeded in distilling the chorionic gonadotropin on which Gonadex was based.

It should be recalled that two days later, Westman contributed to giving Leo and Gonadex even more exposure when, on 12 June, he published the article "Hjärnbihanget och dess hormon" [The pineal gland and its hormone] in the liberal daily paper *Göteborgs Handels- och Sjöfartstidning*.[34] As far as the tests Gonadex had hitherto undergone, Westman wrote that they had "shown that said drug fulfilled all expectations." Exactly what those expectations were is not mentioned, nor *whose* expectations they were. Just like at the press conference, Westman chose to tone down his own involvement in the creation of Gonadex. Instead he emphasized the value of chemical research itself and the successful manner in which the Swedish pharmaceutical industry conducted its work. Gonadex was, Westman wrote, a "testimonial to the achievements of our domestic pharmaceutical industry. Appreciation of the significance of basic research, generosity toward scientists, and job satisfaction are characteristic for the leading men of this industry."[35] This panegyric to the Swedish pharmaceutical industry, now expected to hold its own against tough international competition, can also be seen as a contribution to the contemporary debate on whether it ought to be nationalized. That the politically conservative Westman was against it is clearly apparent.[36]

Westman continued to be involved in the marketing of Gonadex by appearing on radio and at conferences. I have already mentioned the Leo-sponsored Congress of Scandinavian Endocrinologists, which Westman chaired. Two other gatherings at which Leo and Westman made common cause in the autumn of 1948 were the conference of the Swedish Society of Internal Medicine in Helsingborg and a gynecology congress in Stockholm. In August Leo contacted Westman, who was vacationing at the seaside resort of Marstrand, to discuss mounting a display at an exhibition being arranged by the latter. That Gonadex would be the star attraction was a foregone conclusion. "To this end we thought that we would book a corner close to the entrance, and envision a display case with three eye-catching features, with Gonadex prominently displayed in the middle."[37] It would be flanked by mainstays like Ovex or Synsteron, a synthetic estrogen for the treatment of climacteric dysfunction. Apparently Westman approved, because the display ended up looking more or less exactly as proposed.[38] According to the program for the conference on internal medicine, Westman and his colleagues were scheduled to give an account of "the collaboration that led to the creation of a hormone drug."[39] Considering that the speech was planned to take place at a tour of Leo's factory, it is safe to assume that the "drug" in question was Gonadex.

THE IMAGE OF HORMONAL MEDICINE AS A REMEDY FOR STERILITY IN THE PRESS, PART I

"Hormone Drug Cure for Women, Swedish Triumph"; "Swedish Drug Cures Sterility"; "Barrenness Cured, Stunted Grow"; "Swedish Drug for Infertility"; "Swedish Medicine Banishes Infertility." These and many more similar headlines appeared in Swedish newspapers on Friday, 11 June 1948.[40] After the press conference the night before, Gonadex was the topic of the day. A few days later, women's magazine *Husmodern* published a lengthy article entitled, "A Third of All Sterile Women Can Give Birth with New Hormone Drug."[41] Shortly thereafter, popular science magazine *Teknik för alla* featured an article on Leo's modern research and development system, stating that thanks to Gonadex "women who previously could not be treated for sterility have had their barrenness cured by the new preparation."[42]

Thus according to news reports, a unique, Swedish cure for sterility had been discovered. And naturally, it was a sensation. One paper reported that the presentation of the new drug at the press conference was reminiscent of "Old Testament prophecy."[43] This streak of the miraculous was further enhanced by the fact that Gonadex was said to be capable of both increasing and reducing menstrual flow according to need. Moreover, the new drug could also be given to pregnant women in order to prevent miscarriage, to women suffering from climacteric disorders, even to young boys whose biological development had been arrested at the expected advent of puberty.

Usually, preparations touting so many claims were categorized as "panaceas" or "cure-alls" and not unusually associated with quacks and charlatans.[44] But no dissenting voices were raised by the members of the fourth estate. "In context, the final result is less astonishing but no less impressive." The context referred to and which contributed to expectations that Gonadex would fulfill its "lofty promises" can be summarized with the key concepts "Swedish," "science-based" and "industry," and the link uniting them is Axel Westman. As another paper trumpeted, "Gonadex is without doubt a major triumph for Swedish research and Swedish industry!"[45] This triumph, illustrated in many of the papers with a portrait of "inventor" Axel Westman, was of international proportions. "The new drug is of worldwide significance and a major scientific triumph for Sweden," wrote *Husmodern*. "American scientists have already received the news with interest."[46] It was also pointed out that Gonadex, due to its ability to promote nativity, was of such economic interest to the nation that the government ought to seriously consider establishing a special national "sterility clinic" so that it could be maximally exploited.

Fully in line with Leo's PR strategy, news about this remarkable new cure quickly spread abroad, as far as South Africa, where an article entitled "New Swedish Hormone Preparation Remedy for Sterility" circulated, which included a description of Westman's clinical methodology.

> It is reported in the Swedish press that a new hormone preparation has been discovered by Swedish scientists, who claim that it is the most effective remedy known to cure sterility . . . . The original idea which led to the discovery of the preparation came from Professor Axel Westman in Stockholm. He has used Gonadex in more than thirty instances of sterility in woman, and *in most of these cases* the result was that the patients were cured.[47]

The unabashedly enthusiastic articles published in the daily press and widely different household readings like *Husmodern* and *Teknik för alla* certainly appear a bit too sanguine in light of Westman's lecture and his modest, academic publications. The enormous emphasis on sterility also appears hasty, to say the least. The desire to solve the riddle of sterility and contribute to national nativity policy was certainly one aspect of Westman's commitment to the development of the new hormone preparation. The conviction that crystalline chorionic gonadotropin would function better than its non-crystalline counterpart was possibly also the main reason Leo chose to invest so heavily in "New Physex." But as the clinical trials proved, Leo was not quite there yet, to use Westman's own expression. When Gonadex was registered, it was intended for use on a variety of genital disorders, of which sterility was but one, and one based on vague assumptions, to boot. And yet it was on the cure for sterility the press focused. Why was this?

In the network of relationships that circumscribe the launching of new, untried medicines, the mass media comprises one of the most important nodes. The media both contribute to drawing attention to the new product, thereby raising awareness of the drug beyond the medical-academic-industrial establishment, and interpreting its possible meaning for society. It is commonly assumed that the mass media exaggerate, simplify and distort the results of scientific study in order to create a "story."[48] While the case of Gonadex can be understood in this fashion, circumstances were actually more complicated than that. The newspapers did indeed mediate a rather one-sided and uncritical image of the possibilities offered by Gonadex, but in my opinion, this image mirrored the original intent of Axel Westman himself, which Leo did its best to inflate at the press conference. The mass media reporting was in other words a result of Leo's marketing tactics.[49]

This interpretation takes its cue from Dorothy Nelkin who, in her book *Selling Science* (1987), argues that the research world "sells" science to society, e.g. by making extravagant claims in its press information, which creates interest among the public and attracts financiers.[50] There is also empirical evidence for this perception in a document comprised of three typewritten pages. As far as can be ascertained, it is a copy of the "pre-interview" with Axel Westman referred to in the "Memo re: Publicity for Gonadex" mentioned above, which was distributed at the press conference.[51] However, a more fitting term would be "press release" or, to borrow Nelkin's term, "a prepackaged source of information."[52] The text features most of the facts and even word-for-word formulations of sentences that would later appear in the newspaper articles. In order to fully comprehend the image of Gonadex in the media, there is good reason to draw attention to this text.

A well-written press release attracting a large number of journalists is absolutely imperative to the success of any press conference. If said press conference deals with research, then, according to sociologist of science Thomas Gieryn, it is essential that the press release meet three criteria: The results to be presented must claim to have huge significance for a large number of people, preferably for everyone everywhere; the results should be seen as a new "discovery" no one has made before; and finally, the results must appear credible, in order for the mass media to believe that they are being given facts, not fed fiction.[53] As we shall see, Leo's press release succeeded in following these guidelines.

The significance of Gonadex for the sterility issue and therefore all mankind is already broached in the title—"Childless Suddenly Pregnant with New Hormone Preparation." After that follows a brief ingress featuring assertations that a longed-for scientific breakthrough has finally taken place: "Sweden first with sensational scientific news"; "Americans spend months trying to crack well-kept chemical secret"; "Preparation also helps men with defective genital development"; "Pregnant women sought as 'suppliers', attracted by handsome remuneration"; and "Professor Westman achieves elusive goal after ten years." The main text opens with the following paragraph, which deserves to be reproduced in full since it elucidates the reliability of the results.

> A Swedish hormone preparation of unheard-of efficacy and utility will be available for sale in the next few days after one and a half years

> of rigorously concealed experimentation. It has proven to stimulate ovarian functions in women, cure a number of cases of sterility, prevent miscarriage, alleviate discomfort brought on by menopause and puberty, and effectively treat some male patients suffering from defective genital development. Furthermore, it can be injected directly into the bloodstream in much stronger doses than similar, previously-utilized hormone preparations without causing any side effects, which was previously *inconceivable.* For the man behind the achievement, our internationally renowned and celebrated gynecologist Professor *Axel Westman,* this drug means a major personal triumph and possible invaluable weapon in the struggle against sterility, to which he has been tirelessly committed for so many years. The value world science places on this discovery, which Sweden is the first country to present, is evident in the efforts of the Americans, who have spent months trying to get their hands on the results after some information about the experiments was leaked. Without success, we should add.[54]

Note how Leo highlights Westman's mission and how the cloak of secrecy under which the project was conducted is described in positive terms. This rhetoric recalls the alchemists of old, who labored idealistically in the shadows to impart upon mankind a better life.[55] Note also that "the Americans" was an important signifier in Swedish research and research policy at a time when not only science but also the national self-image was becoming increasingly oriented toward the States.[56] If scientists in the "First New Nation" were interested in research results from Sweden, the "Second New Nation," then they were by definition of major international significance.[57] Invoking the interest expressed by the international community was a sure-fire method of rousing attention in Sweden. Only after this is a more detailed description of the actual significance of Gonadex for sterility brought up. This was probably the information—not mentioned in the academic articles—which really caught the attention of reporters.

> The preparation has in fact been ready for some six months now, and among the approximately thirty cases of e.g. childless women on whom Professor Westman has hitherto tested the drug, *one* in particular has been especially gratifying. For three years, the professor tirelessly but in vain struggled to cure the sterility that had embittered the marriage of a female patient and her husband. She wanted to leave no avenue unexplored, even though all indications were that she would be forced to give up. However, under the influence of the new hormone preparation she became pregnant almost immediately. She is now well into her second trimester and the overjoyed couple are expecting in the fall.[58]

Much of the rest of the text is reminiscent of Westman's lecture at the press conference, dealing with the internal secretion of the sex and pituitary glands and the interaction between sex hormones, which "ultimately create new life and [assure] the normal course of all the functions of the body," but also that the "sensational preparation" Gonadex has been developed via close collaboration between Leo and Westman. The press release featured a striking concluding observation explaining how urine from pregnant women had been successfully collected thanks to "suppliers" at Westman's clinic, reported to have been paid a not-inconsiderable fee for their efforts. Westman is said to have stated that the Royal Caroline Hospital would continue to show its gratitude for the contributions of pregnant women to the production of Gonadex, which was "on the brink of becoming an international commodity."[59] The impression is that vast quantities of urine is the only thing standing in the way of Gonadex breaking into the world hormone market. As we shall see in the next chapter, it was not quite that simple.

CHAPTER SIX

The Reception of Gonadex

NORMALLY, A BIOGRAPHY deals mainly with its subject's career—what he or she has accomplished in thought, word and deed. Analogous themes in the biography of a pharmaceutical can be said to be its career as innovation, i.e. how it has been received, disseminated and used, and the effects it has had on people and the therapeutic culture to which it belongs. With this chapter, we embark one such a career analysis by studying how Gonadex was received beyond the confines of Leo's corporate headquarters. Instead of sketching a generalized simplification of the "view" of Gonadex, I intend to show that different parties received the new product in different ways.[1] I begin by giving examples of the opinions of the medical profession, including a highly skeptical interjection published in *Svenska Läkartidningen*. By examining letters sent by private citizens to the Women's Clinic at the Royal Caroline Hospital, the reaction of the general public is presented, after which I provide an account of the opinion of the official government inspector, the National Pharmaceutical Laboratory, arrived at after much delay. Finally, I analyze Axel Westman's own assessment of Gonadex. As I intend to show, Gonadex had a hard time living up to expectations, which left Leo in a somewhat precarious position, to say the least.

REACTION OF THE MEDICAL PROFESSION

On the whole, the launch of Gonadex qualifies as a success, generating a huge amount of press. As early as the beginning of September 1948, Leo's hometown paper *Helsingborgs Dagblad* proudly reported that word of the new Swedish hormone drug had drawn representatives of a foreign company to town. "Two renowned French physicians came to Helsingborg yesterday, for the purpose of familiarizing themselves with the sensational hormone preparation from the Leo factory. Negotiations may be undertaken to manufacture the new Swedish drug in Paris."[2] At the same time, marketing Gonadex the way Leo did was a daring move. Axel Westman too had put his reputation on the line by conducting "science by press conference," to use the term coined by sociologists of science Harry Collins and Trevor Pinch.[3]

Some of the claims made about the documentation of the therapeutic value of Gonadex had been somewhat exaggerated. Ten (of thirty) patients was a relatively small test data basis, even back then, and though one of the treated women had indeed eventually gotten pregnant, that was a pretty paltry outcome.[4] Furthermore, it must have been terribly difficult for Westman to determine whether that pregnancy was really the result of taking Gonadex. If anyone at this point of time knew how random the results of sterility treatment could be, it was Westman. For example, he was well aware of a case when a woman who had been tested and recommended for hormone treatment managed to become pregnant before said treatment began.[5] This uncertainty was a well-known fact. In the summer of 1948, Danish physician Jørgen Hoffmeyer published a critical survey based on his own and outside research in the Nordic medical journal *Nordisk Medicin*, in which he questioned whether medicating sterile women had any real effect at all.[6] Thus the marketing of Gonadex was based as much on hope and expectation as it was on clinical facts, which was probably influenced by the fiscal position in which Leo found itself; you had to make yourself heard to compete on the national and international market. But sales not only relied on market demand but on the will of physicians to prescribe Gonadex. It was therefore imperative that Gonadex gain the trust of the medical profession.

In the months immediately following its launch, Leo was bombarded with requests from individuals wishing to try the new wonder drug.[7] Gynecologists wrote asking for samples, especially of the higher-grade dosages, which suggests that the presumptive patients were involuntarily childless women rather than women with more common menstrual or menopausal troubles. General practitioners got in touch asking for samples with which to treat their patients—among whom were their own, infertile spouses—as did researchers who ordered specimens for "scientific purposes."[8] These requests were made both in writing and directly to Leo's salesmen in the field. One of them reported that "[the physician himself] brought up Gonadex, because his wife had become excited by what she had read about it and he now wondered if he could have some in sample form, but most of all, if he could have the dosage recommendations right then and there, at least for the treatment of sterility."[9] Leo was generous in handing out free samples to gynecologists at the major hospitals but otherwise restrictive. Gonadex was expensive to make and Leo still had not built up much stock.

Along with requests for free samples, Leo was inundated with queries from physicians and pharmacists about how Gonadex was actually supposed to be taken, i.e. how much and for how long a patient with a specific diagnosis should be treated with a specific dosage. "I would be extremely grateful," a typical letter stated, "if you could forward a dosage schedule [for Gonadex treatment], since I cannot find the dosage considered appropriate for this condition [amenorrhea] in the available Swedish literature."[10] Questions like these poured in to the Women's Clinic at Caroline Hospital as well. In one, a private person relates that after having read about Gonadex in the daily *Dagens Nyheter*, she went to the drug store to place an order, but found that the staff was completely ignorant of proper dosage and use.[11]

The only problem was that Leo did not have any concrete advice to give them, since dosage schedules had yet to be compiled. As previously mentioned, the official course of treatment as formulated by Axel Westman in the registration documents was rather vague: "To be injected intravenously once or repeatedly, dependent on the nature of the case and obtained effect." Leo could do little else than answer questions like these by supplying doctors with an offprint of articles culled from *Acta Endocrinologica* and *Svenska Läkartidningen* and refer them to the hormone laboratory at the Caroline Hospital.[12] But Westman could not offer any unambiguous directives either, due to his conviction that hormone therapy could not be easily generalized but rather must be tailored to each individual case and always be preceded by thorough hormone analyses. Gonadex therapy demanded the mastery of hard-to-define skills, a kind of medical artisanry, which so far only Westman possessed. It should also be added that physicians soon informed Leo that they were not particularly impressed so far by what they had seen of the effect of Gonadex. An intern at Umeå General Hospital said that Gonadex had been tested on a couple of patients with endocrinal diagnoses and that no side effects had been observed—but then neither had any others.[13]

DR. WALDEMAR GÅRDLUND'S COMPLAINT

One of the general principles of modernity is that new technology is constantly developed and successively replaces older technology, which follows logically from the modern idea that new is by definition better than old.[14] Axel Westman repeated this mantra whenever the opportunity presented itself to describe his endocrinological orientation publically: only through biochemical hormone research could gynecology be modernized. And the most up-to-date result of hormone research was Gonadex. However, not all physicians agreed that the latest was the greatest. Since its inception, endocrinology was circumscribed by doubt, doubt still lingering in the 1940s.[15] It was based on widespread skepticism toward "miracle cures" but also in trepidation that the new science-based drugs posed a threat to the traditional status of the medical profession. This kind of criticism continued to be voiced after the launch of Gonadex, particularly in the pages of *Svenska Läkartidningen*, the house organ of the medical profession in Sweden.

A little over a month after the press conference, Waldemar Gårdlund (1879–1959), a Stockholm-based physician and chairman of the Swedish Association of Private General Practice, delivered an article entitled "Vetenskaplig reklam och praktisk erfarenhet: Ett bidrag till problemet om kvinnans sterilitet" [Scientific advertising and practical experience: A contribution to the issue of female sterility], in which he expressed his deep discomfort at the prospect of hormone therapy. "I have always harbored a profound skepticism toward the current-day search for the cause of almost all inexplicable irregularities of the female sexual sphere in the dysfunction of internal hormonal secretion. Particularly when dealing with sterility."[16] Gårdlund's own experience was that both diagnosis and treatment of infertile women were complicated undertakings, which involved a variety of medical and psychological factors. Examination and treatment according to current mechanical methods, including X-ray, oviduct inflation, curettage and cervical probing, were only occasionally successful. But according to Gårdlund, the overall outcome was hardly inferior to what "Leo-Westman" had achieved with Gonadex. In fact, it was better.[17]

Thus Gårdlund vigorously protested against "the pretentious and ostentatious manner in which [Westman] pounds the advertising drum for his hormone studies. For it might just prove, and in my opinion will prove, that the new preparation is just as ineffective as the old ones at curing the 'functional' sterility of women."[18] Gårdlund himself had read Westman's article "Clinical Testing of the Chorionic Gonadotropin 'Gonadex' Leo" and knew how tentative the clinical results were. In Gårdlund's estimation, there was imminent risk that involuntarily childless couples who had heard the news about Gonadex would be gripped by unrealistic expectations. He was particularly critical of the way in which Gonadex had been portrayed in the material handed out at the press conference, accusing Westman of contributing to the distribution of speculative propaganda, and sneering at the claims of its worldwide significance. Even if Gonadex worked, he warned, treatment would likely be so expensive that it would only benefit a select few patients. Furthermore, he reserved the right to remain

> highly skeptical toward the optimistic statements about Gonadex as a world-class commodity as long as the crystalline form is manufactured from the raw material currently required. To collect and transport liters, indeed tons of human urine should prove to be less simple than the brochures imagine.[19]

Gårdlund allowed for the possibility that Leo and the newspapers had radically misunderstood Westman's message and scientific results. But if that was indeed the case, then why had Westman not first vetted the press release or at least denied the claims during or after the press conference? Why did Westman choose to remain silent? Gårdlund's question was to remain unanswered, for Westman chose to meet it with silence. At least I have not been able to find any published comment from Westman, nor any correspondence between Leo and Westman concerning Gårdlund's article. If Westman felt any remorse, then he kept it to himself.

While newspaper journalists celebrated the progress of Swedish science and industry in the field of hormones, Gårdlund challenged hormone therapy against the backdrop of the scientific proof at hand and his own experience as a practitioner. His critique was aimed at both the tendency of biochemical research to reduce the complexity of the body and its health to a question of hormonal imbalance and the portrayal of the field in a way that risked stirring unrealistic expectations in presumptive patients. For him it was a question of ethics.[20] That Gårdlund used the term "Leo-Westman" can be understood as an attempt to expose and perhaps also cast aspersions on Westman's dealings with private industry. It was almost as if Gårdlund accused Westman of corruption.

However, similar to the previously mentioned critic Törnqvist, who used the expression "Hormon-Vestman," Gårdlund's criticism can also be interpreted as an expression of boundary work between competing and expanding fields in medicine; between the traditional "practitioner" in his clinic and the modern, laboratory-bound "theoretician."[21] For Gårdlund, the former was trustworthy, his expertise acknowledged, while the latter represented uncertainty; for Westman, the reverse was true. The practitioner was out of touch, while the theoretician represented the only way forward. Historian of science Martina Schlünder uncovered a similar tension between different styles of thought and therapeutic strategies in the field of gynecology: between those who think in a morphological (descriptive) style and those whose thought is shaped by molecular endocrinology.[22] The tension between Gårdlund and Westman, however, was not just about status, credibility and cognitive disagreement, but likely also about money. A palpable financial result of Westman's sudden fame was that increasing numbers of patients booked appointments at his clinic instead of the customary women's clinics they previously frequented.

The press conference was a social event, but it was not an isolated incident. As previously discussed, it can be seen as an expression of a new, public-relations trend gaining ground in Swedish society at large. The subsequent deluge of articles on Gonadex, as well as Gårdlund's critique, was one aspect of a social pattern, which had begun to emerge after the Second World War. Articles on new medical breakthroughs—especially ones that were expected to take place "in the near future"—began to be featured so often in the Swedish press that the professional medical community felt compelled to call for a more temperate dissemination of information via the mass media.[23] One critic who aired his grievances publically was Leonard Brahme, a physician from Norrköping. Taking for granted that physicians were a special, gifted class of human being, upon whom providence had bestowed a unique mastery of medicine, Brahme had previously defended the status of the medical corps in society.[24] In an open letter printed in *Svenska Läkartidningen* in 1951, he now urged his honored colleagues to show some restraint. Otherwise they risked creating false illusions, which would only add to the burden of the infirm. His letter, printed under the rubric "Framsteg och publicitet" [Progress and publicity], does not mention the new hormone drugs specifically, but is still worth quoting, as it illuminates the tension with which postwar Swedish therapeutic culture was rife.

> Recently, the undersigned was asked by an influential political figure whether it would not be prudent to refrain from announcing "medical advancements" until they had undergone more thorough critical medical analysis. He continued, "I am fed up with the many newspaper articles about all the wondrous medical progress being made, which are probably also producing hope in the infirm which cannot always be redeemed. Doctors have a great responsibility with regard to the harm such articles may cause." I agree entirely with this individual's opinion. Dubiously reliable recent reports rolling off the daily and weekly presses with conveyor-belt regularity about miracle cures are becoming the rule. This is something we must carefully monitor and something which is certainly far from desirable. For obvious reasons I shall refrain from going into detail but a practiced physician knows the kind of troublesomeness these articles can create and the disillusion they often cause. *In the interest of the sufferers, I feel that it is time for the leadership of the Swedish Medial Association to bark a resounding "Attention!"* We are embarking on the wrong path. We must learn

> to forgo unnecessary publicity. Should some successful result excite the enthusiasm of the physician in question, said enthusiasm should be tempered by a critical mind. In that way, we shall be spared the many sensationalistic articles in the press and liberate sufferers from unnecessary delusion.[25]

HORMONES AND DREAMS

How did the involuntarily childless react to the news that Gonadex and similar preparations had been developed and were now available to consumers? Were they skeptical or was Gårdlund correct in his suspicions that Leo's marketing contributed to inflating reasonable expectations? Did they even absorb the news at all? I consider the answers to these questions fundamental to the relationship between the research, the pharmaceutical industry and concerned members of the public. Management analyst and historian of medicine Jordan Goodman has stated that the Second World War marked a turning point as far as public access to and information on pharmaceuticals was concerned. "Patients were increasingly introduced to medicines not through the traditional sources—pharmacists, advertisements, word-of-mouth—but rather through a consultation with the physician and the delivery of a prescription."[26] The reasons for this is said to lie in the fact that business had assumed the role previously played by pharmacies as manufacturers of drugs, and that advertising was aimed squarely at the physicians, excluding the general public from the most important, direct channels of information. That the mass media could also play a role in conveying information on drugs and a plethora of other medical-related topics is left unmentioned by Goodman. I feel there is good reason not to do so.[27]

It is, however, admittedly difficult to know how the "general public" partook of information on science, technology and medicine via mass media channels like newspapers, radio and television. It is also reasonable to accept the wisdom that the general public is actually most heterogeneous, receiving news in a wide variety of ways.[28] Answering the questions posed above is a complicated task, not the least due to the fact that it is difficult to find adequate sources. Judging from the material in the Leo archives, it seems it was the exception rather than the rule for private individuals to write directly to Leo with queries about the company's hormone preparations.[29] The situation was further complicated by the fact that sexuality and reproduction were still sensitive and extremely personal issues in mid-century Sweden. However, I have found that it was not unusual for private individuals—mostly women, but some men, too—to write to the doctors at the Women's

Clinic at Caroline Hospital asking for information and advice about sterility. The letters are often long, detailed and personal.[30]

Letters dealing with an individual's or particular couple's involuntarily childlessness are in some instances vaguely formulated, stating that the party in question has been childless for a long period of time and is considering seeking medical assistance of some kind. The writer describes her situation and wonders if the doctor has any helpful suggestions.[31] Often the writer discusses or proposes specific forms of analysis or treatment, including X-ray examinations, surgery or insemination.[32] In time it became increasingly common that the letters mentioned the possibility of hormone drugs. I have thus chosen as my source letters received by the hospital during the 1940s and 1950s. While they certainly cannot tell us the whole truth, they do serve to prove that marketing efforts and news reports in the mass media did not fall on deaf ears. Information about hormones caused dreams to awaken.

Thanks to Leo's hormone lab, the women's clinic at Caroline Hospital was transformed into something of a national center for hormone analysis and treatment. Thus it is hardly surprising that medical researchers, gynecologists and physicians recommended patients from throughout the land, and even some from other countries, to seek its advice. Of the women treated for a variety of menstrual imbalances at the women's clinic during the years 1943–48, the majority had been referred by their hometown doctors.[33] That potential patients wrote to the staff of the clinic, more often than not directly to the renowned Axel Westman, was not only due to these expert recommendations, but was motivated also by information gathered from other sources. Sometimes it was relatives or friends who tipped them off about the specialists at the Caroline Hospital. But as I intend to show, the source may just as often have been the mass media, dailies, weeklies and radio programs in which the outgoing Westman appeared or was quoted. Ladies' magazines in particular often featured articles on childlessness during this time, which ethnologist Katarina Saltzman has previously observed.[34] Hence, that so many childless people turned to the Royal Caroline Hospital was the result of a combination of the material resources available at the women's clinic and Axel Westman's celebrity and public persona. This was in fact a development Westman himself had foreseen. In a letter to the Directorate of the Caroline Hospital written in 1943, the year after he arrived at the hospital and the same year Leo's hormone lab was due to be installed, he stated that

> In the preceding year, the clinic treated 214 cases of sterility. We have every reason to believe that this number will increase substantially in

> the coming period due to the fact that the undersigned has specially dedicated himself to matters of sterility and that the clinic will soon be outfitted with a hormone laboratory, where a majority of hormonally-based cases of sterility will be analyzed and treated.[35]

In the case of letters addressed directly to Westman, it was common that the author mentioned one of his essays or books, e.g. *Hormoner*, or a mass media outlet in which he had appeared or been discussed. To clarify what I mean, here are some examples of how the letters could be formulated, followed by a section where a selection of letters specifically dealing with Gonadex will be discussed.

One woman who after several years of marriage had failed to become pregnant opens her letter to Westman with, "Have just read your article in [the woman's magazine] Damernas Värld, which compelled me to write to you. I am 33 years old and have never menstruated, perhaps even I could become a 'normal woman' through your hormone injections?"[36] Another woman expressing the same wish had gathered courage to write to Westman "[a]fter I read in [the cultural magazine] Idun on 11-16-42 that Professor Vessman [sic] had commented that women who want to have children could be helped."[37] A third claiming to suffer from unspecified problems formulated herself in the following manner: "Read a while ago about the miraculous effect of hormones. Now I wonder if it is possible for the professor to send me a prescription . . . ."[38] Yet another referred to *VI*, the house organ of the Swedish Cooperative Union. "I take the liberty of writing to you after reading an article in VI magazine. If you could please provide me with some information and advice about some things concerning my sterility, I would be extremely grateful."[39]

Two articles in 1943 dealing with the treatment of sterile men with hormones were also eagerly devoured throughout the country. For one childless woman, whose husband suffered from malformed sex glands, a spark of hope was ignited. Her letter to Westman began with the following comment: "Since I have read about the Professor numerous times, most recently in an article in Husmodern no. 31, 'Childlessness Due to the Husband', I take the liberty of writing to you."[40] The question of the role of the man in cases of involuntarily childlessness received much attention in general as the practice of sperm diagnosis began to be conducted regularly at some of the country's women's clinics, including the Caroline, where throughout the 1940s, it was policy to first check the quality of the husband's sperm before considering examining the wife.[41] This did not mean, however, that all the men who were diagnosed or showed signs of dysfunction were treated with hormones to the same extent as the women.

In the archives of the Women's Clinic, there are letters whose writers inquire about the possibility of using hormone therapy for other ends than the most common "functional hormone imbalances," including menstrual problems and involuntary childlessness. Through these letters we understand that a faith bordering on the blind had emerged in society. Hormones were beginning to be perceived as a cure-all. The confidence the writers have in Westman, the "leading hormone expert in the country," as dubbed by journalists, is also striking.[42] Like the celebrated biochemist The Svedberg, who received the Nobel Prize for chemistry in 1926, Westman was almost regarded as a "magician."[43]

Some prospective patients craving hormone treatment wished to modify their bodies, or the bodies of others, in the most physical sense. One man, himself a scientist, wondered if it would be possible to influence the gender of a fetus with hormones, in order to create boys instead of girls.[44] Another who had read Westman's book *Hormoner* with great interest related that he considered himself "insufficiently developed" insofar as his male member was concerned. Could a positive change be effected with the help of hormones?[45] A similar question was posed by women who wished to enhance their breasts and wondered if hormone treatments might be the answer.[46] Several adult men wrote Westman asking if it was possible to increase their height with growth hormones.[47] This possibility had been suggested in the "Reader's Queries" in the mass-market magazine *Folket i Bild*, where columnist "Nurse Anna" had cited the prominence of Westman in the field of hormone research.[48] Westman answered questions like these with restraint, usually stating either that it was impossible to say anything concrete until a thorough hormone analysis had been conducted, or that the method of treatment sought simply did not exist. Yet.[49] He might also reply that while effective hormone preparations probably already exist, they were still very hard to get hold of.[50]

Another category seeking help hoped that the representatives of modern hormone research could help them influence their sexuality. One was a man who no longer felt attracted to his wife but remained so to other women, another a woman who was attracted to women, but not to her husband.[51] Others wished to transform their bodies in a more concrete sense. These were individuals who had been born with male genitalia but perceived themselves and sometimes also lived as women, and who wished to change sex with the aid of surgery in combination with hormone therapy.[52] An important source of inspiration for these individuals was the American photographer George William Jorgensen, who garnered worldwide attention when he changed sex in 1952 and became Christine Jorgensen, her new name taken in honor of the Danish endocrinologist Christian Hamburger, who performed both the operation and oversaw the hormone treatment.

Westman was of two minds about requests of this sort. As long as it concerned boosting sexual attraction in accordance with the heterosexual norm, he was of the opinion that sex hormones or gonadotropin drugs might be effective. However, when it came to reassigning sexuality or changing gender, he was hesitant. In such cases, he considered the problem not to be medical or biological but psychological, and advised the writer to try hypnosis or psychotherapy instead.[53]

Finally, there was a group of writers whose number increased in the mid-1940s—women experiencing "the change" seeking the help of endocrinology to ease their menopausal discomforts.[54] For them, Westman's book on the subject, *Övergångsår* [Menopause] (1945), had been a revelation.[55] It is no surprise the book attracted readers, for in contrast to many others who had tackled the subject, Westman stated that menopause in no way represented the final phase of life but rather its ultimate perfection.[56] There was no need to undergo medical therapy; most discomfort could be regulated by simple adjustments in lifestyle, though truly serious problems could be alleviated with hormone treatment. "Physical discomfort and concomitant mental irritability can in many cases be completely eliminated. Much of the periodic panic previously associated with the menopausal period of life have therewith also been eradicated."[57]

GONADEX AND ITS PROSPECTIVE USERS

The letters excerpted above seek access to generic hormones. I have not come across a single reference to a specific brand or type of hormone. After the launch of Gonadex, though, this all changed.

"With reference to an article in the June 12 issue of Göteborgs Handels- och Sjöfarts-Tidning concerning your new medicine, Gonadex, I take the liberty to write to you." So begins one of the first letters to arrive at the Women's Clinic at the Royal Caroline Hospital in the summer of 1948. It is addressed to Axel Westman and dated 14 June, just four days after the press conference. In another letter, dated the same day, the writer states, "I would be extremely grateful to be admitted to the Caroline Hospital's Women's Clinic now or some time in the future in order to be treated acc. to the new method of injecting the drug 'Gonadex'." Both letters were written by women who had had unsatisfactory contact with the clinic, but gained new hope after hearing about the news about Gonadex.[58] A third wrote on 16 June that "since I read the wonderful news about your new hormone drug in the newspaper a few days ago, I have not been able to rid myself of the thought that it might be able to help me, too, and thus I take the liberty of writing and presenting my case to you."[59] The writer in question had taken hormones regularly for several years in an unsuccessful attempt to become pregnant. The articles on Gonadex had however instilled new hope in her and she wanted to see Westman again. Her letter concludes with the plea, "I am fully aware that perhaps hundreds of women write to you these days with similar requests, but I still dare to hope you might consider accepting me, in my capacity of former patient."[60]

The woman was correct in assuming that many others would write to Westman asking to try the new wonder cure. They were not out after hormones in general, but Gonadex specifically. It may not have been hundreds of women, but the extant letters still testify to a sizeable interest. Information about the effects of Gonadex appearing in the news continued to be invoked. Sometimes the sources were mentioned by name, as "with ref. to your article in Husmodern magazine re: the drug Gonadex," at others the writer referred simply to "the press" or "the papers." "Having read about Professor Westman's new discovery, 'Gonadex', I am very interested in seeing if it might be something for me."[61] Or, "When we [the writer and her husband] read about the new discovery, Gonadex, our hopes were renewed, and in our eagerness we decided to consult the Professor as to the prospect that this new, effective remedy could help us overcome sterility, too."[62] The writers of these and other letters received by the clinic during June, July and August of 1948 were informed that Westman was on a leave of absence (or away on business), but that they were welcome to try again at the beginning of September.[63] This was hardly the answer the eager correspondents had expected.

As a rule, the letter-writers were women. In some instances, they did not want their husbands to know that they wrote seeking advice on such matters, explaining that the problem was far too delicate or private, but also that the anticipated positive effect of Gonadex would then come as a delightful surprise.[64] However, there were men who wrote to Westman about Gonadex, too. In a letter dated 20 June 1948, one says that he had heard Westman's remarks about "a new hormone preparation effective against sterility" on the radio news. Since he and his wife had lived in a childless marriage for many years, he wondered if Westman would recommend the hormone drug to them.[65] Another man, living abroad, explained that "by chance, we [he and his wife] read an article in Husmodern re: a new drug, Gonadex, which Prof. Westman has prepared in collaboration with the pharmaceutical firm Leo. The article seems to apply to our case, since we have tried to have children but so far without result."[66] Another reason this particular couple requested Gonadex was the claim that it totally lacked negative side effects. The hormone drugs his wife had previously tried had not only had no positive effect but also induced fever and nausea.

As all these examples attest, Gonadex was perceived as a potent, risk-free medicine primarily designed to treat sterility, which is not surprising considering the manner in which Leo's press releases were composed and the newspapers reported the news. But both Leo's flyers and Westman's own statements made clear that Gonadex had numerous different uses, and that the drug's ability to cure sterility was still an open question. Did no one get that part of the message? Physicians did, most likely, but among the letters remaining from 1948, few are explicitly interested in Gonadex for any other problem than involuntary childlessness. Among the exceptions can be found the request forwarded by a man concerned about the growth of his daughter. What he wanted Westman to tell him was whether Gonadex could affect sexual maturation—not in order to increase her growth, but rather to retard it.[67]

Simultaneously, this survey shows that the marketing of Gonadex had had the desired effect insofar as numerous potential customers had been reached. But the letters also show that private individuals did not remain passive, but took the initiative to acquire more information or request treatment. Cultural researchers have previously warned that people who enter the medical machine can easily be portrayed as victims instead of subjects taking action, and in this case, the warning is well justified.[68] If these people were victims of anything, it was the influence of the mass media, though Axel Westman is certainly not without blame.

I will not delve deeply into the first actual Gonadex treatments and their results. Since I have not systematically studied the patient files, the empirical data is too meager to draw reliable conclusions. However, the statistics Westman compiled on the ninety women with varying diagnoses he treated between 1 June 1948 and 15 March 1949 certify that the overall results were far from satisfactory.[69] This impression is confirmed by letters from some of the first women to whom Gonadex was prescribed (together with Antex) in the autumn of 1948.[70] That Gårdlund's greatest fears were realized is made apparent in no uncertain terms by a letter from a distressed woman who reported regretfully that the treatment had not borne fruit. "I left Stockholm with the hope that I had a high chance of success, which makes my disappointment so much greater. Seeing that I read so much in both the weekly magazines and daily newspapers about this new cure, Gonadex, which cures sterility, I am surprised that it hasn't succeed in our case, in which both partners are healthy and no organic infirmities exist."[71] In a letter to another woman, who sought advice on hormone treatment for her own unwelcome sterility, Westman admitted that the effects of Gonadex had not been particularly positive.[72] "In some circumstances, Gonadex can appear unpropitious, while in others it can attain good results."[73] This was perhaps Westman's way of saying that it was high time to tone down expectations of what Gonadex was capable of accomplishing.

VERDICT OF THE NATIONAL PHARMACEUTICAL LABORATORY

As required by law, the launching of Gonadex had been preceded by tests to measure its strength in comparison with the international standard for human chorionic gonadotropin (hCG), i.e. the hCG preparation chosen as the standard in 1938. The tests were conducted at the hormone laboratory of Lennart Claesson, M.B., under the supervision of Axel Westman. Testing proved difficult, however, which is hinted at in a letter Westman wrote 12 August 1948 on behalf of Leo seeking the assistance of international expertise.[74] These difficulties made the National Board of Health begin to doubt the quality of Gonadex. Leo, Westman and his colleagues were soon faced with a delicate theoretical problem.

On 8 October, four months after the press conference and half a year after seeking a patent, Leo was contacted by Håkan Rydin (1902–1985), director of the Department of Biology of the National Pharmaceutical Laboratory, who informed the firm that Gonadex would probably not be approved as a pharmaceutical specialty.[75] Interestingly, the reason was not that Gonadex lacked the positive effect on patients promised in its advertising, nor that it proved to have harmful side effects. The problem was rather the manner in which the strength of Gonadex was indicated on its packaging. During the biological tests conducted at the NPL, it had emerged that the preparation was "considerably weaker" than its standardized, international counterpart. At least three times weaker.[76]

Rydin believed that the reason for this was that the NPL and Leo had used different methods to determine the strength of Gonadex. The problem was therefore of an epistemological nature and could be solved with a simple revision of measurements. But Rydin also posed the possibility that the fault lay in the very basis of the measurements; that the active substance in Gonadex and the international standard against which Gonadex was calibrated were not identical. Considering that Leo had claimed that Gonadex was purer than all other chorionic gonadotropin preparations, including the international standard, this was not unreasonable. Hence, the problem lay not in Gonadex, but in the "impure" standard preparation. However, this was little help. "Declaring the strength of Gonadex in international units under these conditions cannot be considered correct."[77] In order for the Board of Health to approve Gonadex required clarification of the divergent results and Rydin proposed that Leo and the NPL open a joint investigation into the matter. The forces of state and capital would solve the problem together.

In the partnership of Leo and Axel Westman, responsibility for scientific matters lay with the latter. Thus just a few days after Rydin's unwelcome news, Leo contacted Westman and asked for his opinion.[78] The firm also encouraged Westman to immediately deliver a description of the standardization methods used in the hormone lab in the fall of 1947, which he did.[79] He also saw to it that supplementary testing of Gonadex was expedited, again under the auspices of Lennart Claesson, while he himself continued to provide advice about the clinical application of Gonadex to the best of his ability.[80] However, the procedure of providing personal counseling proved untenable in the end. As turnover rose and the traveling salesmen brought back more and more questions with each trip, Leo's need for precise dosage instructions became increasingly acute.[81] Worst of all, the standardization issue did not appear to have an easy solution. It turned out that not only the NPL had its doubts about Gonadex; on the first of December, Leo's director Svante Wiström revealed to Westman that reports of standardization problems had also been received from two independent instances. These reports were "in no way reassuring" and had prepared him for "rather large difficulties" to come.

> Professor Håkan Rydin, National Pharmaceutical Laboratory, has informed me personally and confidentially that he had received word from both Organon in Holland and Lövens Kemiske Fabrik in Copenhagen about their rather comprehensive study of packages of Gonadex purchased on the Swedish market. He also let it be known that their studies confirm his own findings . . . .[82]

This report, and further information about trials conducted by the NPL, soon arrived at Leo's offices in written form as well. Rydin wrote that the NPL had determined that at least some of the manufactured forms of Gonadex proved weaker than declared, both in tests with cervical-vaginal cultures from rats and studies of ovarian change in mice. The results were always the same, regardless of method. Then came the *coup de grâce.* "The results have been confirmed in both Denmark and Holland! The NPL must therefore recommend that your registration application be rejected."[83]

Of course, Leo was forced to deal swiftly with this problem. Its first move was to systematically scrutinize all the files compiled in the standardizing process undertaken by the hormone lab, a task delegated to Bertil Högberg.[84] A couple of weeks later, Leo accepted the fact that a new, comprehensive standardization process needed to be carried out. A letter to the NPL explained that, "as far as a substance which has never previously been isolated in crystalline form is concerned, a number of consequences with which we had not reckoned occurred."[85] This could not be righted overnight. The experiments were not only complicated and labour-intensive, they also demanded a large number of lab animals of certain species, age and weight, which took time to acquire. In order for Axel Westman and his colleagues, first and foremost Claesson, to have time to conduct comparative studies with varying methods, Leo asked for a three-month deferment, after which Gonadex was expected to be "finished" so that it could be registered on the free list, where only irreproachable, well-defined and easily-controllable medicines were listed.[86]

Alongside the free list existed another list, however, the so-called "licensed list," featuring preparations that could only be sold to physicians with "special competence" in the preparation in question, for example the then-controversial Antabus.[87] In order not to completely throttle sales of its potential international success, Leo suggested that the Board of Medicine provisionally register Gonadex on that list during the coming control period.[88] This was disagreeable, not to say embarrassing for Leo, but was still preferable to being denied registration altogether.[89] At the end of this eventful year, Leo wrote to Westman and informed him that "[t]his application will be approved as a matter of course, and the drug will be sold on license after 1 January 1949." Leo therefore asked Westman to immediately send in the enclosed license application to the Board of Medicine "so that delivery [of Gonadex] to your clinic can continue without disruption."[90] Which he did.[91]

"WE HAVE MADE FOOLS OF OURSELVES, NOT ONLY IN FRONT OF SWEDISH PHARMACISTS AND PHYSICIANS BUT THE WHOLE WORLD"

Physicians, potential users, official and unofficial inspectors—everyone had an opinion about Gonadex. What about Axel Westman himself? What conclusions did he draw and how were they and the findings of the other reviewers greeted by Leo?

While the problems piled up, Westman continued to use Gonadex regularly on his female patients at the Caroline Hospital. All cases were documented and internal statistics on the effect of the drug were duly noted. Treatment was exclusively performed on women between 1 June 1948 and 15 March 1949, largely patients diagnosed with amenorrhea (seventy-five out of a total of ninety). Among the remainder, ten were diagnosed with metropathia haemorrhagica cystica, while only five were said to have been sterile (for three to six years), a total which, against the backdrop of the letters in the archives of the Women's Clinic, definitely seems on the low side. A written account of these efforts, which can be seen as a large-scale clinical test, was submitted to Leo on 1 April 1949.[92]

In his account, Westman admitted that the results were far from unequivocal. Of the seventy-five amenorrhea patients, Gonadex, taken in varying doses and sometimes in combination with Antex, had had some effect in forty-six cases. For patients suffering from metropathia haemorrhagica cystica, similarly varied treatment gave results in four cases of ten and for the sterile women only one out of five.[93] The sole unambiguous outcome was still the fact that in contrast with older hormone drugs, Gonadex appeared not to cause any adverse side effects. Westman could not explain the divergent results. In fact, he could do little more than admit to Leo that "the effects of gonadotropins are exceedingly capricious and we have not been able to determine the reason." On the current level of knowledge, Westman confessed that

> [i]n general, little is known about the theoretical background of the ovarial effect of gonadotropins. Thus it has not been determined whether there is a principal difference between the organic pituitary gland gonadotropin, serum gonadotropin and chorionic gonadotropin, even if it is very likely, nor has the question as to the extent in which the two factors in organic pituitary gonadotropin, namely the follicle-stimulating and luteinizating factors, are dependent upon one another been definitively answered.[94]

Westman appears genuinely frustrated by this problem, which only seems to grow increasingly complicated. At the same time, it was far too interesting from a scientific perspective to resist and there was good reason to press on and study the crystalline chorionic gonadotropin. As far as the results from the women's clinic were concerned, Westman insisted to Leo that continued study was the only logical recourse. It was quite simply a matter of being patient. He also added that it might be a while before the final results of treatment became truly apparent. My interpretation is that Westman by that meant that possible positive results, as opposed to negative results in the form of pernicious side effects, would come to light in the future.

> The material collected in the short time Gonadex has been available is of course far too small to be able to draw any definitive conclusions about the value of the preparation . . . . Thus it seems to me imperative that testing of the drug continue in as comprehensive a fashion as possible. As always when dealing with tests of this nature, precise conclusions cannot be expected until a supplementary examination of the patients has been conducted, two or three years after they have been subjected to the treatment at the earliest.[95]

It should be mentioned that at this point in time, Westman submitted two identical grant applications to subsidize his research. The applications, one addressed to the Royal Caroline Institute and the other to the newly-established Medical Research Council, state that work on the effect of the crystalline gonadotropin on ovarian function has advanced at a "regrettably slow pace," not due to the complexity of the question but rather because the women's clinic had too few technical assistants at its disposal.[96] This was, as they say, not exactly the whole story.

What about the inquiry into the standardization of Gonadex, begun in December 1948? Westman submitted a report in early April 1949, which also showed that the development of Gonadex was far from a closed chapter.[97] During the spring, a long series of animal tests were conducted in order to compare varying strengths of Gonadex with the international standard preparation. In every single case, the results proved that the declared strength of Gonadex had been off. Gonadex was not as "strong" as it was said to be, thereby confirming the critique. However, the blame for this mistake was laid not on crystalline Gonadex but rather the international standard preparation, which was said to contain "impurities"—which influenced its biological effect in a *positive* direction.

Westman rationalized this paradox by explaining that pituitary gland gonadotropin is a compound of two "principals," one follicle stimulating (FSH) and one luteinizing (LH). Achieving full gonadotropic effect seemed to demand the coordination of these two principals, which must furthermore be in exact proportion to one another. Gonadex in its pure form contained only the LH principal, while the older, standard preparations for chorionic gonadotropin, like Physex, also contained traces of the FSH principal. This meant that Gonadex had a lesser effect than the standard preparation since the efficacy of the former was dependent on the FSH production of the lab animal or patient. In other words, when Physex underwent its purification bath and was transformed into Gonadex, some of its old therapeutic ability was washed out.[98] In Westman's defense, a similar argument had in fact been broached in the 1948 article "Crystalline Human Chorionic Gonadotrophin and Its Biological Action," describing how the biological effect of crystalline chorionic gonadotropin varied depending on the constitution of the lab animal. The authors had gone as far as to venture that the biological activity of different chorionic gonadotropin preparations were not necessarily a function of the degree of purity. In fact, the opposite might be the case. "[T]he possibility of an eventual synergism between the hormone and the impurities present could not with certainty be excluded."[99] Yet the fact remains that this does not explain why Gonadex was ascribed the strengths printed on its packaging, nor the efficacy listed in the registration application.

The Gonadex paradox was however not unique. It can be compared with the disappointment wrought when male sex hormones were purified from testicle extract and urine in the early 1930s. That hormone also proved to be significantly weaker than scientists had expected. Producing an "ideally" functional male sex hormone required modification of the pure preparation by adding its female counterpart, estrone.[100] Whether or not Westman was familiar with this state of affairs is unknown, but if he was it might have given him food for thought about how to move forward in dealing with the relatively weak effect of Gonadex. The only thing Westman actually did was to recommend continuing the research.[101] However, this was in all probability hindered by the fact that neither the clinical results nor the standardization tests were published in scientific journals. As they had been conducted on behalf of Leo, Westman was under no obligation to make the results of the studies public. He may even have been forbidden to do so. The question as to whether he would have been *encouraged* to publish if the results had been more positive remains unanswerable. That scientists—and periodicals—are not eager to publish negative results is no secret.[102] In a later example, when two researchers compared one of Leo's hormone drugs (Andradurin) with a similar product manufactured by another company, the results, according to documentary evidence, were "so discouraging . . . that they decided to forget the whole study."[103]

It is not hard to imagine that Leo received Westman's off-the-record reports with disappointment. First of all, it turned out that Gonadex was not as potent as believed. This was a setback that doubtless threatened the company's dreams of having an international sales success on its hands. Secondly, the problem of standardizing Gonadex remained, which meant that it would take even longer for the Board of Medicine to give the drug its final approval. Perhaps Gonadex was not even going to be a success at home, let alone abroad? In an attempt to get around the standardization issue, Leo asked the permission of the Board of Medicine to register Gonadex according to its own standards. Instead of international units, Leo wished to indicate strength in "weight units," a strategy Westman also saw as a solution to the dilemma.[104] But such ad-hoc solutions were not popular. During a telephone conversation on 19 April 1949, Håkan Rydin explained to Svante Wiström, "So you have sent in an application and it has clearly been proven that the drug is four to five times weaker than what the declaration says. While there are some mitigating circumstances, I've also talked to the Board and we cannot deviate from this, partly on grounds of principle and partly in fairness to other manufacturers."[105] If Leo failed to standardize Gonadex in accordance with international guidelines, only two options remained: if it did not withdraw its application voluntarily, the Board of Medicine would be forced to strike Gonadex from the register. Having a drug deregistered in this manner did not look good. It sent a message that Leo was incapable of correctly assessing its own work, which is why Rydin strongly recommended the latter alternative.[106]

Leo followed his advice. At least part of it. On 9 May 1949, Leo asked that the registration applications for Gonadex in all strengths be withdrawn. At the same time, it requested that two veterinary variants of Physex be reintroduced, which was approved.[107] Axel Westman's compilation of the clinical effects of Gonadex, along with his report on standardization efforts, were enclosed with the application. Leo admitted openly that it had not succeeded in replicating the values previously indicated. The company also conceded that the reason for its failure remained a mystery, and that no solution to the standardization problem was in sight. In a cover letter, the procedure was motivated in the following manner.

> Insofar as the possibility that a qualitative discrepancy exists between Gonadex and the international standard for chorionic gonadotropin cannot be dismissed, in which case the current standardization methods cannot be used for a comparison between Gonadex and the international standard, we request that our application to register Gonadex with its strength indicated in international units be respectfully withdrawn.[108]

By the time this letter reached the Board of Medicine, the NPL had already refused to sanction the old applications. On 1 June 1949, the Board of Medicine announced it would deny the applications of all strengths of Gonadex.[109]

Despite this, Leo tried to submit a new one, indicating the strength of Gonadex in weight units according to its own, homemade scale (0.3 to 20 from weakest to strongest) instead of international units. In this way, Leo hoped to circumvent its standardization issues so that Gonadex could immediately be reregistered and at least be sold on license.[110] This last-ditch attempt at creating its own unit of measurement can also be understood from a business economics perspective. In order to increase the strength of Gonadex so that the original declaration would correspond to international standards, the company was forced to considerably increase the amount of hormones the drug contained. Leo calculated that such an adjustment would cause its projected material expenditure on Gonadex to increase as much as tenfold.

This fiddling with declarations was doomed to failure. As Rydin had predicted, the Board of Medicine promptly denied Leo's application; if Leo wanted Gonadex registered, it would have to conform to accepted international standards.[111] This put Leo in a precarious position. Some 12 months after its grand launch, there was no long a registered drug named "Gonadex."[112]

Evidently, Leo was prepared for this setback. At a meeting held on the fourth of May, the board of directors decided that its contents would be modified and Gonadex retained in its original form. According to a directive from Christian Hamburger of the Statens Serum Institut in Copenhagen, the strength of Gonadex needed to be upgraded by a factor of 6.3.[113] Leo sought and secured the assistance of Håkan Rydin of the NPL in dealing with the standardization issue. The problem was that standardization required so many more lab animals that the NPL's supplier could not keep up with demand. Rydin wondered if Leo itself could procure the necessary rats, "so that registration of the preparation would not be delayed for too many months."[114] Thus Leo's Gonadex expenses continued to rise, but despite public criticism from the medical corps and despite all the difficulties encountered in the standardization process, Leo refused to give up the drug. It did not give up its plans to market it abroad, either.[115] But due to these problems, the foreign market offensive had stranded, a fact alluded to in the minutes of a meeting of the board of directors held in October 1949 and attended by Leo's managing director Edward Goldschmidt.[116] Goldschmidt, who was understandably not happy with how the situation had gotten so out of hand, did not pull his punches. "We have made fools of ourselves, not only in front of Swedish pharmacists and physicians but the whole world, which awaits a solution with interest."[117] In the next chapter, we shall see how Leo, with the help of its network, grappled with this situation.

PART III

DEVELOPMENT

CHAPTER SEVEN

New Gonadex

THE BIOGRAPHY OF GONADEX could very well have ended right about here, with a concluding statement that the drug never lived up to expectations and went down in history as a medical and financial failure. But that would be as misleading as ending the story with the launch of the drug in 1948, when Gonadex was regarded as a bona fide success. Encouraged by the exhortation of John V. Pickstone to not only study the genesis of an innovation but also its fate, I have continued to follow the biographical development of the "carrier" of Gonadex in order to find out what happened after the debacle: how its cool reception contributed to the continued development of Gonadex as an artifact and how that artifact in turn influenced the therapeutic culture from which it sprung. This chapter thus investigates the aftermath of the success that never materialized and follows up and contextualizes continued work on Gonadex by members of Leo's network. As will become apparent, Gonadex did not fade away in 1949, but rather changed identities.

SHAKE-UP AT THE WOMEN'S CLINIC

It has been estimated that the global pharmaceutical market grew from 600 million dollars annually in the 1930s to over seven billion in the 1950s.[1] This remarkable increase was accompanied by a powerful collective confidence in the ability of science-based medicine to constantly improve the life of mankind. Universal faith in the capacity of the life sciences to promote health and welfare was probably never greater than immediately following the Second World War, when penicillin had became widely available.[2] The introduction and establishment of hormone drugs in gynecological practice was part of this process.

As the acceptance of endocrine diagnoses and hormone drugs increased in the 1940s, so did the actual and potential tasks undertaken by the hormone lab at the Royal Caroline Hospital, which remained the home of most hormone analysis in central and northern Sweden. More and more often, the diagnosis was found to be hormone imbalance, which thereby increased the number of hormone treatments. Aside from conducting biological pregnancy tests and chemical analyses of sex hormones and gonadotropins, the lab was also analyzing adrenal gland hormones by the end of the decade. Analyses seeking to detect tumors were conducted as well.[3] With this, clinical gynecology and experimental endocrinology had become fully integrated, completely in line with the professional aspirations of Axel Westman.

In order to keep up with demand and fortify the status of sexual endocrine research (which in time had come to be called "reproductive endocrinology"), it was decided to expand both the parameters of hormone research and the size of the premises housing the women's clinic. After pressure from the Caroline Hospital, the Swedish parliament earmarked nearly SEK 300,000 for the project, while the Knut and Alice Wallenberg Foundation donated 60,000 for fittings and equipment. On a new floor, above the former women's clinic's wing, a new research lab was installed, into which Axel Westman and his staff moved in the autumn of 1948.[4] As one daily paper punned, this new investment was a real "hormone injection" for the new science of endocrinology in Sweden.[5] In the midst of this bustle, the old hormone lab on the ground floor was retrofitted to perform sperm analysis. For more than a decade, the male partner had been routinely examined as part of any sterility case, but it was only now that a lab solely dedicated to the purpose was created, with Erik Nordlander, affectionately know to his co-workers as "Spermander," in charge.[6] Expectations were high that men found to be suffering from an insufficient production of sperm could also be treated successfully, with Gonadex, for example. After an interview with Westman, a Stockholm-based newspaper reported that "in recent years, the chances of curing sterility in both men and women with a hormone preparation called gonadotropin have increased significantly . . . . This hormone, closely related to the pituitary gland hormone and produced by the placenta, is now being manufactured in Sweden by the Leo factory in Helsingborg."[7] The "sterility clinic" the daily press loudly called for when Gonadex was first launched was now a reality.

For Leo, the external hormone lab had long been a decisive factor in testing and standardizing hormone medication. It had furthermore put Leo in direct contact with physicians in a number of cities—first Uppsala, then Lund and finally Stockholm—and at the same time created a demand for their products. In time, however, Leo began to question whether this expanding and increasingly costly lab work was worth the investment, while at the same time considering the advantages of concentrating its hormone work to the plant in Helsingborg. In the autumn of 1948, it was finally decided that Leo's funding of the hormone lab at the Caroline Hospital would be discontinued and the staff let go as of 1 April 1949.[8]

One of those forced out was the luckless Lennart Claesson who, not without a certain sense of relief of being released from Gonadex' standardization problems, found his way to Sune Genell's clinic in Malmö.[9] A smaller lab for smaller tasks and routine studies would however remain under Leo's management, provided it kept on budget. Westman was put on a consultant retainer, through which Leo kept him as part of its network.[10] It is worth noting that the decision to liquidate was taken at roughly the same time the company was hit with the news of the erroneous standardization of Gonadex. Might the two be connected? Perhaps there was a connection between Gonadex and the choice to maintain a small lab at Caroline Hospital after all? Leo probably realized that the standardization process threatened to be a prolonged one, with or without Claesson.

Another change was that the downsized hormone lab added Egon Diczfalusy to its staff. Diczfalusy (b. 1920) was a young physician and microbiologist from Hungary who had left his homeland due to the inclement postwar political climate to embark on a research career in Sweden. He started out as an assistant to chemist Hans von Euler at Stockholm University but transferred to Caroline Hospital in the autumn of 1948, where Axel Westman arranged a Leo-financed post at the hormone lab.[11] Diczfalusy eventually became chief of the laboratory and remained in that role until 1967 when he, as newly-appointed Professor of Reproductive Endocrinology, became director of a special section financed by the Swedish Council for Medical Research.[12]

Internationally Diczfalusy is renowned for his long involvement, beginning in the 1970s, in WHO's planned parenthood program, which he accounts for in the anthology *The Contraceptive Revolution: An Era of Scientific and Social Development* (1996).[13] In his introduction, Diczfalusy recalls how the question of overpopulation fuelled increased interest in reproductive endocrinology, how he received large grants from the Ford Foundation during the 1960s to develop that research, and how "contraceptive research became a day-to-day reality in my life." On the other hand, he does not have much to say about his prior engagement doing research on hormone preparations to cure involuntary infertility for Leo, to which I shall shortly return.

Thus big changes were made at the Women's Clinic of the Royal Caroline Hospital at the end of the 1940s. To say that Gonadex alone lay behind these changes would be to exaggerate the significance of the artifact. It is, however, plausible to see the rise and fall of Gonadex as one of many contributing factors. Furthermore, another kind of change took place around the same time. While hormone therapy was becoming established and normalized in clinical gynecological practice, insight grew into the fact that this form of treatment had its less attractive sides. That hormone preparations, like so many other drugs, could be the source of unwelcome side effects was a well-known medical problem and, as has been shown, efforts were made to reduce these to a minimum. It was generally assumed that side effects were caused by undesired "contaminants," not the "pure" hormones themselves. In time, this perception would be challenged from a variety of camps and in a variety of manners.

HORMONE THERAPY FOR BETTER OR WORSE

Experiment had revealed the unsettling connection between sexual hormones and certain kinds of cancer as early as the 1930s, and the worst fears were confirmed in the decade to follow, when an increase in cancer was noted among women who had undergone estrogen therapy.[14] Not long after, a theory was formulated as to a similar connection between the male sex hormone and enlargement of the prostate. However, there was no consensus as to the exact genesis of this connection. In Germany, where manufacture and use of sex hormone drugs was widespread, and where the connection between hormones and cancer was therefore taken extremely seriously, certain researchers concluded that it was not the hormones themselves that brought about illness, but rather that their ability to stimulate tissue growth could hasten the development of cancerous tumors.[15] This issue gave rise to internal bickering between physicians, endocrinologists and pharmaceutical companies, as well as public debate, the most memorable of which are those of the 1960s and 1970s, when hormone treatment intended to prevent miscarriage and the first generation of birth-control pills proved to have serious side effects.[16]

An inquiry into the negative effect of hormones conducted by Håkan Rydin of the National Pharmaceutical Laboratory (NPL) in 1948 had a major impact on the domestic debate. His conclusion was that comprehensive, unchecked use of sex hormones could result in harmful side effects, and he recommended that they only be available through prescription.[17] While most hormone drugs were in fact already only dispensed via doctor's orders, not all were. By the end of the 1940s so-called "hormone creams" based on American products had begun to be sold by Swedish retailers. Paradoxically, advertisements were permitted to mention that the cream contained estrogen but said nothing about the properties or effects of the hormone. In commercial advertising, even common hormone preparations in phial and pill form were depicted almost as if they were over-the-counter cosmetics. An ad for "Female Sex Hormones" from Ciba was illustrated with five young, glamorous, bare-shouldered women posing inside a huge jar of cream.[18] Hormone creams were exclusively marketed as beauty products for women, to be applied to the face and bosom, and became quickly popular. In the first three years, more than 100,000 jars were sold.[19]

Doctors worried that some women self-medicated with these creams, e.g. as contraceptive, and by doing so could harm themselves.[20] Several women who had used the creams did in fact report genital bleeding. Some of these cases were incorrectly diagnosed as symptoms of uterine cancer, and completely unnecessary operations were performed.[21] But, according to the daily *Stockholms-Tidningen* in an article headlined, "Experts Put False Alarms to Rest," the creams were completely harmless as long as they were purchased from reputable Swedish firms who did not use high dosages.[22] One of these "experts" was Sven Rygaard of the foundation "Advertising Standards Authority for Free Medicine," who claimed that hormone doses less than 200,000 IU per kilo were incapable of causing side effects. "If it were the case that such a mild dose could be hazardous, millions of American women would be sick by now—instead of younger and prettier!"[23] Håkan Rydin was of another opinion altogether and wanted to set the allowable limit much lower. Besides, he was convinced that topical application of hormone cream was not the least bit beneficial.[24]

As director of the NPL, Rydin was a commanding presence in the public discourse on the merits and demerits of pharmaceutical products whose opinion could not be easily dismissed.[25] He also had the backing of the former head of gynecology at the Radiation Clinic, Professor James Heyman, who for years had warned against starry-eyed enthusiasm about hormone drugs.[26] In a critical article published in 1950 under the headline "Hormoner bör tas under kontroll" [Hormones should be under control], in the newspaper *Svenska Dagbladet*, Heyman explained that sex hormones could cause bleeding which made correctly diagnosing serious genital diseases all the more difficult.[27] This state of affairs had been pointed out in 1947 in a dissertation by Heyman's student and colleague Hans Ludvig Kottmeier, and even back then *Svenska Dagbladet* wondered whether the use of hormone drugs risked becoming excessive.[28] But Heyman indicated that there was also a risk that the drugs *themselves* could cause serious side effects, and he meant both hormone creams and prescription-only medicines.

Knowledge about the absolute effect of hormones was still tentative at best, he explained, adding that observations had already indicated a connection between hormones and cancer. For this reason, Kottmeier declared that physicians ought to show much more restraint in prescribing hormones. "In my opinion, hormone preparations should only be prescribed in serious cases, when no other treatment has proven effective, and then with the greatest of caution."[29]

Such public debate put Leo and other hormone companies in a precarious position. As if the fact that its hormone drugs did not always perform as expected was not enough, now there were rumors circulating that they could *cause* grave illnesses, including cancer. Leo noted at this point that sales were dropping off, and from reports submitted by its traveling propagandists, the company understood that doubts about the drug had begun to spread throughout the country's medical corps.[30] Leo did what they could to deny these rumors and after consulting with Professor of Histology Hjalmar Holmgren, formulated a stock answer for their agents to use when encountering anxious physicians:

> Synthetic and natal estrogen substances cannot possibly cause cancer, as documentation and experience attests. As we still know nothing about the heredity of cancer, we have been unable to come to any firm conclusions. By way of precaution, however, doctors should be informed that interstitial hemorrhage occurring even in the most prudent hormone treatment undertaken during menopause can be mistaken for the initial symptoms of uterine cancer, thereby causing a delay in proper treatment.[31]

Fears that hormone drugs could have serious side effects were not going to disappear anytime soon. Nor was the possible connection between cancer and estrogen preparations the only issue subject to critical discussion. In Denmark, a debate on gonadotropin treatment and the risk of "overstimulation" of the ovaries was well underway, focusing on no less than Løvens' and Leo's hitherto irreproachable Physex and Antex. That these drugs could bring about enlarged ovaries and cysts if taken in combination with one another first came to attention during the 1940s.[32] But the debate heated up considerably in 1951 when a physician reported that a young female with secondary amenorrhea passed away after a combination treatment.[33] Due to overstimulation, her ovaries rapidly grew to the size of a pair of clenched fists. Emergency surgery was performed but complications arose and her life could not be saved. The probable cause of death was determined to be shock.[34]

The combination of pregnant mare serum gonadotropin and chorionic gonadotropin had long been the standard treatment recommended by Leo with the backing of Axel Westman. This so-called "two-step method" was also described approvingly in numerous articles and mentioned in instruction manuals for physicians. Now it was suddenly being branded hazardous if not downright dangerous. Physician Poul Gøzsche, who reported the death in the Danish medical journal *Ugeskrift for Læger*, added that he had since been informed of other, similar cases and declared that due to the risks involved, he would never perform the treatment again.[35] Gøzsche's article opened the floodgates to a series of reports on more or less serious side effects caused by Antex–Physex.[36] However, the method still had its partisans.[37] One of them was endocrinologist Erik Rydberg of the Women's Clinic at Copenhagen University Hospital, who had helped develop it in the early 1940s and passionately trumpeted its value to the treatment of sterile women.[38] The problem, in his estimation, was not that gonadotropins could lead to overstimulation, but that this side effect was not always dealt with correctly. Despite his protests, the debate roused legitimate concern at Leo, which immediately sought Westman's advice. Weren't gonadotropin drugs free from side effects? Was the new combination of Antex and Gonadex just as dangerous? Westman's curt comment was that he himself had never encountered any "alarming complications" when prescribing Antex, Physex or Gonadex. "In my opinion, there is no reason to issue any warning regarding these preparations in their current dosages."[39]

Summing up, debate on the possible negative aspects of hormone drugs provoked two different reactions. The first was a reminder that the existing scientific knowledge of the endocrine system and the effects of hormone drugs was much less comprehensive than certain researchers had previously claimed. More and more hormones were being discovered and the interplay of endocrinal glands with each other and the nervous system appeared more and more complicated.[40] Uncertainty also reigned insofar as how effective hormone therapy was in actually restoring the function of "unhealthy" endocrinal organs or if only temporary improvement had occurred. This insight was expressed clearly by Westman himself who, in a lecture at the Royal Swedish Academy of Sciences on 13 April 1955, stated, "We now ask ourselves what regulates the functions of the endocrine organs, whose constitution is a precondition for a harmonious development and a normal physical and mental life. At the moment, we know far too little."[41]

The other reaction was more optimistic in tone and was based on the idea that if hormones could in fact cause or accelerate the development of cancer, then the same hormones might also be able to treat and militate the disease. An initial hope was that the rapid cell growth could be checked with the aid of a retardant factor, e.g. that breast cancer could be treated with male sex hormones and prostate cancer with female ones. This method did indeed work at times, but the problem was, as usual, more complicated. Different strategies were tested, like treatment of breast cancer with estrogen or a variety of combinative treatments.[42]

It was through these means that sex hormone preparations moved into a new field of medicine: oncology. Interest for this specialty had increased enormously, particularly in the United States but also in Sweden. At the Royal Caroline Hospital, hormone analyses intended to diagnose cancer, as well as hormone treatment of cancer, became common. From the 1950s on, Leo in particular redoubled its efforts to develop so-called "chemotherapeutic" medicine, intended to treat male sufferers.[43] The risk naturally remained that even these hormone preparations might induce serious side effects, but the long-term problems were weighed against the short-term dividend of delaying the inevitable.

AT THE CROSSROADS

Gonadex came into being at the crossroads where scientific, medical, financial and political hopes converged but were rarely fulfilled. It never became the "international sales success" Leo had hoped it would. The reason had nothing to do with a dearth of raw material, as Waldemar Gårdlund had feared, but simply that the drug did not work like it was supposed to. First of all, Gonadex was no medical success in the fight against involuntary infertility. Judging from Axel Westman's own statistics, it was the exception rather than the rule that women became pregnant with the help of Gonadex. Secondly, while Gonadex could certainly be used to treat many other diagnoses, it proved that the drug was difficult to standardize in accordance with international hCG standards. After tests conducted by the NPL and other pharmaceutical companies, inconsistencies in the declaration of contents were discovered, which radically hampered the ability of Gonadex to compete on the pharmaceutical market. Inquiries were launched but when Leo was unable to meet requirements, the drug was finally withdrawn. A year after its launch, there was no longer a registered preparation on the market called "Gonadex."

This fiasco created an air of tension between Leo, Axel Westman and the hormone lab at the Caroline Hospital, but did not lead to shutting down the Gonadex project altogether. After reconcentrating its strength more than six-fold on the advice of Christian Hamburger, Leo attempted to register Gonadex anew. An application for Gonadex featuring a potency of 600 IU was submitted in the summer of 1949 and another for Gonadex with 1,500 and 3,000 IU the autumn of 1950. As before, registration was temporarily approved pending final test results from the NPL.[44] "New Gonadex" was significantly stronger, but interestingly, strength was not the only difference.

The product description was new, too. Gone was the long list of indication areas, including infertility and sterility. Only primary and secondary amenorrhea and "hyperplasia irregularis glandularum endometrii" were now listed.[45] The original assertion that Gonadex stimulated follicle growth and estrogen production disappeared as well. Instead, the new pharmacological description states, "The existing mature follicles in the woman's ovaries might become *corpora lutea* under the influence of *Gonadex*." With a stroke, Leo (and Westman) made clear that Gonadex only contained the so-called "LH principal," which had a luteinizing effect. Furthermore, it was made clear that treatment of amenorrhea with Gonadex must always be combined with Antex, which contained the so-called "FSH principal," considered essential to follicular development. Moreover, indications for male patients were also somewhat different than in the original list, which included prostatic hyperplasia, i.e. enlarged prostate.[46] However, after receiving directives from the NPL, a more modest formulation stating that only *tests* for that particular diagnosis had been conducted was added.[47] Hence, Gonadex had undergone a distinct change of identity.

With approval of the registration application, Leo's production network went into full swing. A drug that would both fulfill the declaration and be standardized in an acceptable manner had to be delivered. A meeting was held between Leo's Högberg and Birger Ekman and Axel Westman over two days in September 1950. Together, they agreed that a large amount of urine from pregnant women would be reprocessed in order to facilitate a "total investigation" from chemical and biological perspectives. Preparations would begin at the factory in Helsingborg and each step in the process would be double-checked with two disparate biological testing methods at the laboratory in Stockholm. Westman promised that "the full resources of the laboratory will be made available," including the services of new star staffer Egon Diczfalusy.[48] Clinical trials were the next step, whose purpose was to once and for all determine the differences in effect between pure chorionic gonadotropin and ordinary preparations like "old" Physex, and to establish that prolonged treatment with Gonadex did not cause side effects. The report authored by Ekman after the planning session exuded optimism:

> We are convinced that Prof. Westman and Dr. Diczfalusy have every opportunity to conduct the planned work under the best possible circumstances. As arrangements have been made, the investigation ought to lead to a standard work that can definitively chart the biological, clinical, and commercial prospects of Gonadex.[49]

Leo's decision to carry on with Gonadex was however not a foregone conclusion. Dissenting voices from within the company were raised demanding that all ties with Axel Westman be cut immediately. Terminating work on Gonadex was clearly an alternative, freeing up money and time for other projects. Leo's hormone drug sales were also lagging, which was at least in part seen as a consequence of the public debate on their side effects. In order to bring clarity to the situation, Birger Ekman was given the task of performing what today would be called "business analytics." Ekman proceeded from the guiding principles Leo now stuck to in its research and development. The most crucial criterion was that all undertakings must have the potential to result in a commercially viable product. Coming up with patentable innovations for use in broad indication areas naturally had the greatest chance of success, but it was also important to conduct less-exacting projects that could pay out smaller but surer dividends. Either way, in Ekman's opinion, it was essential that Leo show palpable results which either could be used in its propaganda campaigns or lead to new products sooner than later.[50]

Ekman divided what he considered Leo's most pressing tasks into three types: large-scale projects, short-term work and research to shore up already existing preparations. He put Gonadex in the third group. The conclusion was that it would be wisest for Leo to see the project through, so that the resources already invested would not have been in vain. He stated frankly that Gonadex was "a persistent problem that needed to be solved, especially considering the possible financial yield."[51] He also deemed it worthwhile to keep Westman on retainer since he could do invaluable experimental and clinical work for the firm. Furthermore, endocrinology as such continued to expand internationally, both within industry and the university, and Ekman insisted that Leo could not afford to miss that train.

> We can assume that developments in endocrinology will continue and provide better knowledge on the interaction between different hormones. This means that even preparations that Leo is already manufacturing could be assigned completely new indication areas. This includes Gonadex, which might possibly prove useful in the treatment of male endocrine disorder. —The close collaboration between Profes-

sor Westman's laboratory and clinic is already of great significance to our efforts in endocrinology and should prove even greater.[52]

Anticipation that new indication areas for Gonadex would be revealed through continued research and clinical practice was brought up on numerous occasions. Aside from the conviction that the drug should be able to be used to treat male sterility, which had been broached as early as the opening of the sperm lab at the Caroline Hospital, the possibility that it could be used to treat male menopause was also deliberated. If it worked, which Westman apparently considered medically plausible, the potential market for Gonadex would naturally balloon. Thus Gonadex was still a cure "seeking" its diseases, to borrow a term from philosopher Rein Vos.[53] Moreover, hope that Gonadex could be sold to foreign markets remained undiminished; despite all the problems, international demand for a purified chorionic gonadotropin was still supposed to be high.[54] Leo's attitude toward Westman was undeniably instrumental but hardly surprising. For a business to become successful on the free market, it has to make money, and the value of knowledge, in this case Westman's, was ultimately measured by what it could contribute to the bottom line.[55]

MAKING "NEW GONADEX"

The goal was set and the means of achieving it determined. But making a new Gonadex did not go as smoothly as Leo wished. A document from December 1950 listing expenses incurred by Leo's consultants and external research also characterizes collaboration with Westman and his lab staff as problematic.[56] The team had probably not managed to complete its task at the agreed-upon pace. What Leo wanted was a guarantee that "eventual increased income generated by the lab not be used to expand research beyond Leo's sphere of interest, but rather be reinvested in the task set by Leo regarding Gonadex, etc."[57] Leo was not least dissatisfied with Axel Westman's efforts; he just did not seem able to get the work he promised and been paid for done. Still, he continued to almost compulsively take on new projects.[58]

On 6 February 1951, Leo convened a strategy meeting, which was perhaps something of a crisis meeting, too, at which Gonadex, Axel Westman and the future of the lab at Caroline Hospital were discussed. Its purpose was to brainstorm ideas to "get the best results out of the Westman group."[59] Experience had apparently taught them that it was necessary to anchor collaboration in clearly defined tasks and reasonable cost calculations, determined before the work began. The conditions Leo set for agreeing to continue funding Westman after the summer were that the ongoing Gonadex project (and certain complementary work) be wrapped up no later than 1 July 1951; that a preliminary report on the activity of by-products of peptic indigestion be written within two months; and that a plan for revising all of Leo's hormone drugs (including declaration of contents and appropriate packaging) be drawn up. Westman was furthermore to compile a report on a new pituitary gland hormone drug, collate material for a new brochure containing the clinical results of Gonadex treatment, and revise the article on Gonadex in Leo's product catalogue. At the same time, Leo dangled the prospect that Westman's funding could be *increased* provided sales of the hormone drug increased significantly. "In the case of Gonadex, however, it should be said that we are not talking about sales figures below SEK 50,000–100,000 annually." It was high time Gonadex began generating income.

In issuing these directives, Leo's intent was to

> guarantee that work on Gonadex be completed as swiftly as possible (from now on, funding is dependent on the first half-year's work being discharged in a satisfactory manner). Furthermore, it appears that by doing things in this manner, the necessary advertising material in connection with revision of the hormone drug can be produced within a reasonable time frame. Finally, sales of both old and new hormone drugs are coupled with the opportunity for Professor Westman to receive an increase of the reduced subsidy allowance for the year beginning 7 January 1951.[60]

This belt-tightening was intended to get New Gonadex on the market once and for all. And it turned out to be a wise move, as the Medical Board finally approved all three strengths of Gonadex on 21 November 1951.[61] Westman and his staff were not the only decisive factor in this achievement, as Leo had also managed to enroll prominent endocrinologist Christian Hamburger of Statens Seruminstitut in Copenhagen. Hamburger had helped establish the international standard for chorionic gonadotropin in 1938 and had plenty of experience in dealing with the problems that can arise in the standardization procedure. His encyclopedic knowledge of the field had recently been displayed in the monograph *Hypofysens, Kønskirtlernes og Binyrernes Hormoner* [The hormones of the hypophysis, gonads and adrenal glands] (1950).[62] Enlisting Hamburger increased Gonadex' credibility and should, as Leo pointed out in a letter to the Medical Board, "be a sufficient guarantee that the preparation contains the declared amount of chorionic gonadotropin."[63] Standardization, as mentioned above, was as much about trust as it was about facts and figures.

Leo continued to make minor adjustments to the declaration and contents of the drug.[64] They were forced to add a paragraph in the catalogue as to the fact that Gonadex could, despite everything, cause undesirable side effects.

> It cannot be ruled out that lutein cysts may appear at a later stage during or after a combinatory Gonadex treatment . . . . Should the ovaries become enlarged or should other signs of overstimulation be detected (abdominal pain, meteorism, etc.), treatment should immediately be discontinued and the patient prescribed bed rest for a specified period.[65]

Thus the Danish debate on the risks of gonadotropin trumped Westman's assurances that Gonadex was free of side effects. With these measures, it appears that Gonadex' place in the medical arsenal was secured, at least for now. New Gonadex began to be shipped and according to advertising from 1952, it was again being recommended in the treatment of sterility.[66] This time, however, pharmaceutical competitors appear not to have submitted any protests to the NPL, which had been the case when it was registered the first time four years earlier. Perhaps Organon and Løvens conducted their own tests proving to their satisfaction that Gonadex was now indeed standardized. However, it may also be that the competition no longer bothered with Gonadex, since it was no longer much of a threat to Pregnyl and Physex.

For all parties concerned, however, it was clear that the current standard for chorionic gonadotropin had become outdated. In response, an expert committee for biological standardization at the World Health Organization launched an international comparative study of hCG in order to establish a new and better standard, to be conducted at the Department of Biological Standards at the National Institute for Medical Research in London. Twelve laboratories were invited to participate, and thanks to its long experience with Gonadex, the Women's Clinic at the Royal Caroline Hospital was one of them. To be able to afford to accept the offer, Axel Westman applied for a new grant from the Knut and Alice Wallenberg Foundation.[67] A year later, Westman could report that work had proceeded according to plan; new methods of quantification had been developed and a functional standard preparation was within reach.[68] This was of significance to both the manufacture of pharmaceuticals and hCG research. But even if Gonadex was given a new identity and the world a new standard for hCG, far from all the scientific questions had been answered.

Leo's business analytics consultant Birger Ekman was right when he assumed that endocrinology would "keep on" growing. Gonadotropins in particular continued to be the subject of intense international interest for both experimental and clinical endocrinology throughout the 1950s. Interest in gonadotropins was evident in both the increased number of scholarly publications on the topic and the efforts to arrange scientific conferences dedicated to it. A "Gonadotrophin Club" was even founded during a conference in Geneva in 1953, which subsequently arranged a number of international gonadotropin conferences in Europe. Similar conferences were soon held in the United States as well, the first of which was in Gatlinburg, Tennessee in 1959.[69] Thus researchers learned more and more about gonadotropins, not the least about the complexity of the subject, a fact to which Axel Westmen attested in his speech marking the tenth anniversary of the Swedish Endocrine Society in 1956:

> As far as the protein hormone is concerned, we have of course not come as far. This makes it more difficult to adduce the role some play. As an example, we must hasten to set a question mark in place of the question as to the most principal task the chorionic gonadotropin has in the organism.[70]

THE ROYAL CAROLINE HOSPITAL TAKES OVER THE HORMONE LABORATORY

Leo's determined efforts at structuring Westman's tasks can be seen as a symptom of an overall restructuring of Leo's research policy. One after another, the majority of its regular consultants (and other regular, external expenses) were eliminated, and instead, part-time and very precise—"expedient"—research assignments in line with Leo's particular business interests were arranged. Leo also set up its own pharma-biological lab where preliminary animal testing could be conducted, further reducing its dependence on external consultation.[71] Another direct consequence of this policy was that the board of directors (at the behest of its chairman) eventually earmarked funds for a dedicated research foundation, whose purpose was to support only such research "which directly or indirectly falls within the scope of the company's field of interest."[72]

These changes in research policy also affected the hormone lab at the Royal Caroline Hospital. As work on Gonadex ran long, the lab had run into financial difficulties, which worsened for each month that passed. The situation stabilized through rationalization in combination with an increased demand for hormone analysis.[73] But despite becoming as good as self-sustaining, Leo decided to completely liquidate its interests in the lab, since it was no longer considered of evident value to the firm.[74] The first step in breaking with the Caroline Hospital was taken in August 1952, when the director Svante Wiström explained to Westman that it was time for Leo to turn the reins over to the hospital.[75] Within the company there was some concern that Westman's pride would be hurt, which could lead to a break with him, too. Leo was eager to maintain a good relationship with Westman, who not only possessed useful knowledge and valuable contacts but also sensitive information about the internal operations of the firm.[76] To put it another way, Leo wanted to terminate its formal, organizational collaboration with the Caroline Hospital while keeping Westman in its network. After the meeting, Leo sent an ingratiating letter to Westman, explaining the situation.

> Thanks not the least to your pioneering efforts, the Hormone Laboratory has been consolidated to such a degree that it is now an integral and indispensible element in public health care in Sweden. This incorporation is also marked on a budgetary level, insofar as the Hormone Lab is self-sufficient. Thus every sound reason speaks in favor of fiscal responsibility for the lab to be transferred to the trustees of the hospital.[77]

To its relief, Westman accepted the decision, apparently without griping. The importance Leo placed on the relationship between the two parties can be seen in the company's plan to celebrate the sixtieth anniversary of Westman's birth, though it had an ulterior motive. Leo felt that there was a certain "advertising and goodwill value" in marking the occasion, "for Professor Westman incontestably has a solid reputation in Sweden as our foremost hormone expert and his sixtieth birthday will certainly be the object of much publicity."[78] Leo first contemplated giving Westman a research grant as a present, but since it was assumed that his research would be unlikely to result in any new, marketable products, it was instead decided to give him something a little more personal: a free trip to Japan.[79]

This petty attitude toward Westman's usefulness can also be noted in a marked decline in interest in financing his future scientific conferences. In October 1953 Westman submitted a request for funds to arrange an international hormone conference in Stockholm the coming year. Fifteen researchers, mostly from Great Britain and Switzerland, were expected to attend, and Westman asked Leo to cover their travel expenses. In return, two of Leo's own staff members, including Bertil Högberg, would be invited.[80] Previously Leo had gladly supported such events, but this time the answer was no. A report from the board reads that, "in Leo's opinion, the expense is disproportionate to the benefit to the firm."[81] Considering the status the conference could lend to Leo's international reputation, donating a smaller, symbolic sum was suggested, but in the end, Leo chose to decline to participate.[82]

After wrapping up discussions with Westman, Leo contacted the Royal Caroline Hospital to give formal notice of its intention to terminate its contract with the hormone lab.[83] A long term of notice and other bureaucratic red tape meant that the matter was only finally settled on 30 June 1954. At that instant, Leo's arrangement with the Royal Caroline Hospital and the Swedish government was a closed chapter.[84] As a consequence, the lab was incorporated into the Women's Clinic and the small staff, including Egon Diczfalusy, put on the hospital payroll. The inventory was turned over for free. The hormone lab would do just fine on its own thanks to the fact that routine endocrine work steadily continued to expand. Aside from serving the women's clinic and most of the hospital's other clinics, by the end of the decade the lab was associated with close to one hundred hospitals and clinics throughout Sweden, analyzing over ten thousand hormone samples annually.[85] Furthermore, the development of hormone research and therapy at the clinic was significantly aided by the numerous grants received from the Knut and Alice Wallenberg Foundation. Aside from Westman himself receiving five grants between 1951 and 1958, the Caroline received an extraordinary gift just before breaking with Leo.[86]

19 December 1953 marked the one hundredth anniversary of the birth of the banker and politician Knut A. Wallenberg. To consolidate the memory of its founder, the Foundation decided to establish a special bequest in his honor. According to endocrinologist Rolf Luft, the idea was to promote some form of cancer research. Foundation director Axel Wallenberg consulted the head of the Sloan-Kettering Institute for Cancer Research in New York, who suggested investing in endocrinology, which as stated previously, was emerging as a promising route to improved cancer treatment.[87] Once the foundation was convinced that "endocrine research is currently one of the most significant, still relatively unexplored fields of medical research," it put one million crowns at the Caroline Institute's disposal "as a contribution to endocrinological research in our country."[88] The donation would be used to create a research institute to coordinate and develop work being done at the Caroline and Serafim Hospitals.

Plans had been in the works for some time before the actual announcement.[89] Sketches for a new, three-storey building on land adjacent to the Caroline Hospital were produced which would accommodate nursing wards, an out-patient clinic, research labs and an administrative unit. Rolf Luft, head of the division of endocrinology at the Serafim Hospital, who had been named docent of endocrinology in 1949 and had long enjoyed a good relationship with the Foundation, was considered the obvious leading candidate for the position of chief of the new institute.[90] But this vision was only partly realized. When the proposal was up for approval by the faculty board in the summer of 1953, one of its members, Professor Nanna Svartz, asked that it be tabled pending further investigation. A committee was appointed, consisting of several professors with a special expertise in the discipline, among whom we find Axel Westman. The committee recommended a completely different solution. Instead of a new building with a self-contained "Wallenberg Institute," it recommended that a new division of endocrinology be opened at the Caroline Hospital's existing women's clinic, where comprehensive hormone research was already being conducted.[91] Luft was named division chief and awarded the position "Laborator" (Associate Professor), while Westman continued to be head of the Women's Clinic and its only full professor. Luft was crestfallen.[92] But for Westman and the Women's Clinic, it was a boost, which probably eased the pain of breaking with Leo.[93] After writing to thank the Foundation personally for its donation, Westman, together with Sten Friberg, Principal of the Caroline Institute, proposed that Axel Wallenberg be elevated to honorary Doctor of Medicine at the institute in 1954, which he was in due course.[94]

CHAPTER EIGHT

More Than Gonadex

HORMONE THERAPY as practiced in Sweden during the heyday of the Welfare State was not just about mass-produced, state-controlled drugs like Gonadex, but also gonadotropin preparations produced on a more modest scale, which allowed them to avoid government inspection. In this chapter, I shall focus on two of these used by Swedish gynecological clinics in the treatment of involuntarily childless women. In the first case, finely minced pituitary glands of slaughtered calves were used, in the second, extracts from the pituitary glands of deceased humans. From a contemporary medical perspective, these may seem odd, but they are not irrelevant from the perspective of the history of science. For they were part of the process through which endocrinology and gynecology were integrated, and which was also significant to the development of other, "proper" medicines, whose gonadotropin hormones were extracted from the urine of women who had undergone menopause. The chapter provides further insight into the interplay between the development of a drug and clinical practice during the period under investigation, as well as understanding of the complexity of the therapeutic culture to which Gonadex belonged.

AXEL WESTMAN'S BOVINE PITUITARY IMPLANT

One aspect of Axel Westman's hormone therapy which needs to be discussed in order to give a fair and complete account of his work, is that while successively introducing commercial hormone drugs at his gynecological clinic, he also began treating patients with endocrine glands. The preceding chapter may give the misleading impression that such operations were out-moded by the time of factory-made gonadotropins and sex hormones.[1] However, in contrast with the infamous rejuvenation therapists, such as Steinach and Voronoff, and Morris and his colleagues who used ovarian transplants (mentioned in Chapter One), Westman used pituitary, not sexual glands. The method had many names—pituitary transplant, implant, "in-plant" or simply "pituitary transfer." Westman was not alone in using pituitary glands in clinical hormone therapy in Sweden. What's more, this now-forgotten technique was also being performed in Germany.[2]

The most outspoken advocate of glandular transplantation in Sweden was Eskil Kylin (1889–1975), chief of medicine at the Central Hospital in Jönköping, who often—and according to his own testimony, very successfully—used the pituitary glands of slaughtered calves to treat a wide array of complaints, from psoriasis and alopecia to consumption and dwarfism.[3] A large number of pituitary transplants were also performed at the Women's Clinic at Sahlgrenska University Hospital in Gothenburg.[4] Another seemingly unorthodox technique tested by Westman in an attempt to create an artificial gonadotropin effect was blood transfusion, where the hormone-rich blood of pregnant women was transferred to female patients. According to Westman, both of these procedures had a substantial advantage over standard hormone therapy since "one can immediately introduce significant amounts of hormones to the organism, which is not possible with factory-made hormones."[5]

Westman began performing pituitary gland transplants during his time in Lund where he, together with Dora Jacobsohn, conducted both animal experiments and clinical tests on patients.[6] Inspired by Kylin, Westman chose to use fresh pituitary glands recently removed from calf craniums. His initial intention was to investigate the extent to which this glandular tissue could produce gonadotropic hormones and, if it could do so to a satisfactory degree, whether it could be used in the treatment of women suffering from primary or secondary amenorrhea brought on by hormone deficiency. In contrast to Kylin, Westman entertained no notions that the tissue would meld with what function remained. Instead, his goal in using both these unusual techniques was to achieve what he called a "hormone jolt," a temporary effect.[7]

The results of early clinical testing were generally disappointing, though favorable effects could be confirmed in individual cases. It was not that the problem had been eradicated but rather that the women experienced a somewhat improved "overall state of health." Westman reasoned that it might be that the hormone-rich tissue in fact stimulated increased productivity in the patients' own pituitary glands.[8] This small sign of hope was enough to encourage Westman to continue his clinical trials after moving to the Caroline Hospital. He availed himself of bovine pituitary glands ordered directly from the wartime National Food Administration in Stockholm; in 1943 no less than sixteen calf heads per month were being requisitioned. Some were probably used in experimental study but not all. Westman explained that "the pituitary gland is implanted in patients with certain hormonal illnesses. The procedure in question has proven to be the most effective method of treatment."[9] In a letter addressed to a colleague, he describes the operation.

> The technique requires access to as much fresh bovine pituitary material as possible, never more than 1–2 hours after slaughter. It is removed from the cranium and chopped into very fine pieces. These are either injected or a small incision can be made to insert them.[10]

In the same letter, Westman goes on to explain that he usually "places them in the labia maj., where nutrition is particularly abundant." Thus unlike Kylin, who implanted brain tissue in the abdomen, Westman preferred to implant minced bovine pituitary glands into the outer labia of the patient. It could also be injected ventrogluteally. Judging from correspondence between Westman and some of the patients he treated in 1943, he also performed pituitary implants on male patients.[11] While it is not possible to determine why these operations were performed, the letters do reveal that the results were not immediately forthcoming. One of his statements indicates that such delays were not unusual.

> It often happens that the effect of a pituitary implantation can take as long as 5–6 months to manifest itself. Thus it is too early to determine with any certainty whether or not this initial treatment has led to results. Regardless, we should wait until the fall when both [John Doe] and [Jane Doe] can come for a check-up, at which time we may choose to repeat the procedure.[12]

The gentleman in question had undergone several bovine implant operations. He reported that an ulceration appeared on one side of his chest, so we can assume that Westman chose to make his incision there.[13] The positive effects of each attempt seem to have been insignificant. The outcome was the same for a woman who, along with hormone injections, was given pituitary implants on separate occasions during the spring and autumn of 1944. In a letter to Westman, she complains that her health has been "most unsatisfactory" since the operations; her weight had plummeted and she was no longer menstruating. Furthermore, she was experiencing problems with her nerves. In response, Westman provided no more detailed diagnosis than "internal secretory disorder."[14] In other words, the result of the hormone "jolts" was less than impressive. Patients were plagued with suppurating scars and in most cases the body rejected the inserted tissue after only a few days. According to the numbers in Westman's article "Hormonala behandlingsmetoder inom gynekologien" [Hormone therapy in gynecology] (1943), "favorable results" (in treating diagnosed cases of primary and secondary amenorrhea) had been achieved in only five of twenty-four cases.[15]

Using bovine pituitary glands was chancy, which was probably a prime reason why human pituitary glands were also tested in clinical practice, a move not considered uncontroversial. In 1943, Axel Westman was contacted by a woman who said she had tried to persuade a doctor in Lund to perform a human pituitary gland transplant on her, but that he had refused, most likely on ethical grounds. The doctor was apparently afraid that it "could cause offence, if it came out [in public]."[16] Exactly what constituted his moral predicament was not mentioned in the letter. But the physician's hesitancy comes as no surprise since the handling of human tissue was circumscribed by cultural restrictions and taboos.[17] The woman did not ask Westman to personally perform the transplant but rather that he might try and convince the physician in Lund to tackle the task. She stated that she had more than self-interest in mind. "It is certainly also of great scientific interest to find out if the human pituitary gland has a more powerful effect and better result than bovine glands."[18] In a subsequent communiqué, the same woman reported that the desired transplant was finally performed on 4 April 1944. It probably took place at Westman's clinic at the Caroline Hospital, for the woman asked Westman if he thought she should book a new operation there in the fall.[19]

I have not been able to find any more information about Axel Westman's use of human pituitary tissue. Why this operation was performed and where the glands came from is unknown. Most likely they were removed by coroners performing autopsies, eventually routine procedure in Sweden. There is however an example of human pituitary glands being acquired from another source. In 1944, Sten Floderus defended his thesis in histology at Uppsala University on the morphology of the pituitary gland.[20] Most of his study material was gathered from postmortems conducted at Swedish hospitals, though some had a more macabre back story, which became known far beyond the medical world: they came from men who had been beheaded in Nazi Germany. Their pituitary glands had been removed and stored at the Department of Anatomy at the University of Berlin, which is where Floderus found them. Floderus told a reporter from the daily *Dagens Nyheter* that during a visit to Berlin in 1938, he had also been offered pituitary glands from women in order to compare the sexes, but that he had declined since that would have led to the date for the women's execution being set for his sake. German medical experiments, he added, were beginning to turn unsavory.[21]

One of the reasons Westman experimented so persistently with fresh pituitary glands was that he hoped that the method in the end could be used for treating sterility in difficult cases where the usual medicaments fell short. He did not publish much on this subject, but did share his hopes with his colleagues, both in private and in public.[22] When the very first Scandinavian endocrinology congress was held in Stockholm in 1947, Westman used the opportunity to speak about his "clinical experience with pituitary gland implantation." He explained that the method was extremely complicated and could only be performed in certain, intricate cases, but that it was still "proportionately rewarding." Furthermore, he hinted that a commercial product based on pituitary extract was possibly in the offing.[23]

At Leo, interest in transplantations was extremely limited. On the other hand, the prospect of being able to derive and test purified extracts from fresh bovine pituitary glands was enticing. Abattoirs in Stockholm and Malmö were contacted and work began. A clinical study was planned. "There is enough patient material at the women's clinic in order to be able to conduct a clinical test [of bovine pituitary gland extract] in short order," Leo pronounced in January 1948.[24] However, I have not been able to discover whether a systematic clinical test was actually conducted at the Caroline Hospital at this juncture.

By 1949, Westman had prescribed bovine pituitary glands (often in concert with estrogen hormones) for several hundred patients, most of whom were women diagnosed with "menstrual disorders."[25] The results continued to vary wildly, but some of the women eventually became pregnant, which Westman interpreted as proof that their ovarian functions had in fact been restored to normality thanks to the implanted pituitary material.[26] And the method was not abandoned after Gonadex was on the market. The archives disgorge a letter from a woman in Denmark who underwent two pituitary operations in the fall of 1950. Since she preferred injections before the operation and wished to avoid the side effects she had previously suffered, she wondered if it would be possible to replace the glands with a "powerful series" of Gonadex. Westman recommended that she continue the treatment as before.[27]

As far as I can judge, the pituitary transplant method culminated at the beginning of the 1950s, by which time it had received full scientific support in the form of a Ph.D thesis defended at the Caroline Institute by Westman's student and colleague Nils Erik Påhlsson.[28] Påhlsson processed data culled from many of the hormone treatments performed to combat various menstrual disorders at the hospital's women's clinic between 1943 and 1948. The sample consisted of close to four hundred cases treated in accordance with Westman's guidelines, including many who were prescribed bovine pituitary glands. The substance of Påhlsson's survey is an echo of Westman's own thesis: ordinary sex hormone drugs (from Leo) are as a rule serviceable in favorable circumstances, while implants are preferable in cases where endocrine dysfunction is more profound. Transplantation is furthermore lauded as less invasive, since the only side effects reported were abscesses and allergic reactions.[29] Påhlsson's thesis concludes with the words, "In therapy-resistant and prognostically unpropitious cases, as well as in cases with more pronounced hypopituitarism caused by pluriglandualar infiltraton, pituitary gland implantation is the best method of treatment currently available."[30] Thus the advantage of this form of therapy lay in the fact that in one stroke, the patient received all the hormones produced by the pituitary gland, including both the LH and FSH principals. At least, that was the hypothesis.

There are examples of fresh pituitary glands from calves or humans being implanted in the 1950s, but I have not been able to discover any evidence of the method being carried out at the Caroline Hospital after this period. The method certainly hovered in an ethical gray area and likely vanished together with Westman.[31] Relevant to the issue is that its lab conducted analyses of bovine pituitary glands, which proved that they did not contain the abundant quantity of hormones Westman had presumed. In fact, the amount of gonadotropin was negligible, which is perhaps not such a surprise considering that the glands were taken from immature calves. Contrary to what Påhlsson claimed, it could certainly not be ruled out that the implants primarily had a *psychological* effect on patients, what would later be known as the "placebo effect."[32]

So far, the fate of the bovine pituitary gland can be compared to the tale of the remedy THX, manually extracted from the thymus gland of calves. Behind THX stood Elis Sandberg (1910–1989), a Swedish veterinarian who graduated from the School of Veterinary Medicine in 1949 and proceeded to immerse himself in the study of the significance of the thymus gland to the immune system. Sandberg was convinced that it was possible to manufacture a thymus hormone effective against several types of cancer (and other diseases as well). THX treatment was not much different from Westman's concurrent transplants; in both instances, fresh bovine glandular preparations were used in a frankly capricious manner from a scientific point of view. The thymus was certainly not a conventional endocrine gland like the pituitary, but there were differences of a sociological nature as well. Sandberg was neither professor nor physician. He was not associated with an established hospital where the condition of patients was judged and monitored. He did not publish systematic results in academic journals and he was not a member of any network of established medical researchers who could offer their qualified support. On the other hand, there were not hundreds but rather tens of thousands of sufferers who had confidence in his preparation—a patient organization, the "National Association for Thymus Research," established solely to support Sandberg, evolved into something of a popular movement. While Westman was allowed to perform his pituitary transplants in peace and quiet and without much critical scrutiny, Sandberg was subjected to massive criticism from medical health professionals. In time, THX caused an enormous scientific and mass media debate which ultimately concerned the difficulty in objectively confirming the characteristics of a drug and separate it from the body's own capacity for self-healing.[33]

The complex of problems surrounding pituitary glands did not prevent physicians and gynecologists from using them in practice. In other words, the tradition of using both commercial, factory-made hormone drugs and in-house, gland-based hormone preparations persisted. With one significant change. Instead of minced calf glands, the Caroline Hospital switched to purified human pituitary extract, so-called "human pituitary gonadotropins." This new technique and its relationship to contemporary developments in the pharmaceutical industry will be dealt with next. As I hope to show, Leo was one of the first corporations to show interest in this field of expertise. One reason was their need to complement Gonadex, but it was also motivated by the influence exerted by its consultants.

CARL AXEL GEMZELL'S HUMAN PITUITARY EXTRACT

In the early 1950s, two comprehensive British surveys evaluating the preceding decades' therapeutic efforts combating infertility were published. Both reported that nearly every other woman who visited a fertility clinic eventually conceived.[34] However, they also claimed that far from all these pregnancies could necessarily be interpreted as a direct result of medical treatment. Strangely, merely undergoing a routine examination could be just as effective. Statistically, the odds of an involuntarily childless woman becoming pregnant were even greater if she was examined but declined hormone therapy. Researchers in the Unites States came to the same shocking conclusion: in cases of ovulatory failure, untreated women succeeded in becoming pregnant more often than the treated.[35] Hormone drugs, which only a few years previously had been praised as a miracle cure, were now seen in a new light. Many gynecologists, at least in the UK, were of the opinion that their therapeutic value was strictly marginal.[36]

At the same time as the medical value of commercial hormone preparations was being challenged, new avenues of reproductive research were being pursued. Since simply meeting and conversing with an expert seemed so significant, the psychological aspect of infertility garnered increasing attention. Still, the endocrinologists and pharmaceutical companies refused to give up; the dream of discovering a drug that cured involuntary sterility was still alive.

At the Women's Clinic of the Caroline Hospital and its now state-owned hormone lab, research on sex hormones, gonadotropins and diverse endocrine disorders continued unabated throughout the fifties. Axel Westman had hardly finalized his work on Gonadex and the standardization of the chorionic gonadotropin when, in 1954, he submitted a new application to the Knut and Alice Wallenberg Foundation for funds to resume his research on the pituitary gland's production of gonadotropic hormones.[37] Adhering to the original theory of Bernhard Zondek and Selmar Aschheim from the 1920s, Westman had long claimed that the pituitary gland's gonadotropin likely had two distinct principals (possibly even two distinct hormones), one follicle-stimulating (FSH) and one luteinizing (LH), and that both needed to be present in a specific quantitative relationship in order for the "full gonadotropic effect" to be obtained.[38] If not, hormone imbalance would occur, with failure to ovulate and sterility as a result. Westman's intention was to conduct a close study of this circumstance with the aid of the refined analytical methods conceived for determining the new standard for chorionic gonadotropin. In his application, he explained:

> The task the laboratory currently considers the most urgent is quantitatively analyzing the production of the FSH and LH hormones of the pituitary gland under both healthy conditions and functional disorder with the aid of the above-mentioned method. This will be an exhaustive and time-consuming job. If it can be accomplished . . . then we have good reason to expect that profound advances will have been achieved in the matter of pituitary gonadotropin production and our chances of influencing the same.[39]

The grant was awarded and with it and other financial backing, the gaze of hormone research could again be trained on Westman's favorite gland, the human pituitary gland.[40] Biochemical efforts to purify gonadotropin extracts from human pituitary glands (removed at autopsy) were undertaken, as were experimental and clinical studies of the extract. As far as I have been able to discern, Westman himself did not participate much in this research. Not because he was not active in his later years; on the contrary, he was remarkably productive, but his attention shifted to cancer research and the effect hormones had upon the nervous system. Work on the FSH/LH problematic seems to have been taken over instead by a younger generation at the Caroline Hospital, including the troika of Carl Axel Gemzell, Egon Diczfalusy and Karl-Gunnar Tillinger, all of whom may be considered students of Westman. With this changing of the guard, research into the role of gonadotropins in the treatment of sterility also took a new turn.

Carl Axel Gemzell (1910–2007) was a gynecologist and endocrinologist whom latter-day colleagues usually cite (somewhat ahistorically) as the true pioneer in the field of the medical treatment of sterility.[41] When he began his academic and clinical career, it was far from certain that it would take the turn it did. Though Westman was in fact Gemzell's supervisor, their research goals differed radically. Gemzell conducted his dissertation work at the Wenner-Gren Institute, not at the Caroline Hospital, and took delivery of his purified hormones from the company Pharmacia, not Leo. Nor did his dissertation have any direct connection with the issue of sterility, but rather dealt with developing a biochemical method for studying the effect of certain hormones on the adrenal cortex. His dissertation was based on the new isotope methodology and was published as a supplement to the first issue of *Acta Endocrinologica* (which Westman edited), but was not well received.[42] Faculty opponent Mirjam Furuhjelm, herself a former assistant and student of Westman's who became Sweden's first female Associate Professor of Obstetrics and Gynecology (at the Royal Caroline Institute) the same year, was of the opinion that it had so many scientific shortcomings that Gemzell should withdraw his dissertation.[43] While he did not, he received a mediocre grade, which at the time was usually tantamount to putting the brakes on a presumptive academic career.

According to Egon Diczfalusy, Gemzell took the debacle hard and decided to leave not only Stockholm but Sweden altogether.[44] He moved to the United States, where he spent two years as visiting scholar at the San Francisco and Berkeley campuses of the University of California. Under the leadership of renowned biochemists and endocrinologists like Herbert Evans and Choh Hao Li, he increased his familiarity with both gonadotropin research and the art of extracting hormones from pituitary tissue. Gemzell's newly-acquired expertise was much sought-after in Sweden and when he eventually returned he was awarded both an internship at Westman's clinic and a multi-year research contract at the King Gustaf V Research Institute, which was associated with the Caroline Hospital, under the leadership of Professor Nanna Svartz.[45] In his new role, Gemzell resumed his research on pituitary hormones, dedicating himself to purifying gonadotropins extracted from human pituitary glands and conducting biological tests on hypophysectomized lab rats.

Another of this new generation's leading researchers was Egon Diczfalusy. Along with running the hormone lab, Diczfalusy conducted studies on the hormone production of the placenta at the behest of Westman, and in 1953 received his Ph.D and was named Associate Professor of the new field of "Experimental Endocrinology" at the Caroline Institute.[46] His experimental bent was a valuable asset in this otherwise clinical environment, but he also collaborated with others, including an Edinburgh-based research team. Diczfalusy also followed in Westman's footsteps in another respect when he accepted a job as consultant at Leo.[47] In this way, contact between the erstwhile partners was maintained, even after the administration of the hormone lab had been transferred to the Caroline Hospital. According to the contract he signed in the autumn of 1954, Diczfalusy received an annual wage, annual travel expenses and compensation for any other expenses incurred while on assignment for Leo. Diczfalusy could also look forward to royalties for any drug he eventually contributed to producing: one percent of sales and four percent on licensing.[48]

In the mid-fifties, Gemzell initiated a close collaboration with Diczfalusy and gynecologist Karl-Gunnar Tillinger. Westman refrained, or was perhaps kept away, from participating. This collective expertise in combination with the infrastructure at its disposal in Stockholm gave Gemzell the opportunity to conduct experimental and clinical studies of the pituitary gonadotropin he succeeded in producing.[49] An interesting result of the team's efforts was presented at the third *Acta Endocrinologica* congress held in Leiden in the summer of 1958, subsequently accepted for publication as "Clinical Effect of Human Pituitary Follicle-Stimulating Hormone" by the Endocrine Society's *Journal of Endocrinology and Metabolism*.[50] Quite contrary to what Westman and company had claimed ten years ago in "Crystalline Human Chorionic Gonadotrophin and Its Biological Action"—but fully in line with clinical experience—Gemzell, Diczfalusy and Tillinger stated that the biological effect of Gonadex was modest at best. On the other hand the new extract, provisionally named "human pituitary FSH," appeared to exert a potent effect. However, and this was the salient point, *if the two were combined, the results were even more highly tangible.*

One such combined treatment was performed on seven female patients diagnosed with amenorrhea, and in most cases a notable effect on the ovaries, including follicle rupture, ovulation and corpus luteum development, could be confirmed. Encouragingly, no immediate side effects were detected. Though the study was based on a very small patient sample, the authors still drew the general conclusion that the pituitary extract they used contained the much-desired FSH, which together with Gonadex LH produced "full gonadotropin effect." On the other hand, they dared not claim that they had finally solved the mystery of how the pituitary gland produced a gonadotropin hormone which contained both FSH and LH or if it was in fact a case of two different types of gonadotropin hormones.[51]

In a way, the article confirmed Westman's prior opinion that Gonadex should be complemented with other hormone drugs. In clinical use, Gonadex, as well as Physex, was also used regularly in combination with Antex or its analogues. But the results, at least insofar as sterility was concerned, were still hardly encouraging. One school of thought felt that Antex was the problem. At first it was suspected that Antex was not pure, and, that like Physex, needed to be produced in absolutely pure form in order that the brood mare serum gonadotropin could be effective. Thus Leo undertook a purification process aimed at creating a crystalline answer to Gonadex. But it proved complicated. Unlike Gonadex, which contained species-specific chorionic gonadotropin, Antex was manufactured from the blood serum of pregnant horses and thus contained a "foreign" species of hormone. As far back as the early 1940s, apprehension was expressed that foreign hormones could have an "antihormone action," which was confirmed both experimentally and clinically. These antihormone actions made long-term treatment problematic.[52] Similar problems manifested themselves in lab tests when apes were treated with extracts of sheep pituitary glands, though not when given pituitary extracts from fellow simians. Thus there was good reason to believe that the best course of action was to treat humans with species-specific gonadotropins, too.[53]

When Gemzell, Diczfalusy and Tillinger published their article in 1958, their species-specific pituitary extract had only been tested for a short time and they could therefore not guarantee it would not lead to the creation of antihormones over the long term. Nor did they hazard promising that the women who had been helped to achieve ovulation by the new technique would definitely become pregnant. It was conceivable that the artificially stimulated egg could become negatively affected and in the worst case become unfit. When a follow-up study was conducted, it also emerged that one-quarter of the patients responded poorly to FSH treatment, yet another reason for not quite yet committing to the method.[54] However, the trio did not have to wait long for positive reinforcement. Two children soon came into the world, soon followed by more.[55] Naturally, this was not the first time hormone treatment of sterility had the desired effect, but it was still noteworthy.

The collaboration between Gemzell, Diczfalusy and Tillinger was fruitful but not long lasting. In 1960, the same year Westman passed away, Gemzell resigned from the Caroline Hospital. After having failed to be awarded a professor's chair at Sabbatsberg Hospital, he became Professor of Obstetrics and Gynecology at the Women's Clinic in Uppsala. Together with Paul Roos, Leif Wide and others, he continued to practice and refine the technique of human pituitary glands in the service of reproductive endocrinology. In a few short years, nearly over twenty previously infertile women had become biological mothers thanks to this therapy.[56] Reports on the successful new pituitary method were broadcast on Swedish television, *Time* magazine published notices and Gemzell soon became world famous for his so-called "Gemzell kids."[57] In the decade that followed he was probably the internationally most well known Swedish physician, sought after by "the rich, royal and famous." Uppsala, rather than Stockholm, was now the Scandinavian capital of clinical reproductive endocrinology.[58]

In Gemzell's estimation, some six hundred women were treated with human pituitary gonadotropin in Uppsala between 1960 and 1975, with a success frequency of approximately fifty percent.[59] The key was material; Gemzell had access to huge numbers of human pituitary glands, probably more than any other scientist in the world, by sheer circumstance. During his career, all patients who passed away at Swedish hospitals underwent mandatory postmortem examinations (provided the family did not object), in order to confirm the cause of death as accurately as possible. Whenever the cranium was opened, the opportunity for removing the pituitary gland presented itself. Through an informal agreement, Gemzell succeeded in having the pathologists routinize this extraordinary procedure on women who had died during their reproductive years—he paid them five crowns per gland. Gemzell even hired an assistant whose only job was to make regular pick-ups.[60]

Medical historian Naomi Pfeffer notes that this procedure was performed without consulting the patients or their families; in other words, without informed consent. Nor did it seem that Gemzell informed his patients that the fluid he injected into them contained extract from the pituitary glands of dead people. Whether this can be considered ethical behavior is of course debatable. As shown above, some earlier physicians were plagued by moral doubt about using human pituitary hormones, but such hesitation seems to have not existed during Gemzell's era. Objections were made by the Vatican, not about the use of human glands in itself, but rather because the Catholic Church considered that God alone had the right to tamper with the reproductive capacity of His creations. The medical ethics review board of the Uppsala University Hospital, established in the late 1960s, had no such qualms. The only reprimand Gemzell ever received concerned the fact that this treatment involved certain medical risks. Included among these were overstimulated ovaries and multiple births—one of his patients had quintuplets, four of whom died—but these were risks both Gemzell and his patients were willing to take.[61]

At least Gemzell was not breaking the law, which he would have been in the United States, Australia and a number of West European countries. In the Sweden of the 1950s, it was perfectly legal to utilize minor bodily tissues removed during autopsy, including the pituitary glands.[62] The same opportunity existed in certain communist nations in Eastern Europe, including Poland, from whom Swedish pharmaceutical corporation Kabi imported large amounts of human pituitary glands with which to manufacture growth hormones. The pituitary gland was used in this manner up until the late 1980s, when it was discovered that there was a risk that human pituitary-based preparations could transmit the fatal neurological disorder Creutzfeldt-Jakob disease.[63]

GONADOTROPIN FROM URINE—ONE MORE TIME

The use of pituitary gonadotropins in the treatment of sterility raised other issues than those of risks and ethics. The treatment was not cheap. And even if Gemzell's clinic had treated hundreds of women over time, his strictly regional practice was quite modest in the grand scheme of things. The pharmaceutical industry was interested in meeting the demand it knew existed, but mass-producing drugs made out of human pituitary glands was still considered both practically difficult and commercially nigh on impossible. Numerous attempts with extracts from more accessible animal glands had been made, but each failed to have the desired effect on human patients. Developing a cost-efficient preparation with species-specific FSH for large-scale clinical practice would require a different raw material. The circumstances were undeniably reminiscent of the demand for raw materials during the interwar period, for then too urine emerged as a readily available, practicable source of hormones. However, this time it was not urine from pregnant women but urine from women who had undergone menopause, so-called "post-menopausal urine," that was utilized.

That post-menopausal urine contained a gonadotropic hormone that differed from the chorionic gonadotropin found in pregnant women's urine was hardly news to scientists. Zondek had discovered this already in the 1930s and by the end of the following decade chemists had developed a method of extracting the hormone in a relatively pure form. Even Axel Westman was familiar with this hormone, which he mentioned in his book *Övergångsår*, primarily as an example to explain that menopause could not be a result of decreased pituitary hormone production. "In fact, quite the opposite seems to be true," he wrote. "The amount of pituitary gland hormones in the circulation system increase and are even secreted abundantly in urine."[64] The hormone in question was subsequently dubbed "human menopausal gonadotropin" (hMG) by the Gonadotrophin Club.[65] One explanation for the relatively high concentration of hormones in urine was that the ovaries of women who had passed menopause no longer responded to the impulses of the pituitary hormones. Thus the pituitary gland increases its production of gonadotropic hormones, whereupon the percentage of the latter found in urine grows.[66] The conclusion was thus that hMG was a kind of pituitary gonadotropin and therefore contained FSH. Here was a possible plentiful source of raw materials. Just as human chorionic gonadotropin had been extracted from pregnant women in the past, research teams and pharmaceutical companies began attempting to extract hMG from the urine of post-menopausal women.

It is known that researchers and companies in Italy and the Netherlands attempted to manufacture what would prove to be a serious alternative to genuine pituitary gonadotropins. Serono and Organon were first to market commercial hMG drugs with documented follicle-stimulating effect, the very first of which, Pergonal, was patented by Serono in 1950. According to Naomi Pfeffer, scientists in these countries were motivated by the fact that in contrast to Sweden, there were legal, religious and cultural factors which prevented or at least limited the use of human pituitary glands; they were quite simply forced to find alternatives.[67] Pfeffer appears however to be unaware of the fact that the same kind of research was being conducted in Sweden, both before and during the flourishing of Gemzell's clinic in Uppsala.

For even Leo wanted a piece of the hMG pie. In the early 1950s, the first collection of post-menopausal urine was conducted at an old-age home in Helsingborg, from which a small test batch of what was then called "pituitary gonadotropin" was manufactured. Bertil Högberg, who was involved in this pilot project, remained skeptical since certain difficulties had arisen in the course of collection. He confessed to Axel Westman that he entertained little hope that this was the right way to go. But again, just like in the case of Gonadex, Westman was determined. In May 1955, he contacted Svante Wiström at Leo and declared that it "seems to me that it would be of exceeding value to produce a similar preparation [hMG], which could presumably be more useful than chorionic gonadotropin in the majority of cases."[68]

As he had accounted for his reasons why Leo should manufacture purified chorionic gonadotropins a decade earlier, Westman now argued that the new hormone was significant to endocrine research *per se*. "I believe that the results could be of great value both theoretically and clinically."[69] Thus Westman recommended that the temporarily suspended work be resumed, also recommending that a new urine collection campaign be conducted at the Sabbatsberg elder care facility in Stockholm, with which he was in close contact.[70] As always, Leo attempted to oblige Westman but also relayed a message from Högberg: if gonadotropin hormones were to be manufactured from the urine of elderly women, it should be collected during the autumn, not the summer, in order to "avoid disagreeable odors."[71]

Access to and collection of large quantities of post-menopausal urine was but one of many problems with which pharmaceutical corporations were forced to deal. Producing an injectible drug out of urine with human post-menopausal gonadotropins that did not cause side effects turned out, not unexpectedly, to be easier said than done. It was complicated to purify gonadotropic extracts so that all undesirable elements were eliminated or at least drastically reduced, laborious to continuously and swiftly standardize the purified fractions on lab animals, and difficult to verify the finished product's clinical effectiveness with objective methods.[72] Even the question of the relationship between FSH and LH, which first came to the fore in research conducted on the chorionic and pituitary gonadotropins, recurred with reference to hMG; exchanges of views on this matter were often lively at international Gonadotrophin Club conferences.[73] In 1957, the WHO's Expert Committee on Biological Standardization decided to establish an international standard for hMG as well, a task with which the National Institute for Medical Research in London was charged. A standard preparation referred to as "1st IRP" was selected, though shortly thereafter a purer, more potent standard was demanded.[74]

The problems besetting the manufacture of a post-menopausal gonadotropin could however be eliminated, according to Egon Diczfalusy, a founding member of the Gonadotrophin Club. On 23 December 1960, he submitted an application to Leo's internal research foundation. The application proposed collaboration between Bertil Högberg's team at the Leo lab in Helsingborg and a small group consisting of Diczfalusy, his colleague Karl-Gunnar Tillinger and Italian chemist Piero Donini.[75] Donini was a familiar name in reproductive endocrine circles. A member of the staff of Instituto Farmacologico Serono in Rome, he had taken part in the development of Pergonal and was therefore a knowledgeable resource. Note however that Gemzell was not invited to participate in the project. This may have been due to the fact that he had just left Stockholm for Uppsala, or that he quite simply did not consider hMG an adequate replacement for the genuine pituitary gonadotropin he himself used. And of course there might have been other reasons altogether.[76] Whether he subsequently collaborated with any of Leo's competitors is unknown to the present author.

The purpose of Diczfalusy's project was to investigate the possibility of developing clinically- and commercially-viable human post-menopausal gonadotropins, with proven FSH effect, from the urine of women who had passed menopause.[77] Such a preparation could have a variety of uses, but first and foremost function as a substitute for gonadotropins extracted directly from human pituitary glands. For Leo, it was important because it could thereby replace the old antihormonal Antex while simultaneously complementing Gonadex in the treatment of sterile women. With that, Gonadex could perhaps regain some of its faltered glory, not the least financially. For, as Ove Fernö, Leo's director of research put it during a meeting between Leo and Diczfalusy, "the increased interest in HMG-HCG treatment could turn out to be a decent market for purified HCG [Gonadex]."[78] Diczfalusy's application fitted perfectly with Leo's tradition in the field of hormones and was granted by the research foundation on 30 December 1960.[79] In the next chapter, we will follow the project as it unfolded and account for its results. And we will finally be introduced to the drug that came to overshadow Gonadex, Leo's last hormone drug for the treatment of sterility: Homogonal.

CHAPTER NINE

In the Shadow of Homogonal

THIS FINAL EMPIRICAL CHAPTER details how Aktiebolaget Leo (Helsingborg), the reproductive endocrinologists at the Women's Clinic of the Royal Caroline Hospital and a handful of network associates together created a drug from human post-menopausal gonadotropin. Homogonal, Leo's last attempt at a hormone preparation to treat sterility, did not spell the end for Gonadex, but it did change its identity one last time. The story of Homogonal is essential to the present study since it concludes the story of Gonadex (and Antex, too), and because the geneses of both display numerous similarities insofar as consultation, procuration, standardization and mediation are concerned. But it is also noteworthy because it sheds light on the difficulties encountered by a biomedical innovation with its cap set on becoming an "international sales success." In contrast with Gonadex, Leo was within a hair's breadth of rolling out Homogonal on the American market. Why it failed to make it all the way is one of the questions this chapter intends to answer.

POST-MENOPAUSAL GONADOTROPIN PUT TO THE TEST

When Egon Diczfalusy's Leo-financed hMG project commenced in 1961, it was far from certain that post-menopausal gonadotropin would prove to be a clinically applicable and commercially viable preparation. It was also highly uncertain whether hMG really could contribute to ovarian maturation in cases of hormonal sterility, despite the existence of studies indicating the possibility.[1] One year on and the situation was still muddled. From Israel, endocrinologist Bruno Lunenfeld (b. 1927) reported that he had succeeded in effecting two pregnancies, one of which was carried to term, with the aid of Serono's Pergonal in combination with chorionic gonadotropin.[2] Early lab studies at the Caroline Hospital however had produced more discouraging results. Furthermore, it turned out that purifying hMG was extremely tricky.[3]

At a meeting in June 1962, Diczfalusy declared that he himself had begun to have doubts as to whether hMG would ever be able to replace genuine pituitary gonadotropins, since they would probably prove to be two distinct substances. He also revealed the "highly confidential" news that the Department of Pathology in Stockholm had begun collecting human pituitary glands, which would give him access to "rather large amounts" of the coveted but elusive material, keeping the door open on that particular option.[4] As we already know, this was no one-off affair since by this time Carl Axel Gemzell had begun his clinical research in Uppsala. Furthermore, a few years earlier, endocrinologist Rolf Luft had applied for funds from the Knut and Alice Wallenberg Foundation in order to purchase no less than 3,000 human pituitary glands to be supplied by Swedish and foreign pathologists from autopsied cadavers.[5]

As during the 1940s, when the viability of a pituitary preparation was raised by Axel Westman, Leo again insisted that it was impossible to manufacture a marketable product from pituitary material, and that urine would "have to do."[6] In retrospect, it did indeed appear to be a practicable route. The hMG which had first been used in Diczfalusy's project was purchased from the Dutch company Organon, which at that time was putting the finishing touches on the hMG preparation marketed in 1963 as Humegon. However, when Leo tested another preparation purified from raw material acquired from the Italian company Serono, the results were better. A woman treated in 1962 as part of Diczfalusy's project at the Caroline Hospital not only succeeded in ovulating, but also became pregnant. The research group drew two conclusions from this positive outcome. The first was that there was a clear difference between Leo-Serono's hMG and Organon's hMG and that this difference likely lay in the relationship between FSH and LH in the respective preparations (adduced to be 4:1 in the former and 1:1 in the latter). The second conclusion was that it appeared producing a potent drug out of post-menopausal urine for the treatment of sterility was indeed possible.[7]

Though hMG evidently had clinical potential, financial considerations would dictate whether Leo could afford to invest. When Leo and Westman first began developing hormone drugs in the 1930s and 1940s, the population question was at the very centre of welfare state policy debate. In a climate where all means possible were sought to increase and "improve" the Swedish population, it was both politically and financially prudent to invest in a hormone preparation which might cure involuntary childlessness. Two decades later, the population resource situation had been utterly transformed. Amidst alarming threats of global overpopulation in combination with newly discovered ecological problems and growing malnutrition in the Third World, politicians were instead looking for techniques to *prevent* unwanted pregnancy.[8] Numerous countries mounted comprehensive planned-parenthood campaigns within which hormonal and other contraceptive agents were developed in order to control (primarily female) fertility.[9] The Caroline Hospital too increasingly began focusing on family planning research and information, later institutionalized in the form of a dedicated WHO centre attached to the Women's Clinic.[10] Moreover, an increasing number of childless couples now saw adoption as a viable alternative to biological offspring. While the neo-Malthusian debate heated up, the women's movement also contributed to transforming society's view of sexuality as well as ideas about gender roles. "Free love" became more acceptable than ever before, which further increased the demand for reliable contraceptive devices.[11] In contrast to the pronatalist movement of the 1930s and 1940s, an antinatalism movement, advocating personal freedom and environmental care through childlessness, started to grow.[12]

Against this socio-political backdrop it is hardly far-fetched to imagine that if Leo's efforts in the hormone field had commenced in the 1960s, its first, original hormone preparation would have been an oral contraceptive instead of a sterility drug. And Leo did in fact begin conducting hormone research aimed at developing its own contraceptive. The goal was to create a long-term effect contraceptive agent which, in contrast to the common birth-control pill, need not be taken daily and was therefore better suited to the women of the Third World.[13] This new direction was however not entirely independent of the old one. Hope was expressed that the endocrinal reproductive knowledge generated by the hMG project would eventually be applicable to the more lucrative contraceptive market.[14]

Leo had ascertained that domestic demand for a new hMG drug to fight sterility was small. Not even the entire Scandinavian market was now adjudged large enough to motivate production. The European market already featured Serono's Pergonal while Organon was busy launching Humegon. Perhaps other companies were also preparing to roll out their own hMG product? At the same time, Leo evidently could not undo the choices of lines of research and development they had made in the past; rather, they had to make the best of the situation and hMG undeniably lay within the company's sphere of interest—not least as a complement to Gonadex. One reason in favor of investing in hMG was that the finished product could wholesale at a pretty steep price, so even relatively small demand could lead to satisfactory turnover.[15] Another was that the drug would presumably have a significant "goodwill factor." Furthermore, export opportunities were once again dangled; there was a great big world outside Europe. Thus in December 1962 the matter was settled: Leo would continue funding the research and as soon as possible bring hMG into the "Leo family." In order to speed up the process, hMG would be purchased from Serono until the acquisition of post-menopausal urine in Sweden had been properly organized.[16]

The researchers at Leo and the Royal Caroline Hospital proceeded to produce, standardize and test hMG.[17] Diczfalusy and Tillinger were engaged as external researchers while chemist Torstein Perklev, currently head of Leo's Department of Biochemistry in Helsingborg, was put in charge. The purification method used included a first step wherein the urine was mixed with kaolin, a china clay, which absorbed the hormones (and numerous other substances) and isolated the urine. Thereafter followed a series of biochemical purification baths until a "satisfactorily" pure substance remained.[18] Approximately 50 mg could be extracted from 1,300 liters of urine. (In time, the technique was refined so that a thousand liters produced 125 mg.) The purified substance still contained many pollutants but continuing the purification process was considered commercially unviable. One did however need to abide by international standards. Since a gonadotropin conference held in 1960 determined that a new variant of Serono's Pergonal would replace 1st IRP as the international reference standard for hMG, Leo proceeded from that "2nd IRP" (chosen by the WHO in 1964) when it began attempting to standardize its own drug.[19] This was not a particularly straightforward process and as with Gonadex, the company unilaterally decided that a "Leo-standard preparation" chemically superior to the international one would more than suffice.[20] The notion from the 1940s that the hormone needed to be manufactured in "crystalline" form seems no longer to have been a concern, however.[21]

As Leo strove to prepare and standardize hMG, clinical studies on its effect and toxicity were being conducted to determine how strong the dosage should be, how often it should be taken and the degree to which it needed to be complemented with Gonadex.[22] These studies differed from previous clinical studies of crystalline chorionic gonadotropin in two crucial respects. First, tests were not only conducted at the Women's Clinic of the Caroline Hospital but also at two other Swedish clinics. Secondly, male patients were enrolled in the project and tested as well. The drug was primarily tested on women with sterility-related issues, but a few men who failed to produce a sufficient amount of healthy sperm were also used as subjects. Sterile men were tested at Sahlgrenska University Hospital in Gothenburg, and at Lund University Hospital Leo funded a series of studies at its women's and urology clinics.[23] This diversification was not only motivated by scientific thoroughness; a wider field of use also meant greater profits. "A radical change in the assessment of sales prognoses [can be expected] if the preliminary, positive results of the effect of hMG on spermatogenesis can be confirmed," as the notes from one meeting put it.[24] This bears a striking resemblance to the expectations previously harbored for Gonadex.

The first clinical experiments produced both positive and negative outcomes. While a number of women were affected in the desired fashion, some even becoming pregnant, it proved that more powerful doses, where hMG was taken in combination with hCG, led to the rapid development of ovarian cysts. Some patients also became feverish.[25] For now though, it was too early to come to any conclusions about the correct hMG dosage: "It will probably have to be adapted to the individual, as so often in hormone therapy."[26] Still, in October 1964, Leo decided that the clinical material was sufficient to provide the basis for filing for registration.[27] The reason for rushing was probably the same as in the case of Gonadex—fear of domestic competition nipping at its heels. Leo had learned that Frederik Paulsen's company Ferring in Malmö had offered Serono royalties in exchange for Scandinavian distribution rights. Organon, likely through Pharmacia, had also contacted physicians in Gothenburg and Malmö, who conducted clinical tests of Organon's proprietary hMG drug Humegon. There was no time to lose.[28]

LEO'S THIRD URINE COLLECTION CAMPAIGN

The hMG project was the third time Leo set about collecting urine for the purpose of accumulating raw material from which hormones could be extracted. During its first campaign to produce Ovex, Leo had collected urine from pregnant mares in Scania; during the second for Gonadex, from pregnant women via women's clinics at the Caroline Hospital and other health care facilities in southern Sweden. This time Leo set its sights on women who had gone through menopause. In order to access this raw material, Leo was obliged once again to add new members to its production network.

Serono acquired its urine from convents and Italian hamlets where plenty of older women, retired nuns, could be found. Apparently Leo too considered starting its campaign in similar environs before choosing age-old homes and related facilities, precisely as it had done the first time in the 1950s.[29] Initially it concentrated on the Helsingborg region, with the cooperation of the Romare Foundation, Bergaliden Home for the Aged, Bergaliden Nursing Home, St. Maria's Hospital, Kunghult Sanatorium and a home for chronic invalids in Åstorp. The physicians, clinic directors and chief nurses concerned were contacted, and most of them were happy to grant Leo permission. But there were holdouts—not because they had anything against collaborating with local industry but because of all the extra work it would mean.[30]

As with the campaign to collect the urine of pregnant women, this one relied on the active participation of patients and health care personnel, often without first obtaining informed consent.[31] Staff was charged with the daily collection of urine from the female residents in special containers provided by Leo. When the containers were full, they were picked up for further transport to the factory. The logistics were uncomplicated; all that was needed was a Volvo delivery van. In the first year, more than two hundred women contributed approximately three hundred liters of urine a week.[32]

After a medium-sized trial run was satisfactorily completed, Leo felt the hMG project was ready for large-scale industrial production, which required expanding factory capacity. It also decided to construct a large, outdoor receptacle tank near the factory where the urine could be stored before processing. Now the only thing missing was large quantities of postmenopausal urine.[33] Leo contacted care facilities in Malmö and other communities, mostly in Scania.[34] At this juncture, it was estimated that 1,000 liters of urine per week would be required. This amount would suffice to fill the "requirements" in Sweden, calculated to be three to four hundred patients annually. However, Leo was already planning its international sales strategy and hoped production would soon process one to two thousand liters of urine each day.[35]

By this time Leo had learned the significance of keeping health care staff motivated, so during the Helsingborg campaign, it handed out rewards in the form of confectionary, one cake per month to each ward. Judging from one report, this method paid off. "The collected amount has been determined to increase during the period immediately following delivery of the cake."[36] To further stimulate productivity, a system was proposed whereby rewards were based on individual performance, with the prize level rising for every receptacle filled. Each fifty liters earned a coupon; three coupons could be exchanged for a cake or a bouquet of flowers, five a potted plant, and nine coupons entitled the winner to a subscription to either *Allers* or *Femina*, popular contemporary household magazines. The lucky individual who managed to scrape together twenty coupons became the proud owner of a brand-new transistor radio.[37] The degree to which this system of rewards was actually implemented is hard to say. Normally, staff was reimbursed with cash for its efforts. Regardless, beginning in 1966, the established routine was that each ward received 10 öre per liter collected. The money was paid out once a month to its "coffee fund."[38] The women who actually delivered the urine seem not to have been reimbursed this time.

Not only did Leo require personnel to fill its quota, its instructions needed to be followed to the letter. It was crucial that *only* urine from women who had passed through menopause be poured into the receptacles. In both the Ovex and Gonadex campaigns, Leo faced problems with urine diluted with undesirable liquids, and perhaps fretted that the nurses would be tempted to increase the amount they collected by adding water or even their own urine. Leo's chief accountant Hans Ekström, who had been charged with organizing the campaign, stressed the importance of instructing and admonishing personnel to follow strict guidelines, especially at any sign of "waning interest." A staff member with, as they put it, "business-like powers of persuasion," was put in charge of enforcement.[39] Ekström also recommended concise written instructions be issued and information meetings held at Leo. "It is proposed that the doctors and nurses involved be invited to Leo in expediently-sized groups to spend the day (or evening) receiving relevant instruction about the campaign combined with further information to promote sales."[40] Though it was probably considered too logistically complicated to invite all the health care facilities involved to the office, at least one such meeting was indeed held.[41] The primer Leo composed and circulated to the wards was formulated as followed.

> The urine collected thanks to your generous compliance will be used by our research department to produce a gonadotropic hormone called hMG (Human Menopausal Gonadotropin). This hormone is used in the treatment of certain forms of sterility in women. The results of the treatments conducted so far have been very positive. Unfortunately, access to material suitable for the manufacture of this hormone is limited. Urine from women who have passed through menopause contains enough hMG that reprocessing of the hormone can be successfully performed. However, due to its small concentration, large quantities of urine are necessary to manufacture sufficient amounts of hMG. The collection of urine has been underway for several years now and in consultation with hospital staff, we have arrived at the following routine in order to cause the least inconvenience. 25 l plastic bottles outfitted with funnels and lids have been placed in the ward sterilization room. We have added a small amount of antiseptic in order to eliminate any unpleasant odour. Urine from bedpans, bidets or other

> containers should be emptied straight into the plastic bottles rather than being rinsed out. The bottles will be collected once or twice a week and replaced with new ones. *Note that urine from pregnant women may not be poured into the bottles.*[42]

The campaign thrived in Scania and by 1965, as much as 4,500 liters of urine was accumulated every week.[43] From there, activities expanded quickly so that beginning in 1966, drivers were not only picking up urine from health care providers in southern Sweden but also from Stockholm and Uppsala and their suburbs and, to a lesser extent, from Copenhagen. Almost eighty hospitals and nursing homes caring for some five thousand women over fifty eventually became nodes in the company's swelling production network.[44] Forced to enlist private haulage firms and storage facilities, some 450,000 liters of urine was collected in 1966 and more than 600,000 in 1967.[45] Standard transport trailers were replaced with tanker trucks and logistics became more and more complicated. And yet Leo was still not sated. The goal was to continue expanding until reaching a maximum production level based on 100,000 liters of urine a week.[46]

THE IMAGE OF HORMONAL MEDICINE AS A REMEDY FOR STERILITY IN THE PRESS, PART II

"New Swedish Medicine Can Help Childless," "Swedish Drug Give Childless a Chance," "New Hormone Drug Helped," "New Drug Cures Sterility."[47] Sound familiar? On 13 and 14 August 1964, sixteen years after the launch of Gonadex had generated similar headlines in the Swedish press, new articles were published announcing that a hormone preparation to cure sterility had been created in Sweden. The new articles were reminiscent of what was written in 1948 in other aspects as well. The drug in question consisted of gonadotropins (this time post-menopausal rather than chorionic, of course), it had been manufactured by Leo in a coordinated effort with scientists at the Royal Caroline Hospital, and it was without a doubt a "sensational discovery." Likewise, concrete evidence that the drug actually worked was presented. In 1964, just as in 1948, a woman who had previously been completely barren had succeeded in becoming pregnant thanks to Leo's new hormone drug. To underline the significance of this new discovery, the papers compared Carl Axel Gemzell's revolutionary pituitary extract with Leo's new hMG drug. Both were said to be of equal medical value, but while the former was of mere "theoretical interest," the latter could actually be used to help many families in need.[48] For it was about to go into mass production.

> Thanks to this new method, mass manufacture of the hormone is now possible. This means that hundreds of women who wish to have children but have not been able now have the opportunity to do so at practically any women's clinic in the country.[49]

There was, however, one eyebrow-raising difference between 1948 and 1964. The woman just mentioned not only became pregnant, but delivered, twins no less, and these "hormone babies" were featured prominently in a number of papers. Three similar photographs, taken at the family home in Helsingborg when the children were a month old, were printed to attract readers. The implicit message was that all sterile women suffering from a particular type of pituitary hormonal disorder could become mothers to beautiful, healthy babies like these. As in 1948, no paper challenged or problematized Leo's successes in the field of reproductive endocrinology. Nor was any connection made to the previous mass media hysteria over Gonadex. Once again, the press reflected the interests of Leo and its scientists, rather than the general public.[50]

I have not been able to unearth any archive material which sheds light on Leo's media and marketing strategy similar to that formulated for rolling out Gonadex. Though Leo did not call a press conference this time, it is highly probable that the company once again distributed press material for, just like 1948, the newspaper articles about hMG were remarkably similar, as if transcribed from the same source. There is a two-page document in Leo's historical archive, which may have been the original, bearing the caption "HMG—A Hormone Drug for the Treatment of Certain Forms of Sterility" and dated 3 August 1964. The text makes no mention of the twins.[51] And yet, the most likely explanation as to why the press was contacted in August 1964 was that Leo wanted to draw attention to them, because it still had no hMG drug ready for the shelves. On the other hand, the company was well on its way to accumulating data for a drug registration application.[52]

According to Leo's own documentation, the first concrete clinical results of hMG treatment had been achieved in Sweden in 1962. A participant in Egon Diczfalusy's pilot project at the Caroline had, after years of interruption, begun to menstruate again, become pregnant and ultimately delivered a healthy baby boy.[53] In the years that followed, a group of women diagnosed with pituitarial-induced sterility participated in the more formal clinical testing of Leo's hMG. The first of these women to become pregnant had twins on 14 July 1964, and all evidence indicates that these were the children who drew so much media attention the following month. Shortly thereafter, two other participants became pregnant and therapy led to the resumption of regular menstruation in two more.[54] This tiny test group was complemented with other patients and by December 1965, a total of eleven babies (including the twins) were born to women who had undergone hMG treatment. Compared with the meager outcome of the clinical trials preceding the launch of Gonadex, this was an undeniably impressive result. Apparently, Carl Axel Gemzell's pituitary gonadotropin drug now had a worthy challenger.[55]

Leo applied to register its hMG preparation in Sweden in the summer of 1965 under the name "Homogonal."[56] Leo did not expect the drug to be immediately approved since government inspection procedures were now much more rigorous. Moreover, the origin of Homogonal coincided with the so-called "thalidomide disaster." Thalidomide is a synthetic substance developed by German corporation Chemie Grünenthal and was launched worldwide in 1956. The drug was prescribed to pregnant women suffering from nausea and insomnia. While it alleviated these problems, it also damaged the fetus. Not only had Chemie Grünenthal claimed that its science-based product entirely lacked side effects, the company maintained the claim in the face of numerous reports to the contrary. On 1 November 1961, Chemie Grünenthal finally recalled the drug. By then, between eight and ten thousand children had been born with grave deformities.[57]

The revelation that thalidomide caused serious injury to fetuses sent shockwaves through the pharmaceutical community, so also in Sweden, where the preparation was distributed by the company Astra under the product name Neurosedyn.[58] Together with other chemicals characteristic of the time including DDT and PCB, thalidomide came to symbolize the realization that modern science and technology could just as easily lead to dire consequences as spectacular triumphs.[59] The pharmaceutical industry, which since the end of the Second World War had become accustomed to being celebrated for its scientific rigor and progressive spirit, found itself in the 1960s being scapegoated in pharmaceutical journals and the mass media. Two programs broadcast on Swedish television asked bluntly, "Can we trust the pharmaceutical industry?" Along with the problem of undesirable side effects, criticism was also directed at the price of drugs and the increasingly lavish marketing budgets.[60]

The situation created an atmosphere of fear and distrust and led to the swift tightening of inspection and supervision protocols throughout most of the world. In 1962, the Food and Drug Administration (FDA) in the United States was the first to impose strict new demands on animal testing and scientific documentation before a new drug could be tested on humans and finally accepted for use. The WHO established a global system for the reporting of side effects and recall of medicine with known risks the year after. In Sweden, where the question of tougher restrictions had actually been debated since the 1950s, a new legislation took effect 1 January 1964 and stated, "Pharmaceuticals shall be of sound quality and may not cause injury through normal use disproportionate to the intended effect." The legislation also required stricter documentation and clinical proof in connection with the launch of any new pharmaceutical.[61]

The thalidomide disaster cast doubt on the wisdom of manufacturing drugs intended for use by mothers-to-be, including gonadotropins. In England, these doubts led to a proposal that gonadotropins be temporarily banned.[62] But even if Leo realized that it might take some time before Homogonal was approved for sale, it continued to nurture the hope that it would one day prove to be the success Gonadex never was. Such dreams could however never be achieved at home, for that the market was too small. In the contemporary debate about the Swedish pharmaceutical industry in the world marketplace, the necessity of developing products suitable for export was constantly reiterated.[63] The idea was that Homogonal would be one such product—an "international sales success."

"A CONTRACT TO DELIVER HMG TO THE U.S.A. HAS BEEN SIGNED"

Not long after the application for Homogonal had been submitted to the Board of Medicine, Leo's staff could read the following lines in *Tabletten*, the company's internal newsletter: "A contract to deliver hMG to the U.S.A. has been signed. Clinical testing has been conducted by an American pharmaceutical industry. A number of other countries are also interested in purchasing this drug."[64] The "American industry" in question was Ortho Pharmaceutical Corporation of Raritan, New Jersey. What the article failed to mention was that these tests were being conducted after a history of failures in the hMG field. In line with its new guidelines, the FDA had already denied American pharmaceutical company Cutter Laboratories approval of a variant of Serono's hMG drug Pergonal, and Ortho feared it might suffer the same fate.[65]

Several problems with which Leo was intimately familiar lay behind the FDA's restrictive attitude toward hMG. It was difficult to standardize so that the relationship between FSH and LH remained fairly constant, treatment often caused immediate side effects in the form of fever and ovarian cysts, and positive results were often in the form of multiple pregnancies.[66] As when genuine pituitary gonadotropin was used in the treatment of involuntary childlessness, twin, triplet and even quadruplet births were relatively common, which in turn could cause other medical complications. These issues were not only being discussed privately in the pharmaceutical community but also aired publicly in medical journals including *The Lancet*.[67] In what follows, I shall sketch the background of the optimistic article in *Tabletten* before charting the development of the relationship between Leo and Ortho.

Exactly when the two companies first came into contact is hard to say, but in all likelihood it was at a meeting in 1963 mentioned in a letter addressed to Torsten Perklev from an employee of Ortho.

> We discussed the possibility of your sending us a couple of samples of your commercial hCG material so that we might use this in some of our research work. We also asked if we could have samples of your hMG material, again for just research purposes, as well as a very small amount of the human pituitary FSH and human pituitary LH material.[68]

This suggests that Ortho was interested in testing the range of gonadotropins Leo could provide, including Gonadex, not that Ortho agreed to distribute its products. The letter also mentions that Ortho's assistance in acquiring urine in the States was discussed and that regarding any possible commercial collaboration, Leo should contact the board of directors.

Leo evidently followed that advice promptly because on 12 February 1964, Ortho's vice-president Evan Spalt paid a visit to the factory in Helsingborg. Spalt explained that Ortho was interested in purchasing chorionic gonadotropin. Not for the treatment of sterility—Ortho required purified hCG in order to manufacture a pregnancy-test antiserum. Ortho planned on placing a small order but if it proved satisfactory, the company was prepared to order a large quantity of Gonadex. During the meeting, Leo's ongoing efforts to extract hMG were also discussed, and Spalt hinted that Ortho was willing to market it, too, on the condition that they were awarded exclusive North American rights. To begin with, Ortho wanted to order a smaller batch for clinical testing. The question was whether the "highly purified" Swedish hMG preparation functioned in a manner amenable with the FDA's new, restrictive guidelines.[69]

After this tentative complimentary call, the partnership between the two pharmaceutical companies seems to have quickly intensified. Leo delivered successively newer loads of hCG and hMG to Ortho, who tested them both on animals in a laboratory environment and on patients at a number of different clinics. According to a handwritten report, gonadotropins valued at over half a million Swedish crowns were exported to the US between 1964 and 1966.[70] New meetings were arranged on both sides of the Atlantic and Leo was under the impression that negotiations were being conducted in a spirit of equanimity. Furthermore, Ortho's interest shifted gradually from hCG to hMG. Though some small technical problems remained to be ironed out, each contact seem to bring commercialization closer, as long as Ortho was convinced that Leo could deliver the necessary amount of sufficiently high quality.[71] Torsten Perklev optimistically summarized the current situation after one of these meetings.

> If we can supply Ortho with a material which is superior to the one Serono can provide Cutter, and if we can carry out basic clinical research through our collaboration with ED [Egon Diczfalusy], it does not seem improbable that we can reduce the lead Serono has on the American market.[72]

This sanguine interpretation of the situation was confirmed by the minutes of two meetings held in September 1966, when a prominent representative of Ortho named Arnold Cronk visited the factory in Helsingborg, at which time he reported that Ortho's experts had monitored some one hundred clinical tests of Leo's hMG preparation and found the results highly encouraging. It caused few side effects and seemed relatively well standardized. Not everything was functioning perfectly yet, but Cronk's overall impression was that the issues previously causing the FDA concern had largely been solved and thus Leo's hormone drug would soon be available on the American market. Ortho was scheduled to submit a "New Drug Application" for hMG in October of that year.[73] The moment was ripe to draw up a formal contract between Leo and the Ortho Pharmaceutical Corporation.[74]

Apparently, Ortho was prepared to invest considerable financial resources in the project. In sharp contrast to the pessimistic calculations Leo had made concerning the domestic demand for hMG, Ortho's market analysis concluded that some 600,000 women in the US suffered from sterility issues, which could be treated with hMG.[75] On top of this there was a potential clientele in Australia and South America as well. Even though far from all the women in question would be able to afford the costly treatment, the potential market was good. The amount of hMG Leo could expect to sell to Ortho to cover "future needs" was exceptionally large. First Ortho wanted 1,000 phials of pure hMG delivered monthly, to be followed by 30,000 in October and December 1967, respectively, 25,000 more in January of 1968 and then 30,000 per month up to June of the same year.[76]

This added up to a total of a quarter of a million phials of hMG, requiring a net base material of nearly three and a half million liters of post-menopausal urine. Actually, erring on the side of caution to account for a certain amount of loss during collection, handling and storage, the amount was estimated at 4,600,000 liters.[77] As if this number was not staggering enough, shortly thereafter Ortho requested a further 150,000 phials for the second half of 1968, making the grand total of urine Leo required over the course of the next eighteen months close to six million liters![78] That the company was convinced it could successful perform this herculean task says something about the confidence and optimism characterizing the firm at this point in time, which also manifested itself in the new, five-storey research facility erected on its factory grounds in Helsingborg in the spring of 1967.[79]

At a planning meeting held on 14 September 1966, Leo resolved to carry out the hMG project "with every means at our disposal."[80] This would require more rigorous administration and organization, intensified optimization of hormone production and a rapid expansion of the capacity of the synthesis and biochemical production departments. It also meant redoubling urine collection efforts. There was simply not enough urine in Sweden to meet Ortho's needs. But where on earth could Leo find six million liters of post-menopausal urine? The idea of collecting urine abroad had been broached at an earlier stage; Ortho's suggestion was that someone be hired to study the possibilities of doing so in Germany.[81] Plans for such an arrangement, including outfitting a processing plant in Hamburg, had in fact been sketched. However, the 700,000 liters of urine that could be collected per annum, according to the plan, was far from enough. Thus Leo proceeded to investigate the possibility of conducting similar campaigns in other large population centers, including Vienna and Brussels. Another proposal reintroduced into the discussion was to collect urine in the US, a job that could be done directly by Ortho.[82]

Detailed facts and figures for an international campaign had been assembled for the above-mentioned meeting in September, according to which the problem could be solved by establishing a whole series of sites, not only in Hamburg (now estimated at an amount of 520,000 liters per year), but also Copenhagen (260,000), the Ruhr Valley (1,040,000), England (1,040,000), Spain (1,040,000) and Belgium (700,000).[83] The price of foreign operations on this scale would naturally be very high and as an alternative, the possibility of arranging collections in a suitable Third World nation, where the financial reimbursement would not be as burdensome, was broached.[84] Proposals included starting a campaign in the Gaza Strip, where there was a large concentration of refugees.[85] Since there were regular connecting flights between Istanbul and Copenhagen, Turkey also emerged as a possible candidate. A member of staff suggested that a campaign that could produce enough material for a year could be organized there in the following innovative manner.

> Three collection points would be established, manned by 2 consignees and 1 assistant. At each point, 4–5,000 liters would be collected (= 75,000 liters/week = 3,900,000 liters/year). Divided into 3-liter jars this makes 1,350–1,650 women per day. A steady stream, in other words. The vessels are stacked and picked up twice a day by 3.5-ton trucks. The women are each equipped with an ID badge like gasoline station credit cards and a stamp serves as a receipt for the amount of compensation. A factory will be outfitted at one of the collection points with a manager, clerk and 9 manual workers.[86]

The plan was not to dispatch all this urine to Sweden but that the raw material would be processed on site so that only a concentrate need be shipped. Leo was aware that an undertaking of this nature would pose numerous practical challenges. Cheating was one—diluting the sought-after urine with water or unsuitable urine—which could prove more of a problem at foreign collection points than the relatively well-disciplined Swedish care facilities.[87] There might even be cultural barriers to overcome. Acquaintances who had spent extended periods in Turkey were queried and aid workers at the Swedish International Development Cooperation Agency (SIDA) and the United Nations were consulted.[88] Discouragingly, Leo received little encouragement for its offshore plans from the latter. While the proposed Gaza project was in fact discussed at the headquarters of the United Nations Relief and Works Agency for Palestine Refugees (UNRWA) in Beirut, the conclusion was that it was unworkable.[89] Leo thus found itself in a precarious situation. A foreign collection campaign would be costly and risky and was furthermore predicated on co-financing from Ortho.[90] Moreover, it was necessary that Leo receive guarantees from Ortho that it definitely intended to market the hMG produced. Collected urine could not be stored indefinitely and the shelf life of the finished product was estimated at a maximum of two years.[91]

MUCH ADO ABOUT ALMOST NOTHING

The intent was to launch Leo-Ortho's hMG drug on New Year's Day 1968, but in November 1966, almost a year after the thrilling article in *Tabletten*, no binding agreement concerning Ortho's financial commitment had been reached. To get through the opening phase of the planned export for the coming year, Torsten Perklev was prepared to give the green light to the collection campaign in Germany.[92] But lacking board approval, even that had to be put on the back burner. Anxiety spread through the offices of Leo.

In February 1967, Perklev flew to the US to personally find out the reason for Ortho's lengthy hesitation. The answer he received was short and sweet—Ortho could not afford to invest in increased production capacity until it was sure the FDA would approval the new drug. It intended to compose and submit a New Drug Application in the summer, said Arnold Cronk, so any money talk would have to wait until September. However, Cronk was positive that FDA approval was imminent, since Ortho had entered into a strategic collaboration with a respected research group connected to the National Institute of Health. "All in all," wrote Perklev in his report to the board, "it can be said that Ortho is prepared to continue investing in the hMG project, is aware of the difficulties in getting it past the FDA but unwilling to give up."[93] The situation was, in other words, just as muddled as before his trip to the States.

Meanwhile back in Sweden, Leo continued its relentless quest for urine, as the cost for collection and processing grew by leaps and bounds. An unexpected setback occurred in 1967 when a patient at a nursing home in Leo's production network was discovered to have contracted salmonella, thereby rendering a large quantity of urine contaminated.[94] Furthermore, some facilities began tiring of the seemingly unending job, which perhaps ought to have been more expected. A physician at Beckomberga Hospital in Bromma wrote directly to Leo on behalf of his staff to complain about the miserly sum Leo offered as compensation. As long as the urine was being used for research purposes, he stated, he would put up with it, but the moment the company commercialized its hMG, he wanted to see a significant pay raise.[95] On top of all this, Ortho continued to make new demands about the exact composition of the preparation (i.e., the relationship between FSH and LH), how it should be tested, even how it should be packaged. Other intricate matters that needed to be dealt with included how all the hMG produced would be stored and shipped to the US in the safest manner.[96] Leo began to question the profitability of the great hMG project. What if the contract with Ortho never materialized?[97]

Not long after, Ortho cancelled its gigantic order. The reason why is still unclear, though it seems to have depended on more than just an irresolute FDA. What's more, Ortho threw Leo an unexpected curve ball. During a meeting at Ortho's offices in the fall of 1967, Perklev was informed that for some reason, the FDA had urged all clinics involved in testing hMG to "only use it if other drugs failed to have any effect."[98] The term "other drugs" referred to a new substance called clomiphene citrate.

Clomiphene citrate was not a biological gonadotropin hormone but a chemical agent produced synthetically in the 1950s. Initial experiments on lab animals had shown that clomiphene citrate prevented ovulation, thus functioning more like a contraceptive. But when a research group at the Medical College of Georgia tested the substance on women, the results proved the exact opposite, stimulating ovulation instead.[99] Apparently, it was difficult to explain the mechanism of action of the drug but according to prevailing theory, clomiphene citrate functioned as an "antiestrogen" which indirectly stimulated the pituitary gland's own secretion of gonadotropic hormones.[100] In the early 1960s, clinical trials were conducted in several countries that confirmed these initial results, including one involving 3,500 women in England. Thus a new candidate for the treatment of sterility was born.[101]

From a clinical standpoint, hMG and clomiphene citrate appeared essentially equivalent. Both could cause multiple births and ovarian cysts. And yet the FDA ranked clomiphene citrate higher than hMG. This may have been due to price; since clomiphene citrate was synthetic, it was probably cheaper to produce than biologically based hMG. Or it may have had something to do with notions of which were the most "natural" and therefore preferable. According to Naomi Pfeffer, a distinction between exogenous gonadotropin, which originates from a donor, and endogenous gonadotropin, which is produced by the patient's own body, was construed at this time. Endogenous hormones were considered more trustworthy than exogenous ones, even when provoked "artificially" with the aid of clomiphene citrate.[102] The FDA may also have been influenced by scientists who openly declared their doubts about the hMG drugs currently available. In a 1966 interview published in the respected *Journal of Reproduction and Fertility*, famed if aged gonadotropin expert Bernhard Zondek stated that the new gonadotropin drugs manufactured in Italy and Sweden seemed promising. He was also hopeful that research would one day succeed in determining once and for all which combination of FSH and LH was the perfect one for the treatment of sterility. However, Zondek also "want[ed] to stress that much still remains to be done and learned before the gonadotrophins can be safely recommended for treatment of infertility."[103] In his opinion, this goal had yet to be achieved.

When the FDA's directive reached Ortho, management contemplated hitting the brakes. If the FDA saw hMG as nothing more than a "secondary drug," the potential market would shrink drastically.[104] The same fears naturally plagued Leo, but it continued to do everything in its power to keep Ortho interested. In the autumn of 1967, a harried Perklev explained to Ortho's managing board that Leo's hMG drug was, if nothing else, still valuable from a scientific perspective. And its field of use could still be expected to expand. That negotiations had entered a critical phase can be discerned from Perklev's report to Leo, in which he writes "Ortho is obviously planning a meeting, where it will definitely come to a conclusion about the entire hMG project."[105]

Despite the fact that Ortho long dithered about financing the urine collection campaign, the company had submitted an application to register Leo's hMG as a new, American drug. Before that, Leo had on countless occasions provided the requested information on how development and testing was being conducted and Perklev had even attended a hearing at the FDA.[106] While awaiting the FDA's biological and clinical evaluation, new supplementary information was demanded, until finally, Ortho's management lost interest altogether. The first sign that the project would never come to fruition came in March 1968 in the form of a meeting between Perklev and Evan Spalt.[107] The coup-de-grâce was delivered shortly thereafter in a letter where Spalt curtly informed Leo that "our last review has led us to the conclusion that it would not be feasible for Ortho to bring this product to the market." It had been a difficult decision to make, Spalt explained, and assured Leo that Ortho had done everything within its power. "We regret that the hope we had for a mutually profitable project on HMG has ended in this fashion, and you may be sure that in view of the substantial investment, we have not taken this decision without substantial soul searching."[108] In reply, Leo's director of export, Sune Ebberstéen (1922–1972) gave vent to the disappointment he and the company felt over such an ignominious end.[109] But nothing could ameliorate the fact that five years' worth of hard work on behalf of Ortho had been for naught.[110]

It did not take long for Merrell Pharmaceuticals Inc. of Cincinnati, Ohio, to launch clomiphene citrate, or Clomid, which became its brand name. In the end, Cutter Laboratories' approval (for the distribution of Serono's Pergonal) was also finally accepted by the FDA. Although hMG was developed long before clomiphene citrate, Pergonal did not earn approval for general distribution until a decade after Clomid.[111]

HOMOGONAL LAUNCHED IN SWEDEN

If the FDA considered Leo's hMG drug not up to standard as far as "risks versus benefit" was concerned, Swedish authorities were of another opinion altogether. In Sweden, Homogonal was approved for registration as a pharmaceutical specialty on 25 August 1967.[112] The NPL did have a few things to say about the standardization of the drug, i.e. the degree in which the strength jibed with the international standard for hMG and the constancy of the relationship between FSH and LH. It also noted that the drug could cause users to become feverish.[113] However, since Leo had acquired improved purification technology, in part thanks to new external partnerships, the NPL was convinced that these problems were negligible.[114] Also contributing to the NPL's benevolent disposition was the fact that the principles of hMG treatment were already known and accepted. There were positive clinical results from both Sweden and the US, and furthermore, Gemzell was celebrating success after success with gonadotropin treatment at his clinic in Uppsala.[115] The NPL's strongest provisions were that the instructions clearly state that each treatment should begin with a weaker dose which would be increased incrementally as needed, and that the preparation was only to be prescribed by specialists. These requirements were hardly difficult to fulfill.[116]

The launch of Homogonal was a far cry from the grandeur of the launch of Gonadex. I have not found any breathless reports in the daily press, which probably indicates that its launch was no longer considered newsworthy. In

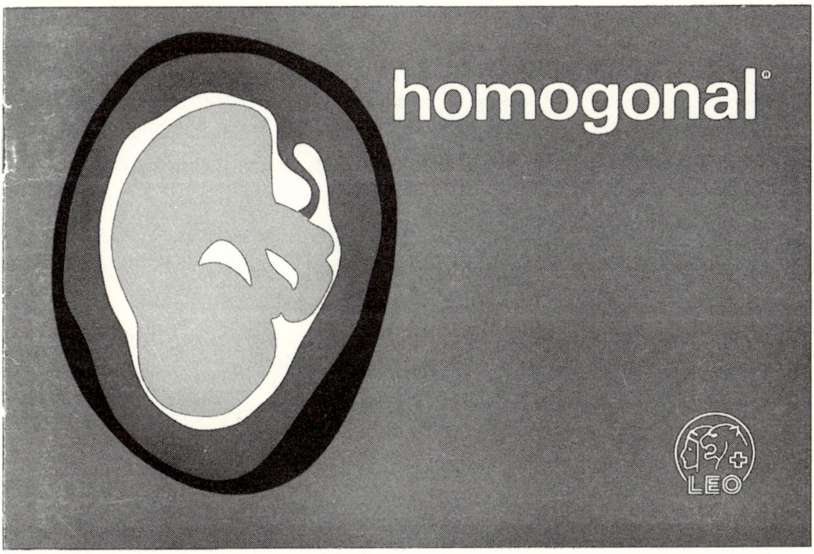

FIGURE 11 It was common during the 1940s and 1950s to illustrate ads for sterility-treatment hormone drugs with a "mother and child" motif. A variation of the theme was used to market Homogonal (1967), though by now, the mother had been reduced to her uterus.

information letters, however, Leo emphasized that this was a new, original drug, the first and only hMG drug manufactured in Sweden, and that it was the result of laudable collaboration between Leo's research laboratories and numerous health care institutions across the country.[117] The participation of Ortho in laboratory and clinical work, to which Leo was eager to draw attention in its application to the NPL, was not mentioned with one word.[118] Homogonal was primarily marketed as a drug to be used by women suffering from sterility caused by insufficient pituitary secretion. The stylized image of a fetus resting in a uterus was chosen as its logo. Sterile men were also said to be treatable with Homogonal, but "more research needs to be conducted before anything definitive can be said."[119]

According to the instructions, each treatment with Homogonal should be combined with Gonadex. The information pamphlet declared that each phial contained 75 IU of FSH and 25 IU of ICSH (a synonym for LH), that FSH and ICSH were two, distinct gonadotropic hormones and that these hormones were pituitary gonadotropins.[120] In order to achieve as exact a relationship as possible, Leo had invented a technique by which both components were purified separately and then joined in the desired proportion. In practice, however, balancing these proportions perfectly was an impossibility, just as it was impossible to determine exactly how the relationship between them actually appeared via biological testing.[121]

The approval of Homogonal meant that Antex, Leo's faithful brood mare serum gonadotropin since the 1930s, would be put out to pasture.[122] Despite being plagued by side effects, Antex had regularly been used with Gonadex in order to achieve full gonadotropic effect. Now its place in the hormonal treatment of sterility would be taken by Homogonal, which functioned well and in concert with Gonadex helped numerous couples become parents. Multiple-birth pregnancies were not unusual. In this manner, the reputation of Gonadex was partly rehabilitated. And yet, Homogonal was not as much of a success as Leo had banked on. Statistics show that sales of Homogonal in Sweden amounted to SEK 88,168 in 1976 and 54,683 the following year. The numbers for Gonadex in the same years were 83, 978 and 117,700, respectively. This modest return on the domestic market can be compared with Leo's cancer treatment hormone, Estracyt Oral, which sold for over SEK 15 million in 1977.[123]

These disappointing numbers can partially be explained by the fact that the demand for drugs to treat sterility was relatively small. Competition also put a dent in sales. Just as Leo rolled out Homogonal, Pharmacia began distributing Organon's hMG drug Humegon in Sweden, a drug more or less identical to Homogonal.[124] It consisted of human post-menopausal gonadotropin (75 IU) extracted from urine; it was intended for the treatment of sterility in women, but also men; it was to be prescribed in combination with highly-purified human chorionic gonadotropin (Pharmacia recommended Pregnyl, Organon's analogue to Gonadex); and its side effects were the same, possible multiple pregnancies and ovarian cysts.[125] Moreover, clomiphene citrate was in the process of conquering the world. Just as Ortho and Leo had feared, it was almost universally proclaimed the drug of choice for treating infertility.

In time, other synthetic drugs for the same area of indication would appear as well. Together with pharmacologist Ernst Barany and his staff at Uppsala University, Ferrosan had been studying a category of chemical substances known as "diphenyl ethenes." They appeared to have certain chemical similarities to synthetic estrogens and one notion was that they could be useful in indicating forms of cancer with hormonal origins. When it proved that one of the substances could influence animal ovaries in a positive manner, the focus of the project changed. Clinical trials were conducted, a concept was drafted and in 1968 Sexovid (containing cyclofenil) was marketed for the treatment of menstrual dysfunction and certain forms of sterility.[126] Later synthetics added to this category include Tamoxifen, Buserelin, Goserelin, Rehibin and Serono's proprietary clomiphene citrate, Serophene.

Despite all the work, despite all the resources that had been expended and the relatively good clinical results, Leo deregistered Homogonal in 1979. Gonadex however hung on for a few more years. That Homogonal be withdrawn so quickly may have been financially motivated; turnover was low at the same time as the collection and handling of the raw material was costly and complicated.[127] But why Leo's oldest original preparation "survived" one of its youngest rather than the other way around remains puzzling. The question of whether Gonadex should be phased out was discussed on numerous occasions.[128] A scientific reference group which conducted a survey of the company's status in the field of hormones at Leo's behest, concluded in 1982 that it would have been unwise to phase out Homogonal before Gonadex, because the latter's foremost task was to complement the former; "a chorionic gonadotropin drug like Gonadex without an analogue in the pituitary or post-menopausal gonadotropin line has very limited value."[129] The reference group did not think that Leo should scrap Gonadex, but that instead it should be modernized. Its laconic judgment of the drug's quality was hardly flattering, but is thought provoking, shedding light on just how much a science-based drug can change over time.

> In FASS [the Swedish Pharmacopeia], it is stated that this is an "electrophoretic homogeneous chorionic gonadotropin." This was so in 1948, when the newly launched periodical Acta Endocrinologica proudly described this drug; now it is patently false. The purification degree is low, some of the stated indications incorrect.[130]

One interpretation of this assertion is that the structure of Gonadex had changed and deteriorated radically over time. However, it might also mean that the quality of Gonadex in itself was unchanged but the techniques for determining the degree of purity had been improved and refined. Despite these harsh words, Leo stuck by its heirloom until 1986, when the company merged with Pharmacia. And Gonadex was finally laid to rest.[131]

CONCLUSION

This has been the story of the origin, marketing and development of Gonadex and the therapeutic culture to which it belonged. Gonadex was a drug containing crystalline human chorionic gonadotropin (hCG), which when introduced to the public in 1948 was attributed extraordinary characteristics, said to be effective in the treatment of diverse hormonal dysfunctions including sterility, and entirely without side effects. It was praised as a triumph for science, a breakthrough for science-based pharmaceuticals, a future financial boon for the pharmaceutical industry, a blessing for involuntarily childless couples, and the silver bullet that would solve Sweden's declining population predicament.

Predictably perhaps, Gonadex failed to live up to the hype. In time, interest in the much-ballyhooed preparation declined and today there are few who know that a drug named Gonadex ever existed, even though it remained on the market until 1986. Gonadex was no miracle drug and it never became an international sales sensation, but that does not mean that the drug lacks value as an object of historical study—actually, quite the contrary. If history only dealt with drugs, which in hindsight have proven to be milestones of biomedicine, then history would be nothing but a celebration of winners. In the present volume, I have tried to rescue Gonadex from oblivion using perspectives and tools borrowed from the History of Science and Ideas and Science and Technology Studies in order to understand what happened and what went wrong.

The study has been guided by the theoretical postulate that modern pharmaceuticals are techno-scientific artifacts developed and used within the framework of a medical-academic-industrial complex where the boundaries between science, technology and medicine are not fixed, and where the evolution of academic knowledge, industrial product development and clinical practice interact rather than act separately. From such a perspective it has not been fruitful to force Gonadex into a predetermined model of innovation theory. With the support of abundant archival material, this study has instead taken the form of an artifact biography, in which Gonadex and its shifting identity has been followed, from cradle to grave. I have consistently combined the biographical imperative with analyses of the production and distribution networks within which Gonadex was created, marketed and refined. Particular attention has thus been paid to some of the main practices of those networks: consultation, procuration, standardization and mediation. Moreover, I have traced the historical roots of the network in a richer industrial, political, socio-economic and mass medial soil.

In this manner I have been able to demonstrate how complicated the innovation process was and how intricate the connection was between Gonadex and Homogonal. I have also illustrated that the potential success of a drug cannot be known until it leaves the laboratory and the factory, for that is when its real life-cycle really begins. Owing to that, this book is an empirical contribution to the debate on innovation theory in the field of pharmaceuticals. But it also has broader historiographical intent. At the same time as the invention of Gonadex has been the main object of study, I have used it as a prism through which to view the development of reproductive endocrinology, its early involvement in the population question, and the introduction and establishment of hormone treatment in Swedish gynecological practice through the period 1930–1970.

One hypothesis tested was that the research that went into creating Gonadex and other, early hormone preparations intended to cure sterility was intimately connected with the political debate on a stagnating population. In the main, the development of sterility treatments has probably been motivated by individual interests and desires. But during the 1930s and 1940s, as the population debate raged, the project was at least partially prompted by the interests of society and the nation. Together with other gynecological techniques, endocrinology was seen as a tool to help reduce the number of infertile couples, which by extension was expected to lead to a baby boom. This outlook likely contributed to the rapid establishment of endocrinology wards at the women's clinics of major hospitals. While there has never been a government-sponsored sterility treatment program similar to the so-called "sterilization program" in Sweden, in my opinion these practitioners can be seen in an historical perspective as two sides of the same coin. In this book I have only cast a cursory glance at exactly how many individuals underwent sterility treatment (whether via hormone therapy or in some other form) and the actual effect it had on reproduction during the period under investigation. There is an undeniable need for more historical research in this field.

MANY LEVELS OF COLLABORATION

A conclusive factor for my interest in Gonadex were details in the press about how the drug had come into being as a result of intimate "collaboration" between the pharmaceutical company Aktiebolaget Leo (Helsingborg) and Professor Axel Westman of the Royal Caroline Hospital in Stockholm. As I acquainted myself with the contents of these reports, I knew that Westman was considered a pioneer in the field of gynecological endocrinology in Europe, but not that he had hobnobbed with the business world. I saw an opportunity to study and exemplify what the interaction between science, industry, medicine and the mass media was like before it registered on the radar of research and innovation policy. The joint efforts on all fronts, mainly within the framework of Leo's production and distribution network, has therefore been a main theme of this book.

Efforts were coordinated on a number of different levels. As far as Gonadex was concerned, Westman was definitely involved in both its design and testing. When Leo chose to invest in a "line of hormones" during the turbulent 1940s, Westman suggested (for both medical and scientific reasons) that human chorionic gonadotropin be rendered in as pure a form as possible and conducted the clinical tests of the substance at the Caroline Hospital's women's clinic. The purification process itself, however, was by all accounts developed and carried out at Leo's chemical laboratory in Helsingborg under the auspices of engineer Bertil Högberg, while standardization was done at the hormone lab by Lennart Claesson.

Westman also participated in the Gonadex project in many other ways. He helped establish the infrastructural arrangements necessary for Leo to gain access to the raw material from which the hormones could be extracted. In its efforts to produce Ovex, Leo already had experience in collecting and using urine from horses for large-scale hormone production. However, to produce Gonadex, the urine of pregnant women was needed. To procure the latter, Leo needed only to deal with local farmers, but for the former contact had to be made with public institutions and Westman's name opened doors. Moreover, he indirectly participated in the marketing campaign by acting as a mediator between the firm and journalists and consumers. If Westman, with his social and symbolic capital, had not agreed to be its poster boy and scientific guarantor, Gonadex would never have attracted the attention it did.

Thus Westman was an invaluable asset for Leo. Furthermore, Gonadex was but one of many company products with which he was involved. But Westman also profited from collaborating with Leo far beyond the fee he was paid for his consultant services. Thanks to Leo, Westman gained access to Sweden's first and foremost hormone lab with all the assistants, lab animals and purified hormones that came with it, which was of great benefit to the medical and scientific studies he and his colleagues were conducting.

Association with that lab, which moved with Westman from Uppsala to Lund and finally to Stockholm, probably also played a decisive role in his securing further research funding from internal and external financiers, especially the generous Wallenberg Foundation. Leo also helped defray the cost of publishing the scientific periodical *Acta Endocrinologica*, edited by Westman, as well as a pair of conferences on endocrinology. Attempting to draw an inviolable line between Westman's consultant work and his basic research must in these circumstances be considered a fool's errand.

The mechanics of the interaction between Leo and Westman must have been hard to grasp for an outsider. Leo often boasted of its alliance with Westman, even if it restricted itself to Westman's strictly scientific contributions. During the launch of Gonadex, Leo explained that it was Westman who was the "man behind the work." This is not so odd since the connection with outside expertise heightened the company's reputation, credibility and competitive edge on the pharmaceutical market. Leo was so eager to be associated with Westman that they continued to nurture the relationship long after it realized that Westman was no longer capable of contributing any research of commercial value to their production efforts.

The image created was that Westman was responsible for the scientific handiwork which was the basis of Leo's hormone drug, an image perpetuated in Lennart Norgren's above-mentioned study, *Kunskapsöverföring från universitet till företag*. While Norgren states that Gonadex was in fact developed by Bertil Högberg together with Westman and that it is difficult to say who first broached the idea, he also claims that "all hormone drugs had their origins, both as product idea and production method, in the hormone lab funded by Leo and run by Professor Westman."[1] However, I have not been able to find any conclusive evidence of such a straightforward, linear transfer of knowledge from the hormone lab to the company.

For his part Westman only rarely mentioned his relationship with Leo in public. His message during the 1948 press conference and in the mass media was that Gonadex was the result of the hard work done by Leo's "chemical research staff." This was not altogether misleading; purification had in fact been achieved by them, if at his urging. But we must not forget that Westman's argument in favor of extracting hCG and hMG not only had commercial motives but that he also needed them to continue his research. Purified hormones were used as tools in his research. Westman's modesty came as no surprise since in the eyes of his professional peers in the life sciences, being connected to commercial industry did hardly enhance his reputation, credibility and competitive capital. Quite the contrary. A relationship of this nature could be seen as something negative, which is suggested by the vehement criticism leveled by physician Waldemar Gårdlund immediately after the launch of Gonadex (not to mention that his accusations can also be interpreted as a boundary feud among gynecologists). Summing up, it can be said that while Leo exaggerated the significance of Westman's science for its product, Westman in turn toned down both his significance for Leo and Leo's significance for his own research. As historians of science Jean-Paul Gaudillière and Ilana Löwy have indicated, it is not unusual for researchers in the life sciences to belittle or ignore the contributions of industry to routine research. The significance of industry was cloaked, a phenomenon reflected in Axel Westman's obituary, which makes no mention whatsoever of his thirty years of collaboration with Leo.[2] This dimension of Westman's scientific work is now brought to light.

THE IDENTITIES OF GONADEX

Another reason my interest in Gonadex was piqued were the grand visions informing the project, like so much other hormone research in the first half of the twentieth century. In its rhetoric about the opportunities offered by hormone therapy I heard an echo of today's chatter about the potential of genetic therapy. Against this backdrop it was tempting to follow the career of such a celebrated hormone preparation like Gonadex and study how its identity was constructed and overhauled over time.

The history of the pharmaceutical industry testifies to the fact that its products develop and "age" in different ways. Due to grave, unforeseen side effects, some drugs have only been available for a few years before being hastily recalled, with thalidomide probably being the most infamous example.[3] Other drugs, like the analgesic Aspirin, have despite tough competition succeeded in thriving for over a century. But even if all drugs are basically unique, there are still certain similarities, allowing generalization on a more abstract level.

According to medical historian Toine Pieters, the life cycles of most modern drugs have a number of common features, which can be most easily analyzed in terms of birth, rise, fall and death. Such a life cycle begins when positive scientific reports, interest from prominent physicians and attention in the media make the market receptive to a new brand of medicine. In instances when the preparation not only proves effective in solving a medical problem but this problem also has great cultural significance, demand can be colossal; the public's enthusiasm can be kindled and the drug fashionable. Increased demand leads to increased use, but when the drug transitions from small, controlled clinical trials to far more complicated everyday practice, heady promises can often prove to have been exaggerated, which in turn leads to disappointment and a successive decline in interest in the drug. As its reputation suffers, a place is created for a new, more promising drug in the particular area of indication, which in turn can result in demand for the first drug declining even more, before eventually being chased off the shelves. The drug disappears from the market and its life cycle comes to an end.[4]

To some extent Gonadex fits the template constructed by Pieters. Gonadex was marketed as an original preparation in the summer of 1948, after Axel Westman and others had confirmed that crystalline chorionic gonadotropin had biological effect and clinical potential. The perception was that Gonadex could stimulate follicle growth in women who produce insufficient amounts of pituitary hormones. Since the preparation—with Westman's assistance—could be associated with the hot button issue of sterility (and the population question as a whole) as well as the dream of postwar expansion of the Swedish pharmaceutical industry, Gonadex garnered plenty of attention in the mass media. This public exposure contributed to creating interest in and demand for Gonadex among both doctors and patients. The goal was to make Gonadex an "international sales success," but this was not to be. Soon after Gonadex began to be used in clinical practice, it proved to be no miracle cure, at least for sterility. Disenchantment began to spread among those involved and interest in the drug abated drastically. It did not take long for Gonadex to be confronted with competition in the form of other gonadotropin drugs. But despite the fact that Gonadex did not deliver on its promise, and despite the tough competition it faced, it took decades before it was finally deregistered and disappeared from the market.

Portraying the life cycle of Gonadex with broad strokes is insufficient to properly appreciate the biography of Gonadex; it is also necessary to be made aware of the fact that it went through several changes in identity during its lifetime. Though Gonadex has gone down in history as Leo's first original product, it must be remember that it was not in fact a wholly new preparation, or at least not the result of a distinct medical "breakthrough." Gonadex was rather an elaboration of Physex, which Leo had been selling since the early 1930s. It would in fact be more accurate to say that it was Physex that changed identity, first becoming "New Physex" and then Gonadex. This means that Gonadex was the continuation of a tradition of producing, distributing and using gonadotropin drugs when it was launched in 1948. It was a "me-too" drug. Once it entered routine clinical use, it became almost immediately apparent that its therapeutic significance for sterility had been grossly exaggerated. However, that was neither the only nor the biggest threat to its existence. Worse news was the fact that the drug had not been standardized in a manner acceptable to external reviewers. At this juncture, Leo could very well have chosen to abandon Gonadex and focused it efforts on another drug. But it did not. Instead, the company poured more resources into getting Gonadex approved, which it eventually was after its strength was adjusted in accordance with Danish endocrinologist Christian Hamburger's recommendations. At the same time, Gonadex went through a distinct change of identity: the description of its efficacy was revised, its area of indication shrank and Leo even admitted that using "New Gonadex" might result in negative side effects.

There are several reasons why Leo chose to cleave to this particular path. One was the claim made by Axel Westman that the difficulties confronting Gonadex would surely be overcome as long as the research was allowed to continue. Future triumphs were, as he said, merely a matter of time and money. Another reason inspired by Westman was the idea that Gonadex' area of indication could re-expand in the future. Perhaps the drug could be used to treat men with low sperm counts or men who were experiencing male menopause. A third reason was the hope that the export market would eventually open up. Furthermore, it was assumed that a drug of Gonadex' stature had much goodwill value attached to it and was therefore priceless from a marketing perspective.

Each of these mentioned reasons is plausible from the company's perspective, but I wonder if Leo's choice cannot also be understood as an example of path dependence. The term "path dependence" has been developed in business and management research but is widely used by historians of technology as well. In brief, it means that visions formulated and strategies devised in the past tend to have a sustained impact that limits or postpones alternative options in the present.[5] A typical example of path dependency is the decision to construct technical systems, like railways or sewers, which are difficult and expensive to modify or replace once they have been fitted.[6] Applied to Leo's situation, it is noteworthy that Leo was a company which ever since the beginning of the 1930s had set its sights on developing hormone drugs manufactured from urine for the treatment of sterility (first in the form of Ovex). The firm had acquired the necessary skills and established an infrastructural arrangement and production and distribution network in which a large number of actors were involved. Such conceptual, material and social circumstances are not changed overnight. In Chapter One, I quoted sociologist of science Adele E. Clarke's remark that developments in academic reproductive research were by and large dictated by the raw material with which scientists were familiar and had easy access.[7] Such was certainly the case with Leo and its long experience collecting and utilizing urine.

Following the process of transformation and change of identity, Gonadex retook its place in the market in 1951, but its status had been significantly altered. An important detail was that it was now apparent that Gonadex was not effective unless combined with Leo's pregnant mare gonadotropin drug Antex. The idea was that the two used jointly could achieve so-called "full gonadotropic effect," equivalent to the genuine pituitary gonadotropins FSH and LH. But even the link with Antex created problems; new obstacles arose in the 1950s when doubt was cast on the therapeutic value of that preparation. Not only was it scrutinized in a public debate on the side effects of sex hormone drugs in general, its content was considered problematic insofar as it was "non-species specific" and thus "generated antihormones." This time, Gonadex' reprieve arrived when Leo developed the menopausal gonadotropin registered in 1967 as Homogonal. And then Gonadex went through another transformation; instead of playing the lead role in the treatment of sterility it was demoted to supporting actor, in the shadow of Homogonal.

Combination treatment with Homogonal and Gonadex apparently helped many involuntarily childless women suffering from dysfunctional ovulation to finally become pregnant. However, the combination did not always function as intended; it was not free of side effects and it sometimes resulted in multiple pregnancies. Moreover, from the very start, Homogonal faced stiff competition from Gemzell's pituitary preparation, similar hMG drugs manufactured by Serono and Organon, and synthetically-produced pharmaceuticals like clomiphene citrate. When the planned stateside launch of Homogonal to be undertaken with American pharmaceutical giant Ortho stranded, turnover proved much smaller than anticipated and that (together with the eternally-convoluted collection of post-menopausal urine) was likely the foremost cause of the end of its life cycle as prematurely as 1979. Given that Gonadex was dependent on Homogonal, it would have been quite possible for Leo to phase out Gonadex simultaneously, but this did not occur until years later. Why things turned out the way they did is hard to say based on the available archival resources, but obviously there was still sufficient demand for Leo's hGC to warrant its continued existence. After all, Gonadex did have areas of indication aside from acting as a support to Homogonal.[8]

THE NEW PHYSIOLOGY AND THE NEW BIOLOGY

For half a century, from the sexual endocrinology of the early thirties to the reproductive endocrinology of the 1970s, a steady industrial, scientific and medical effort to create hormone drugs for the treatment of sterility was undertaken. Many different hormones were tried, many different methods used, but always at the centre of the research and development coordinated by Leo and the Royal Caroline Hospital's women's clinic were the gonadotropin hormones we have come to know as chorionic gonadotropin, brood mare gonadotropin, pituitary gonadotropin and post-menopausal gonadotropin, respectively. Without questioning the ultimate value of the knowledge generated by this research and development, in hindsight it can still be concluded that the pursuit was fairly narrow-minded. Adjustments were certainly made, as when crystalline chorionic gonadotropin was purified and implemented in the form of Gonadex in the late forties, or when a new generation of endocrinologists took over the field at the Caroline Hospital ten years later and contributed to assuring that both purified pituitary gonadotropin and human post-menopausal gonadotropin were tested and adapted to clinical use. However, these changes were no more radical than they remained faithful to what could be called a "hormone therapeutic culture."

This culture accepted the premise of hormone therapy as *the* method of treatment and discussions of alternative methods were few and far between. Its foundational idea was simply that a certain type of sterility was caused by disturbances in hormone balance and that such "functional sterility" was curable (or at least temporarily affected) with the help of hormones. Also typical was that both reproductive endocrinological research and hormone therapeutic treatment were primarily performed on women—despite awareness of the fact that an involuntarily childless marriage could just as well depend on the husband. Insofar as the work with Gonadex and Homogonal is concerned, my impression is also that this culture was manifestly competitive; the highest priority seems to have been to get the product on the market as quickly as possible. I have not come across one instance in the documents that anyone, either at Leo or the Caroline Hospital, ever questioned the medical wisdom of concentrating single-mindedly on hormones year after year, decade after decade. Whenever Leo did raise questions about research and development, it was always on financial grounds.

Sweeping change in the field of infertility treatment began during the 1970s. Thirty years after the Gonadex press conference, another was held in England. This one, held 26 July 1978, did not concern a new hormone drug but rather a new *type* of reproductive technology called "test-tube" or "in vitro fertilization" (IVF). The press flocked to Oldham Hospital in Lancashire not because the technology itself was brand new—the first attempts to fertilize a human egg in vitro was in fact done already in the 1940s, by Harvard physician John Rock and his assistant Miriam Menkin—but that it had produced its first positive result in the form of a living, breathing "test-tube baby," Louise Brown.[9]

The birth of Louise Brown, filmed by a professional television team, implied that a new era of reproductive technology had begun. Author Robin Marantz Henig, who delivered an exhaustive study of the early history of IVF with her book *Pandora's Baby* (2004), speaks of the happy event as the birth of a revolution.[10] It was also the beginning of the huge scientific, bioethical, legal, financial and gender debate, which continues to this day. The event looms so large in the public consciousness that it sometimes seems like the history of reproductive technology actually began in 1978. But as the present book shows, such a picture is a far too simple one of the past.[11] Furthermore, there was a certain connection between the new IVF technique and the old hormone therapy.

The mechanics of IVF involves a mature egg being removed and fertilized outside the woman's body, generally in a prepared Petri dish. Once cell division has begun, the embryo is implanted in the womb and left to develop like a normal fetus. The fertilization process and implantation of the embryo is a touchy moment that can easily fail. One means of increasing the odds of success is removing several eggs during the same operation.[12] Since a woman normally produces only one egg at a time, the demand emerged for a preparation that could stimulate increased development of the ovarian follicles and subsequent ovulation. This is where the existing gonadotropin drugs came in. The fact that using these drugs often resulted in multiple ovulations was now transformed from a medical problem to a reproductive advantage, which further exemplifies how hard it is to know in advance the significance a drug is ultimately going to have. The older technique could also help prevent disruptions in ovulation; treatment with hMG and/or hCG preparations was often the first alternative before proceeding further. Thus hormone drugs continued to be produced, sold and used.

With the growing demand for gonadotropins came an increased need for raw material. In order to fulfill the requirements of the early 1990s, urine from more than 100,000 women from Europe, Korea, China, India and South America was used.[13] This made the situation increasingly complicated on a strictly logistical basis but also brought about new discussion about the risks of spreading infectious proteins, so-called "prions." However, a new technical innovation waited in the wings. In Sweden, it is still possible to buy gonadotropin drugs, which have been extracted from urine. Pregnyl, Organon's hCG drug of 1932, which had long competed with Physex and Gonadex, is still available, and Ferring has been marketing an hMG drug called Menopur for several years now.[14] However, nowadays it is most common for gonadotropin drugs to contain hormones produced via hybrid DNA technology.

The manufacture of hormones by this technology began as far back as the 1970s when it became possible to produce insulin with the aid of genetically-modified bacteria and by the end of the next decade, recombinant gonadotropins were being produced from the altered cells lines of Chinese hamsters. The first recombinant FSH drugs went on sale after several years' clinical trials (Gonal-F in 1995 and Puregon a year later) and were greeted with much acclaim. Compared with the older techniques, the new method of production had undeniable advantages—the final product boasts a consistent structure without any trace of undesirable substances and the pharmaceutical industry, still dominated by Serono and Organon, could finally stop the time-consuming collection of urine. Access to hormones seemed no longer subject to restriction.[15]

In summation, it can be stated that while huge changes have occurred in the field of infertility treatment in recent decades, hormone therapy did not disappear with the advent of IVF and hybrid DNA. In the therapeutic field of "treatment of involuntary childlessness," the "new physiology," as endocrinology once was known, was absorbed by "the new biology." With that, one can concur with the sociologist of science Ludwik Fleck that here, as in so many other fields of medicine, there has been and continues to be a powerful connection between old and new knowledge.[16] The aim of hormone therapy culture may have been myopic, but it was the collective effort of companies like Leo and researchers like Axel Westman, Bertil Högberg, Egon Diczfalusy and Carl Axel Gemzell, together with their patients and staff, which laid the foundation for the in-vitro revolution.

Thanks to IVF treatment, which has been refined and improved in numerous ways over recent decades, it is now technically possible to help far more involuntarily childless individuals than ever before. With the aid of "microinjection," by which a single sperm is mechanically inserted into the egg with a miniscule pipette, many cases of male infertility can also be remedied. Reproductive technology continues to amass facts and figures, and the possibility of diagnosing the causes of infertility increases exponentially, thanks in particular to the introduction of ultrasound technology. This positive trend has even left its mark on the discursive level, insofar as the term "sterile" has today largely been replaced with the less fatalistic-sounding "infertile."[17] But despite all this success, it should be mentioned that technology and knowledge is far from being enough in all cases, either for an exact diagnosis or to achieve a pregnancy carried to term, which says something about how complex the human organism is. Like the hormone therapeutic culture that preceded it, today's IVF culture has it limits, too.[18]

It is customary to conclude a scientific or pedagogical text on the treatment of infertility with a few optimistic words whereby the author speculates about the new possibilities just ahead, on the therapeutic progress expected within "the near future." With the utmost sincerity, I hope that the situation of involuntarily childless individuals becomes better tomorrow than it is today, but I respectfully decline to speculate how. If I have learned one thing working on this book, it is that discretion is the better part of valor in the face of scientifically sanctioned proclamations on the consequences of new research. Vision is an important impulse in both research and industry, but scientists and businessmen (and journalists) ought to avoid raising exaggerated expectations which risk becoming shattered dreams.

NOTES

INTRODUCTION

1. John V. Pickstone, "Introduction," in idem, ed., *Medical Innovations in Historical Perspective* (New York: St. Martin's Press, 1992), p. 1.
2. See for example "Hormonpreparat bot för kvinnor, svensk triumf," *Svenska Morgonbladet* 11 June (1948).
3. "En tredjedel av alla sterila kvinnor kan få barn genom nytt hormonpreparat," *Husmodern* 28 (1948), p. 19.
4. Håkan Lindgren, "Läkemedelsindustri," in *Nationalencyklopedin* (Höganäs: Bra Böcker, 1993), vol. 12. On Dextran (Macrodex) and Xylocain respectively, see Anders Lundgren, "Dextran som blodplasmasubstitut," in Tore Frängsmyr, ed., *Vetenskap och läkemedel: Ett historiskt perspektiv* (Stockholm: Almqvist and Wiksell International, 1987); Anders Lundgren, *Vetenskap till vardags: En historia kring Xylocain* (Stockholm: Stiftelsen Bengt Lundquists minne, 1995).
5. Since the 1960s journalists have become increasingly skeptical toward science, frequently reporting about risks and problems. However, life science journalism in Sweden still seems to promote rather than problematize science. See Malin Ideland, *Dagens gennyheter: Hur massmedier berättar om genetik och genteknik* (Lund: Nordic Academic Press, 2002).
6. Lennart Norgren, *Kunskapsöverföring från universitet till företag: En studie av universitetsforskningens betydelse för de svenska läkemedelsföretagens produktlanseringar 1945–1984* (Uppsala: Uppsala University, 1989), pp. 66, 69–70, 88, 93, 150. Gonadex is described in a similar way in Jerker Ahlin and Rolf Lundgren, *Från Leopiller till nicorette: En industri i Helsingborg under det tjugonde seklet* (Helsingborg: Pharmacia, 2002), p. 115.
7. This is well known within Science and Technology Studies (STS) dealing with the "stabilization" of theoretical or technical innovations. For an introduction to this field, see Jan Golinski, *Making Natural Knowledge: Constructivism and the History of Science* (Cambridge: Cambridge University Press, 1998). An innovation in this sense is something that is introduced not only on the economic market but also in other social systems. Cf. Pickstone, "Introduction," p. 1.
8. See Gunnar Broberg and Mattias Tydén, *Oönskade i folkhemmet: Rashygien och sterilisering i Sverige* (Stockholm: Gidlund, 1991); Maija Runcis, *Steriliseringar i folkhemmet* (Stockholm: Ordfront, 1998); Swedish Government Official Reports (hereafter SOU) 2000:20 *Steriliseringsfrågan i Sverige 1935–1975: Historisk belysning, kartläggning, intervjuer*; Mattias Tydén, *Från politik till praktik: De svenska steriliseringslagarna 1935–1975*, 2d ed., enl. (Stockholm: Almqvist and Wiksell International, 2002).
9. Susanne Lundin, *Guldägget: Föräldraskap i biomedicinens tid* (Lund: Historiska Media, 1997), p. 30.

10. A general introduction to and critique of the policy debate on innovations and innovation systems in Sweden is presented by Sven Widmalm, "Innovationssamhället," in Mats Benner and Sverker Sörlin, eds., *Forska lagom och vara världsbäst: Sverige inför forskningens globala strukturomvandling* (Stockholm: SNS Förlag, 2008).
11. Merriley Borell, "Setting the Standards for a New Science: Edward Schäfer and Endocrinology," *Medical History* 22 (1978), p. 283.
12. Herman H. Rubin, *The Glands of Life: The Story of the Mysterious Endocrine Glands—Their Effects on Our Mental, Physical and Sexual Health, Personality and Behavior* (New York: B.B. Bellaire, 1935).
13. According to the definition cited by Axel Westman, a woman is considered "sterile" if she lacks the biological ability to produce and release eggs that can be fertilized. Eggs can however be produced, released and fertilized without leading to pregnancy, e.g. due to the failure of the egg to develop properly in the uterus or rejection. In such instances, the patient is not considered sterile but "infertile." Today, the definition of sterility is more stringent and the diagnosis more selective than in Westman's time. While "infertility" is the term in general use today, the present book adheres to Westman's definition in order to avoid anachronisms.
14. See Julia E. Rechter, "'The Glands of Destiny': A History of Popular, Medical and Scientific Views of the Sex Hormones in 1920s America" (Ph.D diss., University of California, Berkeley, 1997), p. 25.
15. Christer Nordlund, "Hormoner och visioner i mellankrigstid: Louis Bermans idéer om möjligheten att förädla mänskligheten," *Lychnos: Årsbok för idé- och lärdomshistoria 2004*; idem, "Endocrinology and Expectations in 1930s America: Louis Berman's Ideas on New Creations in Human Beings," *British Journal for the History of Science* 40 (2007).
16. Nicolas Rasmussen, "Steroids in Arms: Science, Government, Industry, and the Hormones of the Adrenal Cortex in the United States, 1930–1950," *Medical History* 46 (2002), p. 299. There were, of course, many other fields of research within the life sciences that claimed to have the answer to the "question of life." See further Timothy Lenoir, *The Strategy of Life: Teleology and Mechanics in Nineteenth-Century German Biology* (1982), new ed. (Chicago and London: University of Chicago Press, 1989); Evelyn Fox Keller, *Making Sense of Life: Explaining Biological Development with Models, Metaphors, and Machines* (Cambridge, Mass. and London: Harvard University Press, 2002); Jane Maienschein, *Whose View of Life?: Embryos, Cloning, and Stem Cells* (Cambridge, Mass. and London: Harvard University Press, 2005).
17. David Cantor, "Cortisone and the Politics of Drama, 1949–55," in Pickstone, ed., *Medical Innovations in Historical Perspective*, p. 173 f; Leo B. Slater, "Industry and Academy: The Synthesis of Steroids," *Historical Studies in the Physical and Biological Sciences* 30 (2000), p. 444.
18. Sheila M. Rothman and David J. Rothman, *The Pursuit of Perfection: The Promise and Perils of Medical Enhancement* (New York: Pantheon Books, 2003).
19. See Annika Nilsson, *Barn till varje pris?* (Stockholm: Atlantis, 1996).
20. Since 1992, the Royal Swedish Academy of Sciences has funded a series of popular-interest books on "the human and the new biology." Nilsson's *Barn till varje pris?*—"A child at any price?"—is part of this series.
21. Rasmussen, "Steroids in Arms," p. 300.

22. Cf. Jean-Paul Gaudillière, "The Pharmaceutical Industry in the Biotech Century: Toward a History of Science, Technology and Business?," *SHPBBS* 32 (2001); idem, "Introduction: Drug Trajectories," *SHPBBS* 36 (2005). For a general overview of the history of biotechnology, see Robert Bud, *The Uses of Life: A History of Biotechnology* (Cambridge: Cambridge University Press, 1993).
23. For an introduction to and overview of this field of research, see Karin Johannisson, *Den mörka kontinenten: Kvinnan, medicinen och fin-de-siècle* (1994), new ed. (Stockholm: Norstedt, 1998); Nelly Oudshoorn, *Beyond the Natural Body: An Archeology of Sexhormones* (London and New York, 1994); Lundin, *Guldägget*; Gary L. Albrecht, Ray Fitzpatrick and Susan C. Scrimshaw, eds., *Handbook of Social Studies in Health and Medicine* (London: Sage, 2000); Adele E. Clarke et al., "Biomedicalization: Technoscientific Transformations of Health, Illness, and U.S. Biomedicine," *American Sociological Review* 68 (2003).
24. The concept "black box" is used in many different ways within science and technology studies. It may, for example, refer to a scientific "fact," which is taken for granted, or to a technical "artifact," whose performance is not called into question. See Bruno Latour, *Science in Action: How to Follow Scientists and Engineers through Society* (1987), new ed. (Cambridge, Mass.: Harvard University Press, 1994), pp. 2–3, 131.
25. Roy Porter, *The Greatest Benefit to Mankind: A Medical History of Humanity from Antiquity to the Present* (London: HarperCollins, 1997).
26. See Harry Collins and Trevor Pinch, *Dr. Golem: How to Think about Medicine* (Chicago and London: University of Chicago Press, 2005), pp. 18–34.
27. See Ivan Wolffers, Anita Hardon and Janita Janssen, *Marketing Fertility: Women, Menstruation and the Pharmaceutical Industry* (Amsterdam: WEMOS, 1989); John Abraham, *Science, Politics and the Pharmaceutical Industry: Controversy and Bias in Drug Regulation* (London and New York: UCL Press, 1995); "Intersections of Pharmaceutical Research and Marketing," special feature issue of *SSS* 34 (2004). For an overview of the history of the pharmaceutical industry, see Louis Galambos and Jeffrey L. Sturchio, "The Transformation of the Pharmaceutical Industry in the Twentieth Century," in John Krige and Dominique Pestre, eds., *Companion to Science in the Twentieth Century* (1997), new ed. (London and New York: Routledge, 2003).
28. Peter Davis, "Introduction: Medicines in a Postmodern World," in idem, ed., *Contested Ground: Public Purpose and Private Interest in the Regulation of Prescription Drugs* (New York and Oxford: Oxford University Press, 1996), p. 7.
29. See Michelle Stanworth, ed., *Reproductive Technologies: Gender, Motherhood and Medicine* (Cambridge: Polity Press, 1987); Lundin, *Guldägget*; Jon Turney, *Frankenstein's Footsteps: Science, Genetics and Popular Culture* (New Haven and London: Yale University Press, 1998); Naomi Pfeffer, "Pioneers of Infertility Treatment," in Lawrence Conrad and Anne Hardy, eds., *Women and Modern Medicine* (Amsterdam and New York: Ropodi, 2001).
30. Gena Corea, *The Mother Machine: Reproductive Technologies from Artificial Insemination to Artificial Wombs* (New York: Harper and Row, 1985). In Sweden, Corea's analysis has been discussed in Anna Weimarck, "Fortplantningsteknologier—etik och kvinnosyn," *Kvinnovetenskaplig tidskrift* 4 (1986).

31. The literature on this topic, especially on IVF fertilization, from 1980 and onward, is extensive. For different views and bibliographical notes, see Maureen McNeil, "New Reproductive Technologies: Dreams and Broken Promises," *Science as Culture* 3 (1993); Elizabeth C. Britt, "Infertility as a Medical Problem: Recasting Feminist Accounts of Nature, Science, and the Law," *Science as Culture* 7 (1998); Adele E. Clarke, *Disciplining Reproduction: Modernity, American Life Sciences, and the "Problems of Sex"* (Berkeley: University of California Press, 1998); Heléna Ragoné and Sharla K. Willis, "Reproduction and Assisted Reproductive Technologies," in Albrecht, Fitzpatrick and Scrimshaw, eds., *Handbook of Social Studies in Health and Medicine*; Charis Thompson, *Making Parents: The Ontological Choreography of Reproductive Technologies* (Cambridge, Mass.: MIT Press, 2005), pp. 55–75.
32. An initiated discussion of historiographical problems related to controversial topics in the history of contemporary medicine is provide by Lene Koch, "On Ethics, Scientists, and Democracy: Writing the History of Eugenic Sterilization," in Ronald E. Doel and Thomas Söderqvist, eds., *The Historiography of Contemporary Science, Technology, and Medicine: Writing Recent Science* (London and New York: Routledge, 2006).
33. Godelieve van Heteren, Marijke Gijswijt-Hofstra and Tilli Tansey, "Introduction," in idem, eds., *Biographies of Remedies: Drugs, Medicines and Contraceptives in Dutch and Anglo-American Healing Cultures* (Amsterdam and New York: Rodopi, 2002), p. 3.
34. See Michael Ludwig et al., "Ovarian Stimulation: From Basic Science to Clinical Application," *Reproductive BioMedicine Online* 5, suppl. 1 (2002).
35. Rein Vos, *Drugs Looking for Diseases: Innovative Drug Research and the Development of the Beta Blockers and the Calcium Antagonists* (Dordrecht and Boston: Kluwer Academic Publishers, 1991), pp. xxiii–xxiv.
36. On how users and their representatives contribute to shaping medical (and other) technologies, see Nelly Oudshoorn and Trevor Pinch, eds., *How Users Matter: The Co-construction of Users and Technology* (2003), new ed. (Cambridge, Mass.: MIT Press, 2005).
37. On the history of artifacts, see Sven Widmalm and Hjalmar Fors, eds., *Artefakter: Industrin, vetenskapen och de tekniska nätverken* (Hedemora: Gidlund, 2004). See further the classical paper by Trevor Pinch and Wiebe Bijker, "The Social Construction of Facts and Artefacts: Or How the Sociology of Science and the Sociology of Technology Might Benefit Each Other," *SSS* 14 (1984). Regarding the complex relationships between science, technology and industry, see also Adele E. Clarke and Joan H. Fujimura, eds., *The Right Tools for the Job: At Work in Twentieth-Century Life Sciences* (Princeton, NJ: Princeton University Press, 1992); Jean-Paul Gaudillière and Ilana Löwy, eds., *The Invisible Industrialist: Manufactures and the Production of Scientific Knowledge* (London and New York: St. Martin's Press, 1998); Karl Grandin, Nina Wormbs and Sven Widmalm, eds., *The Science-Industry Nexus: History, Policy, Implications* (Sagamore Beach: Science History Publications, 2004).
38. Celia Roberts, "'Successful Aging' with Hormone Replacement Therapy: It May Be Sexist, But What If It Works?," *Science as Culture* 11 (2002), p. 55.
39. Toine Pieters, *Interferon: The Science and Selling of a Miracle Drug* (London and New York: Routledge, 2005), pp. 4–5.

40. On the historiography of scientific biographies, see Sune Åkerman, Ronny Ambjörnsson and Per Ringby, eds., *Att skriva människan: Essäer om biografin som livshistoria och vetenskaplig genre* (Stockholm: Carlsson, 1997); Henrik Rosengren and Johan Östling, eds., *Med livet som insats: Biografin som humanistisk genre* (Lund: Sekel, 2007); Thomas Söderqvist, ed., *The History and Poetics of Scientific Biography* (Aldershot: Ashgate, 2007).
41. The classic cultural study on objects is Arjun Appadurai, ed., *The Social Life of Things: Commodities in Cultural Perspective* (Cambridge: Cambridge University Press, 1986). Regarding "scientific objects," see Lorraine Daston, ed., *Biographies of Scientific Objects* (Chicago and London: University of Chicago Press, 2000).
42. Beside van Heteren, Gijswijt-Hofstra and Tansey, eds., *Biographies of Remedies*, mentioned above, I would like to recommend Pieters, *Interferon*; Jean-Paul Gaudillière, "Genesis and Development of a Biomedical Object: Styles of Thought, Styles of Work and the History of Sex Steroids," *SHPBBS* 35 (2004); and *SHPBBS* 36 (2005), a special feature issue on "Drug Trajectories."
43. Vivien Walsh and Jordan Goodman, "The Billion Dollar Molecule: Taxol in Historical and Theoretical Perspective," in van Heteren, Gijswijt-Hofstra and Tansey, eds., *Biographies of Remedies*, p. 247. On exploring artifacts by combining biography and network analysis, see Widmalm and Fors, eds., *Artefakter*.
44. Ylva Hasselberg and Tom Petersson, "Nätverksbegreppets utveckling," in idem, eds., *"Bäste broder!": Nätverk, entreprenörskap och innovation i svenskt näringsliv* (Hedemora: Gidlund, 2006), p. 50.
45. The concepts "production network" and "distribution network" are borrowed from Galambos and Sturchio, "The Transformation of the Pharmaceutical Industry in the Twentieth Century," pp. 232 f. See also Louis Galambos and Jane Eliot Sewell, *Networks of Innovation: Vaccine Development at Merck, Sharp and Dohme, and Mulford, 1895–1995* (Cambridge: Cambridge University Press, 1995).
46. John V. Pickstone, *Ways of Knowing: A New History of Science, Technology and Medicine* (Manchester: Manchester University Press, 2000), pp. 13–15, 162 ff. See also idem, "Working Knowledges Before and After circa 1800: Practices and Disciplines in the History of Science, Technology, and Medicine," *Isis* 98 (2007).
47. Anders Lundgren, "Knowledge and Needs: Some Aspects of the Development of the Chemical Industry," in Anne Kristine Børresen, ed., *Science, Crafts and Ignorance: Perspectives on the History of Knowledge* (Trondheim: Tapir, 2004).
48. Gunnar Eriksson, "Vetenskapens roller i läkemedelsframställningen: Från den galeniska eran till den svenska läkemedelsindustrins framväxt," in Frängsmyr, ed., *Vetenskap och läkemedel.*
49. Nicolas Rasmussen, "The Moral Economy of the Drug Company–Medical Scientist Collaboration in Interwar America," *SSS* 34 (2004), pp. 165–167.
50. John Parascandola, "The Preposterous Provision: The American Society for Pharmacology and Experimental Therapeutics' Ban on Industrial Pharmacologists, 1908–1941," in Jonathan Liebenau, Gregory J. Higby and Elaine C. Stroud, eds., *Pill Peddlers: Essays on the History of the Pharmaceutical Industry* (Madison, Wisconsin: American Institute of the History of Pharmacy, 1990), p. 30.
51. Though it was still common to view positions within industry as the "second best" alternative. See Pickstone, *Ways of Knowing*, p. 183.
52. Rasmussen, "The Moral Economy."

53. Jonathan Liebenau, *Medical Science and Medical Industry: The Formation of the American Pharmaceutical Industry* (Basingstoke: Macmillan in association with Business History Unit, University of London, 1987), p. 9; Galambos and Sewell, *Networks of Innovation*, pp. 54 f; Lennart Paalzow, John Sjögren and Lars Werkö, "Svensk läkemedelsforskning," in Rune Lönngren et al., eds., *Svensk farmaci under 1900-talet*, 3 vol. (Stockholm: Swedish Academy of Pharmaceutical Sciences, 1999), vol. 2, pp. 59 f.
54. Marius Tausk, *Organon: The Story of an Unusual Pharmaceutical Enterprise* (1978), Eng. transl. (Oss: Akzo Pharma, 1984); Nelly Oudshoorn, "On the Making of Sex Hormones: Research Materials and the Production of Knowledge," *SSS* 20 (1990), pp. 14 f.
55. John P. Swann, *Academic Scientists and the Pharmaceutical Industry: Cooperative Research in Twentieth-Century America* (Baltimore and London: Johns Hopkins University Press, 1988), pp. 57 ff.
56. Ibid., pp. 87–93.
57. I have briefly discussed this topic in "Dolda platser i hormonernas historia: Bondgården, kvinnokliniken och vårdhemmet," in Erland Mårald and Christer Nordlund, eds., *Topos: Essäer om tänkvärda platser och platsbundna tankar* (Stockholm: Carlssons, 2006).
58. Oudshoorn, "On the Making of Sex Hormones"; idem, "United We Stand: The Pharmaceutical Industry, Laboratory, and Clinic in the Development of Sex Hormones into Scientific Drugs, 1920–1940," *Science, Technology, and Human Values* 18 (1993).
59. Regarding standardization (or metrology), see Joseph O'Connell, "Metrology: The Creation of Universality by the Circulation of Particulars," *SSS* 23 (1993); Golinski, *Making Natural Knowledge*, pp. 173–177.
60. W. Chas Cockburn, "The International Contribution to the Standardization of Biological Substances: I. Biological Standards and the League of Nations 1921–1946," *Biologicals* 19 (1991); idem et al., "The International Contribution to the Standardization of Biological Substances: II. Biological Standards and the World Health Organization 1947–1990. General Considerations," *Biologicals* 19 (1991).
61. See Eugenia Rosemberg, "Use of Standards: General Considerations," in idem, ed., *Gonadotropins 1968* (Los Altos, California: Geron-X, 1968); Toine Pieters, "Managing Differences in Biomedical Research: The Case of Standardizing Interferons," *SHPBBS* 29 (1998); Christiane Sinding, "Making the Unit of Insulin: Standards, Clinical Work, and Industry, 1920–1925," *Bulletin of the History of Medicine* 76 (2002).
62. Jean-Paul Gaudillière and Ilana Löwy, "General Introduction," in idem, eds., *The Invisible Industrialist*, p. 10.
63. Jennifer R. Fishman, "Manufacturing Desire: The Commodification of Female Sexual Dysfunction," *SSS* 34 (2004), p. 188.
64. Dorothy Nelkin, *Selling Science: How the Press Covers Science and Technology* (1987), rev. ed. (New York: W.E. Freeman and Co., 1995); Toine Pieters, "About Media, Audiences and Marketing Medicines: The Interferons," in van Heteren, Gijswijt-Hofstra and Tansey, eds., *Biographies of Remedies*; Pieters, *Interferon*, pp. 134–157.
65. After merging with Ferrosan in 1984, Leo was absorbed by Pharmacia two years later, first as a subsidiary and then as an integrated component. Pharmacia subsequently

merged with Kabi to form Kabi Pharmacia in 1990, which three years later became simply "Pharmacia." In 1995, another fusion occurred as Pharmacia merged with the Upjohn Company to create Pharmacia and Upjohn, which was subsequently bought by Pfizer in 2003. However, Pfizer almost immediately sold off its Swedish holdings. The plant in Helsingborg was bought by Johnson and Johnson in 2006, creating the subsidiary McNeil Sweden AB.

66. Ahlin and Lundgren, *Från Leopiller till nicorette.*

CHAPTER ONE

1. Oudshoorn, *Beyond the Natural Body.*
2. Bernard was thinking about the liver, and its "external secretion" (of bile) and "internal secretion" (of glycogen), but he indicated that also other organs worked that way.
3. Arnold Josefeson, *Vad betyda insöndringsorganen för vår kropp och själ?: Översikt* (Stockholm: Geber, 1925), p. 12.
4. See Edward Schäfer, "Internal Secretions," *The Lancet* 10 August (1895).
5. See Carl-Herman Hjortsjö, "Inre secretion," in *Svensk uppslagsbok* (Malmö: Förlagshuset Norden, 1950), vol. 14, p. 453.
6. Andrew Cunningham and Perry Williams, eds., *The Laboratory Revolution in Medicine* (Cambridge: Cambridge University Press, 1992).
7. Leonard G. Wilson, "Internal Secretions in Disease: The Historical Relations of Clinical Medicine and Scientific Physiology," *Journal of the History of Medicine and Allied Sciences* 39 (1984); Rasmussen, "Steroids in Arms," p. 301.
8. An analysis of how the perception of the ovary changed with the transformation of the "old physiology" into the "new physiology" is presented in Chandak Sengoopta, "The Modern Ovary: Constructions, Meanings, Uses," *History of Science* 38 (2000).
9. David Hamilton, *The Monkey Gland Affair* (London: Chatto and Windus, 1986); Laura Davidow Hirshbein, "The Glandular Solution: Sex, Masculinity, and Aging in the 1920s," *Journal of the History of Sexuality* 9 (2000). Eugen Steinach presented his research in the book *Hormonerna som forma livet* (1940), Swe. transl. (Stockholm: Bonniers, 1940). In co-operation with urologists Steinach also performed testicular transplants in order to "cure" homosexual men, i.e. make them heterosexual. See Chandak Sengoopta, "Glandular Politics: Experimental Biology, Clinical Medicine, and Homosexual Emancipation in Fin-de-Siècle Central Europé," *Isis* 89 (1998), pp. 465 ff.
10. Sengoopta, "The Modern Ovary."
11. Quotated in Rechter, "'The Glands of Destiny,'" p. 209.
12. Margaret Marsh and Wanda Ronner, *The Empty Cradle: Infertility in America from Colonial Times to the Present* (Baltimore, Maryland: Johns Hopkins University Press, 1996), pp. 131–134.
13. Merriley Borell, "Organotherapy, British Physiology, and Discovery of the Internal Secretions," *JHB* 9 (1976).
14. Idem, "Brown-Séquard's Organotherapy and Its Appearance in America at the End of the Nineteenth Century," *Bulletin of the History of Medicine* 50 (1976).

15. A pamphlet introducing and promoting the new method was published in Boston as early as 1889. Its title was *The "Elixir of Life": Dr Brown-Séquard's own account of his Famous Alleged Remedy for Debility and Old Age, Dr. Variot's Experiments, and Contemporaneous Comments of the Profession and the Press*, and it is mentioned in Borell, "Brown-Séquard's Organotherapy," p. 313. Hormones continued to be described as the "elixir of life," e.g. in the text on the back cover of Axel Westman's book *Hormoner* (Stockholm: Wahlström and Widstrand, 1940).
16. Organ preparations had different components. Some were made from pig ovaries, others from cattle ovaries and still others a mixture of the two. Some preferred using the entire ovary, while others only the extract. A few recommended that the ovaries be removed only when the animal was in heat, others that one should wait until after insemination. Human sex glands were rarely used.
17. Editorial, "Animal Extracts as Therapeutic Agents," *British Medical Journal* 17 June (1893), p. 1279.
18. Oudshoorn, "On the Making of Sex Hormones," pp. 10 f.
19. P. Bergman, "Om adrenalinets terapeutiska användning," *ASL* 3 (1906); Mary Ellen Bowden, "The Rush to Adrenaline: An Excerpt from Pharmaceutical Achievers," *Chemical Heritage* 21 (2003). On the debate concerning the term "adrenaline," see E. M. Tansey, "What's in a Name?: Henry Dale and Adrenaline, 1906," *Medical History* 39 (1995).
20. "Syntetiska binjurepreparater," *SFT* 13 (1909).
21. Rasmussen, "Steroids in Arms," p. 303.
22. Victor C. Medvei, *The History of Clinical Endocrinology: A Comprehensive Account of Endocrinology from Earliest Times to the Present Day* (Carnforth and New York: The Parthenon Publishing Group, 1993), p. 5. Other names suggested in the early twentieth century included "chalones," "autacoids" and "harmozones."
23. Ernest H. Starling, "The Chemical Correlation of the Functions of the Body," *The Lancet* 5 August (1905), p. 340. Starling later developed his view on hormones in the essay "The Wisdom of the Body," *The Lancet* 20 October (1923), the title of which was used by Walter Cannon in his theory of the body as a self-regulating system.
24. Westman, *Hormoner*, p. 5. According to Westman it was, for instance, difficult to distinguish hormones from vitamins.
25. See Edward Schäfer, *An Introduction to the Study of the Endocrine Glands and Internal Secretions: Lane Medical Lectures, 1913* (Stanford: Leland Stanford Junior University, 1914); idem, *The Endocrine Organs: An Introduction to the Study of Internal Secretion* (London and New York: Longmans, Green, and Co., 1916). Previously, endocrine glands were often called "blood glands."
26. Medvei, *The History of Clinical Endocrinology*, p. 5.
27. Endocrinology should be seen more as a wide-ranging field of study than a single discipline. Research over time has come to embrace morphological sciences like anatomy, embryology and histology, and laboratory sciences including physiology, biochemistry, neurology, molecular biology and genetics. Endocrinology has also always had an expressed medical side, and sometimes a distinction is made between experimental and clinical endocrinology. Research in reproductive biology was initially called "sexual endocrinology" and later "reproductive endocrinology." See Arthur F. W. Hughes, "A History of Endocrinology," *Journal of the History of Medicine and Allied Sciences* 32 (1977); Medvei, *The History of Clinical Endocrinology*.

The historiography of endocrinology is discussed in Diana Long Hall and Thomas F. Glick, "Endocrinology: A Brief Introduction," *JHB* 9 (1976).

28. On the development of this society, see Frank M. Pottenger, "The Association for the Study of Internal Secretions: Its Past, Its Future," *Endocrinology* 30 (1942); Hans Lisser, "The Endocrine Society: The First Forty Years (1917–1957)," *Endocrinology* 80 (1967); Alfred E. Wilhelmi, "The Endocrine Society: Origin, Organization, and Institutions," *Endocrinology* 123 (1988). Swedish scientists were also encouraged to join, see Arnold Josefson, "Internationellt samarbete på den endokrina forskningens område: Ett beaktansvärt upprop från Amerika," *ASL* 14 (1917).
29. Marsh and Ronner, *The Empty Cradle*, p. 137.
30. Theodore B. Schwartz, "Henry Harrower and the Turbulent Beginnings of Endocrinology," *Annals of Internal Medicine* 131 (1999).
31. Lewellys F. Barker, "The Study of the Internal Secretions: An Introduction," *Endocrinology* 1 (1917), p. 2. See also A. S. Blumgarten, "The Positive Achievements of Endocrinology," *Endocrinology* 7 (1922).
32. Adele E. Clarke, "Controversy and the Development of Reproductive Sciences," *Social Problems* 37 (1990), pp. 22 f. On the debate on quackery in the USA, see Paul Starr, *The Social Transformation of American Medicine: The Rise of a Sovereign Profession and the Making of a Vast Industry* (New York: Basic Books, 1982).
33. Pottenger, "The Association for the Study of Internal Secretions," p. 846.
34. See "The Present Position of Organotherapy," *The Lancet* 20 January (1923). See further Diana Long Hall, "The Critic and the Advocate: Contrasting British Views on the State of Endocrinology in the Early 1920s," *JHB* 9 (1976); Thomas F. Glick, "On the Diffusion of a New Speciality: Marañón and the 'Crisis' of Endocrinology in Spain," *JHB* 9 (1976); Medvei, *The History of Clinical Endocrinology*, pp. 275 ff.
35. In Soviet Russia an Endocrinological Society was established in 1924 and an Institute of Experimental Endocrinology as well as a journal for endocrinology, *Vestnik Endokrinologii*, was founded in 1925. The German *Endokrinologie: Zentralblatt für das Gebiet der inneren Sekretion und Konstitutionsforschung*, launched in 1928, was probably the first European journal dedicated to the study of endocrinology. The *Journal of Endocrinology* was established in England in 1938 but met with difficulty due to the outbreak of the Second World War. The British Society for Endocrinology was founded after the war, in 1946, the same year as a Section of Endocrinology was attached to the Royal Society of Medicine. See Nikolai Krementsov, "Hormones and the Bolsheviks: From Organotherapy to Experimental Endocrinology, 1918–1929," *Isis* 99 (2008); Peter M. F. Bishop, "The Development of British Endocrinology," *British Medical Journal* 9 April (1955). A similar institutionalization of endocrinology occurred in Sweden when the Swedish Society for Endocrinology as well as a Section of Endocrinology attached to the Swedish Society of Medicine were founded in 1945. In Asia, the first issue of *Endocrinologia Japonica* was published in 1954.
36. Rechter, "'The Glands of Destiny,'" p. 23.
37. Quoted in Rothman and Rothman, *The Pursuit of Perfection*, p. 16. Raw pancreas was however also used in therapy after the launch of insulin. See Martin Edwards, "Good, Bad or Offal?: The Evaluation of Raw Pancreas Therapy and the Rhetoric of Control in the Therapeutic Trial, 1925," *Annals of Science* 61 (2004).

38. The standard book on the history of insulin and diabetes research is Michael Bliss, *The Discovery of Insulin* (1982), 3d ed. (Toronto: University of Toronto Press, 2000). The Swedish counterpart would be Tord Ajanki, *Historien om diabetes och insulinets upptäckt* (Sundbyberg: Swedish Diabetes Society, 1999). On the history of diabetes treatment before insulin, see Robert Tattersall, "Pancreatic Organotherapy for Diabetes, 1889–1921," *Medical History* 39 (1995).
39. Rothman and Rothman, *The Pursuit of Perfection*, p. 16.
40. The CRPS and its context has been analyzed in several historical studies. See Diana E. Long, "Physiological Identity of American Sex Researchers between the Two World Wars," in Gerald L. Geison, ed., *Physiology in the American Context 1850–1940* (Bethesda, Maryland: American Physiological Society, 1987); Merriley Borell, "Biologists and the Promotion of Birth Control Research, 1918–1938," *JHB* 20 (1987); Rechter, "'The Glands of Destiny,'" pp. 48–83.
41. Alfred Flaum, *Lasarettet i Lund 1768–1968: En historik utarbetad på uppdrag av Malmöhus läns landsting till lasarettets tvåhundraårsjubileum* (Lund: Lund County Council, 1968), p. 240. Arne Tiselius' research on the "problem of life" was also funded by the Rockefeller Foundation. On the Rockefeller Foundation, see Robert E. Kohler, *Partners in Science: Foundations and Natural Scientists, 1900–1945* (Chicago and London: Chicago University Press, 1991).
42. Edgar Allen, Charles H. Danforth and Edward A. Doisy, *Sex and Internal Secretions: A Survey of Recent Research* (1932), 2d ed., enl. (Baltimore, MD: The Williams and Wilkins Company, 1939); Borell, "Setting the Standards for a New Science," p. 289.
43. Oudshoorn, "On the Making of Sex Hormones"; Jean-Paul Gaudillière, "Better Prepared than Synthesized: Adolf Butenandt, Schering Ag and the Transformation of Sex Steroids into Drugs (1930–1946)," *SHPBBS* 36 (2005).
44. Rechter, "'The Glands of Destiny,'" p. vi.
45. Merriley Borell, "Organotherapy and the Emergence of Reproductive Endocrinology," *JHB* 18 (1985).
46. Sune Genell, "Nyare rön angående de kvinnliga sexualhormonen: En översikt 1," *SL* 27 (1930), p. 1087.
47. See Diana Long Hall, "Biology, Sex Hormones and Sexism in the 1920s," *Philosophical Forum* 5 (1974); Anne Fausto-Sterling, *Myths of Gender: Biological Theories about Women and Men* (New York: Basic Books, 1985); Nelly Oudshoorn, "Endocrinologists and the Conceptualization of Sex, 1920–1940," *JHB* 23 (1990); Marianne van den Wijngaard, "Feminism and the Biological Construction of Female and Male Behaviour," *JHB* 27 (1994). See also Thomas Laqueur, *Making Sex: Body and Gender from the Greeks to Freud* (Cambridge, Mass: Harvard University Press, 1990).
48. Johannisson, *Den mörka kontinenten*, pp. 109–114.
49. See Nils Erik Påhlsson, *Hormonbehandling av amenorrhe och oligohypomenorrhe* (Stockholm: Caroline Institute, 1951), p. 10.
50. Oudshoorn, "United We Stand," p. 16.
51. Adele E. Clarke, "Research Materials and Reproductive Science in the United States, 1910–1940," in Geison, ed., *Physiology in the American Context 1850–1940*; Oudshoorn, "On the Making of Sex Hormones"; idem, "United We Stand."
52. Idem, "On the Making of Sex Hormones," p. 13.

53. Michael Finkelstein, "Professor Bernhard Zondek: An Interview," *Journal of Reproduction and Fertility* 12 (1966).
54. Bernhard Zondek, "Mass Excretion of Æstrogenic Hormone in the Urine of the Stallion," *Nature* 10 February (1934).
55. Oudshoorn, "Endocrinologists and the Conceptualization of Sex, 1920–1940." The occurrence of "female" sex hormones in the testes had been proposed as far back as the early 1920s. The dualistic division continued however to be the norm, e.g. in neuro-endocrinology and developmental psychology, although it was later accepted that both types of hormones occurred in men and women alike. See Marianne van den Wijngaard, "The Acceptance of Scientific Theories and Images of Masculinity and Femininity. 1959–1985," *JHB* 24 (1991); Nelly Oudshoorn and Marianne van den Wijngaard, "Dualism in Biology: The Case of Sex Hormones," *Women's Studies International Forum* 14 (1991).
56. See Erland Mårald, *Jordens kretslopp: Lantbruket, staden och den kemiska vetenskapen 1840–1910* (Umeå: Umeå University, 2000).
57. Oudshoorn, "On the Making of Sex Hormones," pp. 14 f.
58. Barbara Seaman, *The Greatest Experiment Ever Performed on Women: Exploding the Estrogen Myth* (New York: Hyperion, 2003), p. 21.
59. Urine from men was gathered from factories, garrisons, prisons, and police stations.
60. On hormone replacement therapies for men in Sweden in the early 1940s, see Tore Rilton, "Indikationer för användandet av manligt sexualhormon," *SL* 39 (1942). See further the chapter "Borrowed Manhood," in Rothman and Rothman, *The Pursuit of Perfection.*
61. The cultural and medical history of synthetically manufactured testosterone is discussed in John Hoberman, *Testosterone Dreams: Rejuvenation, Aphrodisia, Doping* (Berkely and Los Angeles: University of California Press, 2005).
62. Clarke, "Research Materials and Reproductive Science in the United States, 1910–1940," p. 326.
63. See Graham Lewis, "Tissue Collection and the Pharmaceutical Industry: Investigating Corporate Biobanks," in Richard Tutton and Oonagh Corrigan, eds., *Genetic Databases: Socio-ethical Issues in the Collection and Use of DNA* (London and New York: Routledge, 2004).
64. Jane H. Murnaghan and Paul Talalay, "H. H. Dale's Account of the Standardization of Insulin," *Bulletin of the History of Medicine* 66 (1992); Nelly Oudshoorn, "On Measuring Sex Hormones: The Role of Biological Assays in Sexualizing Chemical Substances," *Bulletin of the History of Medicine* 64 (1990), pp. 249 f.
65. Henry H. Dale, "Conference on the Standardisation of Sex Hormones: Held at London on July 30th and August 1st, 1932," *Quarterly Bulletin of the Health Organisation* 4 (1935).
66. Idem, "Report of the Second Conference on the Standardisation of Sex Hormones: Held in London, July 15th to 17th, 1935," *Quarterly Bulletin of the Health Organisation* 4 (1935).
67. Chandak Sengoopta, *The Most Secret Quintessence of Life: Sex, Glands, and Hormones, 1850–1950* (Chicago and London: University of Chicago Press, 2006), is one of the most comprehensive studies on this topic.

68. See Torsten Thunberg, "Nyare undersökningar öfver Hypophysis Cerebri: En öfversikt," *ASL* 7 (1910); Philip E. Smith and Earl T. Engle, "Experimental Evidence Regarding the Rôle of the Anterior Pituitary in the Development and Regulation of the Genital System," *American Journal of Anatomy* 40 (1927). These experiments are discussed in Rechter, "'The Glands of Destiny,'" pp. 117–119.
69. Axel Westman, "Den främre hypofyslobens ställning inom den kvinnliga sexualbiologien," *Nord. Med.* 3 (1931), p. 389.
70. Medvei, *The History of Clinical Endocrinology*, p. 224.
71. Drugs made from the pituitary glands of calves had been on the market since the beginning of the twentieth century. See "Pitruitin, Pituglandol, Hypophysin," *SFT* 18 (1914).
72. Westman, "Den främre hypofyslobens ställning inom den kvinnliga sexualbiologien," pp. 390–391.
73. Finkelstein, "Professor Bernhard Zondek," p. 8.
74. Ragnar Björk, "Inside the Nobel Committee on Medicine: Prize Competition Procedures 1901–1950 and the Fate of Carl Neuberg," *Minerva* 39 (2001), p. 399. Such biological pregnancy tests were used in clinical practice until the 1960s.
75. Bernhard Zondek and Selmar Aschheim, "Das Hormon des Hypophysenvorderlappens: I. Testobjekt zum Nachweis des Hormons," *Klinische Wochenschrift* 6 (1927); idem, "Das Hormon des Hypophysenvorderlappens: II. Darstellung, chemische Eigenschaften, biologische Wirkungen," *Klinische Wochenschrift* 7 (1928); Bernhard Zondek, "Über die Hormone des Hypophysenvorderlappens: I. Wachstumshormon, Follikelreifungshormon (Prolan A), Luteinisierungshormon (Prolan B), Stoffwechselhormon?," *Klinische Wochenschrift* 9 (1930).
76. See H. L. Fevold, F. L. Hisaw and S. L. Leonard, "The Gonad Stimulating and the Luteinizing Hormones of the Anterior Lobe of the Hypophesis," *American Journal of Physiology* 97 (1931); H. L. Fevold, F. L. Hisaw, A. Hellbaum and R. Hertz, "Sex Hormones of the Anterior Lobe of the Hypophysis," *American Journal of Physiology* 104 (1933).
77. P. S. Brown, "Anterior Pituitary Hormones: Definition, Measurement and Use," in Michael J. Parnham and Jacques Bruinvels, eds., *Discoveries in Pharmacology: Haemodynamics, Hormones and Inflammation* (Amsterdam and New York: Elsevier, 1984), p. 370; Diana E. Long, "Moving Reprints: A Historian Looks at Sex Research Publications of the 1930s," *Journal of the History of Medicine and Allied Sciences* 45 (1990).
78. Erik Jorpes, "Om handelns 'prólan'-preparat," *SL* 31 (1934), p. 5. See also Fredrik Wendt, "Gammalt och nytt om de kvinnliga sexualhormonen samt deras betydelse för graviditet och abort," *SL* 31 (1934), pp. 399 f.
79. See H. H. Cole and G. H. Hart, "The Potency of Blood Serum of Mares in Progressive Stages of Pregnancy in Effecting the Sexual Maturity of the Immature Rat," *American Journal of Physiology* 94 (1930), p. 57; Wendt, "Gammalt och nytt om de kvinnliga sexualhormonen samt deras betydelse för graviditet och abort," p. 398.
80. Given that prolan/pituitary gonadotropin was considered a general, non-gender specific sex hormone, it can appear in retrospect that the new terminology, which only referred to the effect of hormones on women, was not terribly well thought-out.

81. Medvei, *The History of Clinical Endocrinology*, pp. 224–226. See also Bertil Rönnmark, "Några synpunkter på biologisk bestämning av hormonpreparat," *Farmacevtisk Revy* 39 (1940); Alan S. Parkes, "The Rise of Reproductive Endocrinology, 1926–1940," *Journal of Endocrinology* 34 (1966).
82. Sengoopta, *The Most Secret Quintessence of Life*, p. 159.
83. Clarke, "Controversy and the Development of Reproductive Sciences," p. 27; Jordan Goodman, "Pharmaceutical Industry," in Roger Cooter and John Pickstone, eds., *Medicine in the 20th Century* (Amsterdam: Harwood Academic, 2000), p. 145.
84. Parkes, "The Rise of Reproductive Endocrinology, 1926–1940," p. 33.
85. The authors of one of the first articles on the results of gonadotropin therapy in Sweden were positive about the new method. Still, they assumed a cautious attitude and suggested that the effects could to some extent be due to a "psychic effect." See Märta Adolfsson and Sebastian von Wachenfeldt, "Terapeutiska försök med Prolan och Progynon," *SL* 30 (1933).
86. Jorpes "Om handelns 'prólan'-preparat," p. 5.

CHAPTER TWO

1. Due to his multiple roles and public persona, Westman may be compared with the well-known biochemist Theodor Svedberg (1884–1971) presented in Sven Widmalm, "Trollkarlen från Uppsala: Bilder av The Svedberg och vetenskapen under andra världskriget," in Anders Ekström, ed., *Den mediala vetenskapen* (Nora: Nya Doxa, 2004); idem, "The Svedberg and the Boundary Between Science and Industry: Laboratory Practice, Policy, and Media Images," *History and Technology* 20 (2004); idem, "Ett vetenskapligt nätverk: The Svedberg och hans lärjungar," in Hasselberg and Petersson, eds., *"Bäste broder!"*
2. Westman was born and raised in Stockholm, where he also studied and married Ruth (née Bengtson) in 1924, and with whom he had two daughters. A comprehensive biography of Westman has yet to be written. Biographical detail appearing in this study is taken from Christian Hamburger and Hjalmar Wijnbladh, "Axel Westman," *Acta Endo.* 17 (1954); Christian Hamburger, Kaj Pedersen-Bjergaard and Hjalmar Wijnbladh, "Axel Westman 29.12.1894–29.5.1960," *Acta Endo.* 34 (1960); Hans-Ludvig Kottmeier, "Axel Westman 29.XII.1894–29.V.1960," *Nord. Med.* 65 (1961); Ulf Borell, "Pionjärer inom svensk obstetrik och gynekologi: Axel Westman," *SFOGSs medlemsblad* (1994).
3. On the early history of gynecology in Sweden, see Ulrika Nilsson, *Det heta könet: Gynekologin i Sverige kring förra sekelskiftet* (Stockholm: Wahlström and Widstrand, 2005). The first professorship in gynecology and obstetrics in Sweden was established at the Caroline Institute in 1864. It was followed by professorships at Uppsala University and Lund University in 1891 and 1909 respectively. In 1904, a section for gynecology and obstetrics was founded within the Swedish Society for Medicine.
4. Axel Westman, "Secernierende Zellen im Epithel der Tubae uterinae Falloppii," *Anatomischer Anzeiger* 49 (1916); idem, "Studies on the Influence of the Roentgen and Radium Rays on Phagocytosis," *Acta Radiologica* 2 (1923); idem, "The Results

of the Prophylactic, Postoperative, Radiological Treatment of Carcinoma of the Uterine Cervix at Radiumhemmet in Stockholm," *Acta Radiologica* 3 (1924).

5. Idem, *A Contribution to the Question of the Transit of the Ovum from Ovary to the Uterus in Rabbits* (Stockholm: Caroline Institute, 1926).
6. Ibid., pp. 72 f. Josefeson, *Vad betyda insöndringsorganen för vår kropp och själ?* and Johan August Hammar, *Om den inre sekretionen*, 2 vol. (Stockholm: Bonnier, 1922) were the first books that introduced endocrinology to the Swedish public. Another early Swedish book was Erik Lundberg, *Insöndringskörtlarna och deras viktigaste sjukdomar* (Stockholm: Wahlström and Widstrand, 1934).
7. Axel Westman, "Den moderna hormonforskningens betydelse för gynekologien," *Upsala Läkareförenings förhandlingar* 38 (1933).
8. Ibid., p. 183.
9. Westman's early articles on hormones include "Nyare undersökningar över ovariets biologi," *Hygiea* 90 (1928); "Studien über den Zusammenhang zwischen Corpus luteum und Plazenta als innersekretorische Organe," *Acta Obst.* 10 (1930); "De kvinnliga sexualhormonen," *Hygiea* 93 (1931); "Den främre hypofyslobens ställning inom den kvinnliga sexualbiologien."
10. Idem, "Den moderna hormonforskningens betydelse för gynekologien," p. 187. The importance of the hypophysis for the development and function of the reproduction organs was also discussed in idem, "Den främre hypofyslobens ställning inom den kvinnliga sexualbiologien."
11. Christian Hamburger, *Hypofysens, Kønskirtlernes og Binyrernes Hormoner* (Köpenhamn: Nordiska Bokhandeln, 1950), p. 5.
12. Westman, "Den moderna hormonforskningens betydelse för gynekologien," p. 188.
13. Idem, "Könsutvecklingen och den inre sekretionen," *Tidskrift för Sveriges Sjuksköterskor* 1 (1934).
14. Louis Berman, "Psycho-endocrinology," *Science* 17 February (1928). On this topic, see further Robert A. Cleghorn, "History of Endocrine Psychobiology," in Francesca Brambilla et al., eds., *Perspectives in Endocrine Psychobiology* (London: Wiley, 1978).
15. Westman, "Könsutvecklingen och den inre sekretionen," p. 15.
16. See also idem, *Barnlös: En bok om steriliteten och sterilitetsbekämpandet* (Stockholm: Wahlström and Widstrand, 1940), pp. 74–79.
17. See ibid., p. 33; idem, *Hormoner*, p. 147.
18. During the First World War, Cannon developed a theory on the relationship between hormones, nerves and emotions, published in *Bodily Changes in Pain, Hunger, Fear and Rage: An Account of Recent Researches into the Function of Emotional Excitement* (New York: Appleton, 1915). See further Saul Benison, A. Clifford Barger and Elin L. Wolfe, "Walter B. Cannon and the Mystery of Shock: A Study of Anglo-American Co-operation in World War I," *Medical History* 35 (1991). This theory later evolved into a holistic, materialistic theory of the body's ability to maintain a dynamic physiological balance through self-regulating mechanisms (e.g. in the oxygen, saline and sugar levels of the bloodstream). This ability, called *homeostasis*, is treated in Cannon's popular book *The Wisdom of the Body* (New York: N.W. Norton, 1932). On Cannon and "holistic materialism" in physiology, see

Garland E. Allen, *Life Science in The Twentieth Century* (1975), 2d ed. (Cambridge: Cambridge University Press, 1979), pp. 95–106.

19. Axel Westman, "Sexualhormon för behandling av kvinnosjukdomar," in *Olösta gåtor och aktuella problem: Sjuttiosex uttalanden i Svenska Dagbladets enquête om naturforskningens nuvarande uppgifter och framtida mål* (Stockholm: Wahlström and Widstrand, 1937).
20. A contemporary anthology aimed at shedding light on current scientific problems of vital importance was Gunnar Aspelin and Göte Turesson, eds., *Vetenskap av i dag: Framlagd av svenska forskare* (Uppsala: Gebers, 1940). This book includes a chapter on hormones as well, though the author was not Westman but his colleague Ulf von Euler.
21. Westman, "Sexualhormon för behandling av kvinnosjukdomar," pp. 280–281.
22. Genesis 16 and 30; Ann Ellis Hanson, "Hippocrates: 'Diseases of Woman 1," *Signs: Journal of Women in Culture and Society* 1 (1975).
23. Ann Lalos, "Infertilitetskrisen," in Berndt Kjessler, ed., *Utredning och behandling av ofrivillig barnlöshet* (Linköping: Swedish Society of Obstetrics and Gynecology, 1993), p. 9.
24. On ideas about illnesses and diseases before the breakthrough of medical science in Sweden, see Roger Qvarsell, *Vårdens idéhistoria* (Stockholm: Carlsson, 1991), pp. 46–53.
25. Lundin, *Guldägget*, p. 18.
26. Marsh and Ronner, *The Empty Cradle*, p. 2.
27. Gay Becker and Robert D. Nachtigall, "Eager for Medicalisation: The Social Production of Infertility as a Disease," *Sociology of Health and Illness* 14 (1992); Lalos, "Infertilitetskrisen," p. 9; Naomi Pfeffer, *The Stork and the Syringe: A Political History of Reproductive Medicine* (Cambridge: Polity Press, 1993), pp. 30, 45, 61.
28. Ludwig et al., "Ovarian Stimulation," p. 74.
29. Pfeffer, *The Stork and the Syringe*, pp. 69 f, 143 f. Many examples of such combination therapies (used in the 1940s at the Women's Clinic of the Royal Caroline Hospital) are presented in Påhlsson, *Hormonbehandling av amenorrhe och oligohypomenorrhe*.
30. Axel Westman, "Sterilitet och sterilitetsbehandling," *Hygienisk revy* 24 (1935).
31. On Essen-Möller, see Emma Shirran, *Samhälle, vetenskap och obstetrik: Elis Essen-Möller och kvinnokliniken i Lund* (Uppsala: Uppsala University, 2007).
32. Westman had indicated that the cause of as much as 10–30% of childless marriages could be traced to the male partner and that any examination of a sterile couple should start by determining the husband's fertility. However, he chose to ignore that aspect in his lecture.
33. Westman's ideas about voluntary childlessness are, however, presented in "Den ofrivilliga steriliteten," in SOU 1936:59 *Betänkande i sexualfrågan*, p. 160, where he writes that, "for psychological reasons there are well-founded grounds for assuming that voluntarily zero-offspring marriages are relatively rare, though their number has likely increased in recent years."
34. Idem, "Sterilitet och sterilitetsbehandling," p. 84. Westman exemplifies this as follows. "Experience teaches us that disharmony between the male and female contracting parties can easily lead to an abnormal sexual relationship, which in

not a few cases causes persistent sterility in the wife." He also notes that a certain type of sterility can be cured by psychotherapy.

35. Ibid., p. 83.
36. Ibid., p. 84.
37. Ibid., p. 92.
38. Ibid., p. 92. Portraying the immediate future's hormone therapy as a "positive" development in contrast to routine, "fatalistic" surgery was a rhetorical tactic readily employed by other gynecologists as well. See Rechter, "'The Glands of Destiny,'" pp. 167 f.
39. Emanuel Bergman, "Svenska läkarexlibris med symboler," *SL* 51 (1945).
40. Marsh and Ronner, *The Empty Cradle*, pp. 150–151.
41. George W. Corner, "Laboratory and Clinic in the Study of Infertility," *Fertility and Sterility* 8 (1957), pp. 508–512. See further Borell, "Biologists and the Promotion of Birth Control Research, 1918–1938"; Clarke, "Controversy and the Development of Reproductive Sciences," pp. 21, 29. Cf. Oudshoorn, *Beyond the Natural Body*, p. 115.
42. John Clarke, "The History of Three Scientific Societies: The Society for the Study of Fertility (now the Society for Reproduction and Fertility) (Britain), the Société Française pour l'Étude de la Fertilité, and the Society for the Study of Reproduction (USA)," *SHPBBS* 38 (2007).
43. Tore Frängsmyr, *Svensk idéhistoria: Bildning och vetenskap under tusen år*, 2 vol. (Stockholm: Natur och kultur, 2000), vol. 2, pp. 279–298. On the policies of the Swedish Welfare State, especially concerning public health and the population question, see Ann-Katrin Hatje, *Befolkningsfrågan och välfärden: Debatten om familjepolitik och nativitetsökning under 1930- och 1940-talen* (Stockholm: Allmänna förlaget, 1974); *I framtidens tjänst: Ur folkhemmets idéhistoria* (Malmö: Gidlund, 1986); Yvonne Hirdman, *Att lägga livet till rätta: Studier i svensk folkhemspolitik* (1989), 2d ed. (Stockholm: Carlsson, 2000); Jan Larsson, *Hemmet vi ärvde: Om folkhemmet, identiteten och den gemensamma framtiden* (Stockholm: Arena, 1994); Elin Bommenel, *Sockerförsöket: Kariesexperimenten 1943–1960 på Vipeholms sjukhus för sinnesslöa* (Lund: Arkiv, 2006); Sofia Kling, *Vi våga ej helt leva: Barnbegränsning, sexualitet och genus under den svenska fertilitetstransitionen* (Umeå: Umeå University, 2007).
44. Gunnar Broberg, *Statlig rasforskning: En historik över Rasbiologiska institutet* (Lund: Lund University, 1995).
45. Maria Sophia Quine, *Population Politics in Twentieth-Century Europe: Fascist Dictatorships and Liberal Democracies* (London and New York: Routledge, 1996), p. 9.
46. Pfeffer, *The Stork and the Syringe*, p. 12 f.
47. Alva Myrdal and Gunnar Myrdal, *Kris i befolkningsfrågan* (1934), new ed. (Nora: Nya Doxa, 1997).
48. Ibid., p. 217. A more comprehensive sterilization law came into effect in 1941, citing three indications for sterilization. To the two previously on record was added female "illness" or "feebleness." It was also now possible to volunteer for sterilization.
49. Eva Palmblad, *Den disciplinerade reproduktionen: Abort- och steriliseringspolitikens dolda dagordning* (Stockholm: Carlsson, 2000), p. 35.
50. See *A och O för blivande mödrar* (Stockholm: Allmänna livförsäkringsbolaget Oden, 1943); *Mammas bok* (Uppsala: Henrik Gahns Aktiebolag, 1946).

51. Westman, "Sterilitet och sterilitetsbehandling," p. 81.
52. Westman often referred to this statistic, for example in "Om sterilitetens behandling och resultaten av densamma," *Hygiea* 106 (1944), p. 1162. The same figure was still being referred to fifty years later. See Anna Westerståhl, "Reproduktionsteknologi—vad är det?," *Kvinnovetenskaplig tidskrift* 4 (1986), p. 4.
53. Westman, "Sterilitet och sterilitetsbehandling," p. 81.
54. Idem, "Om fortplantningskontroll och fosterfördrivning," *SL* 32 (1935).
55. See H. Benckert, "Steriliteten hos kvinnan från medicinsk och statistisk synpunkt," *SL* 34 (1937); Lennart Norrlin, "Läkarna och befolkningsfrågan," *SL* 39 (1942). Benckert states that "sterility issues, regardless of their impact on the individual or family, must also be seen in context with another, greater problem which concerns society as a whole—the nativity issue—of which they comprise a small, if far from insignificant detail."
56. Gaudillière, "Genesis and Development of a Biomedical Object," pp. 535–536; Finkelstein, "Professor Bernhard Zondek," p. 12.
57. Westman, "Den ofrivilliga steriliteten," p. 159.
58. Hatje, *Befolkningsfrågan och välfärden*, pp. 55 f, 188 f.
59. Sune Genell, "Den manliga partens roll i sterila äktenskap: Några ord om moderna linjer i spermiediagnostiken," *SL* 40 (1943), p. 1563.
60. Axel Westman to the Population Committee of 1941, 4 April 1945, E1 vol. 6, WCA, SCCA.
61. "Om utredning rörande åtgärder för att häva ofrivillig sterilitet," motion presented to the Upper House of Parliament 1945:286.
62. Axel Westman, "Sterilitet," in Arne Tallberg, ed., *Sexuallivet i modern belysning: Sexton svenska forskare ger vägledning* (Stockholm: Wahlström and Widstrand, 1944).
63. Westman participated in SOU 1944:55 *Betänkande rörande organisatoriska åtgärder för den medicinska forskningens främjande*; SOU 1946:76 *Organisatoriska åtgärder till främjande av medicinsk forskning I*; SOU 1947:66 *Organisatoriska åtgärder till främjande av medicinsk forskning II.*
64. On the establishment of the Medical Research Council, see Thorsten Nybom, *Kunskap, politik, samhälle: Essäer om kunskapssyn, universitet och forskningspolitik 1900–2000* (Hargshamn: Arete, 1997), pp. 66–74.
65. "Några aktuella medicinska forskningsuppgifter av i främsta rummet social eller militärmedicinsk betydelse," in SOU 1944:55, p. 173.
66. Cf. Susan E. Cozzens and Edward J. Woodhouse, "Science, Government, and the Politics of Knowledge," in Sheila Jasanoff et al., eds., *Handbook of Science and Technology Studies*, (1994), rev. ed. (Thousand Oaks, London and New Delhi: Sage, 1995).
67. Pfeffer, *The Stork and the Syringe*, is, however, an important exception.
68. Broberg and Tydén, *Oönskade i folkhemmet*; Runcis, *Steriliseringar i folkhemmet*; SOU 2000:20; Tydén, *Från politik till praktik.*
69. Based on studies of the Women's Clinic in Lund and the efforts of Elis Essen-Möller during the initial phase of practical and political sterilization, historian of ideas Emma Shirran pursues an argument reminiscent of this. Shirran makes a point of the fact that the clinic contributed to "creating" both mothers and sterile individuals, through which process the latter became the negative counterpart of

the former. In both cases the individual went through a metamorphosis considered beneficial to society. However, the "motherhooding" discussed by Shirran concerns just maternity care, not the treatment of sterility. See Shirran, *Samhälle, vetenskap och obstetrik*, p. 182.

70. Similar efforts were made in Germany. During the Second World War, German women judged to be of good "racial quality" but who could not have children were sent to special fertility camps, where they were fed nutritious meals and treated with hormones. One participant in German sterility research was gynecologist and Party member Carl Clauberg (1898–1957), infamous for his experiments in Block 10 at Auschwitz. Camps for treating female sterility were also set up in Mussolini's Italy. See Gaudillière, "Genesis and Development of a Biomedical Object," pp. 535–536.
71. Gunnar Ekelöf, "Till de folkhemske" (1945), in idem, *Samlade dikter* (Stockholm: Bonnier, 2007), p. 165.
72. Eyvind Johnson, *Grupp Krilon* (Stockholm: Bonnier, 1941), p. 114.
73. Ibid., p. 118.
74. Besides his duties as professor and chief physician, Westman acted as editor of the journals *Acta Obstetricia et Gynaecologica Scandinavica* and *Acta Endocrinologica*, and he was also chairman of the Swedish Society of Endocrinology (founded in 1945) as well as of the Scandinavian Society of Endocrinology (founded in 1947). On Dahlberg, see Kjell Jonsson, "Rasbiologi från vänster?: Om Gunnar Dahlbergs vetenskap, politik och popularisering," in Christer Nordlund, ed., *Livsföreställningar: Kultur, samhälle och biovetenskap* (Umeå: Royal Skytte Society, 2004).
75. In addition to the popular books *Hormoner* and *Barnlös*, Westman wrote textbooks in obstetrics and gynecology as well as books on menopause and on the development of the fetus. Furthermore, the book *Endokrinologi*, which for decades served as the Swedish standard work in the field, was undertaken at his initiative. Westman wrote the lion's share of the manuscript, but it was Rolf Luft together with Ulf Borell who finished the text and prepared it for publication. Axel Westman, Rolf Luft and Ulf Borell, eds., *Endokrinologi* (Stockholm: Bonnier, 1963).
76. Cf. Nelkin, *Selling Science*; Terry Shinn and Richard Whitley, eds., *Expository Science: Forms and Functions of Popularisation* (Dordrecht: Reidel, 1985).
77. Cf. Kaj Johansson, *Den torgförda biologin: Studier i populärvetenskapens problem och tematik* (Göteborg: University of Gothenburg, 2003); Kjell Jonsson and Jenny Larsson, "Mellan vetenskap och vers: Ärftlighetsforskare som publika vetenskapsmän 1940–1960," in Ekström, ed., *Den mediala vetenskapen.*
78. Westman, *Barnlös*, p. 8.
79. Steinach, *Hormonerna som forma livet*; Louis Berman, *Människans förvandling: Hur människan kan omskapas genom hormonterapi* (1938), Swe. transl. (Stockholm: Natur och kultur, 1943).
80. Louis Berman, *New Creations in Human Beings* (New York: Doubleday, Doran and Company, 1938), p. 302.
81. See Nordlund, "Hormoner och visioner i mellankrigstid"; idem, "Endocrinology and Expectations in 1930s America."
82. Pehr Henrik Törngren, "Med sirater—och utan," *Dagens Nyheter* 14 December (1940); Torsten Lindner, "Bokanmälan," *SL* 40 (1943), in which Törngren reviews

Steinach and Westman, and Lindner Berman. Steinach's book was also reviewed (more positively) by Arnold Josefson, "Bokanmälan," *SL* 37 (1940).

83. "Barnlösheten i äktenskapet oftast beroende på mannen," *Stockholms-Tidningen* 12 September (1943).
84. Cf. Shirran, *Samhälle, vetenskap och obstetrik*, pp. 16–20. Westman was voted into the Royal Swedish Academy of Sciences and was a member of the Caroline Institute's Nobel Committee. Near the end of his life, he was also chairman of the Swedish Medical Association. While he never received the Nobel Prize, he was nominated in the category for medicine and physiology at least once, in 1951. The nomination was submitted by Heinrich Martius, Professor of Gynecology, Göttingen, for Westman's research on "neurohumoral regulation of female sexual functions and tubal egg transport." Westman himself asked that his candidacy for the prize not be considered. See Axel Westman to Göran Liljestrand, 5 March 1951, E1 vol. 13, WCA, SCCA.
85. Arnold Josefson, "Några ord om hormonterapi," *SL* 38 (1941).
86. Robert T. Frank, "The Sex Hormones: Their Physiologic Significance and Use in Practice," *Journal of the American Medical Association* 114 (1940), p. 1507.
87. "Hormontvist slutade med rättegång: Danska läkare i luven på varandra," *Göteborgsposten* 4 July (1943).
88. Gideon Vilhelm Törnqvist to Elis Essen-Möller, 4 May 1942, Elis Essen-Möller Papers, Lund University Library. Thanks are due to Emma Shirran for providing information about this letter.
89. Ibid. Compare Axel Westman, "Hormonala behandlingsmetoder inom gynekologien," *SL* 40 (1943).
90. Thomas F. Gieryn, *Cultural Boundaries of Science: Credibility on the Line* (Chicago: University of Chicago Press, 1999), pp. 15–18. At the Swedish Society of Medicine papers on hormone therapy for the treatment of menstrual disorders were read for the first time in 1941. That year Westman gave a lecture entitled "Hormonal behandling av amenorrhea," and Sune Genell talked about "Hormonal behandling av blödningar." See *Svenska läkaresällskapet 175 år* (Stockholm: Swedish Society of Medicine, 1983), p. 371. Papers on hormones and hormone therapy in general had, however, been read many times before.

CHAPTER THREE

1. See Stuart Anderson, ed., *Making Medicines: A Brief History of Pharmacy and Pharmaceuticals* (London: Pharmaceutical Press, 2005).
2. "Patent medicines" sold in Sweden were mainly imported from the United States and Germany, where medicine could be patented. In Sweden, the patenting of medicine was not permitted until 1967, although it was possible to patent a production method.
3. Liebenau, *Medical Science and Medical Industry*, p. 5 f.
4. "En ny svensk industri," *SFT* 5 (1901). On the development of the chemical industry in Sweden, see Anders Lundgren, "The Development of Chemical Industry in Sweden and the Contribution of Academic Chemistry after 1900," in Anthony S. Travis et al., eds., *Determinants in the Evolution of the European Chemical Indus-*

try, 1900–1939: New Technologies, Political Frameworks, Markets, and Companies (Dordrecht: Springer, 1998).

5. *SFS* 1913:308 Kungl. Maj:ts nådiga apoteksvarustadga. The pharmacopeia, whose first edition, *Pharmacopoeja Holmiensis*, was published in 1686, describes which medicaments were to be used and how they were to be made. It was superseded in 1775 by *Pharmacopoea Svecica*, which was followed by another six revised editions by the year 1900. The pharmacopeia, like the medicinal rates, was sanctioned and published by the Collegium Medicum, founded in 1663. In 1813, the Collegium Medicum was reorganized as Sundhetskollegium (College of Health and Welfare), which eventually became Kungliga Medicinalstyrelsen (Royal Swedish Board of Medicine) in 1877.
6. A small-scale industry had however already been established by private dispenseries, beginning with Nordstjernan in 1877, generally seen as the first rustlings of a company eventually named Apothecary Product Central Vitrum in 1924. At Kärnan in Helsingborg, similar work began in 1904, which eventually evolved into Paul G. Nordström's factories in Hässleholm, later on AB Hässle.
7. The company AB Ferrosan was established in Malmö in 1920 but their industrical production did not began until 1934. See Stig Nylén, *Leos och Ferrosans rötter* (Helsingborg: Pharmacia Leo Therapeutics, 1992).
8. In Sweden, it was the Swedish Academy of Pharmaceutical Sciences that took the initiative to critically examine preparations not sold at the official pharmacies. The analyses were first conducted by Carl Mörner, a professor of physiology and medical chemistry at Uppsala University, and subsequently published in *SFT*. Mörner was also associated with "Byrån för upplysning av läkemedelsannonser" [Office for information on drug advertising] founded in Uppsala in 1903. See Knut Sjöberg, "Byrån för upplysning om läkemedelsannonser," *SFT* 8 (1904); "Utställningen af reklammedicin i Halmstad," *SFT* 21 (1912); Karin Johannisson, "Bot för en nervtrött generation: Ett läkemedel i idéhistorisk belysning," in Frängsmyr, ed., *Vetenskap och läkemedel*, pp. 96–105.
9. Eva Palmblad, *Sanningens gränser: Kvacksalveriet, läkarna och samhället, Sverige 1890–1990* (Stockholm: Carlsson, 1997), p. 10.
10. Cited in Per Bergström, "En inveckad debut," *SFT* 77 (1973), p. 704.
11. "Løvens kemiske Fabrik—Leo Pharmaceutical Products," *Medicinsk Forum* 36 (1983). In 2002, Løvens kemiske Fabrik was renamed Leo Pharma A/S.
12. Ahlin and Lundgren, *Från Leopiller till nicorette*, pp. 32, 94; Preben Schrøder, "Fra Løveapotekets kemiske Fabik till LEO Pharma A/S," *Theriaca* 36 (2005), p. 34.
13. Acetylsalicylic acid was synthesized at the end of the 19th century. The original preparation, Aspirin, launched by the German dye and drug firm Bayer in 1899, is regarded as the first mass-produced commercial pill.
14. August Krogh, "De nordiske landes forsyning med insulin," *SL* 21 (1924).
15. Nylén, *Leos och Ferrosans rötter*, p. 25. During its first years, Nordisk Insulinlaboratorium was also called "Insulinfabrikken Leo."
16. On the early use and production of insulin in Sweden, see J. Tillgren and Nils Rahm, "Några ord om poliklinisk insulinbehandling vid sockersjuka," *SL* 21 (1924); Erik Jorpes, "Om insulinets natur och dess framställning," *SL* 22 (1925); John Sjöqvist and Erik Jorpes, "Den svenska insulinframställningen," *SL* 28 (1931).
17. "AB Leo's list of drugs" (1924), p. 39, LHA.

18. S. G. Zetterholm, "Erfarenheter med cardiazol—resp. insulinbehandling på ett psykosmaterial," *SL* 36 (1939); A. Norrsell, "Några erfarenheter av insulinbehandling vid schizofreni," *SL* 38 (1941); Gunnar Malmström, "Anorexia nervosa," *SL* 45 (1948).
19. Nylén, *Leos och Ferrosans rötter*, p. 161.
20. "AB Leo's list of drugs" (1926), p. 26, LHA.
21. These were Protamin-Insulin Leo (1936), Protamin-Insulin Leo in crystalline form (1945), Insulin Retard NPH Leo (1953), Zink-Protamin Leo in crystalline form (1958), and Insulin Initard Leo (1966). See Bergström, "En invecklad debut," p. 707. In the 1930s, the Swedish firm Apoteksvarucentralen Vitrum began, in cooperation with the biochemist Erik Jorpes, to produce insulin as well.
22. Cf. Simon Schaffer, "What is Science?," in Krige and Pestre, eds., *Companion to Science in the Twentieth Century*, pp. 32–33.
23. Rasmussen, "Steroids in Arms," pp. 302 f.
24. Along with these hormone preparations, Leo achieved some success in psychopharmacology (with the antidepressant Tymelyt) and anti-smoking therapy (with the nicotine preparation Nicorette).
25. AB Leo to Axel Westman, 3 March 1947, vol. 1368, LHA.
26. *Fortegnelse over Leo Præparater fra Løvens kemiske Fabrik* (Köpenhamn, August 1931). See Nylén, *Leos och Ferrosans rötter*, p. 26; Schrøder, "Fra Løveapotekets kemiske Fabik till LEO Pharma A/S," pp. 22–27.
27. *Leopreparat* (January 1931), LHA. Dystrophia adiposogenitalis is a disease characterized by obesity and undeveloped genitalia.
28. *Leopreparat* (1935), LHA.
29. *Leopreparat*, suppl. (March 1932), LHA.
30. *Leopreparat* (1934), LHA.
31. *Leopreparat* (May 1934), and *Leopreparat* (1935), LHA.
32. *Leopreparat för veterinärer* (1938), LHA.
33. *Leopreparat* (1935), p. 181.
34. Bruno Lunenfeld, "Historical Perspectives in Gonadotrophin Therapy," *Human Reproduction Update* 10 (2004), p. 455. As shown in Chapter 8, Leo considered trying extract of calf pituitary glands. During the 1960s, Leo also conducted veterinary studies where pigs rendered barren by inbreeding were treated with the pituitary extract of other swine. See "Föredrag om Leos HMG-projekt," 10 January 1966, vol. 2621, LHA.
35. "Till ledning vid styrelsesammanträde i första kvartalet 1934," vol. 5097, LHA.
36. AB Leo to Løvens kemiske Fabrik, 13 September 1933, vol. 94, LHA.
37. Løvens kemiske Fabrik to AB Leo, 29 April 1931, vol. 117, LHA.
38. AB Leo to Johan Alm, 22 November 1939, vol. 300, LHA.
39. AB Leo to Anders Andersson, 24 November 1939, vol. 300, LHA.
40. Anders Andersson to AB Leo, 26 November 1939, vol. 300, LHA.
41. AB Leo to Anders Andersson, 8 December 1939, vol. 300, LHA.
42. AB Leo to Anders Andersson, 9 December 1939, vol. 300, LHA.
43. "Den bakteriefria fabriken," *Teknik för alla* 14 (1948), p. 4.
44. AB Leo to Firma Alfred Axelsson, 16 May 1945, vol. 1134, LHA; AB Leo to AB Avfallsråvaror, 16 May 1945, vol. 1134, LHA; "Leo inviger nya forskningslaboratorier," *SFT* 71 (1967), p. 409.

45. Per Bergström, "Grundläggande hormonforskning," *SFT* 77 (1973), p. 709.
46. Quoted in Ahlin and Lundgren, *Från Leopiller till nicorette*, p. 100.
47. The first research scientists contacted by Leo in 1915 and 1917, respectively, were Ivar Bang, Professor of Medical and Physiological Chemistry at Lund University and Ludvig Ramberg, Professor of Organic Chemistry at Uppsala University. They were charged with the quality control of Leo's preparations, but since production came to a standstill during these years, Bang and Ramberg did little actual work for the firm. In 1921, Erik M. P. Widmark (1889–1945), Professor of Medical and Physiological Chemistry at Lund, a nutritional researcher specializing in vitamins, was contracted. With Leo he worked on its fish liver oil Grasinol.
48. "Statsmedicinska anstalten," in *Nordisk familjebok* (Stockholm, 1917), vol. 17, pp. 1089–1090.
49. *SFS* 1934:306 Kungl. Maj:ts kungörelse angående handel med farmaceutiska specialiteter. In many countries, rigorous control of pharmaceutical drugs had already been institutionalized, e.g. Holland 1925, Austria 1925, Norway 1929, and Denmark 1932.
50. Lönngren et al., eds., *Svensk farmaci under 1900-talet*, vol. 1, pp. 184–192. In 1967, the Royal Swedish Board of Medicine merged with the Swedish Board of Health and Welfare (Socialstyrelsen). In 1970, the NPL was replaced by the Swedish Board of Health and Welfare's Department of Pharmaceutical Drugs (Läkemedelsavdelningen), which, in 1990, was replaced by the Medical Products Agency (Läkemedelsverket).
51. Ahlin and Lundgren, *Från Leopiller till nicorette*, pp. 76 f; Finkelstein, "Professor Bernhard Zondek," p. 6. In a letter from 1933, it is mentioned that Zondek himself was looked upon as a possible consultant for Leo. See Løvens kemiske Fabrik to AB Leo, 18 November 1933, vol. 94, LHA. I have, however, found no evidence that Zondek was ever associated with Leo.
52. *Leopreparat* (January 1931); "Dansk läkemedelsindustri III: Løvens kemiske Fabrik," *SFT* 68 (1968), p. 320.
53. Westman, "Den moderna hormonforskningens betydelse för gynekologien," p. 190.
54. Norgren, *Kunskapsöverföring från universitet till företag*, pp. 64–70; Ahlin and Lundgren, *Från Leopiller till nicorette*, p. 75.
55. Cf. Adele E. Clarke and Joan H. Fujimura, "What Tools? Which Jobs? Why Right?," in idem, eds., *The Right Tools for the Job*.
56. Stefan Thorpenberg, "Det tidiga samarbetet mellan Göteborgs medicinska fakultet och industrin—eller födelsen av Mode 2 i det svenska goda samhället," *VEST* 15 (2002). It can also be claimed that collaboration between university researchers and other civic institutions has been around since the seventeenth century.
57. AB Leo to Axel Westman, 6 November 1933, vol. 94, LHA.
58. "Till ledning vid styrelsesammanträde i första kvartalet 1934."
59. Axel Westman, "Hormonlaboratoriernas framtid," *SL* 56 (1959), p. 2076.
60. Axel Westman to the Directorate of the Academic Hospital, 20 October 1933, Directorate protocols 1932–1933, Academic Hospital's Archive, Regional State Archive of Uppsala.
61. Ibid.

62. "Direktionsmöte 1933 den 23 oktober," Directorate protocols 1932–1933, Academic Hospital's Archive, Regional State Archive of Uppsala. In 1934, the Swedish Parliament decided to fund a new building for the women's clinic.
63. Oudshoorn, "United We Stand"; Gaudillière, "Better Prepared than Synthesized."
64. Cf. Fishman, "Manufacturing Desire," p. 205.
65. Axel Westman to the Directorate of the Caroline Hospital, 23 January 1946, E1 vol. 9, WCA, SCCA.
66. See for example Sune Genell, "Nyare rön angående de kvinnliga sexualhormonen: En översikt," *SL* 27 (1930).
67. Idem, "Tre veckors hormonstudier hos Zondek," *Nord. Med.* 4 (1932). As a Jew, Zondek was compelled to flee Germany in 1933. After an invitation from Hans von Euler he arrived in Sweden, where he was temporarily hired by the Department of Biochemistry at Stockholm College. A year later he moved to Jerusalem, where his specific interest in the sterility issue was piqued. See Finkelstein, "Professor Bernhard Zondek," pp. 11–12.
68. "Till ledning för styrelsesammanträde i tredje kvartalet 1933, Bilaga 3," vol. 5097, LHA; Løvens kemiske Fabrik to Sune Genell, 1 December 1933, vol. 94, LHA.
69. *Leopreparat* (1934), p. 86.
70. These theses were defended in 1939, 1945 and 1949, respectively, when Westman's successor John Naeslund was professor at the clinic. See Bo Lindberg, ed., *Kvinnosjukvård under 100 år: En jubileumsbok från Kvinnokliniken, Akademiska sjukhuset* (Uppsala: Academic Hospital, 1994), pp. 138, 187.
71. Westman, "Hormonlaboratoriernas framtid," p. 2077; Flaum, *Lasarettet i Lund 1768–1968*, p. 240; Håkan Westling, *Medicinska fakulteten vid Lunds universitet 1668–2003* (Lund: Lund University, 2003), p. 152.
72. See Axel Westman, "Om den inbördes relationen mellan äggstockens bägge hormon," *SL* 33 (1936); Axel Westman and Dora Jacobsohn, "Experimentelle Untersuchungen über die Bedeutung des Hypophysen-Zwischenhirnsystems für die Produktion gonadotroper Hormone des Hypophysenvorderlappens," *Acta Obst.* 17 (1937); Axel Westman, "Experimentella undersökningar över hypofysens produktion av gonadotropt hormon," *Nord. Med.* 14 (1937); idem, "Experimentella undersökningar över hypofys-mellanhjärnsystemets reglerande inflytande på sexualfunktionerna," *SL* 38 (1941).
73. Nils Emmelin, "Med cello till det nya landet," in Margareta Wirmark et al., eds., *Professorsboken: Fyrtionio Lundakvinnor berättar* (Stockholm: Carlsson, 1996); Westling, *Medicinska fakulteten vid Lunds universitet 1668–2003*, p. 281. Jacobsohn defended her Ph.D thesis in 1948 and was appointed Docent in experimental endocrinology the same year. In 1964, she became the first female professor at the medical faculty of Lund University.
74. *Leopreparat* (1940), LHA, p. 184.
75. Westling, *Medicinska fakulteten vid Lunds universitet 1668–2003*, pp. 156–157.
76. "Avtal mellan direktionen för Karolinska sjukhuset och aktiebolaget Leo angående bolagets hormonlaboratorium vid Karolinska sjukhuset" [signed in Hälsingborg 4 December 1943 and in Stockholm 21 December 1943], vol. 1169, LHA.

77. Harald Johansson had previously been a physician and teacher at the Women's Clinic in Lund and moved to the Caroline Hospital with the hormone lab. He defended his Ph.D thesis at the Caroline Institute in 1946.
78. "Barnlösheten i äktenskapet oftast beroende på mannen"; "Vart åttonde äktenskap utan barn—men varför? 'Medicines vapensmedja' utreder," *Stockholms-Tidningen* 12 September (1943).
79. See "Barnlösheten i äktenskapet oftast beroende på mannen"; "Kampen mod de barnløse Ægteskaber," *Politiken* 8 October (1944). The unit was also used in artificial insemination, see "Provrörsbarnen: En nära släkting till makarna kan få i uppdrag att utpeka lämplig far," *Stockholms-Tidningen* 2 November (1946).
80. Astrid Forsberg, "Barnlöshet beror på mannen," *Husmodern* 31 (1943); Genell, "Den manliga partens roll i sterila äktenskap."
81. Axel Westman to Kungl. Byggnadststyrelsens utredningsbyrå, 28 November 1946, E1 vol. 9, WCA, SCCA.
82. Axel Westman to KAWF, 22 June 1945 (including "P.M. beträffande tillbyggnad för en forskningsavdelning vid Karolinska Sjukhusets kvinnoklinik"), Axel Westman Papers, KAWF Archives.
83. KAWF to Caroline Inst., 6 June 1945, Axel Westman Papers, KAWF Archives. Westman applied for SEK 150,000 to cover the cost for the building and SEK 58,000 for furnishings and equipment. In the end he was granted SEK 60,000.
84. Kungl. Maj:ts proposition 1946:273, 463–466. The grant from the Wallenberg Foundation was requisitioned when the new premises were in place. See Hilding Bergstrand to KAWF, 10 January 1950, Axel Westman Papers, KAWF Archives.

CHAPTER FOUR

1. Christer Ahlberger and Lars Kvarnström, *Det svenska samhället 1720–2000: Böndernas och arbetarnas tid* (Lund: Studentlitteratur, 2004), pp. 290, 338.
2. Adolf Rising, "Den industriella läkemedelstillverkningen och apoteken," *SFT* 30 (1926); Svante Wiström, ed., *Svensk läkemedelsindustri: Mål och medel* (1946), p. 11.
3. Before the war, German companies were a major presence in Sweden. Of the thirty-eight foreign vendors on the Swedish market in 1927, twenty-seven were based in Germany. See Inge Ehrlén et al., "Svensk läkemedelsindustri," in Lönngren et al., eds., *Svensk farmaci under 1900-talet*, vol. 2, p. 108. After the war, German drug patents expired. I. G. Farben remained, however, relatively intact despite wartime activities, see Peter Hayes, *Industry and Ideology: I G Farben in the Nazi Era* (Cambridge: Cambridge University Press, 1987), pp. 375–376.
4. Swann, *Academic Scientists and the Pharmaceutical Industry*, pp. 24–56.
5. Lindgren, "Läkemedelsindustri"; Norgren, *Kunskapsöverföring från universitet till företag*, pp. 20, 34; Lundgren, "Dextran som blodplasmasubstitut"; Lundgren, *Vetenskap till vardags*.
6. *Svensk läkemedelsindustri*, p. 4. The rest of the employees were defined as "salaried" (396) and "laborers" (820).
7. Pickstone, *Ways of Knowing*, p. 181.
8. Paalzow, Sjögren and Werkö, "Svensk läkemedelsforskning," p. 58.

9. "Stadgar och arbetsordning för Svenska Endokrinologföreningen, tillika Svenska Läkaresällskapets sektion för endokrinologi," 5 June 1945, A1a vol. 114, SMS Archive, NAM. Soon thereafter similar societies for the study of endocrinology were established in Denmark, Finland, Norway and Holland. In 1947, these societies together founded the journal *Acta Endocrinologica* and a joint European organization, with which similar societies in Switzerland and West Germany were associated. See Axel Westman, "Editorial," *Acta Endo.* 1 (1948).
10. Frederik Paulsen, who defended his Ph.D thesis at the University of Basel, worked tirelessly to connect physicians and the pharmaceutical industry. He was also editor-in-chief of the Swedish edition of industry journal *Hormoner*, published by Pharmacia.
11. Axel Westman and Frederik Paulsen to the Swedish Society of Medicine, 23 April 1945, A1a vol. 114, SMS Archive, NAM. According to membership rolls, enclosed with the letter, the society initially had sixty-six members, including fifteen professors of natural science and medicine.
12. "Protokoll, fört i nämndens första avdelning av Svenska Läkaresällskapet den 22 maj 1945," A2ca vol. 58, SMS Archive, NAM; "Protokoll, fört i Svenska Läkaresällskapet den 29 maj 1945," A1a vol. 114, SMS Archive, NAM. See also Rolf Luft, "Sektionen för endokrinologi," in *Svenska läkaresällskapet 175 år*. According to Luft, who was one of the founding fathers of the society, the decision to recruit Westman was motivated by his reputation and network of contacts; the society needed a "commanding" personality as chairman. Luft himself was not elected to the first board. Rolf Luft, pers. com., 23 June 2003.
13. Viviane Quirke, "From Alkaloids to Gene Therapy: A Brief History of Drug Discovery in the 20th Century," in Anderson, ed., *Making Medicines*, p. 190.
14. Wolfgang König, "Science-Based Industry or Industry-Based Science? Electrical Engineering in Germany before World War I," *Technology and Culture* 37 (1996).
15. A critic is presented in Arvid Welander, "Tablettfabrikerna på krigsstigen," *SFT* 50 (1946).
16. Lennart Schön, *En modern svensk ekonomisk historia: Tillväxt och omvandling under två sekel* (Stockholm: SNS, 2000), p. 364.
17. Lönngren et al., eds., *Svensk farmaci under 1900-talet*, vol. 1, pp. 236 f. See also Gustaf Myhrman, "Moderna läkemedelsproblem," *Svenska Dagbladet* 8 November (1947).
18. *Svensk läkemedelsindustri*, p. 8.
19. Ibid., p. 8.
20. Ibid., p. 9.
21. "Den bakteriefria fabriken," p. 5. In order to promote their common interests, the leading companies in Sweden combined to form Läkemedelsindustriföreningen (LIF, the Pharmaceutical Industry Association) in 1951. As early as 1947, representatives of several foreign firms trading in Sweden founded Representantföreningen för Utländska farmaceutiska Industrier (RUFI, the Representative Association of Foreign Pharmaceutical Industries). LIF and RUFI merged in 1995 under the name of the former.
22. Astra was by far the largest Swedish corporation and, after buying out Tika in 1939 and Hässle in 1942, was almost the same size as all the other Swedish pharmaceutical concerns combined.

23. "Styrelseprotokoll," 29 October 1945, vol. AX4, LHA. At this point in time, Georg Kahlson, Sven Ingvar and Axel Westman were the consultants receiving the biggest paychecks by Leo.
24. The new factory was ready in 1941. See "Årsberättelse för 1941," undated, LHA; "En stridsfront mot sjukdom och lidande: Leofabriken i Hälsingborg arbetar oförtrutet och intensivt," *Skånska Socialdemokraten* 29 April (1941).
25. "Styrelseprotokoll," 29 October 1945.
26. Ahlin and Lundgren, *Från Leopiller till nicorette*, p. 115.
27. *Sexualhormonpreparat Leo*, 3 ed. (Hälsingborg: Leo, 1944), p. 16.
28. According to the pamphlet, *Ovex Leo* contained pure estrone, while *Ovex B Leo* contained estradiol monobenzoate and *Glycovex Leo* estradiol tetraacetyl glycoside.
29. *Sexualhormonpreparat Leo*, p. 23.
30. *Svensk läkemedelsindustri*, p. 8.
31. Marcie J. Tyre and Wanda J. Orlikowski, "Windows of Opportunity: Temporal Patterns of Technological Adaptation in Organizations," *Organization Science* 5 (1994).
32. "Løvens kemiske Fabrik—Leo Pharmaceutical Products."
33. Axel Westman to Carl Holtman, 3 November 1944, E1 vol. 6, WCA, SCCA.
34. Adam Deutsch and Paul Kallós, "Samtal med professor Axel Westman," undated, vol. 2224, LHA.
35. Ibid.
36. "P. M.," 29 December 1944, vol. 2224, LHA.
37. Adam Deutsch and Paul Kallós, "Rapport över besök hos Överläkare S. Genell, Malmö den 4 april 1945," 5 April 1945, vol. 2224, LHA. Genell also discussed other kinds of pituitary hormones, including growth hormones and prolactin, but cautioned that the clinical value of these substances was still uncertain.
38. "Protokoll vid sammanträdet den 6 april 1945," vol. 2224, LHA.
39. Adam Deutsch and Paul Kallós, "Rapport över resa till Stockholm den 19 t.o.m. 22 oktober," 24 October 1945, vol. 2224, LHA.
40. Westman, *Barnlös*, p. 114. See also idem, "Hormonforskning och praktisk läkekonst," *Tidskrift för Sveriges Sjuksköterskor* 9 (1942), p. 842.
41. Brown, "Anterior Pituitary Hormones," p. 383.
42. Sengoopta, *The Most Secret Quintessence of Life*, p. 163.
43. Westman, "Om sterilitetens behandling och resultaten av densamma," p. 1161.
44. Margaret and Ronner, *The Empty Cradle*, 3.
45. Ibid., p. 1165.
46. *Sexualhormonpreparat Leo*, pp. 20 f.
47. Axel Westman, "Klinisk prövning av choriongonadotropinet 'Gonadex' Leo," *SL* 45 (1948), p. 1157.
48. See Erik Rydberg, "The Use of the Gonadotrophic Hormones in the Therapy and their Dosage," *Acta Obst.* 23 (1943).
49. There were however companies who marketed genuine pituitary extracts after the Second World War, including American firms Searle and Squibb, who launched "Gonadophysin" and "Pituitary-Anterior Pituitary Extract," respectively.
50. Research on chorionic gonadotropin in the 1930s and 1940s is presented in Rydberg, "The Use of the Gonadotrophic Hormones in the Therapy and their Dosage"; Westman, "Klinisk prövning av choriongonadotropinet 'Gonadex' Leo"; "Human

Chorionic Gonadotrophin," *British Medical Journal* 3 April (1948). See also Sengoopta, *The Most Secret Quintessence of Life*, pp. 129–135.

51. Frederik Paulsen, "Hormonterapiens gränser," *Hormoner: Referattidskrift för hormon- och vitaminforskning* 6 (1942), p. 112.
52. See Adolfsson and Wachenfeldt, "Terapeutiska försök med Prolan och Progynon"; Jorpes "Om handelns 'prólan'-preparat"; Elmer L. Sevringhaus, "Commercial Endocrine Preparations," *Endocrinology* 30 (1942), pp. 919–920.
53. See Westman, "Experimentella undersökningar över hypofysens produktion av gonadotropt hormon"; idem, "Untersuchungen über die Wirkung des gonadotropen Hypophysenvorderlappenhormones, Antex (LEO), auf die Ovarien der Frau," *Acta Obst.* 17 (1937); idem, "Über den Luteinisierungseffekt des gonadotropen Chorionhormons auf die Ovarien der Frau," *Acta Pathologica et Microbiologica Scandinavica* 15, suppl. 37 (1938).
54. Oudshoorn, "United We Stand," p. 13.
55. It should however be noted that that which was classified as "pure" was context specific. This becomes apparent by simply reading the description of Physex in *Leopreparat* (1940), p. 214, which explains that though the manufacture of gonadotropic hormones previously had been fraught with problems, all obstacles had now been overcome. "With a brand-new method, it is now possible to manufacture Physex Leo in such pure, sustainable, and concentrated form that it is suitable for clinical use in large doses." As already mentioned, this was not the message on Physex a few years later.
56. There are numerous examples of new drugs that have been used as "scientific instruments," thereby opening new fields of research. On drugs as instruments, see Jordan Goodman, "Can it Ever be Pure Science? Pharmaceuticals, Pharmaceutical Industry and Biomedical Research in the Twentieth Century," in Gaudillière and Löwy, eds., *The Invisible Industrialist.*
57. The standard work on the making of knowledge about hormones in a laboratory environment is Bruno Latour and Steve Woolgar, *Laboratory Life: The Construction of Scientific Facts* (1979), new ed. (Princeton, New Jersey: Princeton University Press, 1986). On the importance of "everyday science" in biochemistry, see Lundgren, *Vetenskap till vardags.*
58. Lennart Claesson, Bertil Högberg, Thomas Rosenberg and Axel Westman, "Crystalline Human Chorionic Gonadotrophin and Its Biological Action," *Acta Endo.* 1 (1948).
59. AB Leo to Axel Westman, 12 February 1947, vol. 1368, LHA. Högberg was not a Ph.D but was awarded an honorary doctorate of medicine by the Caroline Institute in 1960.
60. As early as 1943, Westman and Rosenberg planned to conduct a study on the hormone prolactin. See Axel Westman to the teaching staff at the Caroline Institute, 6 December 1943, E1 vol. 5, WCA, SCCA.
61. Claesson et al., "Crystalline Human Chorionic Gonadotrophin and Its Biological Action," pp. 2–5; Ahlin and Lundgren, *Från Leopiller till nicorette*, p. 113.
62. Claesson et al., "Crystalline Human Chorionic Gonadotrophin and Its Biological Action," pp. 6–7.
63. Ibid., pp. 9–10.

64. On the development of clinical and experimental drug testing, see Abraham M. Lilienfeld, "*Ceteris Paribus*: The Evolution of the Clinical Trial," *Bulletin of the History of Medicine* 56 (1982); Harry M. Marks, *The Progress of Experiment: Science and Therapeutic Reform in the United States, 1900–1990* (Cambridge: Cambridge University Press, 1997). On risk assessment, see Thomas Schlich and Ulrich Tröhler, eds., *The Risks of Medical Innovation: Risk Perception and Assessment in Historical Context* (London and New York: Routledge, 2006).
65. Claesson et al., "Crystalline Human Chorionic Gonadotrophin and Its Biological Action," pp. 10–13.
66. Ibid., p. 13.
67. "P. M. för sammanträde i Hälsingborg lördagen den 17 januari 1948," vol. 1368, LHA.
68. Ibid.
69. Claesson et al., "Crystalline Human Chorionic Gonadotrophin and Its Biological Action," p. 16.
70. Ibid., p. 17.
71. Westman, "Klinisk prövning av choriongonadotropinet 'Gonadex Leo'."
72. Ibid., p. 1159.
73. Rolf Luft, "Kristalliniskt choriongonadotropin (gonadex Leo), *Nord. Med.* 39 (1948), p. 1476.
74. AB Leo to Harald Johansson, 16 February 1948, vol. 792, LHA.
75. AB Leo to Board of Med., 16 and 23 April 1948, vol. 6029, LHA.
76. AB Leo to Board of Med., 17 June 1948, vol. 6029, LHA; Board of Med. to AB Leo, 17 June 1948, E2 vol. 12, NPL Archives, NAA; "Physex," D1a vol. 7, NPL Archives, NAA. Some weeks later, Leo decided to cross Gonadex 300 IU and 600 IU off the register, which was also approved. See Board of Med. to AB Leo, 20 July 1948, E2 vol. 12, NPL Archives, NAA.
77. AB Leo to Board of Med., 16 April 1948. Cryptorchidism is the retention in the abdomen of one or both testicles.
78. AB Leo to Axel Westman, 10 April 1948, vol. 1368, LHA.
79. AB Leo to Board of Med., 16 April 1948.
80. "P. M. beträffande Gonadex-priserna," 6 April 1948, vol. 6029, LHA.
81. *Svensk läkemedelsindustri*, p. 8.
82. Cf. Oudshoorn, "United We Stand."
83. Board of Med. to AB Leo, 13 June 1948, vol. 6029, LHA; Board of Med. to SFT, 13 May 1948, E2 vol. 12, NPL Archives, NAA. This concerned the first application for the strongest potencies. A similar decision on the lower potencies, when Physex became Gonadex, was made on 1 July. See Board of Med. to AB Leo, 17 June 1948, vol. 6029, LHA.
84. AB Leo to Board of Med., 1 July 1948, vol. 6029, LHA. See also the circular concerning Gonadex, enclosed to a letter from AB Leo to Board of Med., 5 June 1948, vol. 6029, LHA. Leo obviously wanted this problem solved as soon as possible. In a letter from Svante Wiström to Håkan Rydin, 5 May 1948, vol. 6029, LHA, Wiström writes: "It is of utmost importance that the preparation be registered and above all that it be entered on the free list."
85. AB Leo to Axel Westman, 27 May 1948, vol. 1368, LHA.

86. Föreningen Skånska Andelsslakterier [Scanian Abbatoir Cooperative] to AB Leo, 16 May 1942, vol. 2190, LHA.
87. Föreningen Skånska Andelsslakterier to AB Leo, 27 May 1942 and 2 April 1942, vol. 2190, LHA.
88. Föreningen Skånska Andelsslakterier to AB Leo, 2 February 1948 and 4 February 1948, vol. 871, LHA. Leo also used (bull) testicles for the production of an enzyme (hyaluronidase), which was used in a preparation called Hyalas, launched in 1949.
89. AB Leo to "stoägare" (horse owners), "Leverantörer av blod från sto," "Deltagarna i blodinsamlingen från dräktiga ston 1948," "P.M. angående blodtappning," "P.M. angående blodtappning," "Utdrag av avtal mellan Skandinaviska Kreatursförsäkringsbolaget, Stockholm och Aktiebolaget Leo, Hälsingborg," and "Utdrag av avtal mellan Skandinaviska Kreatursförsäkringsbolaget, Stockholm och Aktiebolaget Leo, Hälsingborg," all undated, vol. 1169, LHA.
90. "P. M. för sammanträde i Hälsingborg lördagen den 17 januari 1948."
91. "Kalkyl över framställning av chorion-gonadotropin," 6 April 1948, vol. 6029, LHA.
92. "Redovisning för tiden den 11–16 december 1950," vol. 2456, LHA.
93. "Rapport från sammanträde den 14 juli 1950 beträffande urininsamling," vol. 2456, LHA.
94. "Konto nr 304: Råvarukostnader Gonadex," vol. 2456, LHA. Urine collection for the purpose of manufacturing Gonadex continued unabated until 1967 when Leo started purchasing raw material directly from the Dutch corporation Organon, see Ahlin and Lundgren, *Från Leopiller till nicorette*, p. 191.

CHAPTER FIVE

1. Mickey C. Smith, *Principles in Pharmaceutical Marketing* (Philadelphia: Lea and Febiger, 1968), p. 64.
2. See *Svensk läkemedelsindustri*, p. 17.
3. Ibid., p. 15.
4. "Angående propagandan för år 1945," 4 May 1945, vol. 2224, LHA. See also Ahlin and Lundgren, *Från Leopiller till nicorette*, pp. 66, 140; Jeremy A. Greene, "Attention to 'Details': Etiquette and the Pharmaceutical Salesman in Postwar America," *SSS* 34 (2004). Some pharmaceutical companies had their field representatives attend courses offered by bigger, international companies. They could also avail themselves of handbooks written by successful propagandists, such as Thomas H. Jones, *Detailing the Physician: Sales Promotion by Personal Contact with the Medical and Allied Professions* (New York: Romaine Pierson Publishers, 1940).
5. See "En stridsfront mot sjukdom och lidande"; "ABF-besöket hos Leo," *Skånska Socialdemokraten* 21 December (1944); "Leo hade i går besök av blivande apotekare," *Helsingborgs Dagblad* 27 September (1947); "20 professorer såg Hälsingborg," *Helsingborgs Dagblad* 5 September (1948). See also Ahlin and Lundgren, *Från Leopiller till nicorette*, p. 134.
6. "Årsberättelse för 1941."
7. "Angående propagandan för år 1945."
8. Goodman, "Pharmaceutical Industry," p. 149.

9. "World Medical Association International Code of Medical Ethics," www.wma.net/e/policy/c8.htm 11 June 2007.
10. Axel Westman to Christian Hamburger, 26 February 1946, E1 vol. 9, WCA, SCCA.
11. Axel Westman and Hjalmar Wijnbladh to AB Leo, 15 September 1947, vol. 1368, LHA.
12. AB Leo to Axel Westman, 3 May 1948, vol. 1368, LHA.
13. The ad ran in *Acta Endo.* 1 (1948). A design suggested was enclosed with the letter sent by AB Leo to Westman, 3 May 1948.
14. Hjalmar Wijnbladh to AB Leo, 13 October 1948, vol. 1368, LHA. The conference was discussed in several newspaper articles, including Hjalmar Wijnbladh, "Hormoner genom 100 år: Ett forskningsjubileum," *Dagens Nyheter* 2 August (1948); "Forskarmöte i Stockholm diskuterar 'Sändebuden i blodet': Halvt grams hjärnbihang nyckelorgan för kroppen—tillverkar sex hormoner," *Expressen* 24 September (1948); "Svenskt preparat botar sterilitet," *Bergslagernas Tidning* 25 September (1948). The program of the conference, which took place 25–26 September, was reproduced in *Svenska Läkartidningen* 45 (1948).
15. AB Leo to Westman, 3 May 1948.
16. AB Leo to Westman, 27 May 1948.
17. Axel Westman to AB Leo, 31 May 1948, vol. 1368, LHA; "Ett medicinskt sekeljubileum," *Svenska Dagbladet* 16 August (1948).
18. "D-rapport nr 56 från sammanträde på Leo den 29.10.51," 9 November 1951, vol. 5610, LHA. For a similar case, see "D-rapport nr 61 den 11 december 1952," vol. 5610, LHA.
19. AB Leo to Westman, 3 March 1947.
20. Rima D. Apple, *Vitamania: Vitamins in American Culture* (New Brunswick, NJ: Rutger's University Press, 1996), p. 18 f.
21. AB Leo to Axel Westman, 1 March 1948, vol. 1368, LHA.
22. Crystal microphotography had appeared before in advertising. See for example Astra's ad for Sulfatiazol in *SFT* 1942.
23. See *Gonadex*, information booklet distributed by AB Leo (1948), LHA. Aside from an image of "Gonadex Crystals," magnified 250 times, two photos of ovaries after having undergone treatment with Gonadex were used as illustrations.
24. Roger Qvarsell, "Att sälja hälsa," in Roger Qvarsell and Ulrika Torell, eds., *Reklam och hälsa: Levnadsideal, skönhet och hälsa i den svenska reklamens historia* (Stockholm: Carlssons, 2004), p. 16.
25. These advertising pamphlets were also vetted and proofread by Axel Westman before being printed and distributed. See Westman to AB Leo, 31 May 1948.
26. Qvarsell, "Att sälja hälsa," p. 17.
27. "P.M. angående publicity för Gonadex," vol. 792, LHA. The document is undated but was appended to the previously cited letter from Leo to Johansson on 16 February 1948, which mentions that the document concerns the launch of Gonadex, and that it will also be forwarded to Westman for his approval.
28. Larsåke Larsson, *Upplysning och propaganda: Utvecklingen av svensk PR och information* (Lund: Studentlitteratur, 2005), pp. 17–18.
29. Ibid., pp. 49–76.
30. AB Leo to Westman, 27 May 1948; Westman to AB Leo, 31 May 1948.

31. "Professor Westmans anförande vid presskonferensen den 10 June 1948," vol. 1368, LHA.
32. Ibid.
33. Ibid.
34. Axel Westman, "Hjärnbihanget och dess hormon," *Göteborgs Handels- och Sjöfartstidning* 12 June (1948). The article is to some extent similar to Westman's lecture at the press conference.
35. Ibid., p. 8.
36. Westman's enlightened attitude toward contraception might have one conclude that he was a political liberal. However, according to his daughter Ann-Margret Sundius, Westman leaned "farther to the right." Ann-Margret Sundius, pers. com., 8 February 2005.
37. AB Leo to Axel Westman, 2 August 1948, vol. 1368, LHA.
38. Axel Westman to AB Leo, 11 August 1948, vol. 1368, LHA. The exhibition is also discussed in Ahlin and Lundgren, *Från Leopiller till nicorette*, p. 115.
39. AB Leo to Axel Westman, 26 July 1948, vol. 1368, LHA.
40. Headlines appearing in *Svenska Morgonbladet* 11 June (1948); *Dagens Nyheter* 11 June (1948); *Morgontidningen* 11 June (1948); *Svenska Dagbladet* 11 June (1948); *Stockholms-Tidningen* 11 June (1948). Several regional newspapers published similar articles.
41. "En tredjedel av alla sterila kvinnor kan få barn genom nytt hormonpreparat," pp. 19, 34, 35.
42. "Den bakteriefria fabriken," p. 4.
43. "Barnlöshet botas, förkrympta växer."
44. Palmblad, *Sanningens gränser*.
45. "Hormonpreparat bot för kvinnor, svensk triumf."
46. "En tredjedel av alla sterila kvinnor kan få barn genom nytt hormonpreparat," p. 19. However, *Husmodern* published a picture featuring Westman together with colleagues Bertil Högberg and Thomas Rosenberg. The trio was said to be "the three scientists who deserve the lion's share of the credit for creating the new hormone drug."
47. "New Swedish Hormone Preparation Remedy for Sterility," from the Swedish embassy in Pretoria. Copy included with a letter from AB Leo to Axel Westman, 14 August 1948, vol. 1368, LHA. Italics mine.
48. See Sten-Åke Stenberg, "Forskningsresultat och politiska prioriteringar," *Tvärsnitt* 3 (2007).
49. This may be compared with the way biomedical researchers contributed to shaping the image of Interferon in the mass media according to Pieters, *Interferon*, pp. 154–157.
50. Nelkin, *Selling Science*, p. 11.
51. "Barnlös plötsligt gravid med nytt hormonpreparat," vol. 1368, LHA. In his article "Vetenskaplig reklam och praktisk erfarenhet: Ett bidrag till problemet om kvinnans sterilitet," *SL* 45 (1948), p. 1735, Waldemar Gårdlund writes that the organizers of the press conference "delivered several typewritten, stencilled statements to reporters." One of these was titled "Childless Woman Instantly Pregnant Thanks to New Hormone Drug." I have not been able to find any of the other texts in the LHA.
52. Nelkin, *Selling Science*, pp. 119–121.

53. Gieryn, *Cultural Boundaries of Science*, pp. 187–188.
54. "Barnlös plötsligt gravid med nytt hormonpreparat."
55. Thanks to Anders Lundgren for this observation.
56. See Staffan Wennerholm, "'Unga forskare sökes': Att tilltala vetenskapens påläggskalvar i teknikerbristens tidevarv," in Ekström, ed., *Den mediala vetenskapen*, p. 143.
57. See further Arne Ruth, "The Second New Nation: The Mythology of Modern Sweden," *Daedalus* 2 (1984).
58. "Barnlös plötsligt gravid med nytt hormonpreparat."
59. Ibid.

CHAPTER SIX

1. Cf. James A. Secord, "Knowledge in Transit," *Isis* 95 (2004), p. 662.
2. "Hormonpreparat lockar hit framstående fransk läkare," *Helsingborgs Dagblad* 5 September (1948).
3. Harry Collins and Trevor Pinch, *The Golem: What You Should Know about Science* (1993), 2d ed. (Cambridge: Cambridge University Press, 1998), p. 59.
4. From the published articles alone, it is impossible to determine how many of the thirty women were actually sterile. The press release refers to "some thirty cases, e.g. of childless women." If only one or a handful of the women were in fact sterile, the results must be seen in a different light.
5. Name withheld (F) to Axel Westman, 25 January 1944, E1 vol. 6, WCA, SCCA.
6. Jørgen Hoffmeyer, "Resultater af Behandling af Sterilitet hos Kvinden," *Nord. Med.* 39 (1948).
7. AB Leo to Harald Johansson, 10 July 1948, vol. 792, LHA; AB Leo to Axel Westman, 16 August 1948, vol. 1368, LHA. The latter missive states that AB Leo had "recently received lots of queries about Gonadex."
8. See G. Hesselblad to AB Leo, 8 July 1948, vol. 792, LHA; M. Svenmar to AB Leo, undated, vol. 792, LHA; AB Leo to Axel Westman, 28 July 1948 (about a request of a physician who wished to test Gonadex "on a very large clientele" against impotence and decrepitude), vol. 1368, LHA; Gunnar Salmson to AB Leo, 4 August 1948, vol. 1368, LHA; Bertil Olow to AB Leo, 9 August 1948, vol. 1368, LHA; Lars Sundblad to AB Leo, undated, vol. 1368, LHA.
9. Quoted in the letter from AB Leo to Westman, 16 August 1948.
10. Olow to AB Leo, 9 August 1948. See also AB Leo to Harald Johansson, 9 August 1948, vol. 792, LHA.
11. Name withheld (F) to Axel Westman, 22 June 1948, E1 vol. 11, WCA, SCCA.
12. AB Leo to G. Hesselblad, 9 July 1948, vol. 792, LHA; AB Leo to Harald Johansson, 16 July 1948, vol. 792, LHA; AB Leo to Westman, 16 August 1948.
13. AB Leo to Harald Johansson, 11 August 1949, vol. 874, LHA.
14. See Martin Kylhammar, "Bryt upp! Bryt upp! Om den moderna konsten att göra sig kvitt det förflutna," in Martin Kylhammar and Michael Godhe, eds., *Frigörare? Moderna svenska samhällsdrömmar* (Stockholm: Carlssons, 2005).
15. See Clarke, "Controversy and the Development of Reproductive Sciences."
16. Gårdlund, "Vetenskaplig reklam och praktisk erfarenhet," p. 1745. Gårdlund had previously also criticized what he called "the seamy side of modern hormone

therapy," see idem, "Hormoner och fosterfördrivning," *SL* 41 (1944). On Gårdlund, see "Waldemar Gårdlund 23.9 1879–2.8 1959," *SL* 57 (1960); Motzi Eklöf, *Läkarens ethos: Studier i den svenska läkarkårens identiteter, intressen och ideal 1890–1960* (Linköping: Linköping University, 2000).

17. Gårdlund writes that he too had tried hormone therapy, but with no success. "Unfortunately I must say that hopes that encouraging results could be achieved in this manner were quickly dashed, perhaps because, as W. opines, the preparation was apparently not potent enough." Ibid., p. 1739.
18. Ibid., p. 1746.
19. Ibid., pp. 1736–1737.
20. According to Gårdlund "we require certain standards from a representative of science, the highest possible level of trustworthiness, particularly in the case of the holder of a chair in medical studies, inasmuch as he is charged with imparting logical, medical methods, therapy and *medical ethics* to a new generation. He must serve as an inspiration to young people." Ibid., p. 1746.
21. Gieryn, *Cultural Boundaries of Science*, pp. 15–18.
22. Schlünder's results are discussed in Gaudillière, "Genesis and Development of a Biomedical Object," pp. 531–532.
23. News about the progress being made by hormone research was not just about sex hormones and gonadotropins. Another pituitary hormone that generated a lot of buzz in the early 1950s was ACTH. In Sweden, ACTH was first manufactured exclusively by Ferring, founded in Malmö in 1950 under the name Nordiska Hormonlaboratoriet AB (the name change occurring in 1954) under the direction of pharmacologist Frederik Paulsen. Ferring's ACTH drug was called Acton and was based on hormones extracted from the pituitary glands of swine. Leo launched its own porcine-based ACTH drug in 1953, called Reacthin. The "hunt for pituitary glands" was pursued all the way to Tomelilla, home of one of the largest abattoirs in Scandinavia. See "Hypofysjakt i Tomelilla intresserade rotarianer," *Ystads Allehanda* 9 March (1951). Leo also attempted to extract ACTH from the pituitary glands of cattle. See "D-rapport nr 56 från sammanträde på Leo den 29.10.51"; "Miljondels milligram av ACTH och Leos groda blir svart," *Skånska Socialdemokraten* 21 January (1952). There were also attempts at extracting ACTH from whales, see "Hormonforskare på väg lösa ämnesomsättningens gåtor: Valens hypofys framtidens ACTH-källa," *Svenska Dagbladet* 22 June (1950). Another popular topic at this time dealt with the discovery of "agitation hormones" (later referred to as "stress hormones"), which were considered treatable with hormone therapy. See "Jäktskador hormonbotas," *Stockholms-Tidningen* 16 October (1951). On the theory of stress, see Russel Viner, "Putting Stress in Life: Hans Selye and the Making of Stress Theory," *SSS* 29 (1999).
24. Leonard Brahme, "Samhället och läkaren," *SL* 39 (1942). On the self-image of Swedish physician's, see Eklöf, *Läkarens ethos*.
25. Idem, "Framsteg och publicitet," *SL* 48 (1951), p. 415.
26. Goodman, "Pharmaceutical Industry," p. 149.
27. For different views on the relationship between medicine and the mass media, see Virginia Berridge and Kelly Loughlin, eds., *Medicine, the Market and the Mass Media: Producing Health in the Twentieth Century* (London and New York: Routledge, 2005).

28. Bruce V. Lewenstein, "Science and the Media," in Jasanoff et al., eds., *Handbook of Science and Technology Studies*, p. 354.
29. There are however a few isolated examples, see AB Leo to Harald Johansson, 15 May 1950, vol. 874, LHA. This letter mentioned a request for Gonadex from a woman in Peru who wrote directly to Leo.
30. It was also common for people to discuss marital relations and involuntary childlessness in the letters columns of women's magazines, where they could remain anonymous. See Katarina Saltzman, "Barnlöshet och befolkningskris: En studie baserad på veckotidningsmaterial från åren 1935–43" (unpubl. paper in ethnology, Lunds University, Lund 1993).
31. E.g. name withheld (F) to Arne Kinch, 30 August 1942, E1 vol. 2, WCA, SCCA; name withheld (F) to Axel Westman, 4 January 1943, E1 vol. 3, WCA, SCCA; name withheld (F) to Axel Westman, 3 January 1945, E1 vol. 8, WCA, SCCA.
32. E.g. name withheld (F) to the Caroline Hospital, 28 July 1942, E1 vol. 2, WCA, SCCA; name withheld (F) to Axel Westman, 18 November 1945, E1 vol. 8, WCA, SCCA.
33. Påhlsson, *Hormonbehandling av amenorrhe och oligohypomenorrhe*, p. 62.
34. Saltzman, "Barnlöshet och befolkningskris."
35. Axel Westman to the Directorate of the Caroline Hospital, 27 February 1943, E1 vol. 3, WCA, SCCA.
36. Name withheld (F) to Axel Westman, 16 March 1943, E1 vol. 3, WCA, SCCA.
37. Name withheld (F) to Axel Westman, 11 January 1943, E1 vol. 3, WCA, SCCA.
38. Name withheld (F) to Axel Westman, 27 January 1943, E1 vol. 3, WCA, SCCA.
39. Name withheld (F) to Axel Westman, undated 1944, E1 vol. 7, WCA, SCCA. Westman's reply 17 November 1944, E1 vol. 7, WCA, SCCA.
40. Name withheld (F) to Axel Westman, 15 August 1943, E1 vol. 4, WCA, SCCA. See further Forsberg, "Barnlöshet beror på mannen."
41. Gynecologist Ann Lalos is thus wrong in claiming that the participation of the male partner in Sweden was not sought until the 1950s. In actual fact, men were part of the equation as early as the 1930s. See Lalos, "Infertilitetskrisen," p. 9.
42. Name withheld (F) to Axel Westman, 18 September 1943, E1 vol. 4, WCA, SCCA. The writer hoped that Westman would be her "knight in shining armor." On the immense deference shown the medical profession in general, see Shirran, *Samhälle, vetenskap och obstetrik*, pp. 159–160.
43. Cf. Widmalm, "Trollkarlen från Uppsala."
44. Name withheld (M) to Axel Westman, 25 August 1943, E1 vol. 4, WCA, SCCA. Westman answered that he was not familiar with such a method, 30 August 1943, E1 vol. 4, WCA, SCCA.
45. Name withheld (M) to Axel Westman, 4 December 1943, E1 vol. 3, WCA, SCCA.
46. Name withheld (F) to Axel Westman, 3 December 1943, E1 vol. 5, WCA, SCCA.
47. Name withheld (M) to Axel Westman, 23 April 1944, E1 vol. 6, WCA, SCCA; name withheld (M) to Axel Westman, undated 1944, E1 vol. 6, WCA, SCCA; name withheld (M) to Axel Westman, 13 May 1944, E1 vol. 6, WCA, SCCA.
48. "Syster Anna besvarar hälsofrågor," *Folket i bild* 17 (1944), p. 33.
49. Axel Westman to name withheld (M), 30 August 1943, E1 vol. 4, WCA, SCCA; Axel Westman to name withheld (M), 10 December 1943, E1 vol. 5, WCA, SCCA; Axel Westman to name withheld (F), 6 December 1943, E1 vol. 5, WCA, SCCA.

50. Axel Westman to name withheld (M), 26 April 1944, E1 vol. 6, WCA, SCCA; Axel Westman to name withheld (M), 5 May 1944, E1 vol. 6, WCA, SCCA; Axel Westman to name withheld (M), 16 May 1944, E1 vol. 6, WCA, SCCA.
51. Axel Westman to (physician) Torsten Sjögren, 20 January 1943, E1 vol. 3, WCA, SCCA; name withheld (F) to Axel Westman, 22 March 1945, E1 vol. 8, WCA, SCCA.
52. Name withheld (M) to Axel Westman, 13 February 1953, E1 vol. 14, WCA, SCCA; name withheld (M) to Axel Westman, 27 February 1953, E1 vol. 14, WCA, SCCA; name withheld (M) to Axel Westman, 27 March 1953, E1 vol. 14, WCA, SCCA; name withheld (M) to Axel Westman, 13 April 1953, E1 vol. 14, WCA, SCCA; name withheld (M) to Nils Erik Påhlsson 4 September 1953, E1 vol. 14, WCA, SCCA; name withheld (M) to Axel Westman, 27 August 1954, E1 vol. 15, WCA, SCCA.
53. Axel Westman to name withheld (F), 26 March 1945, E1 vol. 8, WCA, SCCA; Nils Erik Påhlsson (writing on behalf of Axel Westman) to name withheld (M), 18 February 1953, E1 vol. 14, WCA, SCCA. Westman realized that the women's clinic lacked competence in psychology and psychiatry and therefore made an effort at hiring a physician with the necessary credentials. See Axel Westman to the Directorate of the Caroline Hospital, 4 April 1955, E1 vol. 15, WCA, SCCA. Toward the end of his life, however, Westman participated in a project in which two men and three women, all transvestites, "changed sex." See John Hertz, Karl-Gunnar Tillinger and Axel Westman, "Report on Five Hormonally and Surgically treated Cases," *Acta Psychiatrica Scandinavica* 37 (1961).
54. E.g. name withheld (F) to Axel Westman, 20 March 1947, E1 vol. 10, WCA, SCCA.
55. Axel Westman, *Övergångsår* (Stockholm: Rabén and Sjögren, 1945).
56. For the debate on menopause in Sweden, see Lena Katarina Swanberg, *Blod, svett och tårar: En ilsken bok om östrogen* (Stockholm: Bokförlaget DN, 2003).
57. Westman, *Övergångsår*, pp. 125–126.
58. Name withheld (F) to Axel Westman, 14 June 1948, E1 vol. 11, WCA, SCCA; name withheld (F) to Axel Westman, 14 June 1948, E1 vol. 11, WCA, SCCA. One of these women had previously undergone several "pituitary transplants" without the desired results. This method is discussed further in Chapter Eight.
59. Name withheld (F) to Axel Westman, 16 June 1948, E1 vol. 11, WCA, SCCA.
60. Ibid.
61. Name withheld (F) to Axel Westman, 12 July 1948, E1 vol. 11, WCA, SCCA.
62. Name withheld (F) to Axel Westman, 24 August 1948, E1 vol. 11, WCA, SCCA. This woman had also used hormone preparations for several years.
63. See clinic assistant to name withheld (F), 16 July 1948, E1 vol. 11, WCA, SCCA.
64. Name withheld (F) to Axel Westman, 13 October 1949, E1 vol. 12, WCA, SCCA.
65. Name withheld (M) to Axel Westman, 20 June 1948, E1 vol. 11, WCA, SCCA.
66. Name withheld (M) to Axel Westman, 15 November 1948, E1 vol. 11, WCA, SCCA.
67. Name withheld (M) to Axel Westman, 8 December 1948, E1 vol. 11, WCA, SCCA. Instead of Gonadex, Westman recommended Leo's synthetic estrogen drug Synsteron in this particular case. See Axel Westman to name withheld (M), 13 December 1948, E1 vol. 11, WCA, SCCA.
68. See Lundin, *Guldägget*, p. 77.

69. Axel Westman to AB Leo, 1 April 1949, vol. 6029, LHA.
70. Name withheld (F) to Axel Westman, 29 December 1948, E1 vol. 11, WCA, SCCA; name withheld (F) to Axel Westman, 5 January 1949, E1 vol. 12, WCA, SCCA.
71. Name withheld (F) to Westman, 5 January 1949.
72. Name withheld (F) to Axel Westman, 19 January 1950, E1 vol. 12, WCA, SCCA.
73. Axel Westman to name withheld (F), 16 February 1950, E1 vol. 12, WCA, SCCA.
74. Westman asked a certain "Professor Dodds" to help in standardization. Axel Westman to Dodds, 12 August 1948, vol. 1368, LHA. Two months later and Dodds still had not replied. See AB Leo to Axel Westman, 25 November 1948, vol. 1368, LHA. This Dodds was most likely British biochemist Edward Charles Dodds, who had succeeded in producing a synthetic hormone in 1938 that functioned similarly to natural estrogen. The drug was called Stilbestrol in England and DES in the US. See Seaman, *The Greatest Experiment Ever Performed on Women*, pp. 31–44.
75. Håkan Rydin was a significant actor with a broad network of contacts within the Swedish pharmaceutical community. He was Associate Professor at the NPL 1938–1947 and later full professor. From 1942 to 1958 he also served as the lab's administrative chief and managing director. He went on to become Professor of Pharmacology and Toxicology at the Institute of Pharmacy (later the Faculty of Pharmacy at Uppsala University) from 1956 to 1969.
76. Håkan Rydin to AB Leo, 8 October 1948, vol. 1368, LHA.
77. Ibid.
78. AB Leo to Axel Westman, 12 October 1948, vol. 1368, LHA.
79. Axel Westman, "P.M. om Gonadexundersökningar," 12 October 1948, vol. 1368, LHA. The document describes both qualitative and quantitative investigations in which Gonadex had been compared with the international standard.
80. Axel Westman to AB Leo, 12 November 1948, vol. 1368, LHA.
81. AB Leo to Westman, 25 November 1948.
82. AB Leo to Axel Westman, 1 December 1948, vol. 1368, LHA. Fragments of the conversation are recorded in the document "Rapport från telefonsamtal mellan professor H. Rydin och apotekare S. Wiström 1 December 1948," vol. 6029, LHA.
83. Håkan Rydin to AB Leo, 3 December 1948, vol. 6029, LHA.
84. AB Leo to Westman, 1 December 1948.
85. AB Leo to NPL, 22 December 1948, vol. 6029, LHA.
86. Ibid.
87. "Antabus och Abstinyl," *SFT* 52 (1948).
88. AB Leo to NPL, 22 December 1948.
89. AB Leo to Axel Westman, 16 December 1948, vol. 1368, LHA.
90. AB Leo to Axel Westman, 31 December 1948, vol. 1368, LHA.
91. The decision to move Gonadex from the free list to the license list was taken on 27 January. See Board of Med. to AB Leo, 27 January 1949, vol. 6029, LHA.
92. Westman to AB Leo, 1 April 1949. It is of course possible that Westman failed to include all the patients he had treated during the relevant period in his statistics.
93. This lone positive outcome was possibly the same one mentioned at the press conference.
94. Westman to AB Leo, 1 April 1949.
95. Ibid.

96. Axel Westman to the teaching staff of the Caroline Institute, 30 March 1949, E1 vol. 12, WCA, SCCA; Axel Westman to the National Medical Research Council, 5 April 1949, E1 vol. 12, WCA, SCCA.
97. Axel Westman, "P.M. beträffande styrkan av preparatet Gonadex Leo," 5 April 1949, vol. 6029, LHA.
98. Ibid; "P.M. rörande standardiseringen av Gonadex," undated 1949, vol. 6029, LHA.
99. Claesson et al., "Crystalline Human Chorionic Gonadotrophin and Its Biological Action," p. 15.
100. Oudshoorn, "On Measuring Sex Hormones," p. 256.
101. Westman, "P.M. beträffande styrkan av preparatet Gonadex Leo."
102. See Parascandola, "The Preposterous Provision."
103. "Leos ställning inom hormonområdet," 6 May 1982, vol. 2792, LHA.
104. Axel Westman to AB Leo, 4 April 1949, vol. 6029, LHA.
105. "Rapport från telefonsamtal mellan professor H. Rydin, Statens Farmacevtiska Laboratorium och apotekare S. Wiström tisdagen den 19 april 1949," vol. 6029, LHA.
106. Ibid.
107. AB Leo to Board of Med., 9 May 1949, vol. 6029, LHA; "Rapport nr D 37," 12 May 1949, vol. 5610, LHA; Board of Med. to AB Leo, 23 May 1949, E2 vol. 13, NPL Archives, NAA. Leo requested changing Gonadex into Physex as early as January, see Board of Med. to AB Leo, 27 January 1949, vol. 6029, LHA; Board of Med. to AB Leo, 23 May 1949, vol. 6029, LHA.
108. AB Leo to Board of Med., enclosed a letter from Svante Wiström to Håkan Rydin, 23 April 1949, vol. 6029, LHA.
109. Board of Med. to AB Leo, 1 June 1949, vol. 6029, LHA; "Gonadex," D1a vol. 4, NPL Archives, NAA.
110. AB Leo to Board of Med., enclosed a letter from Svante Wiström to Håkan Rydin, 23 April 1949.
111. Board of Med. to AB, Leo 1 June 1949.
112. "Rapport nr D 37," vol. 5610, LHA.
113. "Rapport från sammanträde i Köpenhamn den 24 maj 1949," 31 May 1949, vol. 5610, LHA.
114. "Rapport från telefonsamtal mellan professor Håkan Rydin, Statens Farmacevtiska Laboratorium och apotekare S. Wiström," 26 September 1949, vol. 6029, LHA.
115. Contacts were made for instance with endocrinologists in USA, see "Rapport nr D 39 från sammanträde i Köpenhamn den 5.8.49," 3 October 1949, vol. 5610, LHA.
116. Edward Goldschmidt (1901–1950) was part-owner of H. Lundbeck and Co., which took over AB Leo in 1946. In essence, Goldschmidt became the chairman of Leo until 1950. After his death, AB Leo's "own" directors, Alf Eberhard and Jens Nörgård, took over management.
117. "Rapport från fabrikant E. Goldschmidts besök å AB Leo den 13 oktober 1949," vol. 5610, LHA.

CHAPTER SEVEN

1. Goodman, "Pharmaceutical Industry," p. 150. In 2000, the global pharmaceutical market was valued at close to USD 330,000 million. Eighty percent of the market share belonged to American, European and Asian companies. The fifteen largest companies, all based in either the US, Great Britain, Germany, Switzerland or Japan, accounted for almost fifty percent of total sales.
2. Pickstone, *Ways of Knowing*, p. 53.
3. "Sammanfattning av docent Harald Johanssons föredrag på Hormonlaboratoriet i Stockholm den 4 mars 1950," vol. 874, LHA.
4. "Laboratoriebyggnad i Karolinska Sjukhuset," *Svenska Dagbladet* 27 January (1948); Axel Westman and Per Wetterdal, "Obstetrik och gynekologi," in *Karolinska mediko-kirurgiska institutets historia 1910–1960: Utgiven med anledning av institutets hundrafemtioårsdag av dess lärarkollegium*, 4 vol. (Stockholm: Almqvist and Wiksell, 1960), vol. 3, p. 894.
5. "Nya lokaler hormoninjektion för svensk hormonforskning," *Stockholms-Tidningen* 25 September (1948).
6. Egon Diczfalusy, pers. com., 9 November 2007.
7. "Nya lokaler hormoninjektion för svensk hormonforskning."
8. AB Leo to Axel Westman, 29 December 1948, vol. 1368, LHA.
9. Egon Diczfalusy, pers. com., 9 November 2007.
10. "Styrelseprotokoll," 27 January 1949, vol. 5610, LHA; "Rapport nr D 37," vol. 5610, LHA.
11. Axel Westman to the Docent Committee of the Caroline Institute, 27 August 1953, E1 vol. 14, WCA, SCCA. After pressure from Westman, Diczfalusy was granted Swedish citizenship in 1950. See Axel Westman to S. O. Andersson, 30 March 1950, E1 vol. 12, WCA, SCCA.
12. This division later became the Department of Reproductive Endocrinology. Diczfalusy served as Prefect until he retired in 1987.
13. Egon Diczfalusy and Ulf Borell, eds., *Control of Human Fertility: Proceedings of the Fifteenth Nobel Symposium held May 27–29, 1970 at Södergarn, Lidingö, Sweden* (Stockholm: Swedish Royal Academy of Science, 1971); Egon Diczfalusy, *The Contraceptive Revolution: An Era of Scientific and Social Development* (New York and London: Parthenon, 1996).
14. Editorial, "Contraindications to Estrogen Therapy," *Journal of the American Medical Association* 114 (1940). See further Frances B. McCrea and Gerald E. Markle, "The Estrogen Replacement Controversy in the USA and UK: Different Answers to the Same Question?," *SSS* 14 (1984), p. 3.
15. Jean-Paul Gaudillière, "Hormones at Risk: Cancer and the Medical Uses of Industrially-produced Sex Steroids in Germany, 1930–1960," in Schlich and Tröhler, eds., *The Risks of Medical Innovation*, p. 158.
16. Axel Westman to Sten von Stapelmohr, 1 March 1943, E1 vol. 3, WCA, SCCA. Westman hints that a debate on "the matter of hormone treatment" had been conducted within the Swedish Medical Association. On later debates, see Diana B. Dutton, *Worse than the Disease: Pitfalls of Medical Progress* (Cambridge: Cambridge University Press, 1988); Margaret Marsh and Wanda Ronner, *The Fertility Doctor: John Rock and the Reproductive Revolution* (Baltimore, Maryland: Johns Hopkins

University Press, 2008), pp. 247–277; Swanberg, *Blod, svett och tårar*; Seaman, *The Greatest Experiment Ever Performed on Women*.

17. Håkan Rydin to Board of Med., 20 November 1948, B2 vol. 17, NPL Archives, NAA.
18. This advertisement appeared for example in the journal *Endocrinology* 25 (1939).
19. In Sweden, topical hormone creams were manufactured and sold by the company Paulis, which collaborated with Harald Johansson of the Caroline Hospital.
20. Rydin to Board of Med., 20 November 1948.
21. Swanberg, *Blod, svett och tårar*, p. 221.
22. "Experter avlivar alarmrykte: Hormonkrämerna helt ofarliga," *Stockholms-Tidningen* 18 January (1950).
23. Ibid.
24. Håkan Rydin to AB Hässle, 19 January 1949, B3 vol. 4, NPL Archives, NAA.
25. See Håkan Rydin, "Om bedömning av läkemedels medicinska värde," *SFT* 49 (1945).
26. On Heyman, see Axel Westman, "Professor James Heyman in Memoriam," *Acta Obst.* 35 (1956).
27. "Hormoner bör tas under kontroll," *Svenska Dagbladet* 18 January (1950). See also "Kvinnliga hormonpreparat krävs under läkarrecept," *Aftonbladet* 17 January (1950).
28. "Överdrivet bruk av hormonpreparat," *Svenska Dagbladet* 17 May (1947); Hans Ludvig Kottmeier, "Ueber Blutungen in der Menopause, speziell der klinischen Bedeutung eines Endometriums mit Zeichen hormonaler Beeinflussung," *Acta Obst.* 27, suppl. 6 (1947). See also idem, "Behandling med oestrogena hormonpreparat: Indikationer och kontraindikationer," *SL* 45 (1948); idem, "Hormonproducerande ovarialtumörer," *Nord. Med.* 41 (1949).
29. "Hormoner bör tas under kontroll."
30. AB Leo to Axel Westman, 28 May 1947, vol. 1368, LHA; AB Leo to Harald Johansson, 31 May 1950, vol. 874, LHA.
31. AB Leo to Harald Johansson, 8 November 1950, vol. 874, LHA.
32. See Rydberg, "The Use of the Gonadotrophic Hormones in the Therapy and their Dosage"; R. Movin, "Komplikationer ved gonadotropinbehandling af ovarialinsufficiens," *Nord. Med.* 41 (1949); Hamburger, *Hypofysens, Kønskirtlernes og Binyrernes Hormoner*, p. 24.
33. Poul Gøtzsche, "Antex–Physex: En advarsel," *Ugeskrift for Læger* 25 October (1951).
34. Idem, "Antex–Physex," *Ugeskrift for Læger* 22 November (1951).
35. Idem, "Antex–Physex," *Ugeskrift for Læger* 6 December (1951).
36. Erik Rydberg, "Antex–Physex," *Ugeskrift for Læger* 29 November (1951); Christian Hamburger, "Antex–Physex," *Ugeskrift for Læger* 29 November (1951); Frede Jørgensen, "Antex–Physex," *Ugeskrift for Læger* 3 January (1952).
37. Rydberg, "Antex–Physex"; H. Skjoldborg, "Antex–Physex," *Ugeskrift for Læger* 12 December (1951).
38. Rydberg, "The Use of the Gonadotrophic Hormones in the Therapy and their Dosage"; idem, "The Treatment of Functional Sterility with Gonadotropic Hormones," *Acta Obst.* 28 (1949).

39. AB Leo to Axel Westman, 2 February 1952, vol. 911, LHA; Axel Westman to AB Leo, 6 February 1952, vol. 911, LHA.
40. Following the Second World War, the number of substances considered hormones, along with the number of hormone preparations, increased dramatically. An attempt to describe all known hormones and their effect on flora and fauna was undertaken in the form of a comprehensive guidebook, see Gregory Pincus and Kenneth V. Thimann, eds., *The Hormones: Physiology, Chemistry and Applications* (New York: Academic Press, 1948), vol. 1, and (New York: Academic Press, 1950), vol. 2. Some of this information quickly became out-dated; new hormones were regularly discovered and in 1955 the editors presented a third volume including an additional one thousand pages. It was followed by two more, similarly exhaustive volumes, published in 1964.
41. Axel Westman, "Hormoner och nervsystem," in *Kungl. Svenska Vetenskapsakademiens Årsbok 1955*, p. 317.
42. J. W. R. Everse, "Kombinerad behandling med östrogent och androgent hormon," *Hormoner: Tidskrift för hormonforskning* 16 (1952); Gaudillière, "Hormones at Risk," pp. 161–164.
43. Leo introduced Estradurin (long-term effect estrogen) in 1957 and Estracyt (estradiol with nitric mustard attached) in 1972, both used mainly to combat prostate cancer. See Bertil Högberg, "Steroida kvävesenapsgasderivat: Synpunkter mot bakgrunden av hormonernas verkningsmekanism," *SFT* 78 (1974); Norgren, *Kunskapsöverföring från universitet till företag*, pp. 70–72. Estradurin was originally produced for use by gynecologists and was also tested for the treatment of menopause. See Axel Westman, "Behandling av klimakteriska bortfallsbesvär med Estradurin," undated 1959, E1 vol. 17, WCA, SCCA.
44. Board of Med. to AB Leo, 9 November 1949, vol. 6029, LHA; AB Leo to Board of Med., 29 August 1950, vol. 6029, LHA; Board of Med. to AB Leo, 9 November 1950, vol. 6029, LHA.
45. The latter diagnosis indicates "endometrial hyperplasia," a condition that can occur when the mucous membrane is exposed to continuous estrogen stimulation without subsequent menstruation. Thanks to Ulf Högberg for this information.
46. AB Leo to Board of Med., 29 August 1950.
47. NPL to AB Leo, 21 September 1950, vol. 6029, LHA; AB Leo to NPL, 13 January 1951, vol. 6029, LHA; NPL to AB Leo, 6 March 1951, vol. 6029, LHA; AB Leo to NPL, 2 April 1951, vol. 6029, LHA.
48. Birger Ekman, "Rapport från sammanträde med professor A. Westman," 8 September 1950, vol. 2456, LHA.
49. Ibid. See also "D-rapport nr 50 den 16 oktober 1950," vol. 5610, LHA, which states: "Docent Ekman considers the prospect of Gonadex being brought to a favorable conclusion to be good."
50. Birger Ekman, "Leos hormonforskning," 22 September 1950, vol. 2456, LHA.
51. Ibid.
52. Ibid.
53. Cf. Vos, *Drugs Looking for Diseases*.
54. Birger Ekman, "Reseberättelse över köpenhamnskongressen," 29 August 1950, vol. 2456, LHA. Ekman relates that he has been in contact with a number of foreign researchers who expressed interest in Gonadex. According to the article, "Svenskt

hormonpreparat skall lanseras i Amerika," *Svenska Dagbladet* 26 May (1950), there was a definite market for Swedish hormone drugs in the United States. The article is about Axel Westman, who had recently attended an international gynecological conference in New York and a meeting discussing fertility issues and the reasons for sterility with fellow researchers. The "Swedish hormone drug" referred to in the headline is not actually mentioned but may very well be Gonadex.

55. Lundgren, "Knowledge and Needs," p. 26.
56. Birger Ekman and Svante Wiström, "Utgifter för konsulenter och forskningsarbeten i samarbete med institutioner utanför Leo," 19 December 1950, vol. 5610, LHA.
57. Ibid.
58. "D-rapport nr 52: Rapport från sammanträde å AB Leo den 21 december 1950," 22 December 1950, vol. 5610, LHA. Of the five tasks Westman pledged his research team would accomplish in 1951 for AB Leo, three involved Gonadex: "Testing various fractions obtained in the manufacture of Gonadex"; "Preparation of Gonadex from placenta"; and "Study of the effect of Gonadex on different endocrine organs (testes, adrenal glands, thyreoidea)." See Axel Westman to AB Leo, 14 December 1950, vol. 5610, LHA.
59. "Rapport från direktionssammanträde på Leo den 6 februari 1951: Beträffande forskningslaboratoriet i Stockholm," 13 February 1951, vol. 5610, LHA.
60. Ibid. This topic is also discussed in "D-rapport nr 54 över sammanträde på Leo den 1 mars 1951," vol. 5610, LHA.
61. Board of Med. to AB Leo, 21 November 1951, vol. 6029, LHA; "Gonadex," D1b vol. 2, NPL Archives, NAA.
62. Hamburger, *Hypofysens, Kønskirtlernes og Binyrernes Hormoner*. Further evidence of Hamburger's status can be found in the fact that he was elected President of the First International Congress of Endocrinology, held in Copenhagen in 1960.
63. AB Leo to Board of Med., 20 January 1953, vol. 6029, LHA.
64. Gonadex was also registered at 300 IU and its structure somewhat modified. It had contained lactose up until 1935, which was now removed. See AB Leo to Board of Med., 25 April 1953, vol. 6029, LHA; NPL to Board of Med., 29 June 1953, vol. 6029, LHA; Board of Med. to AB Leo, 6 June 1953, vol. 6029, LHA.
65. *Leopreparat* (1952), LHA, pp. 134–135.
66. See Leo's ad in *Acta Endo.* 6 (1952).
67. Axel Westman to KAWF, 17 April 1953, Axel Westman Papers, KAWF Archives; KAWF to Caroline Inst., 18 June 1953, Axel Westman Papers, KAWF Archives. The subsidy was in the amount of SEK 20,000 and intended to pay Westman and Diczfalusy's respective wages and cover the price of lab animals.
68. Axel Westman to KAWF, 14 June 1954, Axel Westman Papers, KAWF Archives. See further Egon Diczfalusy, "An Improved Method for the Bioassay of Chorionic Gonadotrophin," *Acta Endo.* 17 (1954).
69. A second conference on the same theme was arranged in Puerto Vallarta, Mexico in 1965, and three years later another gonadotropin conference was held in the same country, this time in San José de Vista Hermosa. Gonadotropins were also high on the agenda at the fifth Nobel Symposium in Stockholm in 1970, and in 1971 scientists descended on New York for a major, international gonadotropin conference. See Eugenia Rosemberg, "Introductory Remarks," in idem, ed., *Gonadotropins 1968*; W. R. Butt, A. C. Crooke and M. Ryle, "Preface," in idem, eds., *Gonadotrophins*

and Ovarian Development: Proceedings of the two Workshop Meetings on the Chemistry of the Human Gonadotrophins and on the Development of the Ovary in Infancy, Birmingham, 1969 (Edinburgh and London, 1970); Diczfalusy and Borell, eds., *Control of Human Fertility*; Brij B. Saxena, Carl G. Beling and Hortense M. Gandy, eds., *Gonadotropins* (New York et al.: Wiley-Interscience, 1972).

70. Axel Westman, "Synpunkter på endokrinologins utveckling," *SL* 53 (1956), p. 2255.
71. Ekman and Wiström, "Utgifter för konsulenter och forskningsarbeten i samarbete med institutioner utanför Leo."
72. "Leo utökar sin forskningsverksamhet," *Farmacevtisk Revy* 59 (1960); Ahlin and Lundgren, *Från Leopiller till nicorette*, pp. 188 f. In 1962, a second research foundation was established featuring the same board as the first. To aid it, a special "scientific advisory panel" was set up, to be composed of a minimum of three highly qualified research and health care professionals who were not company employees. Axel Westman was appointed chairman. After his demise in 1960, Westman was replaced by Börje Uvnäs, a former student of Georg Kahlson (another Leo consultant). Uvnäs, who was professor of Pharmacology at the Caroline Institute, manned the post of panel chairman for the next twenty-five years.
73. AB Leo to Egon Diczfalusy, 1 November 1951, vol. 3003, LHA; Egon Diczfalusy to AB Leo, 13 November 1951, vol. 3003, LHA; AB Leo to Egon Diczfalusy, 28 November 1951, vol. 3003, LHA; "D-rapport nr 57 den 12.12.51," vol. 5610, LHA; AB Leo to Axel Westman, 11 March 1953 (including documents on the lab budget 1950–1952), vol. 911, LHA.
74. "D-rapport nr 58 den 30.1.52," 5 February 1952, vol. 5610, LHA; "D-rapport nr 60 den 20.8.52," 10 September 1952, vol. 5610, LHA.
75. Svante Wiström, "Rapport från besök i Stockholm den 28–30 augusti 1952," 2 September 1952, vol. 911, LHA.
76. "D-rapport nr 60 den 20.8.52."
77. AB Leo to Axel Westman, 26 September 1952, vol. 911, LHA.
78. "D-rapport nr 71 den 12 oktober 1954," 28 October 1954, vol. 5610, LHA.
79. "D-rapport nr 72 av den 25 november 1954," vol. 5610, LHA; Egon Diczfalusy, pers. com., 9 November 2007.
80. Axel Westman to Svante Wiström, 29 October 1953, vol. 911, LHA. A preliminary program of the conference was enclosed.
81. "D-rapport nr 65 från sammanträde den 24 november 1953," 3 December 1953, vol. 5610, LHA.
82. "D-rapport nr 66 över sammanträde på Leo den 10 december 1953," vol. 5610, LHA. The written reply received by Westman states that the conference concentrated too narrowly on "elementary research." See AB Leo to Axel Westman, 22 January 1954, vol. 911, LHA.
83. AB Leo to the Directorate of the Caroline Institute, 29 September 1952, vol. 2927, LHA.
84. Further funding for the takeover of AB Leo's hormone lab was sought when the Caroline Hospital submitted its supplementary estimate to the government for the fiscal year 1954–55. The relevant departments were favorably inclined to the request but in a referral to Statskontoret [the Agency for Administrative Development] the project met resistance. The agency cited strained state finances and recommended

that AB Leo continue to run the lab for one more year. After a "term of notice" of twenty-one months, Leo was none too pleased with this suggestion, but replied that it was prepared to do so provided the government promised to reimburse possible losses. But Westman did not consider this solution satisfactory either and asked Leo to hold its ground until the government was forced to commit itself. Otherwise, Westman feared, there was a risk that some other hospital in Stockholm be granted funds to build its own hormone lab, thereby worsening the Caroline's chances of taking over Leo's lab. Leo took his advice. Westman was probably specifically worried about Sabbatsberg Hospital, whose women's clinic had contained a small hormone lab since 1949. See Axel Westman to AB Leo, 3 October 1952, vol. 5610, LHA; "D-rapport nr 61 den 11 december 1952," vol. 5610, LHA; "D-rapport nr 65 från sammanträde den 24 november 1953," vol. 5610, LHA; "D-rapport nr 66," vol. 5610, LHA; "D-rapport nr 70 den 29 juni 1954," vol. 5610, LHA; Kjell Carlström, "Kvinnoklinikens hormonlaboratorium," in Valter Holmqvist et al., *Sabbatsbergs sjukhus 111 år* (Stockholm: Sabbatsberg Hospital, 1990).

85. Axel Westman et al., "Hormonanalysernas praktiska värde," *SL* 56 (1959), p. 2050; idem, "Hormonlaboratoriernas framtid," p. 2078.
86. Beside the grant from 1953 (SEK 20,000), Westman received grants from the Wallenberg Foundation in 1951 (SEK 10,000), 1954 (SEK 21,800), 1956 (SEK 19,040), and 1958 (SEK 53,000). See KAWF to Caroline Inst., 24 October 1951, 15 June 1954, 18 December 1956, and 22 December 1958, Axel Westman Papers, KAWF Archives. Endocrinologist Rolf Luft also received several grants from the Wallenberg Foundation during these years. See KAWF to Caroline Inst., 11 March 1953, Rolf Luft Papers, KAWF Archives.
87. Rolf Luft, "Endokrinologi," in Bengt Pernow, ed., *Karolinska sjukhuset 1940–1990: En minnesbok* (Stockholm: Caroline Hospital, 1990), p. 80.
88. KAWF to Caroline Inst., 15 June 1953, Rolf Luft papers, KAWF Archives.
89. Hilding Bergstrand to KAWF, 14 March 1953, Rolf Luft Papers, KAWF Archives; Rolf Luft to KAWF, undated (received 24 March 1953), Rolf Luft Papers, KAWF Archives; Ingrid Uddenberg, "Skiss till Wallenbergs endokrinologiska institution vid Karolinska Sjukhuset, skala 1:100," 28 April 1953, Rolf Luft Papers, KAWF Archives.
90. "Redogörelse betr. utvecklingen av frågan: Stiftelsens 1-miljondonation för byggandet av Karolinska Institutets endokrinologiska laboratorium," 14 September 1954, Rolf Luft Papers, KAWF Archives. See further "Nytt forskningsinstitut för Wallenbergsmiljon," *Svenska Dagbladet* 17 June (1953); "Hormonforskningen får egen institution," *Dagens Nyheter* 19 June (1953); "Hormonforskning med klinik blir ny institution vid Karolinska," *Stockholms-Tidningen* 2 October (1954).
91. "Utdrag ur Lärarkollegiets vid Karolinska Institutet skrivelse till Universitetskanslern i juli 1954 angående budgetåret 1955/56," Rolf Luft Papers, KAWF Archives; "Redogörelse betr. utvecklingen av frågan: Stiftelsens 1-miljondonation för byggandet av Karolinska Institutets endokrinologiska laboratorium," 15 September 1954, Rolf Luft Papers, KAWF Archives. The division was created by literally raising the roof of the women's clinic, building a new floor on top and then putting the same roof back. It opened in September 1958 and was formally unveiled in January 1959. See "'Naturens nyck kan rättas till': Ny hormonavdelning invigd, tre stadsråd bland gästerna," *Dagens Nyheter* 21 January (1959); "Europas första

hormoninstitution invigd: Kan behandla 1200 patienter per år," *Stockholms-Tidningen* 22 January (1959).

92. Rolf Luft, pers. com., 23 June 2003. Luft was the sole applicant for the job, for which Westman was asked to provide expert opinion. Westman's verdict was very positive. See Axel Westman to the teaching staff at the Caroline Hospital, 11 February 1957, E1 vol. 16, WCA, SCCA.
93. However, the relationship changed over time. When Westman passed away in 1960, Luft was appointed Professor of Endocrinology. He was later granted almost SEK 700,000 to refurbish the division, which was then officially upgraded to department. See KAWF to Caroline Inst., 22 June 1964, Rolf Luft Papers, KAWF Archives; KAWF to Caroline Inst., 9 November 1965, Rolf Luft Papers, KAWF Archives. Endocrinology clinics were then established at Sahlgrenska University Hospital and Malmö General Hospital, too.
94. Axel Westman to KAWF, 17 June 1954, E1 vol. 15, WCA, SCCA, LA; Axel Westman and Sten Friberg to the teaching staff of the Caroline Hospital, 5 April 1954, E1 vol. 15, WCA, SCCA.

CHAPTER EIGHT

1. As is well known, the practice of implanting animal tissue into humans has undergone something of a renaissance recently in the form of xenotransplantation. See Anders Persson, "Att överskrida gränser: Om xenotransplantation, risker, värderingar och människouppfattning," *VEST* 11 (1998).
2. Cf. Britt-Marie Landgren and Torbjörn Bäckström, "Reproduktionsendokrinologins utveckling," in Bo Lindberg, ed. *Svensk kvinnosjukvård under ett sekel 1904–2004* (Stockholm: Swedish Society of Obstetrics and Gynecology, 2004), p. 207.
3. During the 1930s and 1940s, Eskil Kylin regularly published his results in *Svenska Läkartidningen*. See his survey article "Tio års hypofystransplantation," *SL* 40 (1943). Kylin's method was headline news, but was also criticized, by e.g. Fride Hylander, "Hypofysheterotransplantationer ad modum Kylin: Några korrigerande och kompletterande randanmärkningar," *SL* 35 (1938).
4. Emil Jerlov, "48 hypofystransplantationer vid gynekologiska åkommor jämte ett förslag till modifikation av ingreppet," *SL* 43 (1946). See also Josefson, "Några ord om hormonterapi."
5. Axel Westman, "Reaktivering av ovarialfunktionen under menopausen," *SL* 31 (1934), p. 339.
6. See Axel Westman and Dora Jacobsohn, "Experimentelle Untersuchung über Kalbshypophysentransplantate bei der Ratte," *Acta Pathologica et Microbiologica Scandinavica* 19 (1942). Pituitary tissue was placed for example in the anterior chamber of the lab animals.
7. Westman, "Hormonala behandlingsmetoder inom gynekologien," p. 1819.
8. Idem, "Kliniska och experimentella undersökningar över hypofystransplantation," *Nord. Med.* 4 (1939).
9. Axel Westman to Statens Livsmedelskommision [National Food Administration], 12 January 1943, E1 vol. 3, WCA, SCCA. The National Food Administration was a government agency responsible for rationing during the Second World War.

10. Axel Westman to Arne Axelsson, 7 June 1945, E1 vol. 8, WCA, SCCA. This method is also described in Axel Westman, "Hypofysimplantation," *Nord. Med.* 41 (1949). Westman claimed that hormones deteriorated rapidly, which is why it was necessary to keep the time between slaughter and operation as short as possible. Special "express transports" between abbatoirs and hospitals were arranged. Egon Diczfalusy, pers. com., 9 November 2007. This routine changed when pituitary glands were flash frozen until needed. See Axel Westman to G. Levander, 2 March 1957, E1 16, WCA, SCCA.
11. Name withheld (F) to Axel Westman, 11 May 1943, E1 vol. 3, WCA, SCCA; name withheld (F) to Axel Westman, 24 May 1943, E1 vol. 3, WCA, SCCA; name withheld (M) to Axel Westman, 27 August 1943, E1 vol. 3, WCA, SCCA.
12. Axel Westman to name withheld (F), 18 May 1943, E1 vol. 3, WCA, SCCA.
13. Name withheld (M) to Axel Westman, 29 September 1943, E1 vol. 3, WCA, SCCA.
14. Name withheld (F) to Axel Westman, 16 January 1945, E1 vol. 8, WCA, SCCA; Axel Westman to name withheld (F), 19 January 1945, E1 vol. 8, WCA, SCCA.
15. Westman, "Hormonala behandlingsmetoder inom gynekologien," pp. 1819–1820.
16. Name withheld (F) to Axel Westman, 20 November 1943, E1 vol. 5, WCA, SCCA.
17. Cf. Pfeffer, "Pioneers of Infertility Treatment," p. 247.
18. Name withheld (F) to Westman, 20 November 1943.
19. Name withheld (F) to Axel Westman, 25 August 1944, E1 vol. 6, WCA, SCCA.
20. Sten Floderus, "Untersuchungen über den Bau der menschlichen Hypophyse mit besonderer Berücksichtigung der quantitativen mikromorphologischen Verhältnisse," *Acta Pathologica et Microbiologica Scandinavica* 21, suppl. 53 (Ph.D diss., 1944).
21. "Svensk läkare fick 'material' från avrättade," *Dagens Nyheter* 19 May (1945). The scientist who acquired pituitary glands for Floderus in Berlin was the notorious anatomist Hermann Stieve (1866–1952), who conducted numerous "medical studies" on women murdered by the Gestapo.
22. Rolf Luft, pers. com., 23 June 2003.
23. "Ny metod hjälper barnlösa," *Stockholms-Tidningen* 6 December (1947).
24. "P. M. för sammanträde i Hälsingborg lördagen den 17 januari 1948."
25. Påhlsson, *Hormonbehandling av amenorrhe och oligohypomenorrhe*, p. 65.
26. Westman, "Hypofysimplantation"; idem, "The Value of Implantation of Hypophyseal Tissue in the Treatment of Hypophyseal Insufficiency," *Acta Medica Scandinavica* 133 (1949).
27. Name withheld (F) to Axel Westman, 30 January 1950 [1951], E1 vol. 13, WCA, SCCA; Axel Westman to name withheld (F), 7 February 1951, E1 vol. 8, WCA, SCCA. In one case, Westman recommended a woman undergo a pituitary transplant after Gonadex treatment caused her hair to fall out, see name withheld (F) to Axel Westman, 17 January 1954, E1 vol. 15, WCA, SCCA; Axel Westman to name withheld (F), 18 January 1954, E1 vol. 15, WCA, SCCA. See also Ulf Borell, Egon Diczfaluzy and Axel Westman, "The Effect of Pituitary Gland Implantation on the Excretion of 17-Ketosteroids in Women," *Acta Medica Scandinavica* 142 (1952).
28. Påhlsson, *Hormonbehandling av amenorrhe och oligohypomenorrhe.*

29. Ibid., pp. 61, 65.
30. Ibid., p. 91.
31. I have found two examples from 1960 in which individuals contacted the Women's Clinic of the Caroline Hospital about the possibility of being treated with pituitary glands, see name withheld (M) to Nils Pålsson, 14 June 1960, E1 vol. 18, WCA, SCCA; name withheld (M) to "Professor A. Westmans efterträdare," 5 September 1960, E1 vol. 18, WCA, SCCA. The replies suggest that the method was still being practiced at the clinic, but that it was not recommended (for the treatment of alopecia). Nils Erik Påhlsson to name withheld (M), 20 September 1960, E1 vol. 18, WCA, SCCA; Nils Erik Påhlsson to name withheld (M), 17 October 1960, E1 vol. 18, WCA, SCCA.
32. Påhlsson, *Hormonbehandling av amenorrhe och oligohypomenorrhe*, p. 58; Egon Diczfalusy, pers. com., 9 November 2007. According to Diczfalusy, the analyses of the hormone content of calf pituitary glands were never published.
33. "The THX Affair" was discussed in numerous newspaper articles and specialty periodicals, including *SFT* and *Farmacevtisk Revy*, and has also been recounted in a pair of books, e.g. Anders Otterland, *THX-rörelsen i teori och praktik* (Stockholm: Bonnier, 1966); Åke Ohlmarks, *THX och makthavarna* (Mjölby: National Association for Thymus Research, 1972). Thanks to Motzi Eklöf for her views on this subject.
34. Cf. Folke Holtz, "Sterility and Its Treatment," *Acta Obst.* 30, suppl. 7 (1950). Here Holtz details nearly one thousand cases, of which sixty-six percent were reported as having their inability to conceive cured after some form of medical or psychotherapeutic treatment.
35. Marsh and Ronner, *The Empty Cradle*, p. 209.
36. Pfeffer, *The Stork and the Syringe*, pp. 133–136.
37. Axel Westman to KAWF, 29 May 1954, Axel Westman Papers, KAWF Archive.
38. Just like Zondek, Westman earlier named these principals A and B, see Westman, "Hormonala behandlingsmetoder inom gynekologien," p. 1816.
39. Westman to KAWF, 29 May 1954.
40. KAWF to Caroline Inst., 15 June 1954. This time Westman applied for SEK 41,000 but received only SEK 21,800.
41. See Ulf Pettersson, Leif Wide and Martin H:son Holmdahl, "Carl Gemzell till minne: En av medicinens banbrytare har gått ur tiden," *Dagens Nyheter* 9 March (2007). In this article Gemzell is described as the "undisputed pioneer."
42. Carl Axel Gemzell, "The Effect of Corticotrophic Hormone and Oestrogen on Liver Glycogen Content and Phosphate Metabolism in the Adrenal Cortex," *Acta Endo.* 1, suppl. 1 (Ph.D diss., 1948).
43. Kerstin Hagenfeldt, "Mirjam Furuhjelm," *SFOGs medlemsblad* 2 (2005).
44. Egon Diczfalusy, pers. com., 9 November 2007.
45. Pfeffer, "Pioneers of Infertility Treatment," p. 252; *Meddelanden om Konung Gustaf V:s 80-årsfond* (Stockholm: Royal Caroline Institute, 1954–58). Thanks to Olof Ljungström for this information.
46. Egon Diczfalusy, "Chorionic Gonadotrophin and Oestrogens in the Human Placenta," *Acta Endo.* 11, suppl. 12 (Ph.D diss., 1953). The cost for printing the thesis was covered by a grant from Leo, and Christian Hamburger was appointed Diczfalusy's opponent. See "D-rapport nr 61 den 11 December 1952"; Westman to

the Docent Committee of the Caroline Institute 27 August 1953; "Havandeskap och hormoner," *Stockholms-Tidningen* 9 February (1953).

47. "D-rapport nr 69 över sammanträde på Leo den 18 maj 1954," vol. 5610, LHA.
48. "D-rapport nr 71 den 12 oktober 1954." Diczfalusy continued to work for Leo until the 1970s, when he became a consultant on human reproduction for the World Health Organization. Considering the politically sensitive information of which he partook on a daily basis, he was urged by the WHO to sever or gradually phase out his involvement with the pharmaceutical industry, which he also did. Egon Diczfalusy, pers. com., 9 January 2008.
49. Egon Diczfalusy, pers. com., 9 November 2007.
50. Carl A. Gemzell, Egon Diczfalusy and Gunnar Tillinger, "Clinical Effect of Human Pituitary Follicle-stimulating Hormone (FSH)," *Journal of Clinical Endocrinology and Metabolism* 18 (1958).
51. Ibid., p. 1344.
52. See Erling Østergaard, *Antigonadotrophic Substances: Experimental and Clinical Studies on the Formation of Antigonadotrophic Substances under Treatment with Gonadotrophic Hormones* (Köpenhamn: Ejnar Munksgaard, 1942), pp. 157 f; Erling Østergaard and Christian Hamburger, "The Formation of Antihormones in Women treated with Pregnant Mares' Serum Hormone (Antex)," *Acta Endo.* 2 (1949).
53. Gemzell, Diczfalusy and Tillinger, "Clinical Effect of Human Pituitary Follicle-stimulating Hormone (FSH)," p. 1346.
54. Carl A. Gemzell, Egon Diczfalusy and Karl-Gunnar Tillinger, "Further Studies of the Clinical Effects of Human Pituitary Follicle-stimulating Hormone (FSH): Lack of Response in Ovarian Insufficiency," *Acta Obst.* 38 (1959).
55. Carl. A. Gemzell, Egon Diczfalusy and Karl-Gunnar Tillinger, "Human Pituitary Follicle-stimulating Hormone: I. Clinical Effect of a Partially Purified Preparation," *Ciba Foundation Colloquia on Endocrinology* 13 (1960).
56. See Carl Gemzell, "Human Pituitary Gonadotopins in the Treatment of Sterility," *Fertility and Sterility* 17 (1966); Carl Gemzell and Paul Roos, "Pregnancies following treatment with Human Gonadotropins: With special reference to the Problem of Multiple Births," *American Journal of Obstetrics and Gynecology* 94 (1966); Carl Gemzell, Paul Roos and F. E. Loeffler, "The Clinical Use of Pituitary Gonadotrophins in Women," *Journal of Reproduction and Fertility* 12 (1966); Paul Roos, "Human Follicle-stimulating Hormone: Its Isolation from the Pituitary Gland and from Postmenopausal Urine and a Study of some Chemical, Physical, Immunological, and Biological Properties of the Hormone from these Two Sources," *Acta Endo.* 59, suppl. 131 (1968).
57. "Graviditetsforskning—sterila kvinnor kan få barn: Lennart Winblad intervjuar professor Carl Axel Gemzell vid Akademiska sjukhuset i Uppsala om tillförsel av hypofyshormoner och tillväxthormoner," *Aktuellt* 24 February (1962), Swedish Media Archive; "Hormones for Fertility," *Time Magazine* 9 October (1964); "The Multiple-Birth Hormone," *Time Magazine* 6 August (1965).
58. Pfeffer, "Pioneers of Infertility Treatment," p. 253; Karl-Gösta Nygren, "Infertilitet," in Lindberg, ed., *Svensk kvinnosjukvård under ett sekel 1904–2004*, p. 191.
59. Carl A. Gemzell, "Genombrott i reproduktionsforskningen mellan 1960 och 1975," in Lindberg, ed., *Kvinnosjukvård under 100 år*, p. 155.

60. Pfeffer, "Pioneers of Infertility Treatment," pp. 254–259.
61. Ibid.
62. Pituitary glands were also utilized in these countries, but the use was heavily regulated by domestic authorities: Medical Research Council in Great Britain, Australian Human Pituitary Agency Committee in Australia, and National Pituitary Agency in the United States. C. Lee Buxton and his group at Yale was the first in the United States to report the use of Gemzell's method (together with hCG). In 1963, they had treated eleven patients of which two became pregnant. See Marsh and Ronner, *The Empty Cradle*, p. 208.
63. Ludwig et al., "Ovarian Stimulation," p. 76. See further L. J. Dumble and R. D. Klein, "Creutzfeldt-Jakob Legacy for Australian Women Treated with Human Pituitary Gonadotropins," *The Lancet* 3 October (1992).
64. Westman, *Övergångsår*, p. 65. However, Westman indicated that there was no way of knowing if the pituitary hormone produced during menopause was identical with the one produced prior to menopause.
65. Ludwig et al., "Ovarian Stimulation," p. 77.
66. "Sterilitet kan botas! Massproduktion av nytt hormon," *Tabletten* (December, 1965), p. 5.
67. Pfeffer, "Pioneers of Infertility Treatment," p. 253.
68. Axel Westman to Svante Wiström, 14 May 1955, vol. 911, LHA.
69. Axel Westman to Svante Wiström, 27 June 1955, vol. 911, LHA.
70. Westman to Wiström, 14 May 1955.
71. Svante Wiström to Axel Westman, 17 June 1955, vol. 911, LHA.
72. Egon Diczfalusy, "Ansökan om anslag," 23 December 1960, vol. HE 82, LHA.
73. Brown, "Anterior Pituitary Hormones," p. 380.
74. Rosemberg, "Use of Standards," pp. 384 f; Ludwig et al., "Ovarian Stimulation," p. 77.
75. Diczfalusy, "Ansökan om anslag."
76. According to Diczfalusy, this cooperation ended due to "logistic reasons." See idem, *The Contraceptive Revolution*, p. 5.
77. Idem, "Ansökan om anslag."
78. "Rapport från forskningssammanträde fredagen den 15 juni 1962," 21 June 1962, vol. 2615, LHA.
79. Leo's research foundation invested considerable sums in hormone research in the years to follow, see Per Bergström, "Leo i dag—i går—i framtiden," *SFT* 77 (1973), p. 727. The foundation also published a substantial handbook on hormones and hormone therapy, Björn Sjögren, ed., *Om hormoner och hormonterapi* (Helsingborg: AB Leo, 1962), which although intended for general consumption contained an appendix in which Leo's own products were presented. A revised, expanded edition was published in 1973.

CHAPTER NINE

1. Bruno Lunenfeld, Annette Menzi and Blaise Volet, "Clinical Effects of Human Postmenopausal Gonadotrophin," *Acta Endo.* 34, suppl. 51 (1960).
2. Bruno Lunenfeld, "Treatment of Anovulation by Human Gonadotrophins," *International Journal of Obstetrics and Gynecology* 12 (1963), p. 158.

3. "Rapport från forskningssammanträde onsdagen den 29 augusti 1962," 4 September 1962, vol. 2615, LHA.
4. "Rapport från forskningssammanträde fredagen den 15 juni 1962."
5. Luft was not interested in pituitary gonadotropins but growth hormones. The application was not accepted. Rolf Luft to KAWF, 24 October 1958, Rolf Luft Papers, KAWF Archives; KAWF to Caroline Inst., 22 December 1958, Rolf Luft Papers, KAWF Archives.
6. "Projektsammanträde inom forskningsavdelningen den 19 december 1962," 7 January 1963, vol. 2615, LHA.
7. Ibid.
8. For the debate on the population explosion in the 1960s, see Björn-Ola Linnér, *The World Household: Georg Borgström and the Postwar Population-Resource Crisis* (Linköping: Linköping University, 1998), pp. 191–209.
9. The idea that endocrinologists should be able to contribute to help solve overpopulation was already broached in the 1950s, see Warren O. Nelson, "Endocrinology: Achievement and Challenge," *Endocrinology* 59 (1956).
10. Egon Diczfalusy was the director of this center from 1970 to 1984. Egon Diczfalusy, "WHO-center: Internationell familjeplaneringsforskning vid Karolinska sjukhuset," in Pernow, ed., *Karolinska sjukhuset 1940–1990*.
11. See Lena Lennerhed, *Frihet att njuta: Sexualdebatten i Sverige på 1960-talet* (Stockholm: Norstedt, 1994).
12. Marsh and Ronner, *The Empty Cradle*, pp. 214–215.
13. See Nelly Oudshoorn, "From Population Control Politics to Chemicals: The WHO as an Intermediary Organization in Contraceptive Development," *SSS* 27 (1997).
14. "Leo inviger nya forskningslaboratorier," p. 410; "Några svenska industriers läkemedelsforskning," *SFT* 73 (1969), p. 720.
15. A single treatment with Serono's Pergonal or Organon's Humegon cost roughly SEK 950 in 1964.
16. "Projektsammanträde inom forskningsavdelningen den 19 december 1962."
17. "Rapport över besök i Stockholm den 23 och 24 april 1963," 30 April 1963, vol. 2615, LHA.
18. Torsten Perklev, "HMG-framställningen," 10 December 1965, vol. 2615, LHA. On the development of the purification technique up to 1964, see P. Donini, D. Puzzuoli and R. Montezemolo, "Purification of Gonadotrophin from Human Menopausal Urine," *Acta Endo.* 45 (1964).
19. Rosemberg, "Use of Standards," p. 385.
20. "Rapport över Stockholms-besök den 8 april 1964: Besök hos lab. E. Diczfalusy för diskussion av olika forskningsproblem inom gonadotropinområdet," 10 april 1964, vol. 2615, LHA.
21. Leo was aware that urine contained numerous different substances, including growth hormones, and one notion was to make use of them as a bi-product in the production of hMG. A research group at the Biochemical Department of Uppsala University was charged with the task of investigating the possibility. See Torsten Perklev, "Rapport från besök i Uppsala och Stockholm den 7–8 oktober 1965," 7 October 1965, vol. 2615, LHA.

22. "Projektsammanträde inom forskningsavdelningen den 9 maj 1963," 17 May 1963, vol. 2615, LHA; Torsten Perklev, "P.M. angående HMG," 18 October 1963, vol. 2615, LHA. The first to be granted access to Leo's hMG was Karl-Gunnar Tillinger of the Caroline Hospital and gynecologist Per Lundström of Umeå General Hospital.
23. B. Carlström, "Telefonsamtal den 9 oktober 1964 med Dr. Sigvard Persson, Sahlgrenska Sjukhuset, Göteborg, rörande erfarenheter med HMG-LEO vid manlig sterilitet," 12 October 1964, vol. 2621, LHA; Lennart Andersson and Torsten Perklev, "Gonadotropinbehandling vid oligo-teratospermi" (Paper presented at the Nordic Fertility Society in Lund 29 January 1966), vol. 2621, LHA.
24. "Projektsammanträde inom forskningsavdelningen den 9 maj 1963."
25. See "Telefonrapport rörande HMG-LEO," 9 May 1964 (Report from Mirjam Furuhjelm of Sabbatsberg Hospital in Stockholm, where the therapy was tested on seven women), vol. 4710, LHA; "Telefonsamtal den 9 oktober 1964 med Dr. Sigvard Persson." See also Egon Diczfalusy et al., "Comparison of the Clinical and Steroid Metabolic Effect of Human Pituitary and Urinary Gonadotrophins in Amenorrhoeic Women," *Acta Endo.* 45, suppl. 90 (1964).
26. "Rapport från HMG-sammanträde den 14 oktober 1964," 15 October 1964, vol. 4710, LHA.
27. Ibid. All these "cases" were women diagnosed as sterile.
28. "Projektsammanträde inom forskningsavdelningen den 9 maj 1963"; Torsten Perklev, "Rapport över Stockholms-besök den 4–5 mars 1964," 10 March 1964, vol. 2615, LHA.
29. "Projektsammanträde inom forskningsavdelningen den 9 maj 1963."
30. Åke Pihl to Hans Ekström and Torsten Perklev, 8 December 1963, vol. HE 82, LHA; Hans Ekström, "Förslag till organisation av urininsamlingen för HMG-tillverkningen," 2 January 1964, vol. HE 82, LHA.
31. According to Christina Lärkner, an orderly at Bergaliden Home for the Aged from 1964 to 1969, patients were not informed that their urine was being used by Leo. Lärkner herself was told that the urine was intended for "hormone research," not that it was the raw material for a commercial product. Christina Lärkner, pers. com., 21 May 2007.
32. Ekström, "Förslag till organisation av urininsamlingen för HMG-tillverkningen."
33. Ibid; "Preliminärt apparatförslag för framställning av H.M.G. (ca 1000 lit. råvara per dag) i byggnad IV på Syntesen," 18 November 1963, vol. 2615, LHA; Torsten Perklev, "Sammanträde om HMG den 28 januari 1964," 28 January 1964, vol. 2615, LHA.
34. See Bertil Högberg to Erik Asker, 30 June 1964, vol. 4710, LHA. According to plans from 25 August 1964, urine was collected in Helsingborg, Lund, Höganäs, Väsby, Brunnby, Ängelholm, Farhult and Landskrona. See "Nuvarande HMG-runda med lastbilen," vol. HE 82, LHA.
35. Ekström, "Förslag till organisation av urininsamlingen för HMG-tillverkningen."
36. Ibid.
37. Ibid.
38. Arne G. Olsson, "Kassan," 21 April 1966, vol. 2615, LHA.

39. Ekström, "Förslag till organisation av urininsamlingen för HMG-tillverkningen." See also "Rapport över sammanträden om HMG-projektet," 22 November 1963, vol. 2615, LHA.
40. Ekström, "Förslag till organisation av urininsamlingen för HMG-tillverkningen." Ekström also investigated the possibility of constructing a specially-fit toilet bowl, which would insure that not a drop of urine would go to waste. On the significance of inviting health care staff to information meetings at Leo's plant, see "Beträffande urininsamlingen för HMG-tillverkningen," 16 February 1965, vol. 2615, LHA.
41. "Föredrag om Leos HMG-projekt." From the text of the lecture it is apparent that it was held at Leo for an audience of health care staff involved in the urine collection campaign. After an introduction to Leo's work in reproductive endocrinology, the text continues, "You have been kind enough to help us collect this urine and together with many Swedish other health care facilities, you have helped gather approximately 10,000 liters of urine each week."
42. "Angående insamling av urin för AB Leo, Hälsingborg," undated, vol. 4710, LHA.
43. Torsten Perklev, "Rapport om HMG-projektet," 20 October 1965, vol. 2610, LHA.
44. Åke Phil and Arne G. Olsson, "Meddelande," 14 September 1965, vol. 4710, LHA; Arne G. Olsson, "Rapport angående insamling av HMG-urin," 1 September 1966, vol. 4710, LHA; idem, "HMG-kostnadsredovisning Stockholm," 7 July 1966, vol. HE 82, LHA.
45. Aktiebolaget Svenska Godscentraler [Swedish transport company] to AB Leo, 10 September 1965, vol. 2621, LHA; "Urininsamling," 1 December 1966, vol. 2615, LHA.
46. "Sterilitet kan botas!," p. 5.
47. *Aftonbladet* 13 August (1964); *Arbetet* 14 August (1964); *Helsingborgs Dagblad* 13 August (1964); *Dagens Nyheter* 14 August (1964).
48. "Nytt hormonmedel hjälpte," *Helsingborgs Dagblad* 13 August (1964).
49. "Svenskt preparat ger barnlösa chans," *Arbetet* 14 August (1964).
50. Cf. Lewenstein, "Science and the Media," p. 345.
51. "HMG—ett hormonpreparat för behandling av vissa former av sterilitet," 3 August 1964, vol. 4710, LHA.
52. The choice to publicize its success with hMG at this particular point in time may also be due to the fact that in August 1964, Leo celebrated its fiftieth anniversary with pomp and circumstance. King Gustav Adolf came to visit the plant and director Ove Färnö used the opportunity to account for the work done on hMG in a lecture delivered in his presence. See Ahlin and Lundgren, *Från leopiller till nicorette*, p. 172. Thanks to Jerker Ahlin for this information.
53. "Sterilitet kan botas!," p. 6.
54. "Samlingsrapport rörande klinisk prövning av HMG-LEO," 10 November 1964, vol. 2615, LHA.
55. "Ang. klinisk utprövning av HMG-LEO," 17 November 1964, vol. 2615, LHA; "Sterilitet kan botas!," p. 6.
56. "Homogonal," D1b vol. 3, NPL Archive, NAA. The first formal description of "Homogonal, amp. à 70 I.E. (FSH)," is from 1 June 1965. It was later changed to

"Homogonal, amp. à 75 I.E. (FSH)," see declaration of 22 April 1966, vol. 2615, LHA.

57. Gordon E. Appelbe, "From Arsenic to Thalidomide: A Brief History of Medicine Safety," in Anderson, ed., *Making Medicines*, pp. 253–255.
58. "Neurosedynkatastrofen," *SFT* 68 (1964); "Tillverkarens ansvar," *SFT* 69 (1965).
59. See Arthur Engel, "Läkemedlen i det moderna samhället," *SFT* 63 (1959). On the burgeoning criticism of science and technology during the 1960s, see Andrew Jamison, *The Making of Green Knowledge: Environmental Politics and Cultural Transformation* (Cambridge: Cambridge University Press, 2001), pp. 71–87.
60. Rune Westerling, "Sökarljus på läkemedelsindustrin," *SFT* 67 (1963); "Kan vi lita på läkemedelsindustrin?" part 1, *SFT* 67 (1963); "Kan vi lita på läkemedelsindustrin?" part 2, *SFT* 67 (1963); Folke Lundin, "Läkemedelsindustri och läkemedelsreklam," *SFT* 67 (1963); J. M. Barnes, "Förgiftningsrisker i samband med läkemedel," *SFT* 67 (1963).
61. Lönngren et al., eds., *Svensk farmaci under 1900-talet*, vol. 1, pp. 325–337. Furthermore, a special committee on side effects was appointed by the Swedish Medical Board in 1965.
62. Pfeffer, *The Stork and the Syringe*, p. 147.
63. See Arne Wegerfelt, "Svensk läkemedelsindustri på världsmarknaden," *SFT* 68 (1964).
64. "Sterilitet kan botas!," p. 6. On a galley proof with the working title "Vad är hMG?" [What is hMG], vol. 2621, LHA, the initials "TP/GS" appear, indicating that Torsten Perklev was the author of the article in *Tabletten*.
65. The first trials with Pergonal in the United States were under the direction of Eugenia Rosemburg, in Worcester, Massachusetts. See Marsh and Ronner, *The Empty Cradle*, p. 208.
66. Torsten Perklev, "Sammanträde med G.A. Cronk, M.D., Director of Pharmaceutical Research, Ortho Research Foundation, U.S.A., den 24 september 1965," 24 September 1965, vol. 2615, LHA.
67. M. Mozes et al., "Thromboembolic Phenomena after Ovarian Stimulation with Human Gonadotrophins," *The Lancet* 11 December (1965), pp. 1213–1215. The term "OHSS," which stands for "Ovarian Hyperstimulation Syndrome," was coined to designate problems encountered in hMG therapy. At the behest of the WHO, a list of typical indications of OHSS and directives for how they were to be treated was compiled in 1973. The opportunity to cause "super-ovulation" with the help of gonadotropins was welcomed in the field of animal husbandry, where the technique of having "high quality pedigree" cattle mass produce eggs which after insemination could be implanted in cows of "lower quality" came into common use. Harry A. Herman, *Improving Cattle by the Millions: NAAB and the Development and Worldwide Application of Artificial Insemination* (Columbia, Missouri and London: University of Missouri Press, 1981), pp. 98 f.
68. Heron O. Singher to Torsten Perklev, 23 September 1963, vol. 4710, LHA. See also Perklev "P.M. angående HMG."
69. Toresten Perklev, "Sammanträde med Mr. E. R. Spalt, Ortho Pharmaceutical Corp., U.S.A., onsdagen den 12 februari 1964," 25 February 1964, vol. 4710, LHA.
70. "Betr. försäljning av HMG och HCG," 9 December 1966, vol. 2621, LHA. A small amount of hMG was also exported to Norway during this period.

71. Perklev, "Sammanträde med G.A. Cronk"; idem, "Rapport om HMG-projektet"; Bertil Högberg, "Rapport från besök på Ortho Pharmaceutical Co. den 22 oktober 1965," 22 October 1965, vol. 2615, LHA; "Rapport från besök i USA den 28 januari–4 februari 1966," 14 February 1966, vol. 2615, LHA; Torsten Perklev, "Rapport från diskussioner med Mr. Spalt, Ortho Pharmaceutical Corp., den 5 september 1966," 7 September 1966, vol. 2615, LHA; idem, "Sammanträde med Mr. Spalt, Ortho Research Foundation, Raritan," 5 May 1966, vol. 4710, LHA.
72. Idem, "Rapport från möte med representanter för Ortho Pharmaceutical Corp. i Raritan, N. J., den 1 februari 1966," 1 February 1966, vol. 4710, LHA.
73. Idem, "Rapport från dr. Cronks besök torsdagen den 8 september 1966 angående HMG," 13 September 1966, vol. HE 82, LHA.
74. Idem, "Delrapport från möte med representanter för Ortho Pharmaceutical Corp. den 8 september 1966," 13 September 1966, vol. 4710, LHA.
75. Idem, "Sammanträde med G.A. Cronk"; idem, "Rapport om HMG-projektet." According to Marsh and Ronner, *The Empty Cradle*, p. 1, about 600,000 Americans a year visited a physician to discuss infertility problems at this point of time. By the early 1990s, that number had increased to 1.5 million.
76. Torsten Linderot, "Rapport från projektmöte HMG den 14 september 1966," 15 September 1966, vol. HE 82, LHA.
77. "Svinnmöjligheter urin HMG," 13 September 1966, vol. HE 82, LHA.
78. "Beräknat behov av menopausurin för framställning av HMG under produktionsperioden 1 januari 1967–30 juni 1968," 3 October 1966, vol. 4710, LHA.
79. "Leo inviger nya forskningslaboratorier." AB Leo's turnover more than quintupled 1961–1973, with some twenty percent of its in-house production (mostly hormone preparations) going to export, mainly to other Scandinavian countries. Construction was simultaneously underway to more than double the total floorage of the facility from 25,000 to 56,000 square meters. In total, foreign sales of Swedish pharmaceuticals increased from 32 to 41 percent over the course of the 1960s.
80. Linderot, "Rapport från projektmöte HMG den 14 september 1966."
81. Perklev, "Rapport om HMG-projektet"; idem, "Sammanträde med Mr. Spalt."
82. "Kostnader för insamling av urin, samt utfällning i kaolin, i Hamburg," undated, vol. 2621, LHA; Perklev, "Rapport om HMG-projektet"; Högberg, "Rapport från besök på Ortho Pharmaceutical."
83. "HMG-kostnader vid insamling av urin utanför Sverige," 13 September 1966, vol. 2621, LHA.
84. Linderot, "Rapport från projektmöte HMG den 14 september 1966." The financial angle of this proposal is apparent in a letter written by Torsten Perklev to Gerda Kärnström, 14 October 1966, vol. HE 82, LHA. Perklev writes, "When we considered collecting urine in a developing nation, we based our calculations on existing economic discrepancies. We estimated paying 20 öre/liter of post-menopausal urine and envisioned that this sum would attract women of the desirable age group to save their urine in the containers we would provide, and deliver them regularly to our local representatives."
85. Torsten Perklev, "Rapport från Stockholmsbesök onsdagen den 5 oktober 1966," 10 October 1966, vol. HE 82, LHA.

86. Document written for Torsten Perklev, "Betr. din idé om urininsamling i U-land," 26 September 1966, vol. HE 82, LHA. Hans Ekström was probably the author of this document.
87. "Svinnmöjligheter urin HMG."
88. Perklev, "Rapport från Stockholmsbesök"; Perklev to Kärnström, 14 October 1966.
89. Gerda Kärnström to Torsten Perklev, 2 November 1966, vol. 4710, LHA.
90. "Förslag till avräkning med Ortho beträffande HMG," 13 September 1966, vol. 2621, LHA.
91. "Protokoll från sammanträde beträffande HMG-orderrutin m.m. den 25 augusti 1965," 26 August 1965, vol. 2615, LHA. Subsequent testing proved that its shelf life could be stretched to three years. See "Betr. Homogonal, hållbarheten," 8 May 1969, vol. 2621, LHA.
92. Torsten Perklev, "Rapport om HMG-projektet," 28 November 1966, vol. HE 82, LHA.
93. Idem, "Besök på Ortho onsdagen den 8 februari 1967," 8 February 1967, vol. 4710, LHA.
94. "Rapport angående salmonella-innehåll i urin för HMG-produktion insamlad i Södertälje," 14 April 1967, vol. 4710, LHA; "H.M.G.," 15 April 1967, vol. 2615, LHA.
95. Stig Waldton to AB Leo 2 October, 1967, vol. 4710, LHA. Leo replied that there were no plans to increase the fee "since cost estimates are already pressed." Börje Nordh to Stig Waldton, 16 October 1967, vol. 2615, LHA.
96. Torsten Perklev, "Angående planeringen av ampullering av nya HMG-ampuller," 9 June 1967, vol. 2615, LHA; Börje Nordh, "Rapport från sammanträde rörande Homogonal den 4 september 1967," vol. 2615, LHA; idem, "Planering av försök rörande olika konserveringsmedel vid urininsamling," 6 September 1967, vol. 2615, LHA.
97. Torsten Perklev, "Synpunkter på kalkylen för Homogonal," 24 July 1967, vol. 2621, LHA. In this confidential report, which was probably intended for corporate management eyes only, Perklev writes, "It is our hope that expenses incurred in production and distribution can be kept within a framework which will enable the company to reap some profit through sales of this drug."
98. Idem, "Rapport från besök på Ortho Research Foundation, Raritan, fredagen den 29 september 1967," vol. 2615, LHA.
99. Walter Sneader, *Drug Discovery: The Evolution of Modern Medicines* (Chichester et al.: Wiley, 1985), p. 199.
100. Marsh and Ronner, *The Empty Cradle*, p. 208.
101. Medvei, *The History of Clinical Endocrinology*, p. 5; Pfeffer, *The Stork and the Syringe*, p. 150. In pharmaceutical literature, clomiphene citrate has served as an example of how tricky it is to come to clinical conclusions from laboratory experiments. See Brown, "Anterior Pituitary Hormones," p. 384. On this problem, see further the issue "The Right Organism for the Job," *JHB* 26 (1993).
102. Pfeffer, *The Stork and the Syringe*, p. 151.
103. Finkelstein, "Professor Bernhard Zondek," p. 10.
104. Long before, Ortho had suspected that clomiphene citrate might constitute a "threat." During a meeting held at Leo in 1965, Cronk reported that they were

"aware that there is a certain risk in the form of competition from substances with an anti-estrogen effect." Ortho was however unconvinced by the clinical effect of clomiphene citrate and considered the chance of FDA approval minimal. See Perklev, "Sammanträde med G.A. Cronk." The threat ostensibly posed by clomiphene citrate was also discussed at Leo, but Cronk's words apparently had a reassuring effect and management was "certain" that Leo's hMG had a superior effect. See idem, "Rapport om HMG-projektet." Clomiphene citrate was the object of a great deal of attention at the Fifth World Conference on Fertility and Sterility held in Stockholm in the summer of 1966. Afterward, Perklev reported that clomiphene citrate appeared to be effective in treating sterility, and that the drug could be expected to be relatively inexpensive since it was synthetic. However, due to its side effects, there was doubt it would receive FDA approval. Aside from the usual problems, several cases of fetal damage were reported. Perklev recommended that Leo closely monitor developments in the field in case clomiphene citrate proved successful. See idem, "Rapport från Fifth World Congress on Fertility and Sterility i Stockholm den 16–22 juni 1966," vol. 2615, LHA.

105. Idem, "Rapport från besök på Ortho Research Foundation."
106. "Besök av Mr. Spalt, Ortho Pharm. Corp., den 21 mars 1968," 22 March 1968, vol. 2615, LHA; Torsten Perklev, "Rapport från möte med FDA i Washington den 28 januari 1966 ang. HMG," 28 January 1966, vol. 2615, LHA; idem, "Rapport från sammanträde om HMG den 15 februari 1966," vol. 2615, LHA; idem to Thomas C. Smith, 11 September 1967, vol. 4710, LHA.
107. "Besök av Mr. Spalt, Ortho Pharm. Corp."
108. Evan R. Spalt to Sune Ebberstéen, 5 June 1968, vol. 4710, LHA.
109. Sune Ebberstéen to Evan R. Spalt, 28 August 1968, vol. 4710, LHA.
110. For the sake of clarity, it should be added that the fate of hMG was in no way unique to the latter-day history of hormone drugs. For example, Leo abandoned its attempt to market poly-stilbetrol phosphate (PSP) to veterinarians in 1970 after fourteen years (!) of hard work. See Ahlin and Lundgren, *Från Leopiller till nicorette*, p. 124. Nowadays, the risk of encountering "setbacks" is inscribed in the pharmaceutical industry's rulebook.
111. Marsh and Ronner, *The Empty Cradle*, pp. 221–222.
112. "Homogonal."
113. Bertil Högberg to NPL, 20 September 1965, vol. 2615, LHA, Ada Elmqvist to AB Leo, 17 November 1965, vol. 2615, LHA; "Rapport från besök vid SFL den 1 december 1965 ang. Homogonal," 1 December 1965, vol. 2615, LHA; Torsten Perklev to Ada Elmqvist, 13 December 1965, vol. 2615, LHA; Gunilla Nyberg to AB Leo 1 January 1966, vol. 2615, LHA; Torsten Perklev, "Telefonrapport från samtal med laborator Ada Elmqvist, SFL," 24 August 1966, vol. 2615, LHA.
114. One of the recruits to the improved purification process was Paul Roos of the Biochemical Department of Uppsala University. Torsten Perklev, "Rapport över besök i Uppsala och Stockholm den 21–22 mars 1967," 21 March 1967, vol. 2615, LHA. Roos, who collaborated with Gemzell, defended his thesis "Human Follicle-stimulating Hormone" in 1968.
115. See Mirjam Furuhjelm, Nils-Olov Lunell and Erik Odeblad, "Ovarian Stimulation by Human Menopausal Gonadotrophin in Patients with Amenorrhæa and Anovu-

lation," *Acta Obst.* 45 (1966). For this study, conducted at Sabbatsberg Hospital's women's clinic, Leo's hMG was used.

116. Perklev, "Rapport över besök i Uppsala och Stockholm den 21–22 mars 1967."
117. Letter from AB Leo, with an information booklet on Homogonal enclosed, 7 September 1967, vol. 2621, LHA.
118. See AB Leo to NPL, 24 November 1966, vol. 2615, LHA.
119. *Homogonal*, information booklet published by AB Leo (1967), p. 1.
120. The reason for this synthesis was that clinical studies preceding the launch (of some three hundred patients), many of which were conducted in the United States, had indicated that hMG was mostly effective if the relationship between FSH and LH was precisely 3-to-1. Ortho first tested a preparation with a relationship of 10:1 or more, before realizing that 3:1 was optimal. After comparing various strengths, Tillinger also concluded that 3:1 was "clinically superior." See Torsten Perklev, "Meddelande angående HMG," 9 January 1967, vol. 2615, LHA.
121. Differences in the relationship between FSH and LH was discovered simultaneously by the pharmaceutical division of Socialstyrelsen [National Board of Health and Welfare] and Leo while conducting follow-up studies. Gunilla Eneroth to AB Leo, 14 June 1973, vol. 2615, LHA; "Betr. Homogonal, intressanta satser i samband med SLA's protokoll," 23 July 1973, vol. 2615, LHA; Torsten Perklev to Gunilla Eneroth, 1 August 1973, vol. 2615, LHA; Torsten Perklev to Gunilla Eneroth, 28 September 1973, vol. 2615, LHA; Gunilla Eneroth to Torsten Perklev, 3 April 1974, vol. 2615, LHA; Torsten Perklev to Gunilla Eneroth, 23 April 1974, vol. 2615, LHA.
122. The registration of Antex expired on 1 June 1969. "Antex," D1a vol. 1, NPL Archive, NAA.
123. "Försäljningsstatistik 1976–77," LHA.
124. Homogonal and Humegon were officially presented at the same time in *SFT* 71 (1967).
125. *Humegon*, information booklet published by Pharmacia (1967). After meeting with Nils Erik Påhlsson, Westman's former student at the Caroline Institute, a representative of Leo reported that a patient treated with Humegon had developed a cyst so large that she resembled a woman well into her second trimester. Påhlsson had also used Humegon successfully ("3–4 pregnancies"). See "Rapport från besök hos överläkaren, docent Erik Påhlsson, KK, Lasarettet, Kristianstad, den 23 januari 1969," vol. 2615, LHA. Similar reports about Homogonal also appeared. Karl-Gunnar Tillinger reported that ovaries could grow "as big as oranges" and that hypertrophy (enlargement) "could be so extreme that many times it could present falsely as pregnancy." Bertil Högberg, "Rapport från diskussion med doc. K.-G. Tillinger, Karolinska Sjukhuset, Stockholm, fredagen den 28 januari 1966," 28 January 1966, vol. 2615, LHA.
126. Norgren, *Kunskapsöverföring från universitet till företag*, pp. 80–81.
127. This was cited as "one of several reasons" in ibid., p. 70. The other reasons are not mentioned.
128. "Ang. eventuell avregistrering av Leo-produkter," 7 January 1980, vol. 6029, LHA.
129. "Leos ställning inom hormonområdet." The document does not mention the names of the members of this consultant group. It may possibly have been the

same experts belonging to Leo's scientific advisory board. However, the page header bears the seal of the Caroline Institute.

130. Ibid.

131. Gonadex in strengths of 3000 IU and 6000 IU was deregistered on 1 January 1986. The 600 IU and 1500 IU variants were deregistered on 1 April 1967 and 1 July 1978, respectively. Humegon, on the other hand, was not deregistered until 1998. See www.lakemedelsverket.se 11 June 2007.

CONCLUSION

1. Norgren, *Kunskapsöverföring från universitet till företag*, pp. 65, 93. The sole sources cited by Norgren are two former Leo employees, Torsten Linderot and Imre Könyves.
2. Gaudillière and Löwy, "General Introduction," p. 4.
3. Lately thalidomide has begun to be used again, for example in the treatment of bone-marrow cancer.
4. Pieters, *Interferon*, pp. 4–5.
5. James Mahoney, "Path Dependence in Historical Sociology," *Theory and Society* 29 (2000). See also Nik Brown, Brian Rappert and Andrew Webster, eds., *Contested Futures: A Sociology of Prospective Techno-Science* (Aldershot: Ashgate, 2000).
6. See Martin V. Melosi, *The Sanitary City: Urban Infrastructure in America from the Colonial Times to the Present* (Baltimore, MD: Johns Hopkins University Press, 2000); Petri S. Juuti and Tapio S. Katko, eds., *From a Few to All: Long-term Development of Water and Environmental Services in Finland* (Pieksämäki: KehräMedia Inc., 2004). A similar argument about the inherent "inertia" of socio-technical systems is made by Thomas P. Hughes. For an introduction, see Thomas P. Hughes, "The Evolution of Large Technological Systems," in Mario Biagioli, ed., *The Science Studies Reader* (New York and London: Routledge, 1999).
7. Clarke, "Research Materials and Reproductive Science in the United States, 1910–1940," p. 326.
8. According to Jerker Ahlin, Leo sold Gonadex mainly to two countries, Spain and East Germany, with most going to the latter in the form of bulk vials. What it was used for is unknown, but the staff of the export division joked that there might be a connection to rumours of hormone doping which had begun to circulate in athletic circles, particularly in reference to the GDR. Jerker Ahlin, pers. com., 7 May 2008. Today, it is known that human chorionic gonadotropin was in fact used to enhance performance; hCG was regarded as increasing the production of testosterone and was often taken together with growth hormones in an effort to increase strength and muscle mass.
9. Biologist Robert G. Edwards at Cambridge University reported his first successful IVF attempt (without implantation) as early as 1969. Together with Patrick Steptoe, a physician working at a hospital in Oldham, he began implanting embryos in female patients in 1972, and three years later, the first IVF pregnancy was achieved (which by the way came about with the aid of hMG treatment), though it was terminated due to complications. The first IVF baby in Sweden was born at Sahlgrenska University Hospital in 1982. In 2010, Edwards was awarded the Nobel Prize

in Physiology or Medicine for the development of IVF. On Rock and Menkin, see Marsh and Ronner, *The Fertility Doctor.*

10. Robin Marantz Henig, *Pandora's Baby: How the First Test Tube Babies Sparked the Reproductive Revolution* (Houghton Mifflin: Cold Spring Harbor Laboratory Press, 2006).
11. See Pfeffer, *The Stork and the Syringe.*
12. Previously, the routine was to inseminate and implant numerous eggs all at once, which could lead to multiple pregnancies. Today it is more common to inseminate several eggs, but implant only one embryo per procedure. The rest are frozen and stored in case the procedure needs to be repeated, or for the use on a later occasion. Another advantage of harvesting and inseminating numerous eggs is that one then has a selection from which to choose.
13. Lunenfeld, "Historical Perspectives in Gonadotrophin Therapy," p. 461.
14. www.fass.se/LIF/home/index.jsp 28 May 2008.
15. Ludwig et al., "Ovarian Stimulation," pp. 79–81; Lunenfeld, "Historical Perspectives in Gonadotrophin Therapy," pp. 461–462.
16. Ludwik Fleck, *Uppkomsten och utvecklingen av ett vetenskapligt faktum: Inledning till läran om tankestil och tankekollektiv* (1935), Swe. transl. (Stockholm and Stehag: Symposion), p. 48.
17. Julius Hreinsson, Lars Hamberger and Thorir Hardarson, eds., *Infertilitet: Utredning och behandling genom assisterad befruktning* (Lund: Studentlitteratur, 2005).
18. It is difficult to provide exact statistics on the results of IVF treatment, since they vary from country to country, even from clinic to clinic. Between 1991 and 2001, the number of successful treatments increased from approximately 13% to 22%. See Karen Throsby, *When IVF Fails: Feminism, Infertility and the Negotiation of Normality* (New York: Palgrave Macmillan, 2004), p. 1. In Sweden the frequency of pregnacy (regardless of result) per egg reimplantation was approximately 40% in 2004. Some twenty percent of the involuntarily childless couples examined today still receive the diagnosis "undetermined infertility." All infertile couples, even those diagnosed as mentioned, are offered the option of treatment. See Nygren, "Infertilitet," pp. 187, 199.

SOURCES AND LITERATURE

ABBREVIATIONS

Acta Endo.	*Acta Endocrinologica*
Acta Obst.	*Acta Obstetricia et Gynecologica Scandinavica*
ASL	*Allmänna Svenska Läkartidningen*
JHB	*Journal of the History of Biology*
Nord. Med.	*Nordisk Medicin* (before 1939 *Nordisk Medicinsk Tidskrift*)
SHPBBS	*Studies in History and Philosophy of Biologcial and Biomedical Sciences*
SFS	Svensk författningssamling [Swedish Statute Book]
SFT	*Svensk Farmaceutisk Tidskrift*
SL	*Svenska Läkartidningen*
SOU	Statens offentliga utredningar [Swedish Government Official Reports]
SSS	*Social Studies of Science*

UNPUBLISHED SOURCES

Archive Material

The Knut and Allice Wallenberg Foundation's (KAWF) Archives. Stored at the Foundation for Economic History Research within Banking and Enterprise in Stockholm.

Rolf Luft Papers. Letters, documents and press clippings 1946–1965.

Axel Westman Papers. Letters, documents and press clippings 1945–1958.

The Leo Historical Archives (LHA). Stored at the Scanian Industrial Archives in Helsingborg.

Vol. 94, 117, 300, 792, 871, 874, 911, 1134, 1169, 1368, 2190, 2224, 2456, 2615, 2651, 2792, 2927, 3003, 4710, 5097, 5610, 6029, AX4 and HE82. Documents without volume number: AB Leo's lists of drugs and catalogues (after 1930 named *Leopreparat*) 1924, 1926, January 1931, March 1932, 1934, May 1934, 1935, 1940 and 1952; "Försäljningsstatistik 1976–77"; *Gonadex*, information booklet published by AB Leo (1948); *Homogonal*, information booklet published by AB Leo (1967); *Humegon*, information booklet published by Pharmacia (1967); *Leopreparat för veterinärer* (1938); *Sexualhormonpreparat Leo*, 3 ed. (1944); "Årsberättelse för 1941."

Lund University Library, Lund.

Elis Essen-Möller Papers. Gideon Vilhelm Törnqvist to Elis Essen Möller, 4 May 1942.

National Archives in Arninge (NAA), Stockholm.

National Pharmaceutical Laboratory's (NPL) Archives. B2 vol. 17, B3 vol. 4, D1a vol. 1, D1a vol. 4, D1a vol. 7, D1b vol. 2, D1b vol. 3, E2 vol. 12 and E2 vol. 13.

National Archives in Marieberg (NAM), Stockholm.

Swedish Medical Society's (SMS) Archives. A1a vol. 114 and A2ca vol. 58.

Regional State Archive of Uppsala.

Academic Hospital's Archive. Directorate protocols 1932–1933.

Stockholm County Council Archives (SCCA).

Archives of the Women's Clinic (WCA) of the Royal Caroline Hospital. E1 vol. 2–18. Diary papers 1942–1960.

Royal Caroline Hospital's "collection of press clippings." Ö1 vol. 4–6 1939–1955.

Swedish Media Archive, Stockholm.

"Graviditetsforskning—sterila kvinnor kan få barn," *Aktuellt* 24 February 1962.

Unpublished Texts

Rechter, Julia E., "'The Glands of Destiny': A History of Popular, Medical and Scientific Views of the Sex Hormones in 1920s America" (Ph.D diss., University of California, Berkeley, 1997).

Saltzman, Katarina, "Barnlöshet och befolkningskris: En studie baserad på veckotidningsmaterial från åren 1935–43" (unpubl. paper, Lund University, Lund, 1993).

Informants

Ahlin, Jerker, e-mail, 7 May 2008.

Diczfalusy, Egon, interview, 9 November 2007, and e-mail, 9 January 2008.

Luft, Rolf, interview, 23 June 2003.

Lärkner, Christina, telephone interview, 21 May 2007.

Sundius, Ann-Margret, telephone interview, 8 February 2005.

Internet

www.fass.se/LIF/home/index.jsp 28 May 2008.

www.lakemedelsverket.se 11 June 2007.

www.wma.net/e/policy/c8.htm 11 June 2007.

PRINTED SOURCES AND LITERATURE

Official Documents

1945 Motion presented to the Upper House of Parliament nr 286. "Om utredning rörande åtgärder för att häva ofrivillig sterilitet."

1946 Kungl. Maj:ts proposition nr 273.

SFS 1913:308 Kungl. Maj:ts nådiga apoteksvarustadga.

SFS 1934:306 Kungl. Maj:ts kungörelse angående handel med farmaceutiska specialiteter.

SOU 1936:59 *Betänkande i sexualfrågan.*

SOU 1944:55 *Betänkande rörande organisatoriska åtgärder för den medicinska forskningens främjande.*

SOU 1946:76 *Organisatoriska åtgärder till främjande av medicinsk forskning I.*

SOU 1947:66 *Organisatoriska åtgärder till främjande av medicinsk forskning II.*

SOU 2000:20 *Steriliseringsfrågan i Sverige 1935–1975: Historisk belysning, kartläggning, intervjuer.*

Newspapers

Aftonbladet 17 January 1950, 13 August 1964.
Arbetet 14 August 1964.
Bergslagernas Tidning 25 September 1948.
Dagens Nyheter 14 December 1940, 19 May 1945, 11 June 1948, 2 August 1948, 19 May 1953, 21 January 1959, 14 August 1964, 9 March 2007.
Expressen 24 September 1948.
Göteborgsposten 4 July 1943.
Helsingborgs Dagblad 27 September 1947, 5 September 1948, 13 August 1964.
Morgontidningen 11 June 1948.
Politiken 8 October 1944.
Skånska Socialdemokraten 29 April 1941, 21 December 1944, 21 January 1952.
Stockholms-Tidningen 12 September 1943, 2 November 1946, 6 December 1947, 11 June 1948, 25 September 1948, 18 January 1950, 16 October 1951, 9 February 1953, 2 October 1954, 22 January 1959.
Svenska Dagbladet 17 May 1947, 8 November 1947, 27 January 1948, 11 June 1948, 16 August 1948, 18 January 1950, 26 May 1950, 22 June 1950, 17 June 1953.
Svenska Morgonbladet 11 June 1948.
Ystads Allehanda 9 March 1951.

LITERATURE

A och O för blivande mödrar (Stockholm: Allmänna livförsäkringsbolaget Oden, 1943).

Abraham, John, *Science, Politics and the Pharmaceutical Industry: Controversy and Bias in Drug Regulation* (London and New York: UCL Press, 1995).

Adolfsson, Märta and Sebastian von Wachenfeldt, "Terapeutiska försök med Prolan och Progynon," *SL* 30 (1933).

Ahlberger, Christer and Lars Kvarnström, *Det svenska samhället 1720–2000: Böndernas och arbetarnas tid* (Lund: Studentlitteratur, 2004).

Ahlin, Jerker and Rolf Lundgren, *Från Leopiller till nicorette: En industri i Helsingborg under det tjugonde seklet* (Helsingborg: Pharmacia, 2002).

Ajanki, Tord, *Historien om diabetes och insulinets upptäckt* (Sundbyberg: Swedish Diabetes Society, 1999).

Åkerman, Sune, Ronny Ambjörnsson and Per Ringby, eds., *Att skriva människan: Essäer om biografin som livshistoria och vetenskaplig genre* (Stockholm: Carlsson, 1997).

Albrecht, Gary L., Ray Fitzpatrick and Susan C. Scrimshaw, eds., *Handbook of Social Studies in Health and Medicine* (London: Sage, 2000).

Allen, Edgar, Charles H. Danforth and Edward A. Doisy, *Sex and Internal Secretions: A Survey of Recent Research* (1932), 2d ed., enl. (Baltimore, MD: The Williams and Wilkins Company, 1939).

Allen, Garland E., *Life Science in The Twentieth Century* (1975), 2d ed. (Cambridge: Cambridge University Press, 1979).

Anderson, Stuart, ed., *Making Medicines: A Brief History of Pharmacy and Pharmaceuticals* (London: Pharmaceutical Press, 2005).

"Antabus och Abstinyl," *SFT* 52 (1948).

Appadurai, Arjun, ed., *The Social Life of Things: Commodities in Cultural Perspective* (Cambridge: Cambridge University Press, 1986).

Appelbe, Gordon E., "From Arsenic to Thalidomide: A Brief History of Medicine Safety," in Stuart Anderson, ed., *Making Medicines: A Brief History of Pharmacy and Pharmaceuticals* (London: Pharmaceutical Press, 2005).

Apple, Rima D., *Vitamania: Vitamins in American Culture* (New Brunswick, NJ: Rutger's University Press, 1996).

Aspelin, Gunnar and Göte Turesson, eds., *Vetenskap av i dag: Framlagd av svenska forskare* (Uppsala: Gebers, 1940).

Barker, Lewellys F., "The Study of the Internal Secretions: An Introduction," *Endocrinology* 1 (1917).

Barnes, J. M., "Förgiftningsrisker i samband med läkemedel," *SFT* 67 (1963).

Becker, Gay and Robert D. Nachtigall, "Eager for Medicalisation: The Social Production of Infertility as a Disease," *Sociology of Health and Illness* 14 (1992).

Benckert, H., "Steriliteten hos kvinnan från medicinsk och statistisk synpunkt," *SL* 34 (1937).

Benison, Saul, A. Clifford Barger and Elin L. Wolfe, "Walter B. Cannon and the Mystery of Shock: A Study of Anglo-American Co-operation in World War I," *Medical History* 35 (1991).

Benner, Mats and Sverker Sörlin, eds., *Forska lagom och vara världsbäst: Sverige inför forskningens globala strukturomvandling* (Stockholm: SNS Förlag, 2008).

Bergman, Emanuel, "Svenska läkarexlibris med symboler," *SL* 51 (1945).

Bergman, P., "Om adrenalinets terapeutiska användning," *ASL* 3 (1906).

Bergström, Per, "En invecklad debut," *SFT* 77 (1973).

Bergström, Per, "Grundläggande hormonforskning," *SFT* 77 (1973).

Bergström, Per, "Leo i dag—i går—i framtiden," *SFT* 77 (1973).

Berman, Louis, *Människans förvandling: Hur människan kan omskapas genom hormonterapi* (1938), Swe. transl. (Stockholm: Natur och kultur, 1943).

Berman, Louis, *New Creations in Human Beings* (New York: Doubleday, Doran and Company, 1938).

Berman, Louis, "Psycho-endocrinology," *Science* 17 February (1928).

Berridge, Virginia and Kelly Loughlin, eds., *Medicine, the Market and the Mass Media: Producing Health in the Twentieth Century* (London and New York: Routledge, 2005).

Biagioli, Mario, ed., *The Science Studies Reader* (New York and London: Routledge, 1999).

Bishop, Peter M. F., "The Development of British Endocrinology," *British Medical Journal* 9 April (1955).

Björk, Ragnar, "Inside the Nobel Committee on Medicine: Prize Competition Procedures 1901–1950 and the Fate of Carl Neuberg," *Minerva* 39 (2001).

Bliss, Michael, *The Discovery of Insulin* (1982), 3d ed. (Toronto: University of Toronto Press, 2000).

Blumgarten, A. S., "The Positive Achievements of Endocrinology," *Endocrinology* 7 (1922).

Bommenel, Elin, *Sockerförsöket: Kariesexperimenten 1943–1960 på Vipeholms sjukhus för sinnesslöa* (Lund: Arkiv, 2006).

Borell, Merriley, "Biologists and the Promotion of Birth Control Research, 1918–1938," *JHB* 20 (1987).
Borell, Merriley, "Brown-Séquard's Organotherapy and Its Appearance in America at the End of the Nineteenth Century," *Bulletin of the History of Medicine* 50 (1976).
Borell, Merriley, "Organotherapy and the Emergence of Reproductive Endocrinology," *JHB* 18 (1985).
Borell, Merriley, "Organotherapy, British Physiology, and Discovery of the Internal Secretions," *JHB* 9 (1976).
Borell, Merriley, "Setting the Standards for a New Science: Edward Schäfer and Endocrinology," *Medical History* 22 (1978).
Borell, Ulf, "Pionjärer inom svensk obstetrik och gynekologi: Axel Westman," *SFOGSs medlemsblad* (1994).
Borell, Ulf, Egon Diczfaluzy and Axel Westman, "The Effect of Pituitary Gland Implantation on the Excretion of 17-Ketosteroids in Women," *Acta Medica Scandinavica* 142 (1952).
Bowden, Mary Ellen, "The Rush to Adrenaline: An Excerpt from Pharmaceutical Achievers," *Chemical Heritage* 21 (2003).
Brahme, Leonard, "Framsteg och publicitet," *SL* 48 (1951).
Brahme, Leonard, "Samhället och läkaren," *SL* 39 (1942).
Britt, Elizabeth C., "Infertility as a Medical Problem: Recasting Feminist Accounts of Nature, Science, and the Law," *Science as Culture* 7 (1998).
Broberg, Gunnar, *Statlig rasforskning: En historik över Rasbiologiska institutet* (Lund: Lund University, 1995).
Broberg, Gunnar and Mattias Tydén, *Oönskade i folkhemmet: Rashygien och sterilisering i Sverige* (Stockholm: Gidlund, 1991).
Brown, Nik, Brian Rappert and Andrew Webster, eds., *Contested Futures: A Sociology of Prospective Techno-Science* (Aldershot: Ashgate, 2000).
Brown, P. S., "Anterior Pituitary Hormones: Definition, Measurement and Use," in Michael J. Parnham and Jacques Bruinvels, eds., *Discoveries in Pharmacology: Haemodynamics, Hormones and Inflammation* (Amsterdam and New York: Elsevier, 1984).
Bud, Robert, *The Uses of Life: A History of Biotechnology* (Cambridge: Cambridge University Press, 1993).
Butt, W. R., A. C. Crooke and M. Ryle, "Preface," in W. R. Butt, A. C. Crooke and M. Ryle, eds., *Gonadotrophins and Ovarian Development: Proceedings of the two Workshop Meetings on the Chemistry of the Human Gonadotrophins and on the Development of the Ovary in Infancy, Birmingham, 1969* (Edinburgh and London, 1970).
Butt, W. R., A. C. Crooke and M. Ryle, eds., *Gonadotrophins and Ovarian Development: Proceedings of the two Workshop Meetings on the Chemistry of the Human Gonadotrophins and on the Development of the Ovary in Infancy, Birmingham, 1969* (Edinburgh and London, 1970).
Børresen, Anne Kristine, ed., *Science, Crafts and Ignorance: Perspectives on the History of Knowledge* (Trondheim: Tapir, 2004).
Cannon, Walter B., *Bodily Changes in Pain, Hunger, Fear and Rage: An Account of Recent Researches into the Function of Emotional Excitement* (New York: Appleton, 1915).
Cannon, Walter B., *The Wisdom of the Body* (New York: N.W. Norton, 1932).
Cantor, David, "Cortisone and the Politics of Drama, 1949–55," in John V. Pickstone, ed., *Medical Innovations in Historical Perspective* (New York: St. Martin's Press, 1992).

Carlström, Kjell, "Kvinnoklinikens hormonlaboratorium," in Valter Holmqvist et al., *Sabbatsbergs sjukhus 111 år* (Stockholm: Sabbatsberg Hospital, 1990).

Claesson, Lennart, Bertil Högberg, Thomas Rosenberg and Axel Westman, "Crystalline Human Chorionic Gonadotrophin and Its Biological Action," *Acta Endo.* 1 (1948).

Clarke, Adele E., "Controversy and the Development of Reproductive Sciences," *Social Problems* 37 (1990).

Clarke, Adele E., *Disciplining Reproduction: Modernity, American Life Sciences, and the "Problems of Sex"* (Berkeley: University of California Press, 1998).

Clarke, Adele E., "Research Materials and Reproductive Science in the United States, 1910–1940," in Gerald L. Geison, ed., *Physiology in the American Context 1850–1940* (Bethesda, Maryland: American Physiological Society, 1987).

Clarke, Adele E. and Joan H. Fujimura, eds., *The Right Tools for the Job: At Work in Twentieth-Century Life Sciences* (Princeton, NJ: Princeton University Press, 1992).

Clarke, Adele E. and Joan H. Fujimura, "What Tools? Which Jobs? Why Right?," in Adele E. Clarke and Joan H. Fujimura, *The Right Tools for the Job: At Work in Twentieth-Century Life Sciences* (Princeton, NJ: Princeton University Press, 1992).

Clarke, Adele E. et al., "Biomedicalization: Technoscientific Transformations of Health, Illness, and U.S. Biomedicine," *American Sociological Review* 68 (2003).

Clarke, John, "The History of Three Scientific Societies: The Society for the Study of Fertility (now the Society for Reproduction and Fertility) (Britain), the Société Française pour l'Étude de la Fertilité, and the Society for the Study of Reproduction (USA)," *SHPBBS* 38 (2007).

Cleghorn, Robert A., "History of Endocrine Psychobiology," in Francesca Brambilla et al., eds., *Perspectives in Endocrine Psychobiology* (London: Wiley, 1978).

Cockburn, W. Chas, "The International Contribution to the Standardization of Biological Substances: I. Biological Standards and the League of Nations 1921–1946," *Biologicals* 19 (1991).

Cockburn, W. Chas et al., "The International Contribution to the Standardization of Biological Substances: II. Biological Standards and the World Health Organization 1947–1990. General Considerations," *Biologicals* 19 (1991).

Cole, H. H. and G. H. Hart, "The Potency of Blood Serum of Mares in Progressive Stages of Pregnancy in Effecting the Sexual Maturity of the Immature Rat," *American Journal of Physiology* 94 (1930).

Collins, Harry and Trevor Pinch, *Dr. Golem: How to Think about Medicine* (Chicago and London: University of Chicago Press, 2005).

Collins, Harry and Trevor Pinch, *The Golem: What You Should Know about Science* (1993), 2d ed. (Cambridge: Cambridge University Press, 1998).

Conrad, Lawrence and Anne Hardy, eds., *Women and Modern Medicine* (Amsterdam and New York: Ropodi, 2001).

Cooter, Roger and John Pickstone, eds., *Medicine in the 20th Century* (Amsterdam: Harwood Academic, 2000).

Corea, Gena, *The Mother Machine: Reproductive Technologies from Artificial Insemination to Artificial Wombs* (New York: Harper and Row, 1985).

Corner, George W., "Laboratory and Clinic in the Study of Infertility," *Fertility and Sterility* 8 (1957).

Cozzens, Susan E. and Edward J. Woodhouse, "Science, Government, and the Politics of Knowledge," in Sheila Jasanoff et al., eds., *Handbook of Science and Technology Studies*, (1994), rev. ed. (Thousand Oaks, London and New Delhi: Sage, 1995).

Cunningham, Andrew and Perry Williams, eds., *The Laboratory Revolution in Medicine* (Cambridge: Cambridge University Press, 1992).

Dale, Henry H., "Conference on the Standardisation of Sex Hormones: Held at London on July 30th and August 1st, 1932," *Quarterly Bulletin of the Health Organisation* 4 (1935).

Dale, Henry H., "Report of the Second Conference on the Standardisation of Sex Hormones: Held in London, July 15th to 17th, 1935," *Quarterly Bulletin of the Health Organisation* 4 (1935).

"Dansk läkemedelsindustri III: Løvens kemiske Fabrik," *SFT* 68 (1968).

Daston, Lorraine, ed., *Biographies of Scientific Objects* (Chicago and London: University of Chicago Press, 2000).

Davis, Peter, ed., *Contested Ground: Public Purpose and Private Interest in the Regulation of Prescription Drugs* (New York and Oxford: Oxford University Press, 1996).

Davis, Peter, "Introduction: Medicines in a Postmodern World," in Peter Davis, ed., *Contested Ground: Public Purpose and Private Interest in the Regulation of Prescription Drugs* (New York and Oxford: Oxford University Press, 1996).

"Den bakteriefria fabriken," *Teknik för alla* 14 (1948).

Diczfalusy, Egon, "An Improved Method for the Bioassay of Chorionic Gonadotrophin," *Acta Endo.* 17 (1954).

Diczfalusy, Egon, "Chorionic Gonadotrophin and Oestrogens in the Human Placenta," *Acta Endo.* 11, suppl. 12 (Ph.D diss., 1953).

Diczfalusy Egon, *The Contraceptive Revolution: An Era of Scientific and Social Development* (New York and London: Parthenon, 1996).

Diczfalusy, Egon, "WHO-center: Internationell familjeplaneringsforskning vid Karolinska sjukhuset," in Bengt Pernow, ed., *Karolinska sjukhuset 1940–1990: En minnesbok* (Stockholm: Caroline Hospital, 1990).

Diczfalusy, Egon and Ulf Borell, eds., *Control of Human Fertility: Proceedings of the Fifteenth Nobel Symposium held May 27–29, 1970 at Södergarn, Lidingö, Sweden* (Stockholm: Swedish Royal Academy of Science, 1971).

Diczfalusy, Egon et al., "Comparison of the Clinical and Steroid Metabolic Effect of Human Pituitary and Urinary Gonadotrophins in Amenorrhoeic Women," *Acta Endo.* 45, suppl. 90 (1964).

Doel, Ronald E. and Thomas Söderqvist, eds., *The Historiography of Contemporary Science, Technology, and Medicine: Writing Recent Science* (London and New York: Routledge, 2006).

Donini, P., D. Puzzuoli and R. Montezemolo, "Purification of Gonadotrophin from Human Menopausal Urine," *Acta Endo.* 45 (1964).

"Drug Trajectories," special feature issue of *SHPBBS* 36 (2005).

Dumble, L. J. and R. D. Klein, "Creutzfeldt-Jakob Legacy for Australian Women Treated with Human Pituitary Gonadotropins," *The Lancet* 3 October (1992).

Dutton, Diana B., *Worse than the Disease: Pitfalls of Medical Progress* (Cambridge: Cambridge University Press, 1988).

Editorial, "Animal Extracts as Therapeutic Agents," *British Medical Journal* 17 June (1893).

Editorial, "Contraindications to Estrogen Therapy," *Journal of the American Medical Association* 114 (1940).
Edwards, Martin, "Good, Bad or Offal?: The Evaluation of Raw Pancreas Therapy and the Rhetoric of Control in the Therapeutic Trial, 1925," *Annals of Science* 61 (2004).
Ehrlén, Inge et al., "Svensk läkemedelsindustri," in Rune Lönngren et al., eds., *Svensk farmaci under 1900-talet*, 3 vol. (Stockholm: Swedish Academy of Pharmaceutical Sciences, 1999), vol. 2.
Ekelöf, Gunnar, "Till de folkhemske" (1945), in idem, *Samlade dikter* (Stockholm: Bonnier, 2007).
Eklöf, Motzi, *Läkarens ethos: Studier i den svenska läkarkårens identiteter, intressen och ideal 1890–1960* (Linköping: Linköping University, 2000).
Ekström, Anders, ed., *Den mediala vetenskapen* (Nora: Nya Doxa, 2004).
Emmelin, Nils, "Med cello till det nya landet," in Margareta Wirmark et al., eds., *Professorsboken: Fyrtionio Lundakvinnor berättar* (Stockholm: Carlsson, 1996).
"En ny svensk industri," *SFT* 5 (1901).
"En tredjedel av alla sterila kvinnor kan få barn genom nytt hormonpreparat," *Husmodern* 28 (1948).
Engel, Arthur, "Läkemedlen i det moderna samhället," *SFT* 63 (1959).
Eriksson, Gunnar, "Vetenskapens roller i läkemedelsframställningen: Från den galeniska eran till den svenska läkemedelsindustrins framväxt," in Tore Frängsmyr, ed., *Vetenskap och läkemedel: Ett historiskt perspektiv* (Stockholm: Almqvist and Wiksell International, 1987).
Everse, J. W. R., "Kombinerad behandling med östrogent och androgent hormon," *Hormoner: Tidskrift för hormonforskning* 16 (1952).
Fausto-Sterling, Anne, *Myths of Gender: Biological Theories about Women and Men* (New York: Basic Books, 1985).
Fevold, H. L., F. L. Hisaw and S. L. Leonard, "The Gonad Stimulating and the Luteinizing Hormones of the Anterior Lobe of the Hypophesis," *American Journal of Physiology* 97 (1931).
Fevold, H. L., F. L. Hisaw, A. Hellbaum and R. Hertz, "Sex Hormones of the Anterior Lobe of the Hypophysis," *American Journal of Physiology* 104 (1933).
Finkelstein, Michael, "Professor Bernhard Zondek: An Interview," *Journal of Reproduction and Fertility* 12 (1966).
Fishman, Jennifer R., "Manufacturing Desire: The Commodification of Female Sexual Dysfunction," *SSS* 34 (2004).
Flaum, Alfred, *Lasarettet i Lund 1768–1968: En historik utarbetad på uppdrag av Malmöhus läns landsting till lasarettets tvåhundraårsjubileum* (Lund: Lund County Council, 1968).
Fleck, Ludwik, *Uppkomsten och utvecklingen av ett vetenskapligt faktum: Inledning till läran om tankestil och tankekollektiv* (1935), Swe. transl. (Stockholm and Stehag: Symposion).
Floderus, Sten, "Untersuchungen über den Bau der menschlichen Hypophyse mit besonderer Berücksichtigung der quantitativen mikromorphologischen Verhältnisse," *Acta Pathologica et Microbiologica Scandinavica* 21, suppl. 53 (Ph.D diss., 1944).
Forsberg, Astrid, "Barnlöshet beror på mannen," *Husmodern* 31 (1943).
Fortegnelse over Leo Præparater fra Løvens kemiske Fabrik (Köpenhamn, August 1931).

Frank, Robert T., "The Sex Hormones: Their Physiologic Significance and Use in Practice," *Journal of the American Medical Association* 114 (1940).

Frängsmyr, Tore, ed., *Vetenskap och läkemedel: Ett historiskt perspektiv* (Stockholm: Almqvist and Wiksell International, 1987).

Frängsmyr, Tore, *Svensk idéhistoria: Bildning och vetenskap under tusen år*, 2 vol. (Stockholm: Natur och kultur, 2000), vol. 2.

Furuhjelm, Mirjam, Nils-Olov Lunell and Erik Odeblad, "Ovarian Stimulation by Human Menopausal Gonadotrophin in Patients with Amenorrhæa and Anovulation," *Acta Obst.* 45 (1966).

Galambos, Louis and Jane Eliot Sewell, *Networks of Innovation: Vaccine Development at Merck, Sharp and Dohme, and Mulford, 1895–1995* (Cambridge: Cambridge University Press, 1995).

Galambos, Louis and Jeffrey L. Sturchio, "The Transformation of the Pharmaceutical Industry in the Twentieth Century," in John Krige and Dominique Pestre, eds., *Companion to Science in the Twentieth Century* (1997), new ed. (London and New York: Routledge, 2003).

Gaudillière, Jean-Paul, "Better Prepared than Synthesized: Adolf Butenandt, Schering Ag and the Transformation of Sex Steroids into Drugs (1930–1946)," *SHPBBS* 36 (2005).

Gaudillière, Jean-Paul, "Genesis and Development of a Biomedical Object: Styles of Thought, Styles of Work and the History of Sex Steroids," *SHPBBS* 35 (2004).

Gaudillière, Jean-Paul, "Hormones at Risk: Cancer and the Medical Uses of Industrially-produced Sex Steroids in Germany, 1930–1960," in Thomas Schlich and Ulrich Tröhler, eds., *The Risks of Medical Innovation: Risk Perception and Assessment in Historical Context* (London and New York: Routledge, 2006).

Gaudillière, Jean-Paul, "Introduction: Drug Trajectories," *SHPBBS* 36 (2005).

Gaudillière, Jean-Paul and Ilana Löwy, "General Introduction," in Jean-Paul Gaudillière and Ilana Löwy, eds., *The Invisible Industrialist: Manufactures and the Production of Scientific Knowledge* (London and New York: St. Martin's Press, 1998).

Gaudillière, Jean-Paul, "The Pharmaceutical Industry in the Biotech Century: Toward a History of Science, Technology and Business?," *SHPBBS* 32 (2001).

Gaudillière, Jean-Paul and Ilana Löwy, eds., *The Invisible Industrialist: Manufactures and the Production of Scientific Knowledge* (London and New York: St. Martin's Press, 1998).

Geison, Gerald L., ed., *Physiology in the American Context 1850–1940* (Bethesda, Maryland: American Physiological Society, 1987).

Gemzell, Carl Axel, "The Effect of Corticotrophic Hormone and Oestrogen on Liver Glycogen Content and Phosphate Metabolism in the Adrenal Cortex," *Acta Endo.* 1, suppl. 1 (Ph.D diss., 1948).

Gemzell, Carl A., "Genombrott i reproduktionsforskningen mellan 1960 och 1975," in Bo Lindberg, ed., *Kvinnosjukvård under 100 år: En jubileumsbok från Kvinnokliniken, Akademiska sjukhuset* (Uppsala: Academic Hospital, 1994).

Gemzell, Carl, "Human Pituitary Gonadotopins in the Treatment of Sterility," *Fertility and Sterility* 17 (1966).

Gemzell, Carl and Paul Roos, "Pregnancies following treatment with Human Gonadotropins: With special reference to the Problem of Muliple Births," *American Journal of Obstetrics and Gynecology* 94 (1966).

Gemzell, Carl A., Egon Diczfalusy and Gunnar Tillinger, "Clinical Effect of Human Pituitary Follicle-stimulating Hormone (FSH)," *Journal of Clinical Endocrinology and Metabolism* 18 (1958).
Gemzell, Carl A., Egon Diczfalusy and Karl-Gunnar Tillinger, "Further Studies of the Clinical Effects of Human Pituitary Follicle-stimulating Hormone (FSH): Lack of Response in Ovarian Insufficiency," *Acta Obst.* 38 (1959).
Gemzell, Carl. A., Egon Diczfalusy and Karl-Gunnar Tillinger, "Human Pituitary Follicle-stimulating Hormone: I. Clinical Effect of a Partially Purified Preparation," *Ciba Foundation Colloquia on Endocrinology* 13 (1960).
Gemzell, Carl, Paul Roos and F. E. Loeffler, "The Clinical Use of Pituitary Gonadotrophins in Women," *Journal of Reproduction and Fertility* 12 (1966).
Genell, Sune, "Den manliga partens roll i sterila äktenskap: Några ord om moderna linjer i spermiediagnostiken," *SL* 40 (1943).
Genell, Sune, "Nyare rön angående de kvinnliga sexualhormonen: En översikt," part 1 and 2, *SL* 27 (1930).
Genell, Sune, "Tre veckors hormonstudier hos Zondek," *Nord. Med.* 4 (1932).
Genesis 16 and 30.
Gieryn, Thomas F., *Cultural Boundaries of Science: Credibility on the Line* (Chicago: University of Chicago Press, 1999).
Glick, Thomas F., "On the Diffusion of a New Speciality: Marañón and the 'Crisis' of Endocrinology in Spain," *JHB* 9 (1976).
Golinski, Jan, *Making Natural Knowledge: Constructivism and the History of Science* (Cambridge: Cambridge University Press, 1998).
Goodman, Jordan, "Can it Ever be Pure Science? Pharmaceuticals, Pharmaceutical Industry and Biomedical Research in the Twentieth Century," in Jean-Paul Gaudillière and Ilana Löwy, eds., *The Invisible Industrialist: Manufactures and the Production of Scientific Knowledge* (London and New York: St. Martin's Press, 1998).
Goodman, Jordan, "Pharmaceutical Industry," in Roger Cooter and John Pickstone, eds., *Medicine in the 20th Century* (Amsterdam: Harwood Academic, 2000).
Grandin, Karl, Nina Wormbs and Sven Widmalm, eds., *The Science-Industry Nexus: History, Policy, Implications* (Sagamore Beach: Science History Publications, 2004).
Greene, Jeremy A., "Attention to 'Details': Etiquette and the Pharmaceutical Salesman in Postwar American," *SSS* 34 (2004).
Gårdlund, Waldemar, "Hormoner och fosterfördrivning," *SL* 41 (1944).
Gårdlund, Waldemar, "Vetenskaplig reklam och praktisk erfarenhet: Ett bidrag till problemet om kvinnans sterilitet," *SL* 45 (1948).
Gøtzsche, Poul, "Antex–Physex," *Ugeskrift for Læger* 6 December (1951).
Gøtzsche, Poul, "Antex–Physex," *Ugeskrift for Læger* 22 November (1951).
Gøtzsche, Poul, "Antex–Physex: En advarsel," *Ugeskrift for Læger* 25 October (1951).
Hagenfeldt, Kerstin, "Mirjam Furuhjelm," *SFOGs medlemsblad* 2 (2005).
Hamburger, Christian, "Antex–Physex," *Ugeskrift for Læger* 29 November (1951).
Hamburger, Christian, *Hypofysens, Kønskirtlernes og Binyrernes Hormoner* (Köpenhamn: Nordiska Bokhandeln, 1950).
Hamburger, Christian and Hjalmar Wijnbladh, "Axel Westman," *Acta Endo.* 17 (1954).
Hamburger, Christian, Kaj Pedersen-Bjergaard and Hjalmar Wijnbladh, "Axel Westman 29.12.1894–29.5.1960," *Acta Endo.* 34 (1960).
Hamilton, David, *The Monkey Gland Affair* (London: Chatto and Windus, 1986).

Hammar, Johan August, *Om den inre sekretionen*, 2 vol. (Stockholm: Bonnier, 1922).

Hanson, Ann Ellis, "Hippocrates: 'Diseases of Woman 1,'" *Signs: Journal of Women in Culture and Society* 1 (1975).

Hasselberg, Ylva and Tom Petersson, eds., *"Bäste broder!": Nätverk, entreprenörskap och innovation i svenskt näringsliv* (Hedemora: Gidlund, 2006).

Hasselberg, Ylva and Tom Petersson, "Nätverksbegreppets utveckling," in Ylva Hasselberg and Tom Petersson, eds., *"Bäste broder!": Nätverk, entreprenörskap och innovation i svenskt näringsliv* (Hedemora: Gidlund, 2006).

Hatje, Ann-Katrin, *Befolkningsfrågan och välfärden: Debatten om familjepolitik och nativitetsökning under 1930- och 1940-talen* (Stockholm: Allmänna förlaget, 1974).

Hayes, Peter, *Industry and Ideology: I G Farben in the Nazi Era* (Cambridge: Cambridge University Press, 1987).

Henig, Robin Marantz, *Pandora's Baby: How the First Test Tube Babies Sparked the Reproductive Revolution* (Houghton Mifflin: Cold Spring Harbor Laboratory Press, 2006).

Herman, Harry A., *Improving Cattle by the Millions: NAAB and the Development and Worldwide Application of Artificial Insemination* (Columbia, Missouri and London: University of Missouri Press, 1981).

Hertz, John, Karl-Gunnar Tillinger and Axel Westman, "Report on Five Hormonally and Surgically treated Cases," *Acta Psychiatrica Scandinavica* 37 (1961).

Heteren, Godelieve van, Marijke Gijswijt-Hofstra and Tilli Tansey, eds., *Biographies of Remedies: Drugs, Medicines and Contraceptives in Dutch and Anglo-American Healing Cultures* (Amsterdam and New York: Rodopi, 2002).

Heteren, Godelieve van, Marijke Gijswijt-Hofstra and Tilli Tansey, "Introduction," in Godelieve van Heteren, Marijke Gijswijt-Hofstra and Tilli Tansey, eds., *Biographies of Remedies: Drugs, Medicines and Contraceptives in Dutch and Anglo-American Healing Cultures* (Amsterdam and New York: Rodopi, 2002).

Hirdman, Yvonne, *Att lägga livet till rätta: Studier i svensk folkhemspolitik* (1989), 2d ed. (Stockholm: Carlsson, 2000).

Hirshbein, Laura Davidow, "The Glandular Solution: Sex, Masculinity, and Aging in the 1920s," *Journal of the History of Sexuality* 9 (2000).

Hjortsjö, Carl-Herman, "Inre secretion," in *Svensk uppslagsbok* (Malmö: Förlagshuset Norden, 1950), vol. 14.

Hoberman, John, *Testosterone Dreams: Rejuvenation, Aphrodisia, Doping* (Berkeley and Los Angeles: University of California Press, 2005).

Holmqvist, Valter et al., *Sabbatsbergs sjukhus 111 år* (Stockholm: Sabbatsberg Hospital, 1990).

Holtz, Folke, "Sterility and Its Treatment," *Acta Obst.* 30, suppl. 7 (1950).

"Hormones for Fertility," *Time Magazine* 9 October (1964).

Hreinsson, Julius, Lars Hamberger and Thorir Hardarson, eds., *Infertilitet: Utredning och behandling genom assisterad befruktning* (Lund: Studentlitteratur, 2005).

Hughes, Arthur F. W., "A History of Endocrinology," *Journal of the History of Medicine and Allied Sciences* 32 (1977).

Hughes, Thomas P., "The Evolution of Large Technological Systems," in Mario Biagioli, ed., *The Science Studies Reader* (New York and London: Routledge, 1999).

"Human Chorionic Gonadotrophin," *British Medical Journal* 3 April (1948).

Hylander, Fride, "Hypofysheterotransplantationer ad modum Kylin: Några korrigerande och kompletterande randanmärkningar," *SL* 35 (1938).

Högberg, Bertil, "Steroida kvävesenapsgasderivat: Synpunkter mot bakgrunden av hormonernas verkningsmekanism," *SFT* 78 (1974).

I framtidens tjänst: Ur folkhemmets idéhistoria (Malmö: Gidlund, 1986).

Ideland, Malin, *Dagens gennyheter: Hur massmedier berättar om genetik och genteknik* (Lund: Nordic Academic Press, 2002).

"Intersections of Pharmaceutical Research and Marketing," special feature issue of *SSS* 34 (2004).

Jamison, Andrew, *The Making of Green Knowledge: Environmental Politics and Cultural Transformation* (Cambridge: Cambridge University Press, 2001).

Jasanoff, Sheila, et al., eds., *Handbook of Science and Technology Studies*, (1994), rev. ed. (Thousand Oaks, London and New Delhi: Sage, 1995).

Jerlov, Emil, "48 hypofystransplantationer vid gynekologiska åkommor jämte ett förslag till modifikation av ingreppet," *SL* 43 (1946).

Johannisson, Karin, "Bot för en nervtrött generation: Ett läkemedel i idéhistorisk belysning," in Tore Frängsmyr, ed., *Vetenskap och läkemedel: Ett historiskt perspektiv* (Stockholm: Almqvist and Wiksell International, 1987).

Johannisson, Karin, *Den mörka kontinenten: Kvinnan, medicinen och fin-de-siècle* (1994), new ed. (Stockholm: Norstedt, 1998).

Johansson, Kaj, *Den torgförda biologin: Studier i populärvetenskapens problem och tematik* (Göteborg: University of Gothenburg, 2003).

Johnson, Eyvind, *Grupp Krilon* (Stockholm: Bonnier, 1941).

Jones, Thomas H., *Detailing the Physician: Sales Promotion by Personal Contact with the Medical and Allied Professions* (New York: Romaine Pierson Publishers, 1940).

Jonsson, Kjell, "Rasbiologi från vänster?: Om Gunnar Dahlbergs vetenskap, politik och popularisering," in Christer Nordlund, ed., *Livsföreställningar: Kultur, samhälle och biovetenskap* (Umeå: Royal Skytte Society, 2004).

Jonsson, Kjell and Jenny Larsson, "Mellan vetenskap och vers: Ärftlighetsforskare som publika vetenskapsmän 1940–1960," in Anders Ekström, ed., *Den mediala vetenskapen* (Nora: Nya Doxa, 2004).

Jorpes, Erik, "Om handelns 'prólan'-preparat," *SL* 31 (1934).

Jorpes, Erik, "Om insulinets natur och dess framställning," *SL* 22 (1925).

Josefson, Arnold, "Bokanmälan," *SL* 37 (1940).

Josefson, Arnold, "Internationellt samarbete på den endokrina forskningens område: Ett beaktansvärt upprop från Amerika," *ASL* 14 (1917).

Josefson, Arnold, "Några ord om hormonterapi," *SL* 38 (1941).

Josefson, Arnold, *Vad betyda insöndringsorganen för vår kropp och själ?: Översikt* (Stockholm: Geber, 1925).

Juuti, Petri S. and Tapio S. Katko, eds., *From a Few to All: Long-term Development of Water and Environmental Services in Finland* (Pieksämäki: KehräMedia Inc., 2004).

Jørgensen, Frede, "Antex–Physex," *Ugeskrift for Læger* 3 January (1952).

"Kan vi lita på läkemedelsindustrin?" part 1 and 2, *SFT* 67 (1963).

Karolinska mediko-kirurgiska institutets historia 1910–1960: Utgiven med anledning av institutets hundrafemtioårsdag av dess lärarkollegium, 4 vol. (Stockholm: Almqvist and Wiksell, 1960), vol. 3.

Keller, Evelyn Fox, *Making Sense of Life: Explaining Biological Development with Models, Metaphors, and Machines* (Cambridge, Mass. and London: Harvard University Press, 2002).

Kling, Sofia, *Vi våga ej helt leva: Barnbegränsning, sexualitet och genus under den svenska fertilitetstransitionen* (Umeå: Umeå University, 2007).

Kjessler, Berndt, ed., *Utredning och behandling av ofrivillig barnlöshet* (Linköping: Swedish Society of Obstetrics and Gynecology, 1993).

Koch, Lene, "On Ethics, Scientists, and Democracy: Writing the History of Eugenic Sterilization," in Ronald E. Doel and Thomas Söderqvist, eds., *The Historiography of Contemporary Science, Technology, and Medicine: Writing Recent Science* (London and New York: Routledge, 2006).

Kohler, Robert E., *Partners in Science: Foundations and Natural Scientists, 1900–1945* (Chicago and London: Chicago University Press, 1991).

Kottmeier, Hans-Ludvig, "Axel Westman 29.XII.1894–29.V.1960," *Nord. Med.* 65 (1961).

Kottmeier, Hans Ludvig, "Behandling med oestrogena hormonpreparat: Indikationer och kontraindikationer," *SL* 45 (1948).

Kottmeier, Hans Ludvig, "Hormonproducerande ovarialtumörer," *Nord. Med.* 41 (1949).

Kottmeier, Hans Ludvig, "Ueber Blutungen in der Menopause, speziell der klinischen Bedeutung eines Endometriums mit Zeichen hormonaler Beeinflussung," *Acta Obst.* 27, suppl. 6 (1947).

Krementsov, Nikolai, "Hormones and the Bolsheviks: From Organotherapy to Experimental Endocrinology, 1918–1929," *Isis* 99 (2008).

Krige, John and Dominique Pestre, eds., *Companion to Science in the Twentieth Century* (1997), new ed. (London and New York: Routledge, 2003).

Krogh, August, "De nordiske landes forsyning med insulin," *SL* 21 (1924).

Kylhammar, Martin, "Bryt upp! Bryt upp! Om den moderna konsten att göra sig kvitt det förflutna," in Martin Kylhammar and Michael Godhe, eds., *Frigörare? Moderna svenska samhällsdrömmar* (Stockholm: Carlssons, 2005).

Kylhammar, Martin and Michael Godhe, eds., *Frigörare? Moderna svenska samhällsdrömmar* (Stockholm: Carlssons, 2005).

Kylin, Eskil, "Tio års hypofystransplantation," *SL* 40 (1943).

König, Wolfgang, "Science-Based Industry or Industry-Based Science? Electrical Engineering in Germany before World War I," *Technology and Culture* 37 (1996).

Lalos, Ann, "Infertilitetskrisen," in Berndt Kjessler, ed., *Utredning och behandling av ofrivillig barnlöshet* (Linköping: Swedish Society of Obstetrics and Gynecology, 1993).

Landgren, Britt-Marie and Torbjörn Bäckström, "Reproduktionsendokrinologins utveckling," in Bo Lindberg, ed. *Svensk kvinnosjukvård under ett sekel 1904–2004* (Stockholm: Swedish Society of Obstetrics and Gynecology, 2004).

Larsson, Jan, *Hemmet vi ärvde: Om folkhemmet, identiteten och den gemensamma framtiden* (Stockholm: Arena, 1994).

Larsson, Larsåke, *Upplysning och propaganda: Utvecklingen av svensk PR och information* (Lund: Studentlitteratur, 2005).

Laqueur, Thomas, *Making Sex: Body and Gender from the Greeks to Freud* (Cambridge, Mass: Harvard University Press, 1990).

Latour, Bruno, *Science in Action: How to Follow Scientists and Engineers through Society* (1987), new ed. (Cambridge, Mass.: Harvard University Press, 1994).

Latour, Bruno and Steve Woolgar, *Laboratory Life: The Construction of Scientific Facts* (1979), new ed. (Princeton, New Jersey: Princeton University Press, 1986).

Lennerhed, Lena, *Frihet att njuta: Sexualdebatten i Sverige på 1960-talet* (Stockholm: Norstedt, 1994).

Lenoir, Timothy, *The Strategy of Life: Teleology and Mechanics in Nineteenth-Century German Biology* (1982), new ed. (Chicago and London: University of Chicago Press, 1989).

"Leo inviger nya forskningslaboratorier," *SFT* 71 (1967).

"Leo utökar sin forskningsverksamhet," *Farmacevtisk Revy* 59 (1960).

Lewenstein, Bruce V., "Science and the Media," in Sheila Jasanoff et al., eds., *Handbook of Science and Technology Studies* (1994), rev. ed. (Thousand Oaks, London and New Delhi: Sage, 1995).

Lewis, Graham, "Tissue Collection and the Pharmaceutical Industry: Investigating Corporate Biobanks," in Richard Tutton and Oonagh Corrigan, eds., *Genetic Databases: Socio-ethical Issues in the Collection and Use of DNA* (London and New York: Routledge, 2004).

Liebenau, Jonathan, *Medical Science and Medical Industry: The Formation of the American Pharmaceutical Industry* (Basingstoke: Macmillan in association with Business History Unit, University of London, 1987).

Liebenau, Jonathan, Gregory J. Higby and Elaine C. Stroud, eds., *Pill Peddlers: Essays on the History of the Pharmaceutical Industry* (Madison, Wisconsin: American Institute of the History of Pharmacy, 1990).

Lilienfeld, Abraham M., "*Ceteris Paribus*: The Evolution of the Clinical Trial," *Bulletin of the History of Medicine* 56 (1982).

Lindberg, Bo, ed., *Kvinnosjukvård under 100 år: En jubileumsbok från Kvinnokliniken, Akademiska sjukhuset* (Uppsala: Academic Hospital, 1994).

Lindberg, Bo, ed. *Svensk kvinnosjukvård under ett sekel 1904–2004* (Stockholm: Swedish Society of Obstetrics and Gynecology, 2004).

Lindgren, Håkan, "Läkemedelsindustri," in *Nationalencyklopedin* (Höganäs: Bra Böcker, 1993), vol. 12.

Lindner, Torsten, "Bokanmälan," *SL* 40 (1943).

Linnér, Björn-Ola, *The World Household: Georg Borgström and the Postwar Population-Resource Crisis* (Linköping: Linköping University, 1998).

Lisser, Hans, "The Endocrine Society: The First Forty Years (1917–1957)," *Endocrinology* 80 (1967).

Long Hall, Diana, "Biology, Sex Hormones and Sexism in the 1920s," *Philosophical Forum* 5 (1974).

Long Hall, Diana, "The Critic and the Advocate: Contrasting British Views on the State of Endocrinology in the Early 1920s," *JHB* 9 (1976).

Long, Diana E., "Moving Reprints: A Historian Looks at Sex Research Publications of the 1930s," *Journal of the History of Medicine and Allied Sciences* 45 (1990).

Long, Diana E., "Physiological Identity of American Sex Researchers between the Two World Wars," in Gerald L. Geison, ed., *Physiology in the American Context 1850–1940* (Bethesda, Maryland: American Physiological Society, 1987).

Long Hall, Diana and Thomas F. Glick, "Endocrinology: A Brief Introduction," *JHB* 9 (1976).

Ludwig, Michael et al., "Ovarian Stimulation: From Basic Science to Clinical Application," *Reproductive BioMedicine Online* 5, suppl. 1 (2002).

Luft, Rolf, "Endokrinologi," in Bengt Pernow, ed., *Karolinska sjukhuset 1940–1990: En minnesbok* (Stockholm: Caroline Hospital, 1990).

Luft, Rolf, "Kristalliniskt choriongonadotropin (gonadex Leo), *Nord. Med.* 39 (1948).

Luft, Rolf, "Sektionen för endokrinologi," in *Svenska läkaresällskapet 175 år* (Stockholm: Swedish Society of Medicine, 1983).

Lundberg, Erik, *Insöndringskörtlarna och deras viktigaste sjukdomar* (Stockholm: Wahlström and Widstrand, 1934).

Lundgren, Anders, "The Development of Chemical Industry in Sweden and the Contribution of Academic Chemistry after 1900," in Anthony S. Travis et al., eds., *Determinants in the Evolution of the European Chemical Industry, 1900–1939: New Technologies, Political Frameworks, Markets, and Companies* (Dordrecht: Springer, 1998).

Lundgren, Anders, "Dextran som blodplasmasubstitut," in Tore Frängsmyr, ed., *Vetenskap och läkemedel: Ett historiskt perspektiv* (Stockholm: Almqvist and Wiksell International, 1987).

Lundgren, Anders, "Knowledge and Needs: Some Aspects of the Development of the Chemical Industry," in Anne Kristine Børresen, ed., *Science, Crafts and Ignorance: Perspectives on the History of Knowledge* (Trondheim: Tapir, 2004).

Lundgren, Anders, *Vetenskap till vardags: En historia kring Xylocain* (Stockholm: Stiftelsen Bengt Lundquists minne, 1995).

Lundin, Folke, "Läkemedelsindustri och läkemedelsreklam," *SFT* 67 (1963).

Lundin, Susanne, *Guldägget: Föräldraskap i biomedicinens tid* (Lund: Historiska Media, 1997).

Lunenfeld, Bruno, "Historical Perspectives in Gonadotrophin Therapy," *Human Reproduction Update* 10 (2004).

Lunenfeld, Bruno, "Treatment of Anovulation by Human Gonadotrophins," *International Journal of Obstetrics and Gynecology* 12 (1963).

Lunenfeld, Bruno, Annette Menzi and Blaise Volet, "Clinical Effects of Human Postmenopausal Gonadotrophin," *Acta Endo.* 34, suppl. 51 (1960).

Lönngren, Rune et al., eds., *Svensk farmaci under 1900-talet*, 3 vol. (Stockholm: Swedish Academy of Pharmaceutical Sciences, 1999), vol. 1–2.

"Løvens kemiske Fabrik—Leo Pharmaceutical Products," *Medicinsk Forum* 36 (1983).

Mahoney, James, "Path Dependence in Historical Sociology," *Theory and Society* 29 (2000).

Maienschein, Jane, *Whose View of Life?: Embryos, Cloning, and Stem Cells* (Cambridge, Mass. and London: Harvard University Press, 2005).

Malmström, Gunnar, "Anorexia nervosa," *SL* 45 (1948).

Mammas bok (Uppsala: Henrik Gahns Aktiebolag, 1946).

Marks, Harry M., *The Progress of Experiment: Science and Therapeutic Reform in the United States, 1900–1990* (Cambridge: Cambridge University Press, 1997).

Marsh, Margaret and Wanda Ronner, *The Fertility Doctor: John Rock and the Reproductive Revolution* (Baltimore, Maryland: Johns Hopkins University Press, 2008).

Marsh, Margaret and Wanda Ronner, *The Empty Cradle: Infertility in America from Colonial Times to the Present* (Baltimore, Maryland: Johns Hopkins University Press, 1996).

McCrea, Frances B. and Gerald E. Markle, "The Estrogen Replacement Controversy in the USA and UK: Different Answers to the Same Question?," *SSS* 14 (1984).

McNeil, Maureen, "New Reproductive Technologies: Dreams and Broken Promises," *Science as Culture* 3 (1993).

Meddelanden om Konung Gustaf V:s 80-årsfond (Stockholm: Royal Caroline Institute, 1954–58).

Medvei, Victor C., *The History of Clinical Endocrinology: A Comprehensive Account of Endocrinology from Earliest Times to the Present Day* (Carnforth and New York: The Parthenon Publishing Group, 1993).

Melosi, Martin V., *The Sanitary City: Urban Infrastructure in America from the Colonial Times to the Present* (Baltimore, MD: Johns Hopkins University Press, 2000).

Movin, R., "Komplikationer ved gonadotropinbehandling af ovarialinsufficiens," *Nord. Med.* 41 (1949).

Mozes, M. et al., "Thromboembolic Phenomena after Ovarian Stimulation with Human Gonadotrophins," *The Lancet* 11 December (1965).

"The Multiple-Birth Hormone," *Time Magazine* 6 August (1965).

Murnaghan, Jane H. and Paul Talalay, "H. H. Dale's Account of the Standardization of Insulin," *Bulletin of the History of Medicine* 66 (1992).

Myrdal, Alva and Gunnar Myrdal, *Kris i befolkningsfrågan* (1934), new ed. (Nora: Nya Doxa, 1997).

Mårald, Erland, *Jordens kretslopp: Lantbruket, staden och den kemiska vetenskapen 1840–1910* (Umeå: Umeå University, 2000).

Mårald, Erland and Christer Nordlund, eds., *Topos: Essäer om tänkvärda platser och platsbundna tankar* (Stockholm: Carlssons, 2006).

Nelkin, Dorothy, *Selling Science: How the Press Covers Science and Technology* (1987), rev. ed. (New York: W.E. Freeman and Co., 1995).

Nelson, Warren O., "Endocrinology: Achievement and Challange," *Endocrinology* 59 (1956).

"Neurosedynkatastrofen," *SFT* 68 (1964).

Nilsson, Annika, *Barn till varje pris?* (Stockholm: Atlantis, 1996).

Nilsson, Ulrika, *Det heta könet: Gynekologin i Sverige kring förra sekelskiftet* (Stockholm: Wahlström and Widstrand, 2005).

Nordlund, Christer, "Dolda platser i hormonernas historia: Bondgården, kvinnokliniken och vårdhemmet," in Erland Mårald and Christer Nordlund, eds., *Topos: Essäer om tänkvärda platser och platsbundna tankar* (Stockholm: Carlssons, 2006).

Nordlund, Christer, ed., *Livsföreställningar: Kultur, samhälle och biovetenskap* (Umeå: Royal Skytte Society, 2004).

Nordlund, Christer, "Endocrinology and Expectations in 1930s America: Louis Berman's Ideas on New Creations in Human Beings," *British Journal for the History of Science* 40 (2007).

Nordlund, Christer, "Hormoner och visioner i mellankrigstid: Louis Bermans idéer om möjligheten att förädla mänskligheten," *Lychnos: Årsbok för idé- och lärdomshistoria 2004*.

Norgren, Lennart, *Kunskapsöverföring från universitet till företag: En studie av universitetsforskningens betydelse för de svenska läkemedelsföretagens produktlanseringar 1945–1984* (Uppsala: Uppsala University, 1989).
Norrlin, Lennart, "Läkarna och befolkningsfrågan," *SL* 39 (1942).
Norrsell, A., "Några erfarenheter av insulinbehandling vid schizofreni," *SL* 38 (1941).
Nybom, Thorsten, *Kunskap, politik, samhälle: Essäer om kunskapssyn, universitet och forskningspolitik 1900 2000* (Hargshamn: Arete, 1997).
Nygren, Karl-Gösta, "Infertilitet," in Bo Lindberg, ed. *Svensk kvinnosjukvård under ett sekel 1904–2004* (Stockholm: Swedish Society of Obstetrics and Gynecology, 2004).
Nylén, Stig, *Leos och Ferrosans rötter* (Helsingborg: Pharmacia Leo Therapeutics, 1992).
"Några svenska industriers läkemedelsforskning," *SFT* 73 (1969).
O'Connell, Joseph, "Metrology: The Creation of Universality by the Circulation of Particulars," *SSS* 23 (1993).
Ohlmarks, Åke, *THX och makthavarna* (Mjölby: National Association for Thymus Research, 1972).
Olösta gåtor och aktuella problem: Sjuttiosex uttalanden i Svenska Dagbladets enquête om naturforskningens nuvarande uppgifter och framtida mål (Stockholm: Wahlström and Widstrand, 1937).
Østergaard, Erling, *Antigonadotrophic Substances: Experimental and Clinical Studies on the Formation of Antigonadotrophic Substances under Treatment with Gonadotrophic Hormones* (Köpenhamn: Ejnar Munksgaard, 1942).
Østergaard, Erling and Christian Hamburger, "The Formation of Antihormones in Women treated with Pregnant Mares' Serum Hormone (Antex)," *Acta Endo.* 2 (1949).
Otterland, Anders, *THX-rörelsen i teori och praktik* (Stockholm: Bonnier, 1966).
Oudshoorn, Nelly, *Beyond the Natural Body: An Archeology of Sexhormones* (London and New York, 1994).
Oudshoorn, Nelly, "Endocrinologists and the Conceptualization of Sex, 1920–1940," *JHB* 23 (1990).
Oudshoorn, Nelly, "From Population Control Politics to Chemicals: The WHO as an Intermediary Organization in Contraceptive Development," *SSS* 27 (1997).
Oudshoorn, Nelly, "On Measuring Sex Hormones: The Role of Biological Assays in Sexualizing Chemical Substances," *Bulletin of the History of Medicine* 64 (1990).
Oudshoorn, Nelly, "On the Making of Sex Hormones: Research Materials and the Production of Knowledge," *SSS* 20 (1990).
Oudshoorn, Nelly, "United We Stand: The Pharmaceutical Industry, Laboratory, and Clinic in the Development of Sex Hormones into Scientific Drugs, 1920–1940," *Science, Technology, and Human Values* 18 (1993).
Oudshoorn, Nelly and Marianne van den Wijngaard, "Dualism in Biology: The Case of Sex Hormones," *Women's Studies International Forum* 14 (1991).
Oudshoorn, Nelly and Trevor Pinch, eds., *How Users Matter: The Co-construction of Users and Technology* (2003), new ed. (Cambridge, Mass.: MIT Press, 2005).
Paalzow, Lennart, John Sjögren and Lars Werkö, "Svensk läkemedelsforskning," in Rune Lönngren et al., eds., *Svensk farmaci under 1900-talet*, 3 vol. (Stockholm: Swedish Academy of Pharmaceutical Sciences, 1999), vol. 2.
Palmblad, Eva, *Den disciplinerade reproduktionen: Abort- och steriliseringspolitikens dolda dagordning* (Stockholm: Carlsson, 2000).

Palmblad, Eva, *Sanningens gränser: Kvacksalveriet, läkarna och samhället, Sverige 1890–1990* (Stockholm: Carlsson, 1997).

Parascandola, John, "The Preposterous Provision: The American Society for Pharmacology and Experimental Therapeutics' Ban on Industrial Pharmacologists, 1908–1941," in Jonathan Liebenau, Gregory J. Higby and Elaine C. Stroud, eds., *Pill Peddlers: Essays on the History of the Pharmaceutical Industry* (Madison, Wisconsin: American Institute of the History of Pharmacy, 1990).

Parkes, Alan S., "The Rise of Reproductive Endocrinology, 1926–1940," *Journal of Endocrinology* 34 (1966).

Parnham, Michael J. and Jacques Bruinvels, eds., *Discoveries in Pharmacology: Haemodynamics, Hormones and Inflammation* (Amsterdam and New York: Elsevier, 1984).

Paulsen, Frederik, "Hormonterapiens gränser," *Hormoner: Referattidskrift för hormon- och vitaminforskning* 6 (1942).

Pernow, Bengt, ed., *Karolinska sjukhuset 1940–1990: En minnesbok* (Stockholm: Caroline Hospital, 1990).

Persson, Anders, "Att överskrida gränser: Om xenotransplantation, risker, värderingar och människouppfattning," *VEST* 11 (1998).

Pfeffer, Naomi, "Pioneers of Infertility Treatment," in Lawrence Conrad and Anne Hardy, eds., *Women and Modern Medicine* (Amsterdam and New York: Ropodi, 2001).

Pfeffer, Naomi, *The Stork and the Syringe: A Political History of Reproductive Medicine* (Cambridge: Polity Press, 1993).

Pickstone, John V., ed., *Medical Innovations in Historical Perspective* (New York: St. Martin's Press, 1992).

Pickstone, John V., "Introduction," in John V. Pickstone, ed., *Medical Innovations in Historical Perspective* (New York: St. Martin's Press, 1992).

Pickstone, John V., *Ways of Knowing: A New History of Science, Technology and Medicine* (Manchester: Manchester University Press, 2000).

Pickstone, John V., "Working Knowledges Before and After circa 1800: Practices and Disciplines in the History of Science, Technology, and Medicine," *Isis* 98 (2007).

Pieters, Toine, "About Media, Audiences and Marketing Medicines: The Interferons," in Godelieve van Heteren, Marijke Gijswijt-Hofstra and Tilli Tansey, eds., *Biographies of Remedies: Drugs, Medicines and Contraceptives in Dutch and Anglo-American Healing Cultures* (Amsterdam and New York: Rodopi, 2002).

Pieters, Toine, *Interferon: The Science and Selling of a Miracle Drug* (London and New York: Routledge, 2005).

Pieters, Toine, "Managing Differences in Biomedical Research: The Case of Standardizing Interferons," *SHPBBS* 29 (1998).

Pinch, Trevor J. and Wiebe E. Bijker, "The Social Construction of Facts and Artefacts: Or How the Sociology of Science and the Sociology of Technology Might Benefit Each Other," *SSS* 14 (1984).

Pincus, Gregory and Kenneth V. Thimann, eds., *The Hormones: Physiology, Chemistry and Applications*, 2 vol. (New York: Academic Press, 1948), vol. 1.

Pincus, Gregory and Kenneth V. Thimann, eds., *The Hormones: Physiology, Chemistry and Applications*, 2 vol. (New York: Academic Press, 1950), vol. 2.

"Pitruitin, Pituglandol, Hypophysin," *SFT* 18 (1914).

Porter, Roy, *The Greatest Benefit to Mankind: A Medical History of Humanity from Antiquity to the Present* (London: HarperCollins, 1997).

Pottenger, Frank M., "The Association for the Study of Internal Secretions: Its Past, Its Future," *Endocrinology* 30 (1942).

"The Present Position of Organotherapy," *The Lancet* 20 January (1923).

Påhlsson, Nils Erik, *Hormonbehandling av amenorrhe och oligohypomenorrhe* (Stockholm: Caroline Institute, 1951).

Quine, Maria Sophia, *Population Politics in Twentieth-Century Europe: Fascist Dictatorships and Liberal Democracies* (London and New York: Routledge, 1996).

Quirke, Viviane, "From Alkaloids to Gene Therapy: A Brief History of Drug Discovery in the 20th Century," in Stuart Anderson, ed., *Making Medicines: A Brief History of Pharmacy and Pharmaceuticals* (London: Pharmaceutical Press, 2005).

Qvarsell, Roger, "Att sälja hälsa," in Roger Qvarsell and Ulrika Torell, eds., *Reklam och hälsa: Levnadsideal, skönhet och hälsa i den svenska reklamens historia* (Stockholm: Carlssons, 2004).

Qvarsell, Roger, *Vårdens idéhistoria* (Stockholm: Carlsson, 1991).

Qvarsell, Roger and Ulrika Torell, eds., *Reklam och hälsa: Levnadsideal, skönhet och hälsa i den svenska reklamens historia* (Stockholm: Carlssons, 2004).

Ragoné, Heléna and Sharla K. Willis, "Reproduction and Assisted Reproductive Technologies," in Gary L. Albrecht., Ray Fitzpatrick and Susan C. Scrimshaw, eds., *Handbook of Social Studies in Health and Medicine* (London: Sage, 2000).

Rasmussen, Nicolas, "The Moral Economy of the Drug Company–Medical Scientist Collaboration in Interwar America," *SSS* 34 (2004).

Rasmussen, Nicolas, "Steroids in Arms: Science, Government, Industry, and the Hormones of the Adrenal Cortex in the United States, 1930–1950," *Medical History* 46 (2002).

"The Right Organism for the Job," special feature issue of *JHB* 26 (1993).

Rilton, Tore, "Indikationer för användandet av manligt sexualhormon," *SL* 39 (1942).

Rising, Adolf, "Den industriella läkemedelstillverkningen och apoteken," *SFT* 30 (1926).

Roberts, Celia, "'Successful Aging' with Hormone Replacement Therapy: It May Be Sexist, But What If It Works?," *Science as Culture* 11 (2002).

Roos, Paul, "Human Follicle-stimulating Hormone: Its Isolation from the Pituitary Gland and from Postmenopausal Urine and a Study of some Chemical, Physical, Immunological, and Biological Properties of the Hormone from these Two Sources," *Acta Endo.* 59, suppl. 131 (1968).

Rosemberg, Eugenia, ed., *Gonadotropins 1968* (Los Altos, California: Geron-X, 1968).

Rosemberg, Eugenia, "Introductory Remarks," in Eugenia Rosemberg, ed., *Gonadotropins 1968* (Los Altos, California: Geron-X, 1968).

Rosemberg, Eugenia, "Use of Standards: General Considerations," in Eugenia Rosemberg, ed., *Gonadotropins 1968* (Los Altos, California: Geron-X, 1968).

Rosengren, Henrik and Johan Östling, eds., *Med livet som insats: Biografin som humanistisk genre* (Lund: Sekel, 2007).

Rothman, Sheila M. and David J. Rothman, *The Pursuit of Perfection: The Promise and Perils of Medical Enhancement* (New York: Pantheon Books, 2003).

Rubin, Herman H., *The Glands of Life: The Story of the Mysterious Endocrine Glands—Their Effects on Our Mental, Physical and Sexual Health, Personality and Behavior* (New York: B.B. Bellaire, 1935).

Runcis, Maija, *Steriliseringar i folkhemmet* (Stockholm: Ordfront, 1998).

Ruth, Arne, "The Second New Nation: The Mythology of Modern Sweden," *Daedalus* 2 (1984).
Rydberg, Erik, "Antex–Physex," *Ugeskrift for Læger* 29 November (1951).
Rydberg, Erik, "The Treatment of Functional Sterility with Gonadotropic Hormones," *Acta Obst.* 28 (1949).
Rydberg, Erik, "The Use of the Gonadotrophic Hormones in the Therapy and their Dosage," *Acta Obst.* 23 (1943).
Rydin, Håkan, "Om bedömning av läkemedels medicinska värde," *SFT* 49 (1945).
Rönnmark, Bertil, "Några synpunkter på biologisk bestämning av hormonpreparat," *Farmacevtisk Revy* 39 (1940).
Saxena, Brij B., Carl G. Beling and Hortense M. Gandy, eds., *Gonadotropins* (New York et al.: Wiley-Interscience, 1972).
Schaffer, Simon, "What is Science?," in John Krige and Dominique Pestre, eds., *Companion to Science in the Twentieth Century* (1997), new ed. (London and New York: Routledge, 2003).
Schlich, Thomas and Ulrich Tröhler, eds., *The Risks of Medical Innovation: Risk Perception and Assessment in Historical Context* (London and New York: Routledge, 2006).
Schrøder, Preben, "Fra Løveapotekets kemiske Fabik till LEO Pharma A/S," *Theriaca* 36 (2005).
Schwartz, Theodore B., "Henry Harrower and the Turbulent Beginnings of Endocrinology," *Annals of Internal Medicine* 131 (1999).
Schäfer, Edward, *An Introduction to the Study of the Endocrine Glands and Internal Secretions: Lane Medical Lectures, 1913* (Stanford: Leland Stanford Junior University, 1914).
Schäfer, Edward, *The Endocrine Organs: An Introduction to the Study of Internal Secretion* (London and New York: Longmans, Green, and Co., 1916).
Schäfer, Edward, "Internal Secretions," *The Lancet* 10 August (1895).
Schön, Lennart, *En modern svensk ekonomisk historia: Tillväxt och omvandling under två sekel* (Stockholm: SNS, 2000).
Seaman, Barbara, *The Greatest Experiment Ever Performed on Women: Exploding the Estrogen Myth* (New York: Hyperion, 2003).
Secord, James A., "Knowledge in Transit," *Isis* 95 (2004).
Sengoopta, Chandak, "Glandular Politics: Experimental Biology, Clinical Medicine, and Homosexual Emancipation in Fin-de-Siècle Central Europé," *Isis* 89 (1998).
Sengoopta, Chandak, *The Most Secret Quintessence of Life: Sex, Glands, and Hormones, 1850–1950* (Chicago and London: University of Chicago Press, 2006).
Sengoopta, Chandak, "The Modern Ovary: Constructions, Meanings, Uses," *History of Science* 38 (2000).
Sevringhaus, Elmer L., "Commercial Endocrine Preparations," *Endocrinology* 30 (1942).
Shinn, Terry and Richard Whitley, eds., *Expository Science: Forms and Functions of Popularisation* (Dordrecht: Reidel, 1985).
Shirran, Emma, *Samhälle, vetenskap och obstetrik: Elis Essen-Möller och kvinnokliniken i Lund* (Uppsala: Uppsala University, 2007).
Sinding, Christiane, "Making the Unit of Insulin: Standards, Clinical Work, and Industry, 1920–1925," *Bulletin of the History of Medicine* 76 (2002).
Sjöberg, Knut, "Byrån för upplysning om läkemedelsannonser," *SFT* 8 (1904).

Sjögren, Björn, ed., *Om hormoner och hormonterapi* (Helsingborg: AB Leo, 1962).

Sjöqvist, John and Erik Jorpes, "Den svenska insulinframställningen," *SL* 28 (1931).

Skjoldborg, H., "Antex–Physex," *Ugeskrift for Læger* 12 December (1951).

Slater, Leo B., "Industry and Academy: The Synthesis of Steroids," *Historical Studies in the Physical and Biological Sciences* 30 (2000).

Smith, Mickey C., *Principles in Pharmaceutical Marketing* (Philadelphia: Lea and Febiger, 1968).

Smith, Philip E. and Earl T. Engle, "Experimental Evidence Regarding the Role of the Anterior Pituitary in the Development and Regulation of the Genital System," *American Journal of Anatomy* 40 (1927).

Sneader, Walter, *Drug Discovery: The Evolution of Modern Medicines* (Chichester et al.: Wiley, 1985).

Stanworth, Michelle, ed., *Reproductive Technologies: Gender, Motherhood and Medicine* (Cambridge: Polity Press, 1987).

Starling, Ernest H., "The Chemical Correlation of the Functions of the Body," *The Lancet* 5 August (1905).

Starling, Ernest H., "The Wisdom of the Body," *The Lancet* 20 October (1923).

Starr, Paul, *The Social Transformation of American Medicine: The Rise of a Sovereign Profession and the Making of a Vast Industry* (New York: Basic Books, 1982).

"Statsmedicinska anstalten," in *Nordisk familjebok* (Stockholm, 1917), vol. 17.

Steinach, Eugen, *Hormonerna som forma livet* (1940), Swe. transl. (Stockholm: Bonniers, 1940).

Stenberg, Sten-Åke, "Forskningsresultat och politiska prioriteringar," *Tvärsnitt* 3 (2007).

"Syntetiska binjurepreparater," *SFT* 13 (1909).

"Sterilitet kan botas! Massproduktion av nytt hormon," *Tabletten* (December, 1965).

Svenska läkaresällskapet 175 år (Stockholm: Swedish Society of Medicine, 1983).

Swanberg, Lena Katarina, *Blod, svett och tårar: En ilsken bok om östrogen* (Stockholm: Bokförlaget DN, 2003).

Swann, John P., *Academic Scientists and the Pharmaceutical Industry: Cooperative Research in Twentieth-Century America* (Baltimore and London: Johns Hopkins University Press, 1988).

"Syster Anna besvarar hälsofrågor," *Folket i bild* 17 (1944).

Söderqvist, Thomas, ed., *The History and Poetics of Scientific Biography* (Aldershot: Ashgate, 2007).

Tallberg, Arne, ed., *Sexuallivet i modern belysning: Sexton svenska forskare ger vägledning* (Stockholm: Wahlström and Widstrand, 1944).

Tansey, E. M., "What's in a Name?: Henry Dale and Adrenaline, 1906," *Medical History* 39 (1995).

Tattersall, Robert, "Pancreatic Organotherapy for Diabetes, 1889–1921," *Medical History* 39 (1995).

Tausk, Marius, *Organon: The Story of an Unusual Pharmaceutical Enterprise* (1978), Eng. transl. (Oss: Akzo Pharma, 1984).

Thompson, Charis, *Making Parents: The Ontological Choreography of Reproductive Technologies* (Cambridge, Mass.: MIT Press, 2005).

Thorpenberg, Stefan, "Det tidiga samarbetet mellan Göteborgs medicinska fakultet och industrin—eller födelsen av Mode 2 i det svenska goda samhället," *VEST* 15 (2002).

Throsby, Karen, *When IVF Fails: Feminism, Infertility and the Negotiation of Normality* (New York: Palgrave Macmillan, 2004).

Thunberg, Torsten, "Nyare undersökningar öfver Hypophysis Cerebri: En öfversikt," *ASL* 7 (1910).

Tillgren, J. and Nils Rahm, "Några ord om poliklinisk insulinbehandling vid sockersjuka," *SL* 21 (1924).

"Tillverkarens ansvar," *SFT* 69 (1965).

Travis, Anthony S. et al., eds., *Determinants in the Evolution of the European Chemical Industry, 1900–1939: New Technologies, Political Frameworks, Markets, and Companies* (Dordrecht: Springer, 1998).

Turney, Jon, *Frankenstein's Footsteps: Science, Genetics and Popular Culture* (New Haven and London: Yale Univesrity Press, 1998).

Tutton, Richard and Oonagh Corrigan, eds., *Genetic Databases: Socio-ethical Issues in the Collection and Use of DNA* (London and New York: Routledge, 2004).

Tydén, Mattias, *Från politik till praktik: De svenska steriliseringslagarna 1935–1975*, 2d ed., enl. (Stockholm: Almqvist and Wiksell International, 2002).

Tyre, Marcie J. and Wanda J. Orlikowski, "Windows of Opportunity: Temporal Patterns of Technological Adaptation in Organizations," *Organization Science* 5 (1994).

"Utställningen af reklammedicin i Halmstad," *SFT* 21 (1912).

Vetenskap av i dag: Framlagd av svenska forskare (Uppsala: Gebers, 1940).

Viner, Russel, "Putting Stress in Life: Hans Selye and the Making of Stress Theory," *SSS* 29 (1999).

Vos, Rein, *Drugs Looking for Diseases: Innovative Drug Research and the Development of the Beta Blockers and the Calcium Antagonists* (Dordrecht and Boston: Kluwer Academic Publishers, 1991).

"Waldemar Gårdlund 23.9 1879–2.8 1959," *SL* 57 (1960).

Walsh, Vivien and Jordan Goodman, "The Billion Dollar Molecule: Taxol in Historical and Theoretical Perspective," in Godelieve van Heteren, Marijke Gijswijt-Hofstra and Tilli Tansey, eds., *Biographies of Remedies: Drugs, Medicines and Contraceptives in Dutch and Anglo-American Healing Cultures* (Amsterdam and New York: Rodopi, 2002).

Wegerfelt, Arne, "Svensk läkemedelsindustri på världsmarknaden," *SFT* 68 (1964).

Weimarck, Anna, "Fortplantningsteknologier—etik och kvinnosyn," *Kvinnovetenskaplig tidskrift* 4 (1986).

Welander, Arvid, "Tablettfabrikerna på krigsstigen," *SFT* 50 (1946).

Wendt, Fredrik, "Gammalt och nytt om de kvinnliga sexualhormonen samt deras betydelse för graviditet och abort," *SL* 31 (1934).

Wennerholm, Staffan, "'Unga forskare sökes': Att tilltala vetenskapens påläggskalvar i teknikerbristens tidevarv," in Anders Ekström, ed., *Den mediala vetenskapen* (Nora: Nya Doxa, 2004).

Westerling, Rune, "Sökarljus på läkemedelsindustrin," *SFT* 67 (1963).

Westerståhl, Anna, "Reproduktionsteknologi—vad är det?," *Kvinnovetenskaplig tidskrift* 4 (1986).

Westling, Håkan, *Medicinska fakulteten vid Lunds universitet 1668–2003* (Lund: Lund University, 2003).

Westman, Axel, *A Contribution to the Question of the Transit of the Ovum from Ovary to the Uterus in Rabbits* (Stockholm: Caroline Institute, 1926).
Westman, Axel, *Barnlös: En bok om steriliteten och sterilitetsbekämpandet* (Stockholm: Wahlström and Widstrand, 1940).
Westman, Axel, "De kvinnliga sexualhormonen," *Hygiea* 93 (1931).
Westman, Axel, "Den främre hypofyslobens ställning inom den kvinnliga sexualbiologien," *Nord. Med.* 3 (1931).
Westman, Axel, "Den moderna hormonforskningens betydelse för gynekologien," *Upsala Läkareförenings förhandlingar* 38 (1933).
Westman, Axel, "Den ofrivilliga steriliteten," in SOU 1936:59 *Betänkande i sexualfrågan*.
Westman, Axel, "Editorial," *Acta Endo.* 1 (1948).
Westman, Axel, "Experimentella undersökningar över hypofysens produktion av gonadotropt hormon," *Nord. Med.* 14 (1937).
Westman, Axel, "Experimentella undersökningar över hypofys-mellanhjärnsystemets reglerande inflytande på sexualfunktionerna," *SL* 38 (1941).
Westman, Axel, "Hjärnbihanget och dess hormon," *Göteborgs Handels- och Sjöfartstidning* 12 June (1948).
Westman, Axel, "Hormonala behandlingsmetoder inom gynekologien," *SL* 40 (1943).
Westman, Axel, "Hormonforskning och praktisk läkekonst," *Tidskrift för Sveriges Sjuksköterskor* 9 (1942).
Westman, Axel, "Hormonlaboratoriernas framtid," *SL* 56 (1959).
Westman, Axel, *Hormoner* (Stockholm: Wahlström and Widstrand, 1940).
Westman, Axel, "Hormoner och nervsystem," in *Kungl. Svenska Vetenskapsakademiens Årsbok 1955*.
Westman, Axel, "Hypofysimplantation," *Nord. Med.* 41 (1949).
Westman, Axel, "Klinisk prövning av choriongonadotropinet 'Gonadex' Leo," *SL* 45 (1948).
Westman, Axel, "Kliniska och experimentella undersökningar över hypofystransplantation," *Nord. Med.* 4 (1939).
Westman, Axel "Könsutvecklingen och den inre sekretionen," *Tidskrift för Sveriges Sjuksköterskor* 1 (1934).
Westman, Axel, "Nyare undersökningar över ovariets biologi," *Hygiea* 90 (1928).
Westman, Axel, "Om den inbördes relationen mellan äggstockens bägge hormon," *SL* 33 (1936).
Westman, Axel, "Om fortplantningskontroll och fosterfördrivning," *SL* 32 (1935).
Westman, Axel, "Om sterilitetens behandling och resultaten av densamma," *Hygiea* 106 (1944).
Westman, Axel, "Professor James Heyman in Memoriam," *Acta Obst.* 35 (1956).
Westman, Axel, "Reaktivering av ovarialfunktionen under menopausen," *SL* 31 (1934).
Westman, Axel, "The Results of the Prophylactic, Postoperative, Radiological Treatment of Carcinoma of the Uterine Cervix at Radiumhemmet in Stockholm," *Acta Radiologica* 3 (1924).
Westman, Axel, "Secernierende Zellen im Epithel der Tubae uterinae Falloppii," *Anatomischer Anzeiger* 49 (1916).
Westman, Axel, "Sexualhormon för behandling av kvinnosjukdomar," in *Olösta gåtor och aktuella problem: Sjuttiosex uttalanden i Svenska Dagbladets enquête om*

naturforskningens nuvarande uppgifter och framtida mål (Stockholm: Wahlström and Widstrand, 1937).

Westman, Axel, "Sterilitet," in Arne Tallberg, ed., *Sexuallivet i modern belysning: Sexton svenska forskare ger vägledning* (Stockholm: Wahlström and Widstrand, 1944).

Westman, Axel, "Sterilitet och sterilitetsbehandling," *Hygienisk revy* 24 (1935).

Westman, Axel, "Studien über den Zusammenhang zwischen Corpus luteum und Plazenta als innersekretorische Organe," *Acta Obst.* 10 (1930).

Westman, Axel, "Studies on the Influence of the Roentgen and Radium Rays on Phagocytosis," *Acta Radiologica* 2 (1923).

Westman, Axel, "Synpunkter på endokrinologins utveckling," *SL* 53 (1956).

Westman, Axel, "Untersuchungen über die Wirkung des gonadotropen Hypophysenvorderlappenhormones, Antex (LEO), auf die Ovarien der Frau," *Acta Obst.* 17 (1937).

Westman, Axel, "The Value of Implantation of Hypophyseal Tissue in the Treatment of Hypophyseal Insufficiency," *Acta Medica Scandinavica* 133 (1949).

Westman, Axel, "Über den Luteinisierungseffekt des gonadotropen Chorionhormons auf die Ovarien der Frau," *Acta Pathologica et Microbiologica Scandinavica* 15, suppl. 37 (1938).

Westman, Axel, *Övergångsår* (Stockholm: Rabén and Sjögren, 1945).

Westman, Axel and Dora Jacobsohn, "Experimentelle Untersuchungen über die Bedeutung des Hypophysen-Zwischenhirnsystems für die Produktion gonadotroper Hormone des Hypophysenvorderlappens," *Acta Obst.* 17 (1937).

Westman, Axel and Dora Jacobsohn, "Experimentelle Untersuchung über Kalbshypophysentransplantate bei der Ratte," *Acta Pathologica et Microbiologica Scandinavica* 19 (1942).

Westman, Axel and Per Wetterdal, "Obstetrik och gynekologi," in *Karolinska medikokirurgiska institutets historia 1910–1960: Utgiven med anledning av institutets hundrafemtioårsdag av dess lärarkollegium*, 4 vol. (Stockholm: Almqvist and Wiksell, 1960), vol. 3.

Westman, Axel et al., "Hormonanalysernas praktiska värde," *SL* 56 (1959).

Westman, Axel, Rolf Luft and Ulf Borell, eds., *Endokrinologi* (Stockholm: Bonnier, 1963).

Widmalm, Sven, "Ett vetenskapligt nätverk: The Svedberg och hans lärjungar," in Ylva Hasselberg and Tom Petersson, eds., *"Bäste broder!": Nätverk, entreprenörskap och innovation i svenskt näringsliv* (Hedemora: Gidlund, 2006).

Widmalm, Sven, "Innovationssamhället," in Mats Benner and Sverker Sörlin, eds., *Forska lagom och vara världsbäst: Sverige inför forskningens globala strukturomvandling* (Stockholm: SNS Förlag, 2008).

Widmalm, Sven, "The Svedberg and the Boundary Between Science and Industry: Laboratory Practice, Policy, and Media Images," *History and Technology* 20 (2004).

Widmalm, Sven, "Trollkarlen från Uppsala: Bilder av The Svedberg och vetenskapen under andra världskriget," in Anders Ekström, ed., *Den mediala vetenskapen* (Nora: Nya Doxa, 2004).

Widmalm, Sven and Hjalmar Fors, eds., *Artefakter: Industrin, vetenskapen och de tekniska nätverken* (Hedemora: Gidlund, 2004).

Wijngaard, Marianne van den, "The Acceptance of Scientific Theories and Images of Masculinity and Femininity: 1959–1985," *JHB* 24 (1991).

Wijngaard, Marianne van den, "Feminism and the Biological Construction of Female and Male Behaviour," *JHB* 27 (1994).

Wilhelmi, Alfred E., "The Endocrine Society: Origin, Organization, and Institutions," *Endocrinology* 123 (1988).

Wilson, Leonard G., "Internal Secretions in Disease: The Historical Relations of Clinical Medicine and Scientific Physiology," *Journal of the History of Medicine and Allied Sciences* 39 (1984).

Wirmark, Margareta et al., eds., *Professorsboken: Fyrtionio Lundakvinnor berättar* (Stockholm: Carlsson, 1996).

Wiström, Svante, ed., *Svensk läkemedelsindustri: Mål och medel* (1946).

Wolffers, Ivan, Anita Hardon and Janita Janssen, *Marketing Fertility: Women, Menstruation and the Pharmaceutical Industry* (Amsterdam: WEMOS, 1989).

Zetterholm, S. G., "Erfarenheter med cardiazol—resp. insulinbehandling på ett psykosmaterial," *SL* 36 (1939).

Zondek, Bernhard, "Mass Excretion of Æstrogenic Hormone in the Urine of the Stallion," *Nature* 10 February (1934).

Zondek, Bernhard, "Über die Hormone des Hypophysenvorderlappens: I. Wachstumshormon, Follikelreifungshormon (Prolan A), Luteinisierungshormon (Prolan B), Stoffwechselhormon?," *Klinische Wochenschrift* 9 (1930).

Zondek, Bernhard and Selmar Aschheim, "Das Hormon des Hypophysenvorderlappens: I. Testobjekt zum Nachweis des Hormons," *Klinische Wochenschrift* 6 (1927).

Zondek, Bernhard and Selmar Aschheim, "Das Hormon des Hypophysenvorderlappens: II. Darstellung, chemische Eigenschaften, biologische Wirkungen," *Klinische Wochenschrift* 7 (1928).

NAME INDEX